# SANCTIFIED VIOLENCE IN HOMERIC SOCIETY

In *Sanctified Violence in Homeric Society*, Margo Kitts explores the oath-making rituals and narratives of the *Iliad* and articulates a theory of ritualized violence. Analyzing ritual features that are common to acts of religious violence worldwide, she focuses on the paradigms, core metaphors, ritual fictions, and poetic registers of Homeric oath-sacrifices. Kitts sees the oath-sacrificing ritual performance as generating a symbolic text, which is interwoven with the poetic text of the *Iliad*'s oath-sacrificing narratives. The resulting intertextual rendering may be analyzed for semantic tensions. Kitts's interdisciplinary approach enlists ritual and metaphor theory to help explain some of those tensions, including that between sacrificed animals and slain men.

Margo Kitts is lecturer at Iowa State University. A scholar of ancient Near Eastern religions, she has contributed to *Kernos*, *History of Religions*, *Literature and Theology*, *Journal of Ritual Studies*, and *Metis*.

# SANCTIFIED VIOLENCE IN HOMERIC SOCIETY

## OATH-MAKING RITUALS AND NARRATIVES IN THE *ILIAD*

### MARGO KITTS

Iowa State University

CAMBRIDGE
UNIVERSITY PRESS

CAMBRIDGE UNIVERSITY PRESS

Cambridge, New York, Melbourne, Madrid, Cape Town, Singapore, São Paulo

Cambridge University Press
40 West 20th Street, New York, NY 10011-4211, USA

www.cambridge.org
Information on this title: www.cambridge.org/9780521855297

First published 2005

Printed in the United States of America

*A catalog record for this publication is available from the British Library.*

*Library of Congress Cataloging in Publication Data*

Kitts, Margo, 1952–
Sanctified violence in Homeric society : oath-making rituals and narratives in the *Iliad* /
Margo Kitts.
p.   cm.
Includes bibliographical references and index.
ISBN-13: 978-0-521-85529-7 (hardback)
ISBN-10: 0-521-85529-2 (hardback)
1. Homer. Iliad.   2. Epic poetry, Greek – History and criticism.   3. Trojan War – Literature
and the war.   4. Holy, The, in literature.   5. Violence in literature.   6. Ritual in literature.
7. Oaths in literature.   I. Title.
PA4037.K47   2005
883′.01 – dc22         2005014866

ISBN-13   978-0-521-85529-7 hardback
ISBN-10   0-521-85529-2 hardback

To my mother

*whose every story has an epic twist.*

# CONTENTS

*Acknowledgments*                                      *page* ix

Introduction: Why Another
Treatment of Greek Sacrifice?. . . . . . . 1

1. Epics, Rituals, and Rituals in Epic:
   Some Methodological
   Considerations . . . . . . . . . . . . . . 11

2. Premises and Principles of Oath-
   Making in the *Iliad* . . . . . . . . . . . 50

3. Ritual Scenes and Epic Themes
   of Oath-Sacrifice . . . . . . . . . . . 115

4. Homeric Battlefield Theophanies,
   in the Light of the Ancient
   Near East . . . . . . . . . . . . . . . 188

Conclusion . . . . . . . . . . . . . . . . 216

*Appendix: Homeric Texts for the*
*Principal Oaths Discussed*                             219

*Bibliography*                                         229

*Index*                                               241

# ACKNOWLEDGMENTS

At the age of 20, I read Soren Kierkegaard's *Fear and Trembling* for a seminar on existentialism offered by John Williams at Raymond College (UOP Stockton, CA). I had scarcely any theological background, my previous exposure to biblical stories consisting of a beautifully illustrated children's book that I had encountered at a doctor's office when I was eight or nine years old. Kierkegaard's presentation of the possible mental tableaus with which Abraham may have prepared to sacrifice Isaac evoked a puzzling image I remembered from the children's book. It was a backside view of Isaac following his father up a mountain trail. Isaac looked at his father's back; his father, stooped under a bundle of wood, looked straight ahead. The viewer was allowed to perceive neither their faces nor their emotions, much as the reader of Genesis is given no index of either. Lacking those emotional signals, the story confounded me as a child, it fascinated me as a young adult, and it was one trigger for my later investigations of sacrifice and violence in the classroom. Those investigations have culminated in a handful of articles on ritualized violence and now in this book. Although this book is on the *Iliad*, I hope that the theory I present here will be seen to extend beyond Homer into the wider subject of sanctified violence, such as the violence that Abraham was prepared to perpetrate on Isaac.

Of course, a book on Homer cannot be explained away by illustrations in children's books. Other influences were more direct. One important influence was Professor Michael Nagler, who endured many semesters of Homeric Greek and oral traditional studies with me during my graduate school days at UC Berkeley. My debt to him is obvious in this book. Professor Ruggero Stefanini was truly a mentor who endured just as many semesters of Hittite language, rituals, and Homeric cross-over studies with me. Both professors indulged my obsession with the figure of Lykaon with gentle humor. Professor Gary Holland was a big aid in my Hittite studies, offering me an independent course on Hittite prayers and midwifery rituals, as well as courses with other students. On the subject of ritualized violence, and particularly its contemporary relevance, my debt is to Professor Mark Juergensmeyer, a longtime mentor and friend whose support has been inestimably precious to me. On biblical themes, I was stimulated by studies with Professors Norman Gottwald, Jacob Milgrom and Victor Gold, who are not to be held responsible for any simplifications I may have made in Chapter 4. Professor Dan Foxvog taught me what little I know of Akkadian and Sumerian, and his independent course with me on the Emesal dialect of Sumerian was terrific bait for studies I would like to continue someday. It was Professor David Stronach's gentle prodding that made me realize that the end of graduate school is not the end of one's studies, and he was right, as the ideas I have put forth in this book bear only remotely on ideas I put forth in my dissertation.

Yet writing is a lonely task, and the above friends and mentors assisted with my creation of this book primarily in the form of memories. Concurrent with the writing of this book, I fell in love with Paul Ricoeur's work on metaphor and Roy Rappaport's work on ritual. Unfortunately, it is too late to meet and thank either scholar. More recently I have been stimulated by the friendships of Classicist Madeleine Henry, who hosted my presentation of some arguments from this book before members of the Classics and Foreign Language Department here at Iowa State University, and of Hector Avalos, a fellow member of the Department of Philosophy and Religious Studies who took my ideas seriously enough to read and contemplate my articles from *Kernos* and the *Journal of Ritual Studies*. Phil Sellew's sessions on Greco-Roman religions at the 2004 and 2005 Upper Midwestern Regional meetings of the American Academy of Religion provided a wonderful forum for presenting my ideas before a rare group of AAR members who actually knew what I was talking about. I have him to thank for arranging that. In addition, I would like to thank longtime friends Joe Illick and Brian George for their enduring confidence in my ability to think. I also must remember Father Tom Casey (now deceased) and Padraic O'Hare (quite alive), two former colleagues who provided riotous humor and moral support during my travail at a small New England Catholic college in the 90s.

My greatest debt is to Cambridge University Press Humanities Editor Beatrice Rehl, who, then as Senior Editor in Classics, read the first chapter of this book in rough form and gambled on my ability to write something of interest. It was she who encouraged me to write this book, read the manuscript in its entirety when I first wrote it, facilitated its review by anonymous reviewers, and promoted it into production. I am grateful to her beyond words. I also thank those anonymous reviewers whose suggestions for improvement I took seriously. Then I thank Eric Crahan, Assistant Editor in Social Sciences who took over for Editor Rehl and helped me to maneuver the field of copyrights and other details. I am grateful, further, to Peter Katsirubas of TechBooks for masterminding the copyediting and production of this book and for reading it, too.

Final gratitude must go to my 11-year-old son Giordan, who had to share me with some old Greek books for a number of years, and to Molly Maqquire and Liza Doolittle, our fuzzy, oversized companions whose need for romps and cuddles brought us right down to earth on a regular basis. I am also blessed with the friendships of Sita Zarnegar and Margaret Olson, with whom I have enjoyed many hours of diversionary play and politics.

Needless to say, no one of these benefactors is responsible for what I have written in this book. All errors of prose, thought, and Greek translation are mine.

Margo Kitts
Ames, Iowa
July 1, 2005

# WHY ANOTHER TREATMENT OF GREEK SACRIFICE?

G REEK SACRIFICE HAS RECEIVED A GREAT DEAL OF ATTENTION OVER the past century, particularly over the last three decades. Nearly the entire corpus of Greek literature, archaeology, and art history has been surveyed for the meanings possibly attributed to sacrifice, from Mycenaean archeology through Classical texts and artifacts to early Christian complaints about the inaccessibility of meat that was not the product of pagan sacrifice (1 Corinthians 8:10). The curious relationship between *thusia* (commensal sacrifice) and *phonē* (murder or slaughter) practically dominated Classical scholarship in Italy and France during the 1970s and 1980s, for instance.[1] Yet, with a few exceptions,[2] sacrifice in the context

---

[1]  Classic treatments include J.-P. Vernant's and M. Detienne, eds, *The Cuisine of Sacrifice among the Greeks*, trans. Paul Wissing (Chicago: University of Chicago Press 1989), Detienne's *Gardens of Adonis: Spices in Greek Mythology*, trans. Janet Lloyd (Atlantic Highlands, NJ: Humanities 1977), Walter Burkert's *Homo Necans*, trans. Peter Bing (Berkeley: University of California Press 1983), René Girard's *Violence and the Sacred*, trans. Patrick Gregory (Baltimore: Johns Hopkins University Press 1977), Pierre Vidal-Naquet, *The Black Hunter; Forms of Thought and Forms of Society in the Greek World*, trans. Andrew Szagedy-Mazak (Baltimore: Johns Hopkins University Press 1986), Luc deHeusch, *Sacrifice in Africa* (Bloomington: Indiana University Press 1985), Cristiano Grottanelli and N. F. Parese, eds., *Sacrificio nel societa' nel mondo antico* (Roma: Laterza 1988).

[2]  Among them Paul Stengel's short comments on oath-sacrifice (*Die Griechischen Kultusaltertumer* (Munich: Oskar Beck: 1920, 136–38), Michael H. Jameson's work on significant cultural acts ("Sacrifice and Ritual: Greece," in *Civilization of the Ancient Mediterranean* (ed. Michael Grant 1988), 959–79, n.b. 972–75, E. J. Bickerman's "Couper une alliance," in *Studies in Jewish and Christian History, Vol. I* (Leiden: E. J. Brill 1976) 1–32, Chris Faraone's "Molten Wax, Spilt Wine and Mutilated Animals: Sympathetic Magic in Near Eastern and Early Greek Oath Ceremonies," *Journal of Hellenic Studies* cxiii, 1993, 60–80, and, in passing, Moshe Weinfeld's "The Covenant of Grant in the Old Testament and in the Ancient Near East," *JOAS* 90, 1970, 184–203.

of Homeric oaths has been given scant attention. More often it is treated peripherally in wider studies of Greek treaty-making, promising, reciprocity, and friendship.[3] While these studies shed much light on their respective topics, they tend to eclipse the sacrifice in oath-making for the end results, and more often than not the persuasive strategies of ritualized violence are not fully addressed.

Yet violence is a conspicuous theme in Homeric oath-making. Oath-sacrifices are striking dramatizations of ritualized violence, and oaths without sacrifices commonly invoke analogies that are symbolically violent, for instance, Achilles swearing by his own life (1.88), or Odysseus swearing by his life and also by his fatherhood of Telemachos, as if to stake his identity as a generator of life (2.257–64).[4] The relative neglect of the subject is surprising when one considers how comparable are the rhetoric and symbolic actions of oath-sacrifice with the rhetoric and symbolic actions of religious terrorism, recently described as cosmic dramatizations on a world stage.[5] Dramatic, too, are the imagined consequences of violated oaths: cosmic vengeance on oath-violators, administered by gods, often on the battlefield, in both Homeric and Near Eastern literature. It is not quite enough to attribute oath-making violence to analogical thinking[6] or to a theological substitute for the lack of international treaty sanctions.[7] Both explanations certainly have merit, but the rhetoric of divine vengeance for oath-violation is so emphatic that it forces one to ponder also the wider issues of ritually configured commitments and the idea of cosmic responsiveness to amplified registers

---

[3] See the excellent *Promise-Giving and Treaty-Making*, by Peter Karavites (Leiden: E. J. Brill 1992), *Ritualized Friendship and the Greek City*, by Gabriel Herman (Cambridge: Cambridge University Press 1987), *The Stranger's Welcome*, by Steve Reece (Ann Arbor: The University of Michigan Press 1993), and "The Common Heritage of Covenantal Traditions in the Ancient World," by Moshe Weinfeld, in *I Trattai nel mondo antico, forma, ideologica, funzione*, eds. Luciano Canfora, Mario Liverani, Carlo Zaccagnini (Rome: L'Erinna di Bretschneider 1990) 175–91.

[4] The speech of Odysseus is not called an oath explicitly, but clearly his speech act denotes an oath as well as a threat when he says to Thersites, "But I tell you and this shall be completed. If I come across you still as mindless as you are now, then no longer will the head of Odysseus remain on his shoulders, and let me no longer be called the father of Telemachus, if I do not take you and strip from you your clothes, your cloak and tunic, which hide your shame, and I send you to the swift ships crying, driving you from the agora with vicious blows."

[5] See for instance, Mark Juergensmeyer, *Terror in the Mind of God* (Berkeley: University of California Press 2000).

[6] See P. Stengel 1920: 136–38, C. Faraone 1993: 65.

[7] P. Karavites 1992: 98.

of speech and gesture. Nor can oath-making violence be explained adequately by regional and historical idiosyncracies. E. J. Bickerman, focusing on the ancient Mediterranean in particular, has demonstrated that, far beyond the Mediterranean in geography and in history, oath-making is linked with symbolic acts that are deemed sealing and often life-risking at their core.[8] But even if the *Iliad's* ritualized killing of animals and the threat of death to seal oaths were strictly regional or somehow primitive, it still would be worthwhile to ponder the violence in oath-making for at least four reasons.

The first is that there are more than two dozen references to oath-making and cursing customs and two precise oath-sacrificing rituals in the *Iliad*, evidence enough that oath-making was understood as a foundational institution in Homeric society and surely penetrated the ancient world beyond the epic.[9] Second, in its emphasis on the death of a sacrificial victim, oath-sacrifice stands at the very opposite end of the dramatic spectrum from the commensal sacrifices in the *Iliad*, which never mention the animal's blood, collapse, last gasps, or even that it is dead before being slaughtered. (I am taking funeral feasts as falling under a different *topos*.) In contrast, the narrative of oath-sacrifice in *Iliad* 3 is powerful enough that the ominous tone generated by its symbolic actions and curses persists through four books after the sacrifice. The ritual's violation is referred to at least six times in the subsequent four books (4.67, 4.72, 4.155–65, 4.236, 4.271, 7.351–52), which helps to establish a ritual leitmotif for the devastation of the Trojans as a consequence of their violating a divinely witnessed oath. Third, and more profoundly, the subject is worthy of attention because a handful of human killings and dyings on the battlefield are rendered in such a way as to elicit comparisons with the killing and dying of the animal victims of oath-sacrifice in Books 3 and 19, insinuating a figurative equation of killing in war with killing in sacrifice. The same figurative equation is clear in the biblical traditions of *herem*[10] and in the records of Neo-Assyrian kings, whose treaty curses and war rhetoric often attribute the slaughter of enemies precisely to divine retribution for violated oaths.[11] Fourth, this pan-Mediterranean theme

---

[8]  E. J. Bickerman 1976: 1–32.
[9]  This is an unstated assumption in most treatments of cultural conventions in Homer. See, for instance, the scholars cited in footnote 2, and Gabriel Herman 1987.
[10]  Susan Niditch, *War in the Hebrew Bible* (New York: Oxford University Press 1993).
[11]  See, for instance, the inscriptions of Sargon (section 155), Esarhaddon (sections 503, 509, 596), and Ashurbanipal (sections 773, 828) in Daniel David Luckenbill's *Ancient Records of Assyria, Vol.* II, *Historical Records of Assyria, From Sargon to the End* (New

is supported obliquely by myriad examples of deities marching in battles to show divine favor or discontent. Not only the Homeric familiars
(such as Ares, Athena, Apollo, and Poseidon) but also the sun goddess of
Arinna, Ashur, Shamash, Marduk, Nergal, Enlil, Ninlil, Ishtar of Arbela,
Yahweh, and other gods from the Levant to Mesopotamia march in front
of their favorites in war. Indeed, envisioning battlefield slaughter as a
religious spectacle on a cosmic stage is an enduring motif in Western war
literature, from early Mesopotamian poetry right into our own time.[12]
In short, oath-sacrificing rhetoric in the *Iliad* is tied to a multiplicity of
themes having to do with cosmic punishment for perjury and with the
notion of sanctified violence in war. For all of these reasons, it is important to examine oath-making rituals and oath-making violence in the
*Iliad*. This book will explore these themes.

Scholars who would explore oath-sacrifice as ritual killing in the *Iliad*
have the immense task of integrating oral poetic studies, ritual theories,
and the oath-making rituals and rhetoric to be found in the evidence
from surrounding cultures. This book is a step in that direction. It begins
in Chapter 1 by discussing the intersection of epic, anthropological, and
oral traditional theory in the study of Homeric rituals. The epic genre all
by itself permits discussion of a full range of literary devices that might
color battlefield killings as ritual killings, but the *Iliad* is also reputedly an
oral poetic epic, and its origins in oral traditional performance require
another set of considerations regarding ritual scenes in the poem as they
may have resonated orally with audiences. Given the millennia that stand
between us and the Homeric audiences for whom the poem was cast,
one of the first methodological considerations will be the extent to which
we can grasp the cultural repercussions of oath-sacrificing rituals through
their reflections in the text. It should be noted that this approach is somewhat anthropological (enlisting Rappaport, Tambiah, Bloch, and Valeri),
and hermeneutic (enlisting Gadamer, Ricoeur, Jakobson, and Johnson
and Turner). It is not in any formal sense archeological or historical-
linguistic. This approach to the study of Homeric rituals relies in fact on
an intertextual theory, presuming the existence of symbolic dimensions in

---

York: Greenwood Press 1968). All references to Luckenbill henceforth are to Volume II.

[12] A few of the contemporary authors who recognize some kind of religious fervor to
war would include John Glen Gray, *The Warriors, Reflections on Men in Battle* (New
York: Harper & Row 1959, 1970), Chris Hedges, *War Is a Force that Gives Us Meaning*
(New York: Random House 2002), and Oliver McTernan, *Violence in God's Name*
(New York: Orbis Books 2003).

oath-making ritual practices as well as in oath-making scenes in Homeric poetry. I believe the semantic spheres of these symbolic performances
and poetic scenes must interpenetrate in the way that semantic spheres in
texts may be said to interpenetrate. That is, both ritual performances in
cult and ritual scenes in epic poetry may be regarded as symbolic modes
of communication that produce a kind of text, and the ancient audience's
experience of the sticky interface between the actual ritual performance
and the poetic ritual scene, however elusively rendered in the fixed text
we have today, is also where semantic tensions between ritual killing and
battlefield killing must have originated.

The primary means for grasping this intertextuality will be through
an examination of the anthropology of the oath-making ritual qua ritual as communication. It is a fair charge that epic cannot be treated as
anthropology, but the interactive nature of oral traditional performance
nonetheless permits exploring ritual scenes for the far-reaching symbolic
matrices those scenes may have attracted to the text from actual cultural
practices in antiquity.[13] Of course there is a degree of ambiguity deriving
from the presentation of a ritual embedded within a ritual, that is, from
an oath-making ritual performance narrated as part of an oral-poetic
ritual of composition in performance. But both layers of ritualization
serve the communicative ends that anthropologists Tambiah, Rappaport,
Bloch, and Valeri ascribe to rituals in general. Yet, as will be argued, the
communicative efficacy of ritual differs qualitatively from the communicative efficacy of ordinary speech, due in large part to the formalized
and paradigmatic nature of ritual communication.

A related consideration will be the fixity of features in the oath-
sacrificing ritual scene. Contemporary scholars of traditional verse tend to
emphasize the fluidity of the oral traditional poet in composing verse, and
envision the poetic use of typical scenes, motifs, formulae, single words –
an array of differently conceived lexical items – as a much more creative
process than they did some 80 years ago, when the study of oral traditional
verse was emerging as a recognized field of study. Valuable as are these
more contemporary approaches for probing poetic signification and for
discovering the deep structures beneath the surface manifestations of certain scene types, it so happens that the typical scene for oath-sacrificing

---

[13] Most Classical scholars simply assume this point. Peter Karavites unabashedly asserts the
historical significance of Homeric poetry and in particular the promising conventions
represented within it, pointing out that "such poetry derives its themes from reality,
from which it forms a new synthesis" (1992: 3).

rituals is the most fixed in the entire *Iliad*, with whole verses repeated in precisely the same sequences and featuring a predictable vocabulary of seemingly marked words. My own perspective is that this ritual scene is neither an empty shell nor a grouping of individually meaningful words but instead a semantically weighty phrase and idea-cluster reflective of a ritual form deemed by the audience to be encoded largely by forces other than the human ritual participants. Because of oath-sacrifices' formality as "liturgical orders" (Roy Rappaport's phrase[14]), oath-sacrificing scenes in the *Iliad* arguably preserve ritual gestures and idea clusters from cultural contexts beyond the epic. They reflect patterns of behavior and thought regarded as immutable and perduring ("canonical," as Rappaport would see it) by the poet and his audience. The fixity of their elements arguably makes the ritual scenes more semantically weighty, and not merely rote. Notably, some ritual paradigms that emerge through oath-making scenes in the *Iliad* are reflected in ancient literature beyond the Homeric epic, in Hittite, Neo-Assyrian, and Biblical oaths. Such reflections speak to the perduring nature of some ritual forms outside of the Homeric context.

Chapter 2 will explore the cultural foundations of Homeric oath-making. An oath will be regarded as the ritualized configuration of a relationship between two or more individuals – a configuration specified by solemn utterances, gestures, and sometimes artifacts – that may be sealed by a symbolic act. It will be shown that oaths often entail the overcoming of estrangements between individuals and may involve a ritualized act of violence that fixes the new relationship in place. Chapter 2 is *not* dedicated to a dissection of linguistic elements involved in oath-making: It will not focus on, for instance, the finer distinctions among *horkos, horkion, omnymi, pistoō* and *horkon temnein*. Such terms have been discussed by Karavites and others and I will make use of the rich literature on the figures of speech connected to oath-making patterns across Near Eastern and Mediterranean languages. However, the primary focus of Chapter 2 is not the precise terminology but the underlying ritual patterns to which that terminology is attached. Moshe Weinfeld and E. J. Bickerman, among others, have demonstrated cross-Mediterranean patterns for oath-making rituals and rhetoric, and a number of the features they describe are manifest in a handful of speeches and narratives

---

[14] Most fully explained in *Ritual and Religion in the Making of Humanity* (Cambridge: Cambridge University Press 1999).

in the *Iliad*. I aim to investigate the oath-making references in the *Iliad* that shed light on underlying cultural assumptions and ritual logic and, where applicable, to examine those assumptions and practices for shared assumptions and practices with ancient Anatolian, Assyrian, and biblical oaths as revealed by texts.

Chapter 2 begins with a discussion of the cultural premises on which Homeric oath-making is based, examining their inverse prefigurations in narratives that portray warriors in the heat of battle, oblivious to cultural constraints such as oaths. Then it proceeds to a discussion of *poinē* as a ritual leitmotif that barely shapes and configures behavior, in particular the behavior of Achilles. The discussion of *poinē* aims to demonstrate the power of Homeric ritual leitmotifs to suggest an engagement of individuals in common conventions and to portray an overcoming of antipathy to common cultural forms. This discussion is based on the ritual theory outlined in the Chapter 1. Finally, Chapter 2 examines ritual principles and Near Eastern comparisons for Homeric oath-making gestures and themes, beginning with the features outlined by Rappaport as constituting liturgical orders and proceeding through an array of different features of Homeric oaths.

It should be pointed out that Near Eastern materials are used in this study only for loose comparisons, largely to contextualize the Homeric material. The lines of historical transmission for particular features of Near Eastern and Homeric diplomatic and religious traditions have been much discussed,[15] but are problematized by the historical and cultural parameters of the Near Eastern traditions involved.[16] The Hebrew Bible, for instance, describes at least three broad phases in religious–political history and presents glimpses into a variety of ideologies and cultural practices that vary in clarity from the conspicuous ideology of the religious elite to the

---

[15] See, for instance, Ann C. Gunter, "Models of the Orient in the Art History of the Orientalizing Period," in *Achaemenid History V: The Roots of the European Tradition*, ed. S. Sancisi-Weerdenburg and J. W. Drijvers (Leiden: Nederlands Institutuut Voor Het Nabije Oosten, 1990) 131–47, and Sarah Morris, "The Sacrifice of Astyanax: Near Eastern Contributions to the Siege of Troy," in *The Ages of Homer: A Tribute to Emily Townsend Vermeule*, eds. Jane B. Carter and Sarah P. Morris (Austin: University of Texas 1995) 221–44. For a short summary of the field, see also Morris's "Homer and the Near East," in *A New Companion to Homer*, ed. Ian Morris and Barry Powell (Leiden: E.J. Brill 1997) 599–623.

[16] Hence, Robert Mondi's emphasis on tracing themes rather than precise features, in "Greek Mythic Thought in the Light of the Near East," in *Approaches to Greek Myth*, ed. Lowell Edmunds (Baltimore: Johns Hopkins University Press 1990) 142–98.

muted cultural practices of, say, outlying peasants.[17] The bits and pieces of biblical prose used to highlight Homeric materials are, therefore, just that, and should not be taken as representing any monolithic biblical religious tradition. The biblical materials instead are cited as suggestive for broad, shared traditions represented in classical literatures from the Western and Eastern sides of the Mediterranean Sea. Similarly, Hittite texts present a daunting maze of traditions, deities, ritual personae, genres, and theological notions, and this intricate web does little to facilitate the task of reconstructing lines of influence with Homeric texts. Although collected primarily from the ancient Hittite capital of Hattusa in Bogazkoy, the Hittite texts are written in languages from all over ancient Anatolia – Hittite (more properly Nesite), Luvian, Hattian, and Hurrian – and seem to reflect cultic behaviors from a variety of ethnic and geographical pockets whose populations may have enjoyed some degree of religious and cultural autonomy. Some, such as the rebellious Kaska people, put up continuous resistence to overarching Hittite control.[18] The outcome of this profusion of Anatolian languages and cultural practices is that whereas Hittite diplomatic texts, royal apologies, and some prayers display consistent structures and phrasing, ritual texts appear remarkably promiscuous as to form, language, ritual personae, and even performance compulsions.[19] For instance, an elaborate recipe of ritual procedures may begin with a disclaimer such as the one that introduces the 16th day of the 38-day AN.TAH.SUM festival: "If there is a wish to the king, he does the following. Nothing at all is in force."[20] With their thousand gods of Hatti and their permissiveness regarding ritual forms, the populations who made up Hittite Anatolia in the second millennium BCE apparently did not suffer from a narrow theological perspective![21] Generalizations

---

[17] See, for instance, Norman Gottwald, "Proto-Globalization and Proto-Secularization in Ancient Israel," forthcoming in *Out of the Cloister: a Festschrift in Honor of William G. Dever,* eds. S. Gifin J. E. Wright, and J. P. Dessel (Winonalake, MD: Eisenbrauns) (in press).

[18] For a summary of some of the problems, see Ruggero Stefanini, "Toward a Diachronic Reconstruction of the Linguistic Map of Ancient Anatolia," in *Anatolia Antica* 11: *Studi in Memoria di Fiorella Imparati* (Florence: LoGisma 2002) 783–806, and Theo van den Hout, "Another View of Hittite Literature," from the same volume, 857–78.

[19] See the encyclopedia of ritual personae collected by Pecchioli-Daddi, *Mestieri, professioni e dignita' nel'Anatolia ittita* (Roma: Edizioni dell'Ateneo 1982).

[20] GÌM-an LUGAL-i ZI-za, nu QA-TAM-MA i-i̯a-zi U-UL ku-it-ki du-uq-qa-ri. Kbo.IV 9 I:8–10.

[21] On the playful nature of Hittite religion generally, see Ahmet Unal, "Hittite Architect and A Rope-Climbing Ritual," *Turk Tarih Kurumu Belleten* LII:205 (1988b) 1469–1503.

about Hittite ritual practices therefore are problematic and we proceed with an awareness that there is no monolithic Hittite religious tradition, either. The Assyrian and particularly Neo-Assyrian evidence presents virtually the opposite set of problems, as one gets the impression from the royal annals between the time of Tiglath Pileser 1 to the end (1114 to 610 BCE), presumably a period of relevance for the Homeric texts, of an imperialistic propagandizing machine that suffocated much evidence of private cultic behaviors.[22] The royal reports seem strikingly formulaic in their religious, war-mongering, and avenging language, and it is precisely the formulaic nature of the Assyrian royal rhetoric that lends itself to comparison with Homeric material. Ann Gunter has argued persuasively for the plausibility of a Greek and Neo-Assyrian interchange in imagery for the visual arts, and a rhetorical interchange would seem just as plausible.[23] At any rate, conspicuously similar theophanic motifs are evident in the *Iliad* and in the annals of the Assyrian kings. (Assyrian rhetorical traditions will be germane mostly to Chapter 4.)

Chapter 3 dissects the oath-sacrificing rituals of Books 3 and 19 into the various steps that comprise the oath-sacrificing ritual, and then attempts to explore the metaphorical movement promoted by the whole ritual performance for the participants in the ritual. The first part of the chapter explores each feature of the oath-sacrificing ritual against the other instances of the same ritual feature elsewhere in the epic and, on

---

On the integrative feature of Hittite state religion, see Alfonso Archi, who observes that men from rural districts (LÚ.MEŠ.KUR) are included in lists of recipients of food offerings intended for the gods, from which can be inferred the regional participation of villagers in seasonal festivals: "L'elenco mosta come i membri delle communita' (si veda anche gli "uomini della regione": (LÚ.MEŠ.KUR) partecipino in particolare alla celebrazione delle feste stagionali locali, legate al ripetersi del ciclo agricolo, e dunque direttamente connesse alla vita del villagio. Sono questi tra i pochissimi elementi attraverso i quali e' dato provare l'esistenza di tali comunita'." "L'Organizzazione amministrative ittita e il regime delle offerte cultuali," *Or An* XII 3 (1973) 209–26, 220.

[22] See Steven W. Holloway, *Ashur Is King! Ashur Is King! Religion in the Exercise of Power in the Neo-Assyrian Empire* (Leiden: E. J. Brill 2002), 80–216, n.b. 80–93. It is interesting, for instance, that according to Assyrian kings' "letters to Ashur," the Assyrians never lost a battle.

[23] Gunter's conclusion: "Reexamination of Near Eastern elements in Greek art of this period suggests instead that Neo-Assyrian royal imagery and narrative traditions were known to, and emulated by, contemporary Greek artists for illustration of both secular and mythological subjects. Neo-Assyrian palace art was a principal source for the Greek visual tradition of aristocratic behavior. A key monument of Orientalizing vase painting serves to illustrate the kinds of images selected and their narrative treatment" (1990: 147).

a few occasions, against other instances of the same feature in Hittite, Assyrian, and biblical texts. The possible tension between the fixity of actual ritual performances and the fixity of verses in a typical ritual scene is also explored, and various levels of possible audience recognition are analyzed. This is essentially a demonstration of the principles outlined in Chapter 1. The second part of Chapter 3 is more abstract in that it attempts to argue for the emanation of the oath-sacrificing ritual motif beyond the actual sacrifices in Books 3 and 19 into other narratives. This argument relies on an exploration of some of the vocabulary of sacrifice as it filters into battle scenes, and also on a subtle etiology of oath-avenging that seems to permeate some battlefield slaughters after the failed oath of Book 3. On the surface, the failed oath-sacrifice of Book 3 is a facile illustration of James Fernandez's theory of ritual as metaphorical transformation. However, to promote a theory of metaphorical transformation in a poetic text inevitably involves a deeper discussion of metaphor, the basis for which I have drawn primarily from Paul Ricoeur. In Chapter 3, then, I propose a theory of ritual as poetry and examine the oath-making ritual for its poetic texture, its register, and finally the "ritual fictions" created by the oath-sacrificing performance. This is an elaboration of an argument I presented in *Kernos*, in 2003.[24]

Chapter 4 is a survey of battlefield theophanies in the *Iliad* and in the literary traditions of the Near East. It is a shorter chapter, whose theoretical aim is less ambitious: to show a shared Mediterranean imagination regarding the roles of gods on the battlefield. Principally, I explore literatures on both sides of the Mediterranean for figurations of deities leading battles, arousing fighting spirits, stunning and bewitching warriors on the battlefield, and finally punishing those who violate oaths and other conventions of trust. Common themes in Homeric, biblical, Assyrian, and occasionally Hittite curses and battlefield theophanies will be shown to exist. Some of these themes are the total annihilation of the families of perjurers, the reduction of cities to desolate tells, and the rending of bodies as carrion for wild animals.

[24] M. Kitts, "Not Barren Is the Blood of Lambs," *Kernos* 16 (2003) 17–34.

# CHAPTER ONE

# EPICS, RITUALS, AND RITUALS IN EPIC: SOME METHODOLOGICAL CONSIDERATIONS

## EPICS AND RITUALS

Since most epics are replete with combats, battles, wars and assassinations, the killing scene is often an epitome or multivocal symbol of the scheme of values underpinning the whole work.                    (Victor Turner[1])

I T HAS BEEN ARGUED THAT THE WAY A HERO ENGAGES THE TERMS OF his or her destiny is the very stuff of epic literature.[2] The nature of fate and the cosmic principles which shape it penetrate the personal narrative of the epic hero usually at that point when he or she is close to death. Such is the case in the *Iliad*, especially in the poignant dying scenes of Sarpedon, Patroklos, and Hector — major heroes beloved by gods and men alike, whose deaths elicit pondering by divinities, foreshadow one another, and point ahead to the death of Achilles. Unlike those heroes, Achilles chooses to die young, and his coming to terms with his fate is a measure of his truly heroic stature. Yet the pathos of his fate is built up by the pathos of the other heroes, whose deaths in turn are built up by shorter dying scenes of lesser characters.[3] So, for instance, the death of young Polydoros, Priam's "most beloved son" who is stabbed in the back while fleeing from Achilles (20.407–18), anticipates the longer dying scene of his brother Lykaon, who begs Achilles to spare him because his mother

---

[1] "Comparative Epic and Saga," p. 7 (unpublished essay), quoted by Alf Hiltebeitel, *The Ritual of Battle* (New York: SUNY Press 1990) 37.

[2] Hiltebeitel 1990: 34–5.

[3] George Duckworth, *Foreshadowing and Suspense in the Epics of Homer, Apollonius, and Vergil* (Princeton: Princeton University Press 1933), Bernard Fenik on doublets, *Typical Battle Scenes in the Iliad* (Wiesbaden: Franz Sterlag 1968) 214, and Agathe Thornton, *Homer's Iliad: Its Composition and the Motif of Supplication* (Gottingen: Vandenhoeck and Ruprecht, H.81 1984).

already has lost her other son and has just received Lykaon home again, after Achilles had abducted him (21.54–135). Lykaon's death at the hands of Achilles anticipates in turn the death of Hector, also Priam's favorite son (22.424–25), remembered by his own mother as a tender, nursing infant (22.79–85), and whose subsequent dying scene is virtually the climax of the epic. Then the ransom of Hector's corpse by Priam reminds Achilles of the toll his oncoming death will take on his own father, and the weeping together of the Trojan father and Achaian son is simply the quintessential expression of despair and reconciliation in western epic. And so the anticipatory echoes and intricate themes of fathers, mothers, love, youth, death, and despair which are tied to minor characters, generate tone for the death of a major hero and texturize his personal encounter with fate.

The dying scenes of minor characters, then, may condense and also radiate themes embellished more fully in longer narratives about major characters.[4] Short, formulaic dying scenes exist by the hundreds in the *Iliad*. Regardless of where one stands on the semanticity of these shorter formulae, the cumulative effect of formulaic dying scenes clearly projects the tragic character of the whole work. Men fall gasping for breath (for instance in 5.585; 13.396–9; 13.571; 20.403; 21.182), clutching the earth in their fists (13.508, 13.520, 14.452, 16.486, 17.315), their armor clatters on top of them (5.42, 5.58; 5.294, 5.540; 17.311), their limbs are loosened (7.12; 7.16; 16.312, 16.341, 16.465; 17.349); and darkness, dark night, hateful death, or purple fate covers their eyes (4.461–2, 4.503, 4.526, 5.68; 5.82–3; 5.310; 5.659; 6.11; 15.578). The great number of such dying scenes is what distinguishes Homeric war rhetoric from, say, Neo-Assyrian war rhetoric, which is similarly formulaic but whose triumphant tone mutes the plight of the victims. The *Iliad* has its own share of vengeful boasting and gory slaughter, of course, but even the most unsophisticated listener will notice that death tends to be focalized with an ear for the victim's last breath. Sometimes that focalization occupies only half a verse, sometimes 20. The impact of death is measured from many different points of view – parents,' wives,' siblings,' friends,' even horses' (as in the immortal horses who grieve for Patroklos [17.426–428, 23.280–284]). On occasion, a victim's last moments are compared to those of an animal resisting or finally yielding to death. Victims may meet death as stunned fawns (21.29), as belching bulls (20.402–06), as fish fleeing a voracious dolphin (21.22–26), or as an ox: "gasping as an

---

[4] A point established well by Bernard Fenik in *Typical Battle Scenes*.

unwilling ox whom oxherds in the mountains bind with twisted cords and lead by force, so, being struck, he gasped only for a little, not very long, while Meriones came near and pulled back the spear from his flesh. Then darkness covered his eyes" (13.568–75).

Given that the *Iliad*'s dying scenes, both large and small, appear to serve an epic ideology pertaining to war, peace, and destiny, what are we to make of the poem's dying scenes that fall within religious rituals, or mimic them in some way? It is a curious fact that the *Iliad*'s commensal sacrifices, which may anticipate bloody battles and be initiated by ominous prayers to inflict death (such as at 2.412–18), never acknowledge the dying of the sacrificial victim.[5] Instead, the death is eclipsed by an abundance of formulaic phrases and microadjusting finite verbs that describe the throat-slitting (*sphazdō* – usually a culinary verb in Homer), flaying, butchering, skewering, roasting, and finally dining on the animal (see 1.446–74; 2.410–432). The blood, intrinsic to battle scenes and an emphasized element in several major theories of Greek sacrifice, is never mentioned, nor are the animal's last gasps and collapse. Instead the mood is one of harmony and jubilant feasting.

The same jubilation is notably ironic, however, when a sacrificial context is conjured in this simile for a dying warrior:

> . . . [Achilles] stabbed him in the upper back with his spear.
> Then Hippodamus gasped out his spirit and belched, as when a bull
> belches as he is being dragged for the Helikonian lord
> by young men, and the Earthshaker is happy with them.
> So as Hippodamas was belching, the manly spirit left his bones.
>
> (20.402–06)

And there is little jubilation in this simile, seemingly based on a sacrificial paradigm:

> As when a vigorous man holding a sharp ax
> strikes behind the horns of a field ox,
> so he may cut clear through, and the ox plunges forth and falls,
> so [Aretos] plunged forth and fell on his back, and the sharp spear
> in his bowels quite loosened his quivering limbs.
>
> (17.520–24)

---

[5] I am considering funeral feasts to fall under a different *topos*.

How are we to explain the silence regarding the animal's plight in commensal sacrifices and the conspicuousness of the same plight in similes that render the fighter as a dying sacrificial victim?

On the one hand, the disparity between the focalization on dying warriors as sacrificed animals on the battlefield and the focalization away from dying animals in commensal sacrifices may be explained simply by the needs of epic. It is obvious that the *Iliad*'s focalizations, figurative expressions, and also rituals serve the story; they build tension, layer meanings, generate themes, and stir the imaginations of audiences. As suggested by Victor Turner in our opening quote, killing scenes in epic tend to sensitize audiences to the impact of violence and death. By a similar logic, commensal scenes may diffuse it. The commensal sacrifices in *Iliad* Books 1 and 2, for instance, follow Achilles' quarrel with Agamemnon, which sets the stage for the carnage that will befall the Greeks while Achilles is away. The audience may anticipate this carnage and see the congenial mood of those commensal feasts as a striking contrast, albeit dimmed by the anger of Achilles in Book 1 and by Agamemnon's prayer for Priam's total destruction in Book 2 (412–18). Likewise, the commensal feasts hosted by Achilles elsewhere in the epic (Books 9 and 24) illustrate the best of human harmony and hospitality, and pose as dramatic counterpoints to battlefield depictions of warriors as raw-flesh-eating predators (see 16.156–63, 17.61–64, 24.41–45, 24.207–8) or as indomitable heroes from a bygone age (1.271–72, 5.302–4, 20.285–87, 12.381–83, 12.447–49). At first glance, then, commensal sacrifices in Homeric epic may be said to offer audiences a respite from the violence of the surrounding battle scenes. The respite throws the battle scenes into crisp relief. In this way of thinking, contrasting poetic purposes may explain quite simply why the dying of animals is rendered vividly in similes for men dying in battle, but not at all in representations of the sacrifices that lead to feasting and the sating of appetites.

To persist in this way of thinking, briefly, the setting of Homeric oath-sacrifices might be appreciated in marked contrast with commensal sacrifices. Notably, oath-sacrificing rituals, too, feature an abundance of microadjusting steps, represented by a fixed cluster of finite indicative verbs and precise detail; yet the obvious effect of these details is to highlight, not to obscure, the dying of the victim. Oath-sacrificing scenes feature striking displays of death, with apparent crescendo. The two complete examples of oath-sacrifice in the *Iliad* will be discussed fully in Chapter 3, but for now they may be broken down into the following ritual steps: (a) the participants assemble respectfully around a leader (3.114–15, 19.255–56); (b) an animal victim is presented for sacrifice (3.268–69, 19.250–51); (c) Agamemnon "draws with his hands the sacrificial knife (*machaira*) which always hung by the great sheath of his sword" (3.271–72, 19.252–53); (d) with the *machaira* he cuts hair from the victim (3.273, 19.254) and distributes it to the participants (3.274); (e) he prays, holding up his hands to Zeus (3.275–76, 19.254–55); (f) the Erinyes are invoked to punish perjurers (3.279, 19.259–260); (g) the terms of the oath are given; (h) oath-violators are cursed, either here (in Book 19) or after the concluding libation of wine (in Book 3); (i) the cinching of the oath occurs when Agamemnon "cuts" (*tame*) the throat of the sacrificial victim with the "pitiless bronze" (*nelei chalkō*, 3.392, 19.266); and (j) the victims die – either they lie on the ground "gasping and emptied of life [*thumos*] for the bronze has taken away their might [*menos*]" (3.293–94), or they die elliptically, as when the herald "hurls [the boar] into the great abyss of the sea" (19.267–68). The somber mood of oath-sacrifices is enunciated by the curses stressing the analogy between the perjurer's and the victim's bodies as well as by analogies between other symbolic substances and acts. For instance, the Achaians and Trojans conclude the oath-sacrifice in Book 3 by pouring cups of wine and praying, each of them.[6]

> Thus each of the Achaians and Trojans would pray:
> "Zeus greatest and best, and the other immortal gods,
> whoever first shall violate the oaths,
> so may their brains pour onto the ground, as does this wine,
> and the brains of their children, and may their wives be subdued by
>     others'. "
>
> (3.297–301)

The same deadly analogy is inferred by the fate Agamemnon invites upon himself in Book 19, right before he slices the neck of the boar:

> "[I]f in any way I have sworn these matters falsely, may the gods
>     give to me pains
> very many, as many as they give to anyone who transgresses against
>     them in swearing."
>
> (19.264–65)

That the somber tone of oath-sacrifice does not relieve but rather infuses the killing scenes that follow is supported by repeated curses on

---

[6] I am assigning the distributive nuance to *epesken*, at 3.297.

oath-breakers after the Trojans violate the oath in Book 3. For instance, Agamemnon assures Menelaos:

> "In no way barren is the oath, the blood of lambs,
> the unmixed libations and the right hands in which we trusted.
> For indeed, if the Olympian does not fulfill it at once,
> he certainly will fulfill it later, and with might he will avenge it,
> with their lives and their wives and also their children."
>
> (4.158–162)

And to the rest of the men:

> Argives, do not give up on your rushing courage.
> For Zeus father will not be a advocate for liars,
> but those who were first in violating oaths,
> vultures surely will devour their own tender skins,
> while we lead their wives and little children
> to the ships, after we take the citadel.
>
> (4.234–39)

Given these deadly analogies and the somberness of the oath-sacrificing ritual, then, it may be tempting to argue that oath-sacrifices are used by the poet primarily to create the opposite poetic effect evoked by commensal sacrifices. Oath-sacrifices may be argued to impart a somber mood to the narrative and to underscore, rather than to contrast, the violence in the surrounding battles.

Of course there is something very tidy about confining the significance of different ritual scenes to poetic stress in an epic poem, and this poetic perspective is certainly not wrong.[7] Nonetheless, it is a contention of this book that the poetic perspective is only part of the story. That is, poetic considerations are *not enough* to explain the violence in Homeric oath-sacrifice, to explain the violence in its after-effects, and to explain the violence in sacrificial similes on the battlefield. The reasons are many, but one of them is this: Not discounting the dramatic tensions in the story, to presume that resonances between dying as represented in Homeric rituals and dying as represented in battle scenes yield no window in to semantic tensions in lived experience beyond the *Iliad* would be to fail to appreciate the origins of the epic as an oral poem performed before an audience already familiar with sacrificial rituals as an everyday practice. That

---

[7] I myself have argued for it, in "Sacrificial Violence in the Iliad," *Journal of Ritual Studies* 16:1 (2002) 19–39.

familiarity may not be easily discerned by us, as readers unfamiliar with animal sacrifice in its various configurations and settings millennia ago. Nonetheless, it is with the ancient audience's probable familiarity with sacrificial traditions in mind that we may note the variety and ambiguity in the depictions of animal sacrifice in the *Iliad*. The ritualized killing of animals there appears to be rendered in four different ways: (a) as butchery in commensal sacrifices, wherein the death of the victim is completely muted; (b) ironically in sacrificial similes for dying warriors, wherein the last gasps of the dying animal (figuratively the warrior) are highlighted, presumably to inject a degree of pathos into the human death; (c) ominously in oath-sacrifice, wherein the drama of death seals irrevocably the oath's terms; and (d) murderously on the battlefield, when references to oath-making curses underscore the analogy of perjurers to sacrificial victims. How is it that the ritualized killing of animal victims may be exploited to such different narrative ends? It is a contention of this book that, in order to grasp the multivocality of ritual killing in the *Iliad*, we must probe beyond strictly epic sensibilities to the semantic domains of the rituals themselves.

To probe the semantic domains of ritual performances requires an approach that combines the lessons of oral traditional theory with those of ritual performance theory, but not necessarily with those theories dedicated strictly to ritual sacrifice. Over the last few decades a number of grand sacrificial theories have been applied to Greek sacrificial traditions. Most well known are the theories of René Girard,[8] Jean-Pierre Vernant and Marcel Detienne,[9] and Walter Burkert,[10] all of which have their virtues but fail to account for oath-sacrifice in the *Iliad*. As I have argued elsewhere, René Girard's mimetic theory of ritualized violence ignores a range of human emotions and capabilities, as well as genres of evidence, in favor of a totalizing picture of ritualized violence as a primordial cathartic impulse that holds individuals at its mercy.[11] It simply cannot account for the lack of blood and observable death in the *Iliad*'s commensal sacrifices,

---

[8] See, Girard 1977.

[9] See J. Vernant and Detienne 1989.

[10] See Walter Burkert, *Homo Necans* and *Creation of the Sacred* (Cambridge, MA: Harvard University Press 1996).

[11] See Kitts 2002. René Girard's groundbreaking work on the social function of sacrifice is in *Violence and the Sacred*, but it is perhaps more accessible in *The Girard Reader* (ed. James G. Williams, New York: Crossroads 2000), especially Chapter 6, "Sacrifice as Sacral Violence and Substitution" (69–93).

nor for the lack of catharsis in the oath-sacrifice of Book 19, which appears to cleanse no one and instead launches Achilles' violent *poinē* against the Trojans. Marcel Detienne and Jean-Pierre Vernant's hypothesis of sacrifice as cuisine has some limited applicability to the *Iliad*, but strictly for its representations of *thusia*, and obviously not of *horkia*, where there is no cuisine at all. Walter Burkert's theory of sacrificial ritual as nonverbal communication has far-reaching utility, but his 1971 idea that sacrificial ritual has roots in paleolithic hunting behavior has been challenged on the basis of ethnographic evidence and, at any rate, the idea surely exceeds epic considerations. Notably, he has continued to refine his theory over the years.[12] Many others have offered their own refinements and alternatives to these theories, and of course the topic of sacrifice has received a great deal of attention in Western intellectual history since at least Robertson-Smith's *Religion of the Semites*.[13] These theories are the topic for another book. For now, we will approach the violence in Homeric *horkia* from a perspective that emphasizes not sacrifice, but ritual performance and metaphorical transformation.

But first a caveat about the study of Greek sacrifice: To study the *Iliad*'s oath-sacrificing rituals at all, we must disentangle ourselves from contemporary assumptions about sacrifice. It has been noted frequently that ancient sacrificial symbolism has an entirely different semantic cast than contemporary sacrificial symbolism.[14] Whereas contemporary sacrificial symbolism tends to draw figurative power from the economic sphere of loss and deprivation – giving something up – ancient sacrificial symbolism, especially in tragedy, draws instead on the vivid reality of animal slaughter for nuance.[15] In order to explore the figurative possibilities generated by the sacrificial ritual of animal slaughter, this study will utilize

---

[12] See, for instance, his "Offerings in Perspective: Surrender, Distribution, Exchange," in *Gifts to the Gods* (Boreas 15, Uppala Universitet 1987) 43–50, and *Creation of the Sacred* (1996).

[13] First published 1889. For an overview of the subject, see Grottanelli 1988: 3–53; deHeusch 1985: 1–25; and John Milbank, "Stories of Sacrifice," *Modern Theology* 12:1 (January 1996) 27–56.

[14] See, Wolfgang Stegemann, "Sacrifice as Metaphor," in *Social Scientific Models for Interpreting the Bible, Essays by the Context Group in Honor of Bruce J. Malina*, ed. John J. Pilch (Leiden: E. J. Brill 2001) 310–27.

[15] Although broader in scope, an interesting and relatively early exploration of this vivid reality as a reference in tragedy is Froma Zeitlin's "The Motif of the Corrupted Sacrifice in Aeschylus' Oresteia," TAPA 96 (1966): 468–508.

a theory that highlights the way semantic domains might adhere to a ritual sphere itself. Semantic domains can adhere to rituals because ritualization may be regarded as a symbolic mode of communication, that is, as communication by means of a coherent pattern of gestures and words. The ritual performance can be said to generate a symbolic "text," which happens, in the *Iliad*, to be interwoven with the poetic text. Ritual narratives in the *Iliad* thus fuse the symbolic dimensions of ritual practice with the symbolic aims of the poet (premeditated or not), resulting in a kind of intertextual rendering that can be analyzed for semantic tensions. Such tensions might originate in the ritual performance, in the poetic scene describing that performance, or in the fusion of the two, against a background of audience expectations regarding epic conventions and actual ritual practices at the same time. A complete dethreading of this intertext is probably impossible, but an appreciation of some aspects of it will be helped by an understanding of ritual performance theory, and to some extent by the theory of ritual as promoting metaphorical transformation.

A combination of the theory of ritual performance as communication and the theory of ritual as promoting metaphorical transformation is uniquely suitable for analyzing rituals in the *Iliad* for at least four reasons. First, the theory of ritual performance as communication allows the *Iliad* to speak about ritual performance in more or less its own terms, violating the text less than some "megatheories" of sacrifice that would impose their own shapes on sacrificial narratives but that the epic just cannot support. Second, as a bridge between anthropological and textual studies, the theory of ritual as promoting metaphorical transformation allows the symbolic dimensions of ritual performance to emerge through the text. Third, the theory of ritual performance as communication permits recognition that the audience to the performance is likely to provide its own analogues for interpretation of those symbolic dimensions. The role of audience participation is thereby highlighted, as befits an originally oral traditional text. Fourth, the emphasis on metaphor allows us to appreciate the transformation of actors in ritual, making visible the dynamic aspects not only of characters in the story but also of characters in the ritual performances. The rest of this chapter will outline some of the ritual and oral traditional considerations necessary to make the upcoming arguments about Homeric oath-sacrifices.

Because the study of ritual is enormously broad, let us set out a preliminary definition of ritual to set the stage for the upcoming arguments, which should expand this definition considerably. It should be noted that this definition is coined not to revolutionize ritual studies, but just to help with the analysis of rituals in the *Iliad*. The theory has two sides: (1) ritual performance, and (2) ritual performers, with whom the audience to an orally performed poem might be expected to identify. So (1) ritual will be regarded as a relatively invariant sequence of words and acts that communicates iconic analogues of primordial events to an audience or to performers, who (2) contribute to the interpretation of those analogues by virtue of their own familiarity with them and who exercise a limited capacity to accept, reject, or modify the paradigms on which the analogues are based. It should be noted right off that the communicative efficacy of ritual performance here is assumed to be different than the communicative efficacy of ordinary speech. Ordinary speech permits greater flexibility and precision in expression, based upon the reciprocity between speakers and upon the inevitable clarifying and contextualizing of statements in conversation. Ritual communication, argues Valerio Valeri, among others, is more restricted in its flexibility and precision by, for one thing, the inchoateness of the original ritual "author," usually projected way back into tradition or into some celestial sphere. The "hearing" performer or audience to the ritual tends to project his or her own understanding upon the ritual intention, which the hearer deems to be the intention of an implicit author.[16] The inchoateness of this implicit author permits some degree of negotiation of meaning by an audience and thus a limited variety of interpretations, but the variety floats along the parameters of established ritual paradigms, which are more restricted in scope than the paradigms of ordinary speech. The degree of negotiation of meaning for ritual paradigms is not unlike that involved in the interpretations of typical scenes by an audience to the *Iliad* as an orally performed text, because the audience putatively recognizes an underlying paradigm in the oral-poetic scene even as it may envision the underlying paradigm somewhat differently, audience to audience, era to era, context to context.

The paradigmatic aspects of ritual communication, too, are different than those of ordinary speech. Similarly to the grammar of ordinary speech, ritual "grammar" involves paradigmatic and syntagmatic associations, but ordinary speech tends to highlight one aspect of a paradigm while excluding others, specifying the aspects that suit

[16] Valerio Valeri, *Kingship and Sacrifice*, trans. Paula Wissing (Chicago: University of Chicago Press 1985) 342.

particular contexts. The interpretation of paradigms by performers and audiences of rituals (imply Valeri, Rappaport,[17] and other anthropologists[18]) is more restricted by the relatively invariant ritual shape and also by the tradition that gives rise to it. As Valeri sees it, ritual performances stress equivalence over difference. Most importantly, they enjoy a poetic property resulting from the projection of the paradigmatic over the syntagmatic axis, as Jakobson might assert about poetic thought.[19] A ritual's poetic property, based on the projection of the paradigmatic over the syntagmatic, may be said to generate a poetic text that, especially in the *Iliad's* ritual scenes but also in some of its killing scenes, may be exploited by the poet of the epic, who weaves the poetic text produced by the ritual performance into the larger poetic text of the *Iliad*.[20]

The remainder of this chapter will examine the assumptions and the repercussions of this definition as they might pertain to ritual scenes in the *Iliad*.

## RITUALS IN EPIC

To begin our investigation of the "intertextual" dimensions between the oath-making ritual spheres in the *Iliad* and oath-making ritual spheres in the experience and imagination of ancient audiences, it is first necessary to appreciate the once open nature of the oral traditional text. Oral traditional theory has gone full circle on a number of its claims since the 1920s, but one claim that remains quite stable is that the *Iliad* and the *Odyssey* were composed not as closed texts, but to be intensely participatory.[21] Based on analogues from Yugoslavia and

---

[17] See Rappaport 1999.

[18] See Catherine Bell's discussion of "Ritual Traditions and Systems," Chapter 6 of *Ritual Theory, Ritual Practice* (New York: Oxford University Press 1992) 118–68, and Maurice Bloch's discussion of ritual oratory in his "Introduction" to *Political Language and Oratory in Traditional Society* (London: Academy Press 1975) 1–28.

[19] See Valeri 1985: 343.

[20] See Kitts, "Not Barren Is the Blood of Lambs," for a preliminary version of this argument.

[21] Standard works on this vast subject include *The Making of Homeric Verse, The Collected Papers of Milman Parry*, ed. Adam Parry (New York: Oxford University Press 1987b), Albert Lord, *The Singer of Tales* (Cambridge, MA: Harvard University Press 1960), Walter Ong, *Interfaces of the Word* (London: Cornell University Press 1977), Michael Nagler, *Spontaneity and Tradition* (Berkeley: University of California Press, 1974), and John Miles Foley, *Immanent Art, from Structure to Meaning in Traditional Oral Epic*

elsewhere,[22] it has long been hypothesized that the Homeric poets probably composed songs in verse during performances for audiences weaned on a story and its themes, its rhythmic cadences, and its epic texture. The audience was thus in a position to intuit certain contextual, semantic, and thematic undertones that a singer didn't need to specify in a particular song. John Miles Foley has coined the expression "traditional referentiality"[23] to refer to the semantic fields called to the minds of the audience by the poet-composers, who evoked them through the use of synecdoche and contoured their songs in each performance to fit audience expectations in a discreet kind of give and take. The *Iliad* apparently enjoyed centuries of popularity as a participatory experience for audiences on two sides of the Mediterranean before it was rendered as a fixed text.[24] From any kind of critical perspective, it is simply unimaginable that these centuries of participatory experience would not have resulted in the attraction of an audience's lived ritual traditions into poetic narratives concerning those traditions.[25] In fact, the comprehension of the audience relies upon it. What Ricoeur points out about the semantic reach of written literature may be applied just as well to oral literature: "If reading [and comprehending] is possible, it is indeed because the text is not closed in on itself but opens out onto other things."[26] The recreating of the story by audience and poet together through performance might be said to establish a three-way tension between tradition, individual singer, and particular audience. The involvement of the audience makes it unlikely that oath-sacrificing narratives, and any ambiguity adhering to them, were not understood as somehow relevant to an audience's lived,

---

(Bloomington: Indiana University Press 1991). Two nice summaries of the implications are "Oral Tradition and Its Implications," John Miles Foley, in *A New Companion to Homer*, eds. Ian Morris & Barry Powell (Leiden: E. J. Brill 1997) 146–73, and "Contemporary Critical Approaches and Studies in Oral Tradition," Mark C. Amodio, in *Teaching Oral Traditions*, ed. John Miles Foley (New York: The Modern Language Association 1998) 95–105.

[22] Parry 1987b; Albert Lord 1960; Agathe Thornton 1984; John Miles Foley (1991) and *Traditional Oral Epic* (Berkeley: University of California Press 1990).

[23] Foley 1991.

[24] See, for instance, Gregory Nagy's *Poetry as Performance* (Cambridge: Cambridge University Press 1996) 107–52.

[25] Peter Karavites is unabashed in finding in the Homeric poems "the format and structure of the treaties and other promise-making conventions that actually obtained in the Mycenaean world" (1992: 3).

[26] Paul Ricoeur, *Hermeneutics and the Human Sciences: Essays on Language, Action and Interpretation* (Cambridge: Cambridge University Press 1981) 158.

cultural experiences, quite in addition to any imagined relevance to ritual practices during an age of heroes. It is this interactive nature of the oral traditional text that encourages exploration of ritual scenes for the far-reaching symbolic matrices those scenes may have attracted to the text from actual cultural practices in antiquity.

Given the *Iliad*'s presumably long history as an oral text, however, it is unlikely that only one understanding of a ritual ever informed a ritual scene's shape. Shifting cultural sensibilities over time, regions, and audiences surely influenced the poem and somehow must bear on its current hypostasis. Such shifts complicate an investigation of ritual patterns and their significance in epic, but do not entirely preclude it. A few helpful keys for unlocking actual oath-sacrificing ritual patterns, their interpenetration with Homeric oath-sacrificing narratives, and their relevance to the poetic rendering of battlefield deaths as sacrificial deaths, may be fitted into three broad areas: (1) a simple view of hermeneutic limitations and the anthropology of the lie; (2) the anthropological study of ritual patterns, particularly those patterns that trigger iconic recognition of primordial paradigms and metaphorical shifts of identity on the part of performers; and (3) the formalization of the ritual scene in oral traditional literature. At least two of these areas are familiar to anthropologists and historians of religion, and the third is certainly well known to Homerists. Although an investigation of these areas takes us away from the poetic impact of dying as a sacrificial victim, the detour is essential background for envisioning the larger cultural frame for oath-sacrifices as they are rendered in the *Iliad*.

## HERMENEUTICS AND THE PROBLEM OF THE LIE

The problem of perspective in analyzing rituals from the *Iliad* or from any other ancient text is to some degree obvious. We may recognize ritual patterns and their implications by closely studying ritual narratives and the narratives that surround them, but how deeply may we gauge a ritual's power as felt by the poet's audience, given the fact that twenty-first century readers are at best very indirect participants in any rituals the text may represent? Of course our understanding will never be identical to that of an ancient audience, given the premise that perspective shapes inquiry and that, basically, we never encounter a bare ritual fact without interpretation. Yet, hermeneutic limitations are less problematic when prejudice is recognized. Gadamer puts it simply: "Prejudices are biases of our openness to the world. They are simply conditions whereby we experience something – whereby what we encounter says something to us."[27] Consequently, we may grasp ritual patterns and even some of their semantic themes insofar as our training – historical research, familiarity with neighboring traditions, a taste for epic, experience with rituals, and so forth – has already prefigured our capacity for recognition.[28] But this prefiguring amounts to a hermeneutic circle, or at least a spiral, which leaves us susceptible to missing what Rappaport and others before him have referred to as the "numinous" dimension of rituals.[29] Secular moderns tend to treat numinous dimensions in Classical texts as a matter of aesthetics. Gadamer relies on Hegel in pointing out that we withdraw into aesthetic judgment "when we are no longer open to the immediate claim of that which grasps us,"[30] which, in the case of Homeric oath-sacrifice, presumably would be the unquestioned authority of the oath-making rituals, as well as of the gods they invoke. What Gadamer has called an aesthetic perspective strips ritual narratives of some of the power presumably understood to adhere to them by audiences still under the ritual tradition's spell.

One response to this hermeneutic limitation is to examine the ontological metaphors implicit in oath-making, particularly metaphors on which we might rely to grasp the meaning of a threat of death for perjury. As discussed by Turner, Johnson, and Lakoff, ontological metaphors are based on the image schemas for universally embodied experiences. In the oath-making case, this would appear to be on a simple but elusive image schema of the *vigor* of the human body.[31] This schema would appear to be as basic

---

[27] Hans-Georg Gadamer, *Philosophical Hermeneutics* (Berkeley: University of California Press 1976); Chapter 9, "The Universality of the Hermeneutic Problem" (written in 1966).

[28] "Only the support of familiar and common understanding makes possible the venture into the alien, the lifting up of something out of the alien, and thus the broadening and enrichment of our experience of the world." Gadamer 1976: 15.

[29] Rudolf Otto is usually credited with this coinage, *The Idea of the Holy* (London: Oxford University Press 1958).

[30] Gadamer 1976: 5.

[31] Although the notion of bodily sanctity may fall under the image schema of body as container – essentially a spatialization metaphor – one might also consider the possibility of a different image schema based on simply the vigor of living in time. To be fair, Lakoff, Johnson, and Turner do not, to my knowledge, discuss ontological recognition based on bodily vigor, per se, but I believe it may be intrinsic to their discussion of narrative and time. It is certainly relevant to a notion from Longinus, discussed by Turner, that "figural understanding is all the more powerful when it is so automatic that we do not recognize its figural nature." Mark Turner, "Design for a Theory of Meaning" in *Nature and Ontogenesis of Meaning*, eds. W. Overton and D. Palermo (Mahwah, NJ: Lawrence Erlbaum Associates 1994) 91–107. See also George

to understanding what a threat of death means as the gravity vector is to understanding the experience of walking around under the burden of one's own weight, by which we comprehend "a heavy load" in our own and other people's metaphors. Ontological metaphors help to explain the cross-cultural recognition of certain very basic rhetorical themes. The relevance of ontological metaphors for understanding oaths and perjury in ancient epic may be summed up neatly: Although few of us fear the wrath of Zeus, we can imagine what it means to be threatened with death. This certainly does not eliminate all distance between our own and ancient perspectives on oaths and perjury, but it does ameliorate it to a degree.

Notwithstanding the specter of punishment for perjurers throughout the ages, history is littered with people who lied anyway. Thus, a perhaps more interesting consideration that bears on an understanding of the *Iliad*'s oath-making rituals, is the problem of the lie. Were willful lying not a common human attribute – and arguably one unique to humans at that[32] – oath-making traditions presumably never would be established. Conversely, threats relating to the consequences of perjury may never arouse anything like a twinge of trepidation, neither for ancient audiences nor for us, were we not all likely to recognize oath-making traditions as somehow compelling, perhaps as a legitimate challenge to unlimited individual freedoms, or perhaps just in response to the threat as speech act. Although its philosophical ramifications are beyond the scope of this study, the subject of lying invites two comments relating to the ubiquity of oath-making institutions and to understanding the oath-conscious society represented in the *Iliad*. The first involves the issue of words and trust and the second involves the affective nature of ritual performances.

First, as "a fence [*herkos*] . . . which confines or constrains,"[33] an oath, *horkos*, is designed precisely to thwart the duplicity of speakers, this duplicity being a fundamental problem in the study of communication itself and one felt keenly in Greek culture and poetry at least as early as Hesiod's invocation of the whimsical Muses. Their boast, "We know how to speak many lies which seem true, and we know also how to sing the truth, when we wish" (*Theogony* 27–28), is emblematic of a felt slipperiness in language, based on, minimally, the potential for deceit and possibly also on a

Lakoff and Mark Johnson, *Metaphors We Live By* (Chicago: University of Chicago Press 1980) 56–68.

[32] Rappaport 1999: 11–17.

[33] See Joseph Plescia, *The Oath and Perjury in Ancient Greece* (Tallahassee: Florida State University Press, 1970) 1, for this definition.

sense of word-magic. As for the deceit, Rappaport has observed that the notion of lying has meaning based upon the presumption of a relationship of trust between individuals in a society.[34] Notably, the Muses who boast of willful lies are outside of the human community, so perhaps are not bound by the "grounds of the trustworthiness requisite to systems of communication and community generally."[35] But everyone else is, despite an unmistakable archaic Greek infatuation with clever liars (such as the high regard for liars Odysseus and Autolycus). The very existence of oath-making customs is an indicator of the potential duplicity felt to reside in speech acts of any sort, and of the recognition that society's stability rests on stymying any such duplicity (notwithstanding Plato's advocation of the noble lie).

As for the sense of spoken words as magical forces, the untrustworthiness of the Muses stems at least in part from a suspicion that words have as an intrinsic property a slight-of-hand potential: they can conceal or they can reveal; they can mask or point out new truths; they can bring new perceptions into being. As Stanley J. Tambiah has pointed out, there is some truth to this suspicion about the magical property of words, because language, as part of our historical and cultural heritage, might well be felt as an outside force, constraining our possibilities for self-expression even as it also enters within us, and can be manipulated freely to our own devices.[36] We will return to the subject of words and magical power when we discuss cursing customs in Chapter 2, but here suffice it to say that an awareness of the compelling and bewitching properties of spoken words is essential for grasping the power of oath-making traditions in the *Iliad*.

Second, and more complexly, aside from the issues of social trust and the compelling force behind spoken words, there is the problem of the distancing effect of ritualized conventions per se, including those conventions dedicated to oath-making. Ironically, a lack of sincerity is perfectly possible in ritual performance, even in rituals designed to ensure conformance to a preset goal. In other words, one may "lie" in some interior way or to some degree as one enters into a ritualized convention

---

[34] Rappaport 1999: 13.

[35] Rappaport 1999: 15.

[36] "[Language] moves us, and we generate it as active agents. Since words exist and are in a sense agents in themselves which establish connexions and relations between both man and man, and man and the world, and are capable of 'acting' upon them, they are one of the most realistic representations we have of the concept of force which is either not directly observable or is a metaphysical notion which we find necessary to use." S. J. Tambiah, "The Magic Power of Words," *Man* 3:2 (1968) 175–208, n.b. 184.

meant precisely to bind a ritual performer to a mandate that precludes lying. Most students of the *Iliad* probably would agree that Agamemnon's commitment to the oath he makes with Achilles in Book 19 is less than personally earnest, given the weak excuse he offers for his earlier folly – which he compares to the *Atē* that once ensnared Zeus (19.108–36)[37] – and given that benefits for the oath accrue to him especially, and not particularly to Achilles – hence, perhaps, Achilles' request that they dispense with whole thing (19:145–53) and his disinterest in the feast that follows (19.198–214, 19.304–8, 19.319–20). Tambiah, Langer, and Rappaport have offered accounts of the distancing effect of ritualized conventions, which permit a degree of hypocrisy in that they "separate the private emotions of the actors from their commitment to a public morality."[38] The institutionalized discourse effected through the stereotyped conventions of ritual, says Tambiah, encodes not private intentions but simulations of intentions, and is publically construed to express and communicate "certain attitudes congenial to an ongoing institutionalized discourse."[39] Thus, "ritual is not a free expression of emotions, but a disciplined rehearsal of right attitudes."[40] The suppression of immediate, personal emotion, further, "enables the cultural elaboration of the symbolic"[41] and, according to Langer, ultimately contributes to "not a simple emotion, but a complex permanent attitude."[42] As Rappaport sees it, the primary function of certain rituals is not to control personal emotions anyway, "but rather to establish conventional understandings, rules, and norms, in accordance with which everyday behavior is *supposed* to proceed."[43]

Rappaport's view of the compelling force of formalized rituals illuminates in great detail the public nature of ritual constraints on behavior, and given the persistent Homeric theme of oaths and oath-violating, is worth

---

[37] See, for instance, Oliver Taplin's discussion of Agamemnon's contradiction: He is not *aitios* and yet he is willing to pay reparation (*Homeric Soundings* [Oxford: Clarendon Press 1992] 205–12).

[38] Stanley Tambiah, "A Performative Approach to Ritual," in *Proceedings of the British Academy*, Vol. 65 (Oxford: Oxford University Press 1979) 124; Rappaport 1999: 122–23; Susanne Langer, *Philosophy in a New Key* (New York: New American Library 1951), cited by Tambiah at page 126–27.

[39] Tambiah 1979: 124.

[40] Tambiah 1979: 126.

[41] Tambiah 1979: 124.

[42] Susanne Langer, *Philosophy in a New Key* (New York: New American Library 1951) 123–4, quoted in Tambiah 1979: 125.

[43] Rappaport 1999: 123.

a bit of development here. As Rappaport sees it, perfidy, reluctance, lack of belief, or any other private orientation does not nullify the social effectiveness of a formalized ritual, whose effectiveness lies instead "in its very lack of profundity, in the possibility of disparity between the outward act and the inward state."[44] Rather than establish interior states, says Rappaport, formalized rituals instantiate conventions that specify canonical ideals for individual behavior, implicating the performers in commitments that are wider than self-interest. The theory turns on a ritual's "metaperformative" power. Metaperformative rituals not only compel recognition of the authority of the conventions they represent, they actually bring those conventions into existence through performance,[45] rather the way performative-constative illocutions bring into being the matters they express, according to the theory of illocutionary "speech acts" usually attributed to J. L. Austin and John Searle.[46] In Austin's terms, illocutions by their nature do something more than just transmit sounds or words to convey meaning. They also inform, warn, threaten, amuse, confuse, congratulate, dub, swear, and so forth. As acts, they have a conventional force.[47] Of special relevance for oath-making rituals are factive illocutions, which establish the matters of which they speak. For instance, "I dub thee knight," uttered by the right person in the right circumstances and not in jest, confers knighthood upon someone who may or may not be up to the tasks of knighthood; the conventional force of the ritual commits him to it anyway. Oaths, too, by being performed, clearly establish the matters of which they speak, which in the *Iliad* tend to be circumstantial facts or a commitment to fulfilling certain terms, the latter interpreted as "commissives" by Austin and Rappaport.[48] Rappaport's illustrations of commissives include dancing at a host's *kaiko* among the Maring: Dancing at one's host's *kaiko* brings into effect an obligation to fight alongside him during the next war. Dancing the *kaiko* has more performative force than just saying one will fight because, unlike words – which

---

[44] Rappaport 1999: 121.

[45] Rappaport 1999: 125. To be fair, Rappaport is referring to "liturgical performances" here, which shall be discussed presently.

[46] Constitutive rules are contrasted with regulative rules in John R. Searle's *Speech Acts* (London: Cambridge University Press 1969, reprint 1974) at pages 34–5.

[47] J. L. Austin, *How To Do Things with Words* (Cambridge, MA: Harvard University Press 1962, reprint (1975) Chapter 1, 3–6.

[48] Commissives differ from factives quite simply in that they do "not bring into being the states of affairs with which they are concerned, but bring into being the commitment of those performing them to do so sometime in the future." Rappaport 1999: 115.

are ephemeral, retractable, and potentially ambiguous – dancing the *kaiko* is an established convention, a public act whose significance permits little ambiguity.[49] Also, once it is performed, the commitment is made, regardless of when or if its promise will be realized. In both cases, factive and commissive, the performance is self-fulfilling. It brings a convention into being, and the ritualized performing of it – the metaperformance of it – creates a conventional truth against which future acts (such as the failure to fulfill one's commitments) are judged.[50] The public fact of commitment is established by ritual performance. In establishing its own authority, then, a ritual performance does not eliminate insincerity, but does render it publically irrelevant. This allowance for insincerity will have an obvious bearing on Agamemnon's oath to Achilles in *Iliad* 19.

It may seem paradoxical that at the same time as a ritual formalizes the intentions of individual participants, stripping their private emotions of relevance, the same ritual may have commissive effects that are indisputably powerful for individuals, and may even put a ritual actor's life at stake. This would seem to apply to the *Iliad* where, for instance, the violation of the oaths sworn, regardless of the reason for violation, is advertised to bring about one's death.[51] These commissive effects may seem to contradict the distancing effect of ritual conventions already discussed. Three considerations help to temper this seeming contradiction.

The first consideration is the possibly variant degrees and motives of engagement among the ritual actors.[52] This first possibility may be glimpsed in *Iliad* 19. There, Achilles seems less interested in his oath with Agamemnon (19.145–53) than are Odysseus, Nestor, and the rest of the troops, who are relieved that Achilles has renounced his *mēnis* and rejoined the war effort (19.74–75). They clearly see the oath as a symbolic commitment to cooperation between their chief leader and their chief

---

[49] Rappaport 1999: 57, 146–7.

[50] Indeed, participation in the ritual, for Rappaport, ensures acceptance of its terms, the subsequent violation of which is tantamount to violating moral dicta, based on the sense of obligation implicit in having performed the ritual. Rappaport 1999: 132.

[51] According to Joseph Plescia, in this respect the *Iliad*'s oaths differ from later oaths in Greek antiquity, in which the religious elements are less pronounced (1970: 83–91). However, any sense of the lethal punishment for perjury is a bit vague in Hector's "false" oath to Dolon (that he should be awarded Achilles' horses), which is based on a hypothetical Trojan victory and which is thwarted by Dolon's death.

[52] I say this in disagreement with Rappaport's performance ideal of fusion between ritual actor and ritual commitment. To be fair, Rappaport's notion of the dissolution of the individual into his ritual persona is applied strictly to the most formalized category of rituals, a category he refers to as "liturgical orders."

hero, regardless of the two chiefs' personal emotions. Rappaport explains the principle behind such variant degrees of ritual engagement: "To recognize that secret denial may hide beneath the acceptance inhering in the act of performance is to recognize that the grounds of acceptance may vary widely, that acceptance is not necessarily founded upon belief, and that it does not even necessarily imply the subject state termed "approval."[53] Bell,[54] Bourdieu,[55] and Bloch[56] touch on another facet of this variance in engagement, which is that a cultivated mastery of ritual schemes enables performers to appropriate and deploy a ritual's power strategies to their own ends. As Bell puts it, a ritual's semantic schemes may be employed to serve "a semicoherent vision of personal identity and action. Socialization cannot be anything less than the acquisition of schemes that can potentially restructure and renuance both self and society."[57] In the *Iliad*, Odysseus and Nestor are represented as particularly discerning of Agamemnon's and Achilles' personal infelicities regarding the oath's performance and also of the way that ritual may be used to manipulate authority and garner popular support.[58] Achilles, too, seems to exercise a fine and subtle grasp of ritual as a nuancing vehicle for behavior, as we shall see in Chapter 2. These two related factors – hidden motives and the use of ritual schemes to manipulate personal identities and power relations – help to account for the variant degrees of engagement by the actors represented in the oath of Book 19.

[53] Rappaport 1999: 121.
[54] Catherine Bell 1992.
[55] Pierre Bourdieu, *Language and Symbolic Power*, trans. G. Raymond and M. Adamson (Cambridge, MA: Harvard University Press 1991).
[56] Maurice Bloch, "Symbols, Song, Dance and Features of Articulation," in *Archives Europeenes*, 1974, cited by C. Bell, 1992.
[57] Catherine Bell 1992: 216.
[58] Compare Hera's ploy in refusing to help Poseidon in Book 20, by blaming it on a prior oath even though she has already demonstrated her willingness to meddle in the war and has solicited the help of Poseidon elsewhere:

> "Earthshaker, you decide yourself in your mind
> whether to protect Aineas or to allow him to be defeated
> even though he is brave, by Achilles son of Peleus
> For once we two swore oaths by many powers [Edwards 1991:327]
> among all the immortals, I and Pallas Athene,
> never to ward off the evil day to Trojans,
> not even when all of Troy is burning and is destroyed
> by powerful fire, when the warlike sons of the Achaians burn it."
>
> (20.310–17)

A second consideration is the fact that some ritual performances simply have more compelling force than others, based on the risk involved – that is, based on the context. This second consideration may be glimpsed in the disparity between the oath-sacrifices in Books 3 and 19. The longer and more tenuous oath between the Achaians and Trojans in Book 3 establishes a truce that, once violated, calls upon the ritual participants to bring to fruition the commitments they made to the messages encoded in the ritual sacrifice and the concluding curse, references to all of which recur numerous times over the next four books. The anticipated untrustworthiness of the Trojans, referred to at 3.105–10,[59] heightens the sense of precariousness in this oath, and the tension after the oath is broken reverberates into surrounding battle scenes, as evidenced by the repeated lambasts against the Trojans as oath-violators. In contrast, the more abbreviated oath-sacrifice between Achilles and Agamemnon in Book 19, in which an implied pledge of alliance is eclipsed by the more superficial pledge that Agamemnon has not slept with Briseis, is less likely to invite repercussions, for four possible reasons borne out in the larger story: (1) everyone presumes that the precise terms of the oath are not violated (if Agamemnon were lying, presumably Achilles would find out), so the formality is a mere one; (2) Achilles has a reputation for trustworthiness, once he agrees to participate in something, so there is no need for high tension and urgency on anyone's part; (3) the audience and presumably the Achaians are aware that Achilles is predicted not to live long enough to realize Agamemnon's earlier promises of land and son-in-law status – promises unmentioned during the actual oath-cutting ritual anyway, and promises Achilles has already rejected as insulting (9.394ff); and (4) in effect, the rest of that book and the next three concern only Achilles, his victims, and the gods. Narratively speaking, they have little to do with Achilles' bond with Agamemnon or with any other living human besides his victims. In short, reliability is not the issue in the surrounding story. The most apparent purpose of this oath-making ritual is to boost the morale of the Achaian troops and to launch

---

"And bring the strength (*Bie*) of Priam, so he may cut the oaths (*horkia*)
      himself, since his children are overbearing and untrustworthy,
      lest someone by overstepping/violence destroy the oath of Zeus.
      For the thoughts of younger men always flutter.
      An old man goes among them, and considers both the past
      and the future, whatever may be the best, by far, for both sides."
      
                                                          (3.105–110)

Achilles into the war. Not all ritual performances are of equal risk and consequence.

Nonetheless – and this is the third and most important consideration that helps to temper the seeming contradiction between the suppression of personal emotions and the formalization of personal commitments – the very formality of the ritual may engage the ritual actor in the ritual's terms, based on the affective force of ritualization itself. We needn't go so far as Rappaport in asserting that the performative ideal creates a fusion of ritual actors (the "transmitter-receivers") with the performances they make.[60] This may be a publically perceived fact, but that there are variant degrees of personal engagement already has been argued. Yet, if ritual performances do not quite create a personalized fusion with conventions for actors, ritualization does exert a forceful influence, an influence that may be argued to correspond in degree to a ritual's formalization.

One might begin to explain this forceful influence by observing that the formality in ritual performance all by itself may influence the performer, who recognizes and intuitively responds to a traditional authority expressed by that formality. According to Maurice Bloch, such authority usually is rooted partly in an appeal to the past and often more specifically in an idea of a preexisting eternal order. This notion of a presumed preexisting eternal order is similar to the Ultimate Sacred Postulates or Rho sentences Rappaport sees reflected in the invariance of a society's ritual cannon.[61] These characterize the primordial basis a society presumes its ritual formalities to have. Yet, for Bloch, the formalization of the performance has an additional efficacy just in itself, regardless of any preexisting postulates. That efficacy is based on an intangible sense of power communicated by the formality of the ritual performance. The sense of power is constituted in part by the fixity of the sequence of ritual gestures and speech acts, and in other part by the stressed register of the performance as a whole (which will be discussed further in Chapter 3). For Bloch, a ritual is efficacious similarly to the conventions of polite speech, the formality of which promotes acceptance and discourages open challenge

---

[60] *"To say that performers participate in or become parts of the orders they are realizing is to say that transmitter-receivers become fused with the messages they are transmitting and receiving. In conforming to the orders their performances bring into being, and that come alive in their performance, performers become indistinguishable from those orders, parts of them, for the time being. Since this is the case, for performers to reject liturgical performances being realized by their own participation in them as they are participating in them is self-contradictory, and thus impossible"* (Rappaport 1999: 119).

[61] Rappaport, "The Idea of the Sacred" in *Ritual and Religion* (1999: 277–312).

on the part of those engaged in polite conversation.[62] Just as polite speech is effective in diffusing the urgency of personal emotion, so is a ritualized oath: The formalization of the convention, when performed, distances an individual performer from the public expression of an immediate impulse, which is checked for the sake of ritual propriety. A performer communicates through established channels and means that substantially narrow the scope of what may be communicated.

A different but somewhat parallel paradigm to polite speech is given by Radcliffe-Brown in a brief description of rhythmic dance among the Andaman Islanders. Similar to the constraints of polite speech, "any marked rhythm exercises on those submitted to its influence a constraint, impelling them to yield to it and to permit it to direct and regulate the movements of body and even those of the mind."[63] Stanley Tambiah applies this model of rhythm and musicality to some ritual performances:

> "Fixed rhythm, fixed pitch are conducive to the performance of joint social activity. Indeed, those who resist yielding to this constraining influence are likely to suffer from a marked unpleasant restlessness. In comparison, the experience of constraint of a peculiar kind acting upon the collaborator induces in him, when he yields himself to it, the pleasure of self-surrender."[64]

In simple terms, it is easier to dance than to resist the beat, or as Bloch says about participation in formalized rituals, it is difficult to argue with a song.[65]

Both paradigms – polite speech and rhythmic music – convey a sense of the constraining force that ritual formality exercises on individual performers. The constraint would seem to be due to the ritual's relatively invariant sequence of acts and utterances, and by the rhythm in which they are performed. The invariance and rhythm are largely unquestioned and give the ritual a higher and more authoritative voice than one would expect to find in nonformalized communication. The rhythm by itself might be said to amplify the formality and also the influence on the individual, affecting a person in the same way that extraordinary registers of speech (such as singing) have affective consequences on the receivers of oral communications. In sum, "ritual registers" (if I may coin a phrase) amplify and enhance the persuasive effects of the ritual, and may

---

[62] Bloch 1975: 1–28, n.b. 6–13.
[63] Quoted by Tambiah 1979: 113.
[64] Tambiah 1979: 113.
[65] Bloch 1974: 55–81, cited by Catherine Bell 1992: 214–15.

overpower individual resistance to their messages. Individuals respond with what has been called a "sense of ritual,"[66] a response enabled by acquaintance with ritual paradigms and an ingrained responsiveness to formality.[67] It is conceivable that individuals may improvise in their responses to some degree, and *may even resist* the ritual altogether by an exercise of will, but they do so only at the price of the "marked unpleasant restlessness" referred to by Tambiah.

As for what particular communicative features produce those amplifications of registers in rituals, it is worth noting that much discussion has been generated on notions such as "heated" discourse and what Malinowski characterized as the "rubbing" effect of repetitive ritual language. As Tambiah puts it, the "magical missile"[68] of heightened communication may be generated by the "hyper-regular surface structure of ritual language,"[69] and its repeated intonations "with modulations of speed, loudness, and rhythm, thereby foregrounding them as well as telescoping or fusing them into an amalgam that is given motion and direction by compelling illocutionary words of command and persuasion or declaration."[70] In Homeric oath-sacrifices, as I will show, the relatively fixed sequence of gestures and verbal illocutions conspire to generate the magical missile and ultimately to heighten formality and ritual effect. The intensity of this heightened effect may be gauged by the ominous threats that follow the breakdown of the oath between the Achaians and Trojans in Book 3, as we shall see.

## RITUAL PATTERNING

Recognizing oath-making or any other kind of ritual narrative in an ancient text also requires an understanding of ritual patterns in general. The spirit and patterns of rituals have been explained by numerous paradigms, including play (Huizinga,[71] Geertz,[72]), performance

---

[66] Bell 1992: 81.

[67] By "an ingrained responsiveness," I am thinking of Bourdieu's habitus" or Bateson's "deutero-learning," that is, a pattern-responsiveness inculcated from the earliest socialization of children.

[68] Tambiah discusses "heated" discourse and Malinowski's "rubbing" effect at p. 137, 1979: 137.

[69] Tambiah 1979: 164.

[70] Tambiah 1979: 137–38.

[71] Johan Huizinga, *Homo Ludens, A Study of the Play Element in Culture* (Boston: Beacon Press 1955, copyrighted 1950).

[72] Clifford Geertz, "Deep Play: Notes on the Balinese Cockfight," *Daedalus* 101:1 (1972) 1–37.

(Turner,[73] Fernandez,[74] Tambiah,[75] Bell[76]), metaphorical transformation (Fernandez,[77] Tambiah,[78] Eilberg-Schwartz,[79] Turner[80]), primal scenes (Freud,[81] Jensen,[82] Girard[83]), cultural revitalization (Wallace,[84] Girard[85]), totemism (Freud,[86] Robertson-Smith,[87] Durkheim[88]), species-specific communication (Lorenz,[89] Burkert,[90] Rappaport[91]), semiotic codes (Vernant and Detienne[92]), catharsis (Girard again), a response to stress (Alexiou[93]), parceling out and repetition (Lévi-Strauss[94]), and the

---

[73] See Victor Turner on "Social Dramas and Ritual Metaphors," in his *Dramas, Fields, and Metaphors: Symbolic Action in Human Society* (Ithaca, NY: Cornell University Press 1974) 23–59.

[74] James W. Fernandez (1977) "The Performance of Ritual Metaphors," and "Persuasions and Performances: Of the Beast in Every Body . . . And the Metaphors of Everyman," *Daedalus* 101:1. (1972) 39–59.

[75] Tambiah 1979.

[76] Bell 1992.

[77] Fernandez 1977.

[78] Tambiah 1979.

[79] Howard Eilberg-Schwartz, *The Savage in Judaism* (Bloomington: Indiana University Press 1990).

[80] Victor Turner, "Sacrifice as Quintessential Process Prophylaxis or Abandonment?" *History of Religions* 16:3 (1977) 189–215.

[81] Most obviously, in "The Infantile Recurrence of Totemism," in *Totem and Taboo* (New York: Random House 1946, originally published 1918) 130–207.

[82] Adolf Jensen, *Myth and Cult among Primitive Peoples*, trans. M. Tax Choldin and W. Weissleder (Chicago: University of Chicago Press 1963).

[83] Girard 1977, 2000.

[84] Anthony Wallace, "Ritual as Revitalization," in *Religion, An Anthropological View* (New York: Random House 1966) 157–66.

[85] Particularly, *Violence and the Sacred*.

[86] Freud 1946 (1918).

[87] Robertson-Smith, *The Religion of the Semites* (New York: Meridian Books 1957 (1889)).

[88] Emile Durkheim, *The Elementary Forms of Religious Life*, trans. J. W. Swain (New York: The Free Press 1915). Originally *Les Formes elementaires de la vie religeuse: la systemed totemique en Australie* (Paris: Alcan 1912).

[89] Konrad Z. Lorenz, *King Solomon's Ring*, trans. M. Kerr Wilson (New York: Harper & Row 1952).

[90] Burkert 1983, 1996.

[91] Rappaport 1996, 1999.

[92] See, for instance, *Gardens of Adonis* (English editions Princeton: Princeton University Press 1977, 1994) and *The Cuisine of Sacrifice Among the Greeks*.

[93] Margaret Alexiou, "Reappropriating Greek Sacrifice: *homo necans* or ἄνθρωπος θυσιάζων?" *Journal of Modern Greek Studies*, 8 (1990) 97–123. Perhaps the most fascinating thing about this article is the role she discerns for women's lamenting rituals in the Eastern and Western Mediterranean worlds. The lamenting rituals "may provide a ritual path to the temporary resolution to the cycle of killing and loss" (1990:115).

[94] See, for instance, "Finale," in *The Naked Man*, trans. J. and D. Weightman (New York: Harper & Row 1981) 625–95.

differentiating and privileging of particular activities (Bell[95]), to enormously simplify just a handful of important theories, many of which overlap. And then there is a whole series of commentators on the spirit and patterns of ritual sacrifice per se. Of the latter theories, the most commonly applied to Greek sacrifice are those of Girard and Burkert, whose studies illuminate some dire aspects of ritual killing, and of Vernant and Detienne, who sketch a broad landscape of Greek sacrificial imagery, emphasizing an implicit tension between *thusia* (commensal sacrifice) and *phonē* (murder, or slaughter). Generally speaking, Homeric narratives of oath-sacrifice (*horkia*) elude the grasp of these sacrificial theories, which fail to account for the formal peculiarities of oral traditional literature, of the epic genre, and of entire semantic domains elicited in oath-sacrifice but ignored in commensal sacrifice. Anthropologists Bloch and deHeusch both insist that the range of cultural practices often subsumed under the category of sacrifice is too broad to fit into a single paradigm,[96] which is a sensible position and the one taken here. Instead of focusing on megatheories of ritual sacrifice, we will explore the Homeric oath-making ritual sacrifices qua ritual, insofar as studying ritual patterns can help us to recognize patterns in the *Iliad*'s oath-making scenes. The killing that stands at the heart of the oath-sacrifice will be discussed as a significant ritual gesture.

Because their stress on communication coincides with our emphasis on discovering meanings in oral traditional poetry, and because oath-making per se falls within the scope of communication theory, the communication-oriented theories of Rappaport and Tambiah will provide preliminary tools for analysis, as they have in the preceding section. Briefly here and more fully in later chapters, Fernandez will provide additional insight into the metaphorical transformation effected by oath-sacrificing rituals. Ricoeur's theory of metaphor will be germane to the discussion in Chapter 3 on oath-sacrifice and the killing scene.

Patterns are, of course, intrinsic to rituals, within or without a text. Stanley Tambiah has postulated pattern recognition as the very foundation of ritual communication. According to Tambiah, rituals may be understood as "iconic analogues"[97] of original creative acts. This iconic

---

[95] Bell 1992.

[96] Maurice Bloch, *Prey into Hunter* (Cambridge: Cambridge University Press 1992) 24–5; Luc de Heusch 1985: 23.

[97] Tambiah leans upon Peirce's use of "icon," described by Rappaport as a sign bearing a relationship to an object in the way a map bears a relationship to a territory. "A map

analogue is recognized at some level by actual participants in rituals and also, one may presume, by audiences to the ritualized oral performance of the *Iliad*, which narrates religious rituals within its own ritualized performances. Although Tambiah doesn't address this doubly tiered recognition of ritual analogues on the part of audiences to an oral performance, he does cite Albert Lord's work on Homeric and Yugoslavian traditional bards in order to compare the oral poet's creation of an iconic analogue of the primordial recitation to the ritual performer's "iconic analogue of the cycles of creations of the cosmic order in their temporal and spatial regularity and cumulative effect."[98] Ritual performance is thus not creation *ex nihilo*, but basically the reinvigoration of primordial events along the lines of paradigmatic configurations. Tambiah also builds on Michelle Rosaldo's suggestion that magical spells, for instance, acquire their effectiveness by invoking images from " 'a number of diverse areas of experience and that these images, in turn, are regrouped and organized in terms of a small set of culturally significant and contextually desirable themes.' "[99] On the basis of Tambiah's synthesis of Lord and Rosaldo, we shall envision ritualization as basically a reinvigoration of primordial events within newer, shifted, metaphoric domains. The ritual participant recognizes the primordial event in its newer constellation, and responds to the ritual in terms of "pattern recognition and configurational awareness,"[100] essentially as one might respond to a work of art. This notion has application to the recognition of rituals by audiences of the orally performed text of the *Iliad*, as well as by participants in rituals within the *Iliad*, as the audience imagines them.

In incarnating certain cosmological "orientating principles and conceptions . . . [that] are held to be sacrosanct, are constantly used as yardsticks, and are considered worthy of perpetuating relatively unchanged,"[101] rituals may display standard but flexible performance features such as staging (special spaces, props), sequential shaping (special successions of steps, tempos, rhythms, the evocation of extramundane

is an icon of a territory, inasmuch as it bears a formal resemblance to it." Rappaport 1999: 462 (note 1).

[98] Tambiah 1979: 137.

[99] Michelle Zimbalist Rosaldo, "It's All Uphill: The Creative Metaphors of Ilongot Magical Spells," in *Sociocultural Dimensions of Language Use*, eds. Mary Sanches and B. G. Blount (New York: Academic Press 1975), 178, quoted in Tambiah (1979) at 138.

[100] Tambiah 1979: 134.

[101] Tambiah 1979: 121.

temporal spheres), stylized discourse with conspicuous sequencing rules,[102] and the communicating by-products of rituals that Victor Turner and others have called *communitas* (compare Durkheim's "effervescence"[103] or the "heated" communication referred to earlier). These and other features combine to provide a quality of formalization that may be said to add a certain "register" to the ritual as a form of symbolic communication, as we alluded to earlier. In positing this element of register to Homeric oath-making rituals I am agreeing with Rappaport that, although form and content may be inseparable from the perspective of the actual performer of a ritual, form is distinct at least for purposes of analyzing ritual's communicational efficacy: "*The ritual form . . . adds something to the substance of the ritual, something that the symbolically encoded substance cannot by itself express.*"[104] The cybernetic logic is patent: "The effectiveness of signals is enhanced if they are easy to distinguish from ordinary technical acts. The more extraordinary a ritual movement or posture, the more easily it may be recognized as a signal and not a physically efficacious act."[105] Of course some rituals may have concrete physical efficacy as well as communicational efficacy and rituals vary in their degrees of formality, but the point is that the formalization flags what is taking place in the ritual as somehow extramundane. This will have obvious relevance for analyzing the seemingly fixed sequences of verses and acts that constitute oath-making ritual scenes in the *Iliad*. Not only considering the ritualized behavior but also considering the poetic narration of it, the fixity of steps, the special vocabulary, and the clustering of finite indicative verbs may combine to create a marked poetic register reserved for extramundane ritual acts in the *Iliad*.

Of equal relevance is the correspondence between the degree of formalization and the degree of policing effect established by ritualized institutions in a society. We have hinted at this in our discussion of the affective qualities of formalization, but Rappaport applies the correspondence to larger matters of culture. According to Rappaport, there is a

---

[102] This item is discussed by Tambiah as sharing features with oral poetry. Tambiah 1979: 139.

[103] Emile Durkheim 1915: 240–45. For an interesting discussion of current approaches to the neurophysiology of *communitas*, see Rappaport 1999: 236–40.

[104] Rappaport 1999: 31. Earlier he says, "Ritual is not simply an alternative way to express any manner of thing, but . . . certain meanings and effects can best, or even only, be expressed or achieved in ritual" (1999: 30).

[105] Rappaport 1999: 50.

proportionality between the most formalized, least variant ritual structures in a society (structures implied to reflect "liturgical orders") and a felt tendency for them to be violated. The degree of formality is actually a measure of the degree of constraint required for the individual entering into the social contract established by the ritual. That is, the degree of constraint corresponds to the degree of temptation: "It may further be suggested that the more highly motivated people are to violate a convention, or the more consequential its violation is deemed to be, the more likely it is to be established in liturgy than in daily practice, or the more closely and strongly will it be associated with the conventional understandings that are so represented."[106] This has obvious relevance to swearing conventions and to the dire consequences of perjury in the *Iliad*. These would appear to mirror a truly universal taboo on the breaching of obligations, the one breach stigmatized as immoral across societies.[107] Thus, the highly formalized communicational register and weighty significance of sequential ritual acts in the *Iliad*'s oath-making scenes may correspond to (a) the degree of tenuousness felt intrinsically to adhere to promising, a tenuousness amplified in the Achaian claims about the hybristic tendencies of Priam's unreliable sons (3.105–10), and (b) the very consequential cosmic vengeance felt to result from perjury, as exemplified in the self-curse in Book 19 – "If I have sworn any of these things falsely, may the gods give to me pains, exceedingly many, as many as they give to anyone who transgresses against them in swearing" (19.265–67). We see an echo of the ritual's force especially after the oath-sacrifice in Book 3, with the repeated curses calling down divine vengeance on the Trojans because of their oath-violation (for instance, at 4.158–62, 4.234–39, and 4.268–71).

The quality of formality and the necessity of performance in establishing a ritual's authority are the two defining features Rappaport ascribes to "liturgical orders," a ritual subset that happens to correspond well to oath-making rituals in the *Iliad*, because oath-making rituals, too, are characterized by formality and their actual performance is what establishes their commissive effects, as we have established. Rappaport defines liturgical orders as "more or less invariant sequences of formal acts and utterances not entirely encoded by the performers,"[108] which

---

[106] Rappaport 1999: 128.

[107] Rappaport 1999: 132.

[108] Rappaport 1999: 24, with slight variation in his "The Obvious Aspects of Ritual," in *Ecology, Meaning and Religion* (Berkeley, CA: North Atlantic 1979) 175–80, reprinted

are "enlivened, realized, or established only when those acts are performed and those utterances voiced."[109] But herein lies the tension: The
liturgical order is enlivened by performance, but the performers are not
understood to be the primary ones encoding the messages in it. The
messages that the liturgical order encodes are dubbed "canonical" by
Rappaport. The canonical messages correspond to a ritual's invariability;
they represent the immutable and perduring aspects of the ritual message
which are felt to be invested by powers other than the performers. If I
understand Rappaport's thesis correctly, the liturgical encoding of canonical messages ultimately mirrors the creative dynamic found in those many
creation stories that conceive of a preexisting inchoate substance *informed*
and, as it were, *temporalized* by a dynamic word – that is, an empowered
liturgical utterance that creates order and directed movement out of an
originary formless and aimless matter (such as in Genesis 1:2). Put differently, the informing and temporalizing of the primordial substance by
a dynamic utterance mirrors the way that liturgy informs and temporalizes a ritual event, infusing the socially prescribed gestures and words
with canonical status and launching the ritual's message, so infused, into
time – hence its effect on the performers. In other words, the liturgical
invariability performs the same role as does the magical voice that creates
order out of chaos.

More complexly, liturgical orders also are said to inform and tem-
poralize the ritual's participants, by infusing the preritualized "inchoate
substance" of the participant (a preritualized identity conceived as formless and atemporal from the perspective of ritual canon) with liturgy's
canonical shape and vitality, and by committing the performer to the
ritual's terms thereafter. To some extent, Rappaport's analysis of these
informing and temporalizing aspects is apt for the sway of oath-making
rituals in the *Iliad* not only for mortals but even for the immortal gods,
who ostensibly exist outside of time but are compelled to honor their
oaths down to the very letter, once they have nodded their heads to them
(for instance, Zeus's promise, Hera's trickery, and the birth of Heracles, at
19.98–131). This movement of performers into alignment with canonical
paradigms coincides with a performance's "indexical messages." For Rappaport, indexical messages reflect, from the performer's perspective, the
changes that were secured for the person by ritual performance. Ancillary

in *Readings in Ritual Studies*, ed. R. Grimes (Upper Saddle River, NJ: Prentice Hall
  1996, 427–40), 428.
[109] Rappaport 1996: 432.

to the canonical messages, indexical messages communicate the immediate and social aspects of ritual events, situating the performers in relation to a certain status quo. This more immediate dynamic element of the oath-making ritual pertains, for instance, to the renewal of the relationship between Agamemnon and Achilles in *Iliad* 19 and to the alliance between the Achaians and Trojans in Book 3.

However, Rappaport's account of a ritual performer's indexical shifts approaches the experience of the performers from what might be considered the top down. The metaphorical transformation theory of James Fernandez more satisfactorily accounts for the changes secured by performances from the bottom up, and is in keeping with the aforementioned notion of ritual performance as fostering paradigmatic communication and self-understanding within reinvigorated metaphorical domains. For Fernandez, the performer's experience in ritual performance is not simply a matter of aligning with a canonical picture of reality, but involves potentially various metaphorical shifts in identity – shifts that rely on a play of the images associated with underlying paradigms. Ritual performance's most basic office for Fernandez is to effect a reenvisioning of the performer within a new metaphorical domain. Ritual performances accomplish movement in a performer's self-image similarly to the way that a metaphor accomplishes a reenvisioning of one thing in terms of another.[110] The semantic movement tends to be from the obscure and inchoate in the subject (or "tenor") to the concrete and ostensive in the metaphoric predicate (the "vehicle").[111]

According to Fernandez, the schemata imposed on performers tend to be either structural, wherein the translation between realms is based on some isomorphism of structure or similarity of relationship of parts, or textural, wherein an assimilation is made on the basis of similarity in feeling tone, contiguities in previous experience, or syntagmatic habit.[112] Formally speaking, these two schemata fall into metaphoric and metonymic camps, but it should be noted that this distinction is loose in ritual imagination, where one may find a play of metaphors and shifting textural undertones and where figures of speech may invoke a multidimensional "network of associations." Such networks highlight

---

[110] Ritual performance effects a "strategic predication upon an inchoate pronoun (an I, a you, a we, a they) which makes a movement and leads to performance." James Fernandez, "The Performance of Ritual Metaphors," 1977: 102.

[111] Fernandez 1977: 104.

[112] Fernandez 1972: 46–7 and 1977: 117–18.

different aspects of the domains of experience,[113] performing for metaphors the same basic function as leitmotifs perform for ritual. Ritual leitmotifs effectively thicken and transform the experiences of participants in a ritual, connecting them to a primordial pattern or canonical ideal. Ritual leitmotifs, says Fernandez, may be penetrated by religious symbols, which are especially "volatile to interpretation" and which "fill out this universe of religious experience giving it resonance, a thick complexity and potency, which the discussion of the paradigm of metaphors – however basic – does not fully capture."[114] Fernandez's theory of metaphorical movement in ritual will help us to appreciate the connotations generated by the use of sacrificial motifs for killing scenes in the *Iliad*. It also will have relevance to the performer's appropriation of ritual schemes to identify behavior and manipulate power, which I mentioned earlier in a brief reference to Catherine Bell's theory of ritual.

Another important aspect of rituals is the relationship between acts and utterances. As Chapter 3 will demonstrate, utterances in oath-making rituals muster a variety of effects: They set out the terms of the oath (essentially constructing the semantic horizons for the performance), invoke mythological analogues, recite prayers and, in effect, engage cosmic response and level curses, thereby establishing the perlocutionary effects on participants and audiences. The contribution of acts to rituals is more elusive, considering the broad range of theories on the subject and considering that ritual gestures have been pondered as having roots as archaic as the ritual displays of nonspeaking animals.[115] The important issue in the *Iliad* is not the ethological origins for ritual gestures, however, but the mindful display of formalized gestures by a ritual's human participants. According to Rappaport, there tends to be an inverted relationship between the weightiness of the words in ritual and the weightiness of acts. That is, when the words spoken in ritual are relatively insubstantial, they must be made "heavy" by acts. When the words are weighty, the gestures that accompany them are less substantial. Of particular relevance to the

---

[113] Fernandez 1977: 104 109, 113, 117. On page 126 he summarizes: "Most metaphoric images potentially imply a set of actions by which they might be realized. The utterance of metaphor itself as well as the actions undertaken to realize it is attended by a set of associations which "belong" to it by reason of contiguities in previous experience. The assertion of metaphor thus provokes a metonymous chain of elements or experiences associated with it as part to whole, cause to effect, or other contiguity in time or space."

[114] Fernandez 1977: 126.

[115] See, for instance, Walter Burkert 1983 and also Rappaport 1999: 139.

ritual killing in oath-sacrifice, "corporeal representation gives weight to the incorporeal and gives visible substance to the aspects which are themselves impalpable, but of great importance in the ordering of social life."[116] If we put this together with the tenuousness felt to adhere intrinsically to the sphere of human obligation, not only for Homer but for human societies in large,[117] we have a measure for the dramatic violence in the ritual killing of oath-sacrifice. To put it another way, the more tenuous the reliability of the swearing parties and the more consequential the oath, the more striking will be the ritual gesture – in some Homeric cases, killing the animal victim – that finalizes it. Rappaport also points out that physical display in rituals often transmits something more or different than what the corresponding words would say or do say.[118] As I have argued elsewhere, the physical act of slicing the victim's throat in Homeric oath-sacrifice has more power than the words of oath because the act of killing is less abstract.[119] Killing is more dramatic and death more final than words can possibly denote. Words may be ambiguous; death is not.

What is striking about the act of ritual killing in Book 3's oath-sacrifice is not just that it symbolizes the fate anticipated for perjurers, but that its killing effects spill over into surrounding narratives and seem to infect the entire war, itself legendarily based on a breach of trust. One may argue that, within the ritual performance of the larger epic narrative, the liturgical order of oath-sacrifice, with its ritualized killing and its ritualized words, informs and infuses the rest of the narrative with a canonical significance.

Rappaport also points out that by encoding canonical messages, liturgical orders appear to preserve them against the vagaries of historical change, a point that helps to explain the preservation of Homeric oath-sacrificing patterns into later antiquity. Regardless of possible shifts in the meanings attributed to ritual patterns over the centuries, the fact that Pausanias invokes the Homeric paradigm (V.24.9–11) to explain the configuration of oath-sacrificing rituals seven to ten centuries after the estimated consolidation of the *Iliad*'s text, attests to that liturgical form's perdurance. One might argue that the Homeric prototype configures the later ritual just because of the lofty position of the *Iliad* as a kind of Greek

---

[116] Rappaport 1999: 141.

[117] Rappaport 1999: 132; see note 49.

[118] "For lack of better terminology, it may be suggested that physical display is 'performatively stronger' or 'performatively more complete' than utterances" (Rappaport 1999: 143).

[119] Kitts 2003.

bible; indeed, some anthropologists have postulated a fixity of cultural forms based on literacy and on the historical consciousness established by having written texts.[120] Although it is difficult to know the deepest sources for Pausanias's ideas or for those of his ritualizing peers, the *Iliad*'s oral traditional origin permits consideration of a deeper historicity for the oath-making ritual. Rappaport argues that predominantly oral cultures that know of written texts nonetheless may maintain relatively stiff and orally transmitted liturgical orders that are regarded as encoded at a primordial stratum of reality, rather than as encoded by an authoritative text or by a guild of performers.[121] If he is right, the perdurance of the oath-sacrificing form may correspond in Greek imagination to the primordial sources the oath seeks to invoke (for example, Zeus and the Erinyes at 19.258–65, and "those who from underneath avenge toiling men, whoever swears a false oath" at 3.276–80; cf. Hesiod's W&D 803–4, Th. 231–32[122]). The ideological rooting of oath-making conventions in a primordial stratum antecedent to their performances would seem to match the well-known Greek tendency, conspicuous in Hesiod and discernible in Homer, to envision the establishment of human institutions as coincident with a fall from a Golden Age.[123]

## THE ORAL TRADITIONAL FORMALIZATION OF THE RITUAL SCENE

In order to make an argument for the shared semantic domains of oath-sacrifice and battlefield killing scenes in the *Iliad*, however, we will need additional tools. Now we will summarize relevant aspects of the oral traditional theory of poetic composition. From this perspective, ritual patterns within the *Iliad* fall under the rubric of what has been called

---

[120] For a discussion, see Bell 1992: 118–42.

[121] For a quick summary of arguments about the coextensive presence of literacy and orality in ancient Greece, see John Miles Foley, "Oral Tradition and Its Implications," 146–73, n.b. 162–65. The reliance on nonwritten forms of traditional authority is attested in Mishnah Eduyot, which cites the traditions recollected by venerable sages. See Moshe Weinfeld 1990: 183.

[122] For an overview, see Alfred Heubeck, "Erinus in der archaischen Epik," *Glotta* 64 (1986) 145–65.

[123] Innumerable are the secondary sources on this topic, but key among them are Pierre Vidal-Naquet 1986: 15–38; J.-P. Vernant 1983: 1–72, 248–70; Marcel Detienne 1994: 37–59, and "Culinary Practices and the Spirit of Sacrifice," in *The Cuisine of Sacrifice among the Greeks* (Chicago: University of Chicago 1989) 1–20.

typical scenes, themes, or motif sequences. Although differently shaded, all three point to a similar compositional tendency to render recurrent scenes as patternings of poetic elements, whether whole verses, formulae, or single "words," however so defined. The poetic generation of typical scenes has been envisioned in several different ways over the last century, and even diminished in relevance altogether by recent theories of oral poetic composition by single words. Nonetheless, as the most formalized sequences of verses and acts in the *Iliad*, oath-sacrificing scenes manifest a coherent pattern that befits analysis of them as typical scenes. Both old and newer accounts of typical scenes will be discussed here, as both bear on discussions in subsequent chapters.

We begin with the newer. Once defined as an aggregate of formulae, phrases, and whole verses used regularly by the poet to aid in the spontaneous composition of recurrent scenes,[124] the typical scene has been reenvisioned by Michael Nagler as an abstract preverbal template, or Gestalt, for the spontaneous generation of a family of meaningful details, which may be compressed or expanded in the service of the story.[125] Each generated family is an allomorph of the preverbal template, and is molded in response to narrative and performance exigencies. It might be noted that this vision of allomorphs emerging from an originary Gestalt to fit different narrative situations bears a loose resemblance to Tambiah's vision of ritual performance as an iconic analogue of an original creative act with reinvigorated metaphoric domains. We seem to have two similar approaches to the same underlying creativity.

The oral poetic analysis doesn't stop there, however. In an effort to capture the spontaneous generation of meanings in orally performed poetry, Nagler elicits Sanskrit grammatical theory to describe the bursting forth (the *sphuṭ*) of meaning upon the mind, a bursting that may be triggered in part by a linguistic symbol or by independent linguistic elements occurring "in the happy synergism of a meaningful pattern" and generating an artistic entity "(a *sphoṭa*), which is somehow greater than the sum of its parts."[126] In between the "inchoate generative impulse (*sphoṭa, Gestalt ab initio*)"[127] and its surface structure as an utterance lies "an intermediate stage consisting of patterns of phonological and syntactic norms"[128] and

---

[124] Walter Arend, *Die Typischen Scenen bei Homer* (Berlin 1933); Bernard Fenik 1968.
[125] Michael Nagler 1974: 64–130.
[126] Nagler 1974: 85.
[127] Nagler 1974: 17.
[128] Nagler 1974: 16.

more generally a "multidimensional network of potentialities of sound, sense, and even of rhythm, which is realized differently and to different effect in each context."[129] The fresh realization of this network triggers a flash of meaning for audiences, and reaches through and beyond tradition to a deeper level of intuition, reminiscent of the fictional genius in Paul Ricoeur's theory of metaphor. One aspect of Ricoeur's very intricate theory is the poetic genius that creates fictions from a split reference: The speaker or hearer suspends the reference proper to ordinary descriptive language and allows the illocutionary force of the metaphor, as speech act, to elicit a more radical way of seeing things. Poetic feeling, which is basically an intentional structure for Ricoeur,[130] allows self-assimilation into what is seen in the metaphor: "We feel like what we see like."[131] We shall return to this dimension of poetic imagination and the self-assimilation of hearers into heard metaphors in Chapter 3, but for now let it be noted that both Ricoeur's and Nagler's descriptions of the kind of sudden intuition elicited by poetic language open up rich possibilities for uncovering the network of associations elicited by sacrificial scenes, similes, and associated single words for an ancient audience already awake to the everyday visceral experience of slaughtering animals in sacrificial rituals.

As for the older analysis of typical scenes as "aggregates of formulae, phrases, and whole verses used regularly in the construction of recurrent scenes in oral poetry,"[132] oath-sacrificing narratives happen to present the longest formalized aggregates of formulae and verses in the entire *Iliad*. This does not mean that the generative process described by Nagler as emanating from an original Gestalt is inapplicable to oath-sacrifices; I intend to show that the oath-sacrificing Gestalt does have phonemic and semantic resonances with certain battlefield killings and dyings. However, the relative fixity of the ritual scene per se, as hypostasized in our current text, suggests that it is identifiable as an autonomous liturgical form bearing its own associative clusters of meanings.

---

[129] Nagler 1974: 33.

[130] I am presuming a basic awareness of the philosophical notion of intentionality as put forth by Husserl and the phenomenologists who came after him.

[131] To feel, says Ricouer, is to make ours what objectifying thought would put at a distance. Poetic feeling is thus an intentional structure. Paul Ricoeur, "The Metaphorical Process as Cognition, Imagination, and Feeling," in *Philosophical Perspectives on Metaphor*, ed. Mark Johnson (Minneapolis: University of Minnesota Press 1981) 228–47. N.b. 242–43.

[132] Arend 1933; Fenik 1968.

By its fixed cluster of verses and precise vocabulary, the typical scene of oath-sacrifice might give the impression of semantic hollowness, based on the notion that the degree of fixity of the scene corresponds to a distance from its sphere of semantic origination, or, in other words, that its recitation is rote. But a better explanation would take into consideration Rappaport's analysis of the proportionality between the more formalized, least variant ritual structures in a society and a felt tendency for them to be violated. Recall that the degree of ritual formality reflects the degree of individual constraint required in entering into the social contract established by the ritual, and that its fixity is a kind of bulwark against violation. If we apply this conception of ritual formality not just to ritual performances but also to ritual scenes performed as part of an oral poetic performance, the formalized oath-sacrificing scene becomes more semantically burdened, not more semantically hollow. That is, in ritual scenes, fixity of phrasing connotes traditional weight. The relevance of this point shall be illuminated in Chapter 3.

As for the patterning of the scene's individual elements, similarly, the tighter and more closed the pattern of elements in the ritual scene would seem to correspond to the tighter semantic matrix with which those elements are associated. Hence, when certain of those elements do get loosened and do appear in narratives that are not obviously ritualistic, they propagate their original matrix, disseminating their initial semantic fields that much more conspicuously into the new narratives. For instance, when a man dying in battle is described as gasping, lying on the ground, and being deprived of *thumos* and *menos* in the same way the lambs are in the oath-sacrificing scene in Book 3, the man's gasping and deprivations of *thumos* and *menos* might seem to attract the sacrificial matrix to the new scene, which takes on a sacrificial overtone. Hence, the seeming fixity of verses in ritual scenes does not mean that the scene is semantically depleted, or that its shape is a happenstance constellation of single words without cultural significance. Instead, the fixity in typical scenes may denote a ritual formality and a cultural depth. Further, the elements that are traditionally attached to a scene such as a sacrifice, once loosened from the originary semantic matrix and embedded in other narratives, may import a sublime nuance into narratives not generally understood as belonging to a religious sphere.

Considering the patterning of those smaller poetic elements usually known as formulae, scholars disagree as to whether or not bards think and compose in these traditional lexical solidarities once regarded as the very building blocks of Homeric verse. It has been argued variously that oral poets compose and even think in idea and lexical clusters (from Parry to Ong), that these clusters represent different allomorphs generated from an inchoate preverbal template (Nagler), that these clusters are not generated differently in oral poetry than they are in everyday speech but occur to different degrees in each (Kiparsky[133]), and that many seemingly formulaic verses in fact are composed in single words (Visser[134]), to sketch but four of many opinions. Metrical exigency figures into all such arguments, although meter is deemed constraining to different degrees in each. It is a basic supposition of this book that oathmaking narratives do manifest both lexical and idea clusters, although some clusters are more loosely cohering than others, and that such clusters in ritual contexts may imply traditional significance and cultural depth.

A more interesting question than whether such clusters exist is whether such lexical clusters may draw upon or resonate beyond the *Iliad* into neighboring cultures, particularly in connection with the rhetorical conventions of oath-making and cursing. Gregory Nagy, for one, has argued that phonemic and lexical associations may cohere through centuries of language change and that they may generate metrical tendencies and even metrical and phonemic lookalikes within language families and across oceans.[135] Phonemic associations may be observed just within the text of the *Iliad*; hence Parry's and after him Nagler's discussion of calembour (such as the end of line phrases *pioni dēmǭ* – (hidden in) rich fat, and *pioni dēmǭ* – (amid the) flourishing populace).[136] It is only sensible to presume that liturgical speech, consisting of the least flexible performative utterances in the ritual sphere, is more likely to preserve formal sequences of lexical elements and also rhythms across cultural boundaries than are other kinds of speech. Walter Burkert has pointed out that oaths and treaties are likely to be occasions for the meeting and exchanging of differing rhetorical and cultic traditions, particularly when the

---

[133] Paul Kiparsky, "Oral Poetry: Some Linguistic and Typological Considerations," in *Oral Literature and the Formula*, eds. Stolz and Shannnon (Ann Arbor, MI: Center for the Coordination of Ancient and Modern Studies 1976) 73–105.

[134] Edzard Visser, "Formulae or Single Words?" *Würzburger Jahrbücher fur die Altertumswissenschaft* 14 (1988) 21–37.

[135] The argument for the persistence of traditional themes and the way they influence meter is summarized in "Formula and Meter," *Greek Mythology and Poetics* (Ithaca, NY: Cornell University Press 1990) 18–35.

[136] Nagler 1974: 5–8.

treaties are international in nature,[137] and Moshe Weinfeld has charted some precise sharings between Greek, biblical, Akkadian, Hittite, and even Egyptian treaty-making formulae.[138] Third, Robert Mondi has explored common Greek and Near Eastern mythological systems not as shared narratives, but as "a structured array of conceptual foci (god names, for instance) around each of which cluster various ideas, images, and narrative motifs."[139] All of these hypotheses support an argument for the coherence of idea clusters beyond the text, as well as within it, an argument that is germane to detecting the semantic domains of oath-sacrificing liturgies and ritual acts both within the *Iliad* and beyond it into the ancient Mediterranean world.

In essence, it would seem that a careful analysis of any kind of sacrificial scene in the *Iliad* must be attentive to the epic themes of the text, while at the same time recognizing that ritual practices have their own features and semantic domains. The sticky relationship between the semantic domains and special registers of ritual practices – which would seem to be intrinsically symbolic – and the epic text that describes those practices, is front and center in this study of oath-sacrifices in the *Iliad*. I hope to have established that the former penetrates the latter and that the intertextual dimensions of the two may be analyzed in the oath-sacrifices of the *Iliad*.

---

[137] Walter Burkert, *The Orientalizing Revolution* (Cambridge, MA: Harvard University Press 1992) 68: "[O]ath-taking rituals of international character have the best chances to cross cultural borders."

[138] See, for instance, Weinfeld 1990: 175–91, and "Covenant Making in Anatolia and Mesopotamia," *Journal of Ancient Near Eastern Studies* 22 (1993) 135–39.

[139] Mondi 1990: 142–98.

# CHAPTER TWO

# PREMISES AND PRINCIPLES OF OATH-MAKING IN THE *ILIAD*

B EFORE WE CAN INVESTIGATE THE VIOLENCE THAT EMANATES FROM oath-making rituals in the *Iliad*, we must have an adequate understanding of the specific cultural premises and principles on which Homeric oath-making is based. In the introduction, an oath was defined as a ritualized configuration of a relationship between two or more individuals, a configuration specified by solemn utterances, gestures, and sometimes artifacts, that may be sealed by a symbolic act. The cultural premises behind such ritualized configurations are amply, if elliptically, demonstrated in the *Iliad*, especially in depictions of warriors who reject oaths, who tend to be in the throes of battle passion and oblivious to the pull of cultural constraints. Such depictions inversely prefigure the paradigm of the oath-honoring man.[1] Exploring these premises will help to illuminate the principles behind oath-making in the *Iliad*. In addition, we will enlist some Near Eastern comparisons to shed light on some ancient Mediterranean oath-making principles, and we will outline the premises and principles of Homeric oath-making against the anthropology of ritual set out in Chapter 1. Achilles' oath by the scepter in Book 1 will be discussed at the end of the chapter as an example of the poetic highlighting and manipulating of some of those ritual principles.

---

[1] Alas, I know of no instance in the *Iliad* where a woman is involved in oath-making conventions or is morally implicated to uphold the commitment behind her own statements. Perhaps the closest thing to a comment on a woman's good faith is Helen's self-castigation for her own infidelity. Briseis does bemoan the fact that Patroklos will not make good on his word to give her to Achilles to marry, but she is lamenting his death, not his good faith. Thus, when I use the word "man" throughout this book, I refer to male human beings, not to generic humanity.

## OATH-MAKING PREMISES

A lie was possible only after a creature, man, was capable of conceiving the
being of truth.                                                      (Martin Buber[2])

It is perhaps ironic that some of the most striking examples of oath-
making premises in the *Iliad* occur in narratives where oaths are anticipated but absent. One notable example is Achilles' denial of Hector's
request for an oath that the victor will respect the loser's corpse. Hector
puts his request in this way:

> "... But now my *thumos* bids me
> to stand up to you. Whether I take you or I be taken,
> but come, and let us swear (*epidōmetha*) by each other's gods, for they
> will be
> the best witnesses and protectors of agreements (*harmoniaōn*).
> I shall not disfigure you terribly, if Zeus should bestow
> endurance upon me and I take away your life (*psukēn*).
> But instead I will strip you of your fine armor, Achilles,
> and give your body back to the Achaians. You do the same."
>
> (22:252–59)

Hector's request is remarkable for its inclusion of the word *epidōmetha*,
which denotes swearing by a cast of gods from both sides – a richly attested
Anatolian convention[3] – and the word *harmoniaōn*, which connotes that
such a tradition may bind together seemingly disparate parties into one
harmonious whole.[4] The choice of these words, plus the whole clause
"for [those gods] will be the best witnesses and protectors of agreements,"

---

[2]  *Good and Evil: Two Interpretations* (New York: Charles Scribner's Sons 1952), 7, cited
by Rappaport 1999: 13.

[3]  The cross-swearing by a cast of divinities from both sides is discussed for its vestiges of
Anatolian customs by Jaan Puhvel, *Homer and Hittite* (Innsbruck: Inst. f. Sprachwiss.
d. Univ. 1991) 9–12. See further examples in Volume I of Gary Beckman's *Hittite
Diplomatic Texts* (Atlanta: Scholars Press 1996), such as the treaty between Hittite king
Suppiluliuma 1 and Shattiwaza of Mittani, translated by Gary Beckman as treaty 6A,
pages 38–44, n.b. 42–3.

[4]  Peter Karavites (1992) explains the word *epidōmetha* as serving "to invoke one another's
gods as witnesses, denoting the offer of a guarantee to the other side exactly as in Il.
3.276, where Zeus, the god of Ida, was named as witness and the local rivers as divinities
invoked to represent the Trojan side" (1992:34). The gloss on *harmonia* as "collecting
and fitting disparate parties together in a harmonious whole" derives from Eustasius.
ad Il. 22.255 (Immanuel Bekker (ed.), *Scholia in Homeri Iliadem* [Berline 1825]), cited
by Karavites at page 34.

gives the impression that Hector (or the narrator) may be invoking an established tradition for mending a great schism.

Yet, despite its traditional force, Hector's request fails:

> "Hector, do not, accursed, speak to me of compacts,
> since trusty oaths (*horkia pista*) are not possible for lions and men,
> and wolves and lambs do not hold a like-minded *thumos*.
> Instead they think ill thoughts, piercing through and through, at each other.
> Just so, it is not possible to bind me and you in *philotēs*, nor will there be
> any oaths (*horkia*) between us, before one or the other shall fall
> and sate Ares, the brave warrior, with blood."
>
> (22.261–69)

In denying the possibility of *harmonia* or *horkia* — apparently equated at line 262 — between Hector and himself, Achilles affirms the very dimension of life that Homeric oaths seek to circumvent. Standing outside of the sphere of trusty oaths, as a wolf to a lamb, as a lion to a man, he thinks piercing evil at Hector. His passion is not to be softened by the conventions which refine and protect social intercourse. Oaths, pacts, and *philotēs* (friendship, alliance, and their various nuances[5]) are impossible for Achilles because he rejects the very foundations they are built upon: compassion, self-restraint, and mutual trust. Similarly to wolves and lambs, he and Hector do not share a like-minded *thumos* (heart, life-spirit).

The contrast between pitiless passion and the softening effect of shared conventions is a familiar theme in the Homeric epics. It is conspicuous in the *Odyssey*, where repeatedly the civilized mores of Zeus are pit against the cannibalistic, monstrous, and unconstrained impulses of creatures living on the dark side of the Golden Age — Laistrygonians, Cyclopes, and the like. It also pervades the *Iliad*, most obviously when martial fury and pleas for pity collide. A battle doesn't have to erode all possibilities for friendship, as Hector suggests after his duel with Ajax:

> "So let someone of the Achaians and Trojans say,
> They fought in heart-rending strife,
> but they parted bound in friendship (*philotēti . . . arthmēsante*)."
>
> (7.301–2)

---

[5] See Karavites for a discussion of the various meanings of *philotēs* in the context of promises and treaties (1992: 48–58).

Yet rarely do they part as friends. The duel between Hector and Ajax does not remedy the ruptured Achaian–Trojan pact, and Hector's vision of friendship after strife belies what usually happens, which is that heart-rending strife culminates not with friendship but with the rending of bodies. Hence in Book 22 Achilles refuses Hector's supplication by emphasizing his desire to eat Hector's flesh raw:

> "Do not, dog, supplicate me by my parents.
> If only my *menos* and *thumos* should bid me to
> cut off your flesh and eat the meat, considering what you have done.
> It is just not possible that someone might ward off the dogs from
> your head,
> not if he should bring here ten times or twenty times
> the ransom and promise me still more."
>
> (22.345–50)

Aptly, Achilles' preference for raw–flesh-eating strife over a pact to respect Hector's body conjoins the themes of violating bodies and violating oaths, or at least violating the very idea of oaths. The homology between the two violations clearly is built on the notion of respect – respect for the integrity of the human body and respect for the integrity of human institutions. Such themes transcend Hector's personal predicament. Despite the disfiguring end by Achilles that awaits Hector, the theme of violating bodies effectively opens the *Iliad*, in what might be described as a eulogy to souls departed for Hades and to corpses left on the battlefield as spoil for dogs and birds (1.3–5).[6] The theme is revived with every graphic description of death in battle. The theme of violating oaths also penetrates the *Iliad* and stands obliquely behind promises not to violate oaths, beginning with Achilles' oath to defend Kalchas as long as the war persists, in Book 1, and continuing through Book 24, when Achilles promises Priam to hold off the raid of Troy until the funeral of Hector is completed (24.671–72). In between are at least two dozen precise references to oaths sworn or violated, and the repeated threat of a painful death for perjury ironically unites the themes of violating bodies and violating oaths. One may argue that the theme of bodily violation consequent to violating oaths sets up a poetic leitmotif for an entire

---

[6] The classic treatment of this theme is Charles Segal's *The Theme of the Mutilation of the Corpse in the Iliad* (Leiden: E. J. Brill 1971).

realm of destructive experience that oath-making and similar conventions can barely constrain.[7]

Admiration for this realm that oath-making and other such conventions can barely constrain is obvious in the *Iliad*. One might even sense a narrator's "lust of the eye," as John Glen Gray called it in another context,[8] in the depictions of battlefield carnage and brute strength. At the same time, there is clearly an attraction–aversion paradox in the *Iliad*'s poetic glorification of men resistant to cultural constraints, and in its alternating antipathy to such men.[9] Understanding the poetic glorification and antipathy to men who defy human conventions will help to identify the deeper premises behind oath-making in the *Iliad*.

On the one hand, the *Iliad* exalts raw power and lack of restraint in numerous comparisons of warriors to raw-flesh-eating predators and to devastating natural phenomena. As predators, warriors are compared to ravening wolves (4.471, 16.156–65, 16.352–56), lions (15.592, 17.61–64, 17.542. 20.164–5, 24.41–45), a raging dog (8.299), and even a tenacious fly who relishes human blood (17.570–72). The positive side of this depiction is obvious when the fight results in victory, but its dearer side is captured by Hecuba: "[Achilles] is a raw-flesh-eater, not to be trusted; he will show you neither pity nor respect" (24.207–8). Similarly, as natural phenomena, warriors are compared to uncontrollably swollen winter rivers (5:85–94), to gusts of strong winds mixed with the sea (13.793–99), to burning flames (13.330, 17.88–89; 19:365–66), and, complexly, to flames and strife, driven by a sand storm (13.330–45), among other motifs. These comparisons of mighty humans to mighty storms are rooted in the

---

[7] A comparable theme in the curses that seal Near Eastern oaths is the rendering of oath-violators as wild asses or other creatures who roam outside of civilization, and are bereft of it (hence Esarhadden's invocation of the God Sin to make oath-breakers roam the desert like lepers and wild asses). On the Assyrian and Biblical parallels, see Delbert Hillers, *Treaty-Curses and the Old Testament Prophets* (Rome: Pontifical Biblical Institute 1964) 15. Comparable is the Hittite imprecation on runaway lovers, discussed by Jos Weitenberg, "You have become a wolf!" ("The Meaning of the Expression to Become a Wolf in Hittite," in *Perspectives on Indo-European Language, Culture and Religion, Studies in Honor of Edgar C. Polomé*, Vol. 1., ed. Roger Pearson, Monograph Number Seven, *Journal of Indo-European Studies* (McLean, VA 1991) 189–98.

[8] John Glen Gray 1970: 25–58. See also Tim O'Brien's account of the "beautiful death" of Curt Lemon ("How to Tell a True War Story," *The Things They Carried*, Boston: Houghton Mifflin, 1990, 75–91).

[9] An enduring motif in Western literature. On the attraction–aversion paradox in Eve's careful study of the forbidden fruit, see commentary on the "lust to the eye" (Genesis 3.6) by Robert Alter, in *Genesis* (New York: W.W. Norton & Company 1996) 12.

paradigm of divine passion and vengeance expressed as natural disasters, common also to the Near East.[10] This paradigm, too, has ambivalent nuance. For instance, it is to punish those who defy divinely sanctioned conventions that Zeus imposes thunderstorms and devastating floods that diminish the works of men, on crooked law judges who refuse to heed the voice of the gods (16.384–93).[11] For similar reasons Zeus, Poseidon, and Apollo famously storm the Achaian wall with crashing waves after the war, because the Achaians built the wall without divine permission (12.8–36). On the other hand, it is a straightforward exaltation of divine power when Poseidon's attack with the Achaians against Hector is rendered as a roaring sea storm compared in devastation to a crackling fire storm (14.384–401). Equally powerful is the epiphany of Skamandros hurling waves, tree trunks, and corpses at raging Achilles, coming after him as a bellowing bull (20.234–315) and perpetrating a water battle that will end with a fire, seemingly crematory, launched by Hephaestus (20.342–45). Regardless of narrative aim,[12] these spectacles of mighty gods in battle

---

[10] Consider, for instance, Sargon II's report: "Adad, the violent, the powerful son of Anu, let loose his fierce tempest against them and, with bursting cloud and thunderbolt (lit. Stone of heaven), totally annihilated them" (D. D. Luckenbill, *Ancient Record*, Vol. II, section 155, page 83). Also see Ashurbanipal's dedicatory text from Esagila of Babylon to Marduk: "To Marduk, the exalted lord, king of the gods, mighty ruler (endowed with) tremendous power, . . . adorned with terror, who holds the bond of heaven and earth, the wise, the prudent, . . . crowned with the crown of a rulership of splendor, the sun of the gods, of fiery mien, mightiest of the mighty, . . . . lord of springs (and) fountains, floods and seas, who created the black-headed race of men, lord of all creation, the merciful lord, who receives petitions, who hears prayer" (Luckenbill, 1968, section 1000, 384–5). For the divine–human warrior parallel, consider Sennacharib's "At the word of Ashur, the great lord, my lord, on flank and front I pressed upon the enemy like the onset of a raging storm. With the weapons of Ashur, my lord, . . . I decimated the enemy host with arrow and spear. All of their bodies I bored through like a sieve (?). . . . like fat steers who have hobbles put on them – speedily I cut them down and established their defeat. I cut their throats like lambs. I cut off their precious lives (as one cuts) a string. Like the many waters of a storm, I made (the contents of) their gullets and entrails run down upon the wide earth. My prancing steeds, harnessed for my riding, plunged into the streams of their blood as (into) a river. The wheels of my war chariot, which brings low the wicked and the evil, were bespattered with blood filth. With the bodies of their warriors I filled the plain, like grass (Luckenbill section 254, 127–8). For a broad analysis, see Simonetta Ponchia, "Analogie, metafore, e similitudini nelle iscrizioni reali assire: semantica e ideologia." *Or.Ant.* XXVI:3–4 (1987) 223–55.

[11] For a discussion of flood metaphors in Near Eastern treaty-curses, see Delbert Hillers, *Treaty-Curses and the Old Testament Prophets*, 70–1.

[12] I, for one, do not think these theophanic episodes were designed to provide an audience with comic relief; rather, they seem to express a world gone awry and on the verge of cataclysm.

are presumed to have a staggering effect upon the humans who witness them. Diomedes, his mortal eyes opened by Athene, is horrified to see Ares cresting as a wave in battle (5.593ff). Hera anticipates the same effect on Achilles during the theomachia, "for it is a terrible thing for gods to manifest in appearance" (20.131).[13] Clearly, the manifestation of divinity as natural disaster is a potent paradigm, which is why it is applied to human heroes in battle passion. The similar poetic effect created by images of warriors as ravening animals and images of them as powerful storms speaks to that place in Homeric imagination where the world of untamed nature and the world of deities may coincide.

A twist on the same adulation of raw power may be found in a handful of Homeric epiphanies of human warriors as superhuman vestiges of a bygone age. But, although admired by the poet, these superhuman spectacles also cast light on the very status quo they violate. On the positive side, Nestor (1.271–72), Diomedes (5.302–4), Ajax Telemonios (12.381–85), Hector (12.449–51), and Aineas (20.285–87) all muster strength inconceivable for Homer's contemporaries, "the sort of mortals there are now." Such strength is quasi-immortal: "No one but a god could have restrained Hector by coming at him, when Hector shone with terrible bronze, leapt over the Achaian gates, and fire burned in his eyes" (12.463–46). But a similar description of Ajax relies on a contrasting status quo: "[Ajax] would not yield to anyone who is mortal and eats the meal of Demeter, who may be broken by bronze and great stones. . . . In no way is it possible to contend with him" (13.321–25). Both descriptions are affirmations of a terrible strength, but in the description of mighty Ajax, the "meal of Demeter" obliquely introduces another mythic theme, that of the humanizing sphere associated with the goddess Demeter. Briefly exploring Demeter's cultural sphere as represented in the *Iliad* will help to define human mortality and frailty and the civilizing conventions shattered by the harsh realities of brute strength.

In the *Iliad* Demeter is more than a goddess of the barley-harvest "who separates the fruit from the chaff on the sacred threshing floor" (5.499–502); she is also one figurehead for a range of humanizing customs associated with agriculture, such as communal laws, compassion, and breaking bread together around a common hearth.[14] Her sovereign sphere

[13] The same effect is implied in numerous Assyrian examples; hence Marduk appears in battle "adorned in terror" and Ishtar of Arbela appears "clothed in fire," "raining fire," and "bearing aloft an awful splendor." See Luckenbill 1968.

[14] See M. Kitts, "Two Expressions for Human Mortality in the Epics of Homer," *History of Religions* (1994) 132–51.

complements that of Zeus in his persona as the patron god of hospitality and also of suppliance, law, and dietary custom. Together, the two gods promote the human conventions that make possible the authentic human society situated around the hearth in the Homeric *oikos*.

The conventions promoted by the two gods are highlighted in Book 21, when Lykaon begs Achilles to pity him, to spare him as a suppliant (*hikētēs*), and to respect the "meal of Demeter" they once ate together (21.74–79) in an earlier time, when Achilles abducted Lykaon from his father's orchard, took him to Lemnos, and later sold him for a price. Whatever actually may have occurred between Achilles and Lykaon during their trip to Lemnos – whether, for instance, they dined as companions around the same table, whether hostage Lykaon merely ate his host's bread, or whether they together underwent some kind of initiatory rites to Demeter at Lemnos[15] – Lykaon's appeal to their shared "meal of Demeter" clearly invokes some kind of obligation, as does his appeal for pity and for recognition as Achilles' suppliant. As established by Leonard Muellner, a suppliant, *hikētēs*, or "'one who comes [*hikanei*],' ... in the formal language of reciprocity means a *xeinos* [guestfriend] in need of his first favor." This favor cannot be refused, even by Achilles, without incurring the wrath of Zeus.[16] However, this is not Lykaon's first request as a suppliant. His life having been spared by Achilles once, Lykaon is appealing now for second favor, which strengthens his appeal to their former "meal of Demeter" and to the convention of suppliance, and also renders him a shadowy kind of guestfriend to his former host. Lykaon has already established a relationship with Achilles. Now, in appealing to the conventions of suppliance, pity, and the meal of Demeter, Lykaon is appealing to the humanity of Achilles, a compassionate humanity that would respect the conventions sanctioned by gods and would allow Lykaon to live.

But in the face of Achilles' emerging "*mēnis* of the gods" (21.523), Lykaon's plea is futile, which perfectly illustrates Homer's contrast.

---

[15] On cults at Lemnos, see Walter Burkert's *Greek Religion* (Cambridge, MA: Harvard University Press, 1985) 281–2.

[16] *The Meaning of Homeric ἐύχομαι Through Its Formulae* (Innsbruck: Institut fur Sprach-wiseenschaft der Universitat Innsbruck 1976) 87–8. Zeus, protector of suppliants and guestfriends, shall vindicate those who are dishonored in this request. See also my discussion in M. Kitts, "Killing, Healing, and the Hidden Motif of Oath-Sacrifice in *Iliad* 21," *Journal of Ritual Studies* 13(2) 1999 42–57, and "The Wide Bosom of the Sea as a Place of Death – Maternal and Sacrificial Imagery in *Iliad* 21," *Literature and Theology* 14:2 (June 2000) 103–24.

Achilles has refused to honor most communal conventions since Patroklos died, refusing to join in commensal feasts (19.198–214, 19.304–8, 19.314–21; cf. 19.345–54), vowing to fast until vengeance is paid (19.203–14),[17] and only reluctantly participating in the oath-ceremony mending his rift with Agamemnon (19.146–53, 19.188–205). In Books 21 and 22, Achilles defies all human customs except the one of *poinē*, or retribution, for the fallen Patroklos (21.134). Aptly, his *poinē* is undertaken with utmost singularity – he shares the stage only with his victims and with gods. Lykaon understands this. Realizing that he cannot possibly escape Achilles' wrath (21.92–4), Lykaon gives up (*luto . . . philon ētor*) (21.114), loosens his grip on Achilles' knees and spear, sits back, and awaits death, his arms at his sides (21.115–16). Similarly, in the next book Hector perceives that Achilles is beyond pity. "He will not pity me nor respect me at all, but will kill me unarmed, as if I were a woman" (22.123–5). In these books, Achilles surpasses Demeter's sphere of compassionate humanity and of breaking bread around a common hearth, a fact epitomized by his fasting (19.198–214, 19.304–8, 19.314–21) as well as, implicitly, by the immortal nectar and ambrosia applied to him by Athene (19:345–54) – herself one of the breadless and bloodless immortals (5.339–42). Monstrous in his breadless strength, Achilles is here the very paragon of Hesiod's men of the third age, who were excessive in hubris and lacked bread: "They ate no bread at all but, unrefined (*aplastoi*), they possessed the dauntless hearts of the untamed (*adamantos*)" (*Works and Days* 146–48). As early as Book 9 Agamemnon compares Achilles to Hades because of his refusal to be tamed: "Hades, you know, cannot be softened or tamed (*adamastos*). For this reason, to mortals he is the most hateful of all the gods" (9.158–61). Hades' hardness stems, of course, from his personification of death, the one experience that, at least in Homer, nullifies the softening effect of Demeter's conventions. Untamed like Hades, Achilles in these examples inversely prefigures the civilizing institutions he rejects. His battle fury will so transcend mortal limits that it will provoke retaliation by the river god and a cosmic clash of gods on earth (21.383–413).

Achilles in these manifestations thus epitomizes also the asocial man reproved by Nestor in Book 9: "Without clan, without law, and without hearth is he who loves chilling civil strife [*aphrētōr athemistos anestios estin ekeinos, hos polemou eratai epidēmiou ikruoentos*]" (9.63–64). In context, Nestor's rebuke seems directed at the obstinacy of both Agamemnon and

---

[17] Compare Saul's vow, at 1 Samuel 14.24: "A curse be on the man who eats any food before nightfall, until I have taken vengeance on my enemies."

Achilles (the latter at least implicitly), but it also casts light on an implied and general link between the hearth, the clan, and legal institutions. The hearth is a multifaceted symbol in Greek antiquity[18] and central to the ideological domain of Demeter, who oversees the sharing of bread around a common hearth.[19] In Nestor's platitude, to be without hearth (*anestios*) seems virtually a synonym for being without clan (*aphrētor*), which harks back to the social isolation of the man who rejects pity, suppliance, and Demeter's meal around a common hearth. This symbolic link between clan and hearth extends beyond the *Iliad* at least into Hittite Anatolia, where, to be sure, the hearth has a wide range of significations, but is the vehicle par excellence for communicating with ancestors and gods.[20] Even there, to be without hearth is to be without clan and without

[18] On the hearth in Greek thought, see, famously, J.-P. Vernant, "Hestia-Hermes: The Religious Expression of Space and Movement in Ancient Greece," in *Myth and Thought Among the Greeks* (London: Routledge & Kegan Paul 1983) 127–75. See also Louise Bruitt Zaidman and Pauline Schmitt Pantel's *Religion in the Ancient Greek City* (Cambridge: Cambridge University Press 1994 [1992, 1989]) 93.

[19] See, for instance, I. Chirassi-Colombo, "I doni di Demeter: mito e ideologia nella Grecia arcaica," in *Studi Triestini di Antichita' in Onore di Luigia Achillea Stella* (Trieste: Universita' degli studi antichi di Trieste, 1975), H. Foley, *The Homeric Hymn to Demeter* (Princeton: Princeton University Press 1994), and D. Sabbatucci, *Il Mito, Il Rito e La Storia* (Rome: Bulzoni 1978) 225–26.

[20] In Hittite texts, the hearth has a wide range of religious offices, and lies at the nucleus of a Hittite domestic ideology similar to but delineated somewhat from the Greek. The Anatolian hearth represents a source of divine and domestic beneficence. In the myths of the disappearing god Telepinu, for instance, the smothered hearth is a key symbol of desolation, and the return of its fire significant for domestic renewal. (See Alfonso Archi, "Il Culto del Focolare presso gli Ittiti," *SMEA* XVI (1975) 77–87, and the sections 2 and 24 of the first version of the myth of the disappearing god Telepinu, as translated by Harry Hoffner *(Hittite Myths*, Society for Biblical Literature Vol. 2, Atlanta: Scholars' Press 1990: 14–7.) Similarly, Hestia's hearth in the Greek city was kept burning to signify civic vitality, presumably on the same principle as the hearths of *oikoi*, which were temporarily extinguished at the proprietor's death (Bruit Zaidman and Schmitt Pantel 1994: 93). Relatedly, the hearth is a virtual synonym for "domicile" in Hittite law 24, which prescribes the repayment due the owner of a slave who has escaped "to the hearth" of someone else (discussed in Archi 1975).

Similarly to Greek ideology, Hittite ideology of the hearth also includes "vertical" dimensions. Libations are poured at the hearth because the smoke of the hearth was thought to forge divine–human pathways. Hence a handful of chthonic gods were libated at the hearth, as were the spirits of dead sovereigns. The hearth also conveyed meat offerings to the gods, either by smoke from cooking the meat or by complete combustion in a cultic situation thought to be Hurrian. The hearth is entreated to supplicate various tutelary deities on behalf of humans, usually at night, because "As by day, oh hearth, humankind continuously surrounds you, by night the gods surround

access to the ancestors to whom hearth smoke conducts human petitions. In the same vein, Nestor also conjoins being "without hearth" with being "without law" (*athemistos*). That a man without hearth eludes the legal standard for civic membership – however that might be conceived in Homer – is implied in Agamemnon's hypothetical census for native dwellers at Troy: "If we Achaians and Trojans should wish to cut trusty oaths and to count out both sides, to collect the Trojans, as many as there are *at the hearth . . .*" (2.123–25) (italics mine). Here, being "at the hearth" apparently identifies householders in the *polis*'s milieu, as Agamemnon is about to contrast the numbers of Trojans "at the hearth" (2.125) with the numbers of their allies from outside of the *polis* (2.131). His use of the phrase "to cut trusty oaths" further illuminates the legalistic focus of his comment, because oath-making is the commissive prerequisite for the truce that would have to come before any such census (see truces at 3.66–323, 6.232–36, 7.411ff, 19.250–68). Despite the uncertainty as to how Agamemnon's speech about a *polis* fits into an authentic version of the poem,[21] the use of the phrase "at the hearth" to designate civic membership, in our extant poem, at least illustrates an ancient link among compassionate, domestic, and civic spheres of experience (with clan, with hearth, and with law). That the link of hearth, clan, and law holds also in Anatolia is suggested by Hittite Law 24, which prescribes the lawful repayment due the owner of a slave who has escaped "to the hearth" of someone else, presumably of a benefactor who will protect and shelter him.[22] Given the long-suspected cultural borrowings between Hittite customs and the Homeric poems,[23] then, to be with hearth appears

you" (Kbo XVII 105). The vertical channel between gods and humans at the hearth is also a means by which the gods are encouraged to establish the roots and draw up the shoots of the royal family, in KUB XXIX III 37–IV 3. These examples illustrate the enormously important role of the hearth for both familial and theological discourse, among the Hittites as among the Greeks. In short, the hearth enables human-to-human and human-to-divine communication. Around it humans come together and through it they offer to and entreat their ancestors and their gods. For a contextualization of the Hittite cites and a summary of Hittite domestic ideology, see Archi 1975.

[21] Aristarchus atheticized some of these lines as out of place or illogical. G. S. Kirk, *The Iliad: A Commentary*, Vol. 1 (Cambridge: Cambridge University Press 1985) 131.

[22] Analyzed by Archi 1975. On the law of *hurkel* and the wide embrace of the notion of family in Hittite sociology, see Harry Hoffner, "Incest, Sodomy and Bestiality in the Ancient Near East," *Alter Orient und Altest Testament*, Vol. 22 1973, 81–90.

[23] See, for instance, Faraone 1993: 60–80, Mauro Giorgieri, "Aspetti magico-religiosi del giuramento presso gli ittiti e i Greci," in *La questione delle influenze vicino-orientali sulla religione greca*, ed. Sergio Ribichini, Maria Rocchi (Rome: Paolo Xelle. 2001), 421–40,

to be linked to being with clan (widely defined) and with protective legal institutions, not only within the *Iliad* but beyond it. When Nestor reproves the clanless, hearthless, and lawless supermen who reject the social and legal standards upon which treaties and oaths are based, he appears to be setting a cross-Mediterranean social standard in crisp relief.

By implication from these inverse figurations, then, the virtues upon which oath-making is based – civility, compassion, and willingness to break bread around a common hearth – are the marks of a cultivated man who shuns chilling strife. Yet the *Iliad* provides ample evidence to suggest that oath-making and similar conventions are seen as exercising but a fragile hold over human passions, at least during wartime. It is clearly the chaos of battle and the lack of battlefield restraint that make the hold of oath-making and other such conventions seem fragile. To grasp the precarious boundary between battlefield passion and the stability bestowed on the social order by oath-making and similar ritual conventions in the *Iliad*, we need to review the constraining effects and authoritative voice of ritual, as well as the tenuous ability of individuals to resist a ritual's taming effects.

In Chapter 1 we compared the constraints of ritual performance to the compulsions of polite conventions and of rhythmic or musical performances, stressing the tendency for ritual performers to respond to the special registers of the authoritative voice embedded in ritual formality, the way that rituals bestow authority on conventions by formalization, and the way that formalization distinguishes ritual behavior from casual behavior. It may seem obvious that enactments of conventions such as oath-making, suppliance, pity, and hospitality in the *Iliad* constrain individual impulses and passions in this way, although with differing degrees of formality and compulsion. Gould,[24] Thornton,[25] Muellner,[26] Edwards,[27] Karavites,[28] and others have explored the compelling nature of such conventions, all of which appear to have been ritualized and deeply rooted in Homeric sociology. There is also a history of scholarship on the more

---

Hans Gutterbock, "Troy in Hittite Texts? Wilusa, Ahhiyawa and Hittite History," in *Troy and the Trojan War*, ed. Machteld J. Mellink (Bryn Mawr, PA: Bryn Mawr College 1996) 33–44, Mondi 1990: 142–98, and Puhvel 1991: 9–12.

[24] John Gould, "Hiketeia," *Journal of Hellenistic Studies* 93 (1973) 74–103.

[25] Thornton 1984.

[26] Muellner 1976.

[27] Mark Edwards, "Type-Scenes and Homeric Hospitality," *TAPA* (1975) 105: 51–72.

[28] Peter Karavites 1992.

abstract issues of socialization through ritualization – Bourdieu's "habi-tus,"[29] Bateson's "deutero-learning,"[30] Rappaport's "deutero-truth,"[31] and others – some of which was touched upon in Chapter 1. But the power of a ritual to constrain and to temper exuberant behavior is per-haps most simply explained by the reinstantiating and preserving effects of rituals, as Rappaport discusses in the context of liturgical orders.

> The orders of societies, like the order of the universe in general, tend to degenerate into disorder. . . . Liturgy does not simply remind people of the orders which usage – behavior and history – violates and dissolves. It establishes and ever again reestablishes those orders. Liturgy pre-serves the conventions it encodes inviolate in defiance of the vagaries of ordinary practice, thereby providing them with existence independent of, and insulated against, the statistical averages which characterize behavior.[32]

It is against this establishing and reestablishing of liturgical orders that we might begin to appreciate Hector's, Lykaon's, or Agamemnon's efforts to "tame" Achilles by binding him in conventions based on mutual trust. We have already probed the "metaperformative" nature of oath-making rituals, whose performance establishes commitments in the same way that factive illocutions bring certain conventions into existence by their very utterance. Participation in such rituals, Rappaport argues, entails acceptance of their terms, regardless of any secret doubt or inner qualms about the moral imperatives of the conventions enacted. Violation of the terms enacted is a violation of the obligation implicitly established when one engages in the ritual's performance, even if the ritual is not an oath-making one. Violation of obligation, we may remember, is the one breach universally held to be immoral across societies. Agamem-non, Hector, Lykaon, and others would bind Achilles to the obligations implicit in common conventions by urging him to engage in those con-ventions. By refusing to engage in common conventions, Achilles escapes the obligations and the morality entailed therein.

It may seem obvious that the binding power of many such rituals, especially oath-making rituals, is mired in spoken language – hence "liturgical" rituals. We already have discussed the inverted relationship

[29] Bourdieu 1995.
[30] Gregory Bateson, *Steps to an Ecology of Mind* (New York: Ballantine Books (Random House) 1972, 1985) 159ff.
[31] Rappaport 1999.
[32] Rappaport 1999: 129–30.

between utterances and acts in rituals, in Chapter 1, particularly those rituals characterized as liturgical orders ("more or less invariant sequences of
formal acts and utterances not entirely encoded by the performers"). Such
rituals do more than bind participants to their terms; their expository elements also help to establish common realities by constructing a semantic
horizon for the ritual performance and by enunciating and repeating what
Rappaport has called "Ultimate Sacred Postulates."[33] Especially in rituals where the utterances are performatively stronger than acts, these most
invariant verbal pronouncements basically select out from the myriad possibilities of discourse what is real, sacred, and true, and pronounce those
postulates with a voice of authority that is directly proportional to the relatively fixed and unquestioned order of the ritual performance. As Bloch
has observed, we tend to respond in kind to pronouncements formally
made, and it is difficult to resist messages communicated in heightened
speaking registers and especially in archaic syntactical patterns, particularly if they are communicated with rhythm and vocal inflection, or if they
bear some other marked feature. As he notes, it is difficult to argue with a
song.[34] In the context of Rappaport's liturgical orders, the repetition of an
Ultimate Sacred Postulate in a special speaking register accompanied by
a formalized sequence of ritual acts is persuasive in a different way than is
ordinary speech. Unlike ordinary speech, which permits a variety of possibilities of expression and response, Ultimate Sacred Postulates restrict
the field of alternatives. As Rappaport and many others see it, one of
religion's sociological purposes is precisely to ameliorate the problems of
conflicting realities and allegiances to those realities, problems that arise at
least in part from the power of language to signify alternatives, a problem
intrinsic to the flexibility of everyday language and to the loose connection between verbal symbols and the things they signify. He points out, "If
there is enough grammar to think and say 'YHVH is God and Marduk is
not,' or 'Socialism is preferable to capitalism,' there is, obviously, enough
to imagine, say and act upon the opposite."[35] By establishing liturgical
orders whose traditional messages are communicated formally through
ritualized utterances and that resist challenge by virtue of their formality, religion works to ameliorate the problems that arise from alternative

---

[33] "[T]he recurrent, punctilious, and perduring expression of a particular sentence or set
of sentences in ritual selects it out of the infinite possibilities of discourse and represents
it as an Ultimate Sacred Postulate. This is one of the most fundamental and crucial
entailments of canonical invariance." Rappaport 1999: 290–91.

[34] Bloch 1974, cited by Bell 1992: 214–15.

[35] Rappaport 1999: 17, see also 321.

conceptions and world views. It is because of this work of religion that human sociability can be developed and maintained.[36]

As "fences" (*herkoi*) against the lie and disorder, oaths (*horkoi*) do exactly the same. Oaths might be envisioned as formalized testaments of allegiance to a common reality. The messages they encode stand against what Rappaport calls the dissolving power of lie and alternative, the two vices intrinsic to language.[37] The function of oaths to establish allegiances to a common reality is applicable to the attempts of Agamemnon, Nestor, Hector, Lykaon, and others to bind Achilles to the prevailing order and to the obligations such a bond would entail. To persuade Achilles to accept the constraints of established customs is to persuade him to accept a liturgically constructed reality. By refusing to engage in established customs, Achilles is able to resist the postulates they pronounce and to resist becoming engaged in the realities and obligations they establish as factive.

In this, Achilles is a special figure. More complexly than other characters in the *Iliad*, Achilles demonstrates an acute "sense of ritual" while also demonstrating his resistance to the authoritative voice of convention. We hear that he has a reputation for honoring social conventions (21.67–69; 24.186–87), and we see two well-developed examples of his hospitality in Books 9 and 24. But we also see his frequent resistance to traditions, such as in his Hades-like refusal to be "tamed" by Agamemnon's gifts (9.158–9), in his refusal to be bound by an oath to spare Hector's corpse (22.252–69), and in his refusal to be moved by Lykaon's pleas that he respect suppliance, based on their past experiences together as host and hostage (21.74ff). The example with Lykaon is particularly telling, as in it Achilles also rejects Lykaon's plea of compassion for Lykaon's mother (21.89–92), to whom the boy has just returned, who has just lost her other son, and whose plight elicits a number of themes that apply to Achilles' own mother. Both mothers soon will be bereft of sons, both bore their

---

[36] Rappaport 1999: 15, 326–29. The establishment of what is real has moral implications as well:

> In societies in which such matters are contested, such reality, or truth is not, moreover merely a matter of the civil establishment of one or the other possibilities, nor necessarily, the outcome of an easy tolerance, . . . . It is not merely a question of what order does prevail but which one should prevail. For at least some of the world's symbolically contingent elements "reality" or "truth" has a moral as well as social dimension, and, historical states of affairs at variance with that reality are taken to be false.                    (1999: 18)

[37] Rappaport 1999: 11–17.

sons "to be but brief" (1.352 and 21.84–85),[38] and both expect to mourn their sons with ceremony; but Lykaon's will not – "your mother will not lay you on a bier and wail for you but eddying Skamander will bear you into the wide bosom of the sea" (21.124). The sea, of course, is where Thetis, at last mention, was wailing for Achilles, and where she once received Dionysos "to her bosom" (6.136), which completes the ironic circle. In just this one vignette, many themes come together and help to layer the depiction of a man who endorses chilling strife at the cost of his own clan, customs, and the compassion associated with the hearth (9:63–64).[39]

It is interesting that it is against the prospect of his own death, with all of its universalizing and particularizing aspects, that Achilles rejects clan, custom and hearth. He explains his position starkly and lucidly to Lykaon:

> You must die too, friend (*philos*), why lament in this way?
> Even Patroklos died, and he was far better than you.
> Do you not see what a great and fine man also am I?
> I am of a good father and the mother who bore me is a goddess.
> But even so, death and strong fate are on me.
> It will be at dawn or afternoon or the middle of the day
> when someone will take my life in battle,
> striking me either by spear or by an arrow from a bow.
>
> (21.106–13)

Achilles' point is clearly that death renders everybody equal – Patroklos, Lykaon, and eventually himself – and against the prospect of imminent death the appeal of human customs fades.

Yet even as his approaching death diminishes the appeal of human customs, Achilles envisions his battlefield slaughter as falling within the bounds of at least one last human convention, which is *poinē* – retribution, expiation, the paying back (*epitinō*) of reparations. A brief examination of *poinē* as a ritual leitmotif will illustrate the power of ritualization to configure and signify behavior. It will also demonstrate Achilles' (or perhaps the narrator's) keen sense of the dynamic between ritualization and

---

[38] See Mark Edwards on the universality of this theme and its attraction to the figure of Achilles in the *Iliad*. *The Iliad: A Commentary, Vol. V* (Cambridge: Cambridge Unviersity Press 1991) 7.

[39] On the dialogue between Achilles and Lykaon and the comparison of the plights of their respective mothers, see Kitts 2000: 103–24.

resistance,[40] and the way that ritual codes may be appropriated or manipulated, based on personal acuity and what Catherine Bell has called "a sense of ritual."[41]

But before launching into a discussion of Achilles' *poinē* as a ritual leitmotif, it should be pointed out that the link of the Homeric theme of *poinē* with the verbs *tinō*, *apotinō*, *tinomai*, and *apotinomai* (as well as verbs of the *didomi* and *legō* families) has been established in a recent book by Donna Wilson,[42] who examines the economic, social, and political pathways behind *poinē* as ritualized exchange. Her argument is cogent and far-reaching in that it illuminates the politics and economics of Homeric reciprocity and compensation, and traces the exchange of *timē* (honor, prestige) in terms of both concrete and symbolic capital. She demonstrates, among other things, that ransom and revenge, the usual candidates for translations of *apoina* and *poinē*, correspond to two different types of compensation in the *Iliad*, but are comprehended semantically and thematically within a unified traditional theme. Considering Achilles' predicament after the death of Patroklos, it might seem to be symbolic capital that is accruing with his practice of *poinē* from Book 18 on. On the other hand, the distinction between concrete and symbolic capital would seem to blur, or perhaps fuse, in Books 21 and 22, due as much to the poetic expression of his *mēnis* as to the cultural conventions of exchange represented there. Examining *poinē* as a ritual leitmotif in Homeric poetry may shed some light on an aspect of *poinē* not fully comprehended within the concept of exchange.

Achilles' *poinē* arguably begins as early as his promise that he will *appodeirotomeō*, cut the throats, of twelve Trojan youths in his anger (*cholōtheis*) for Patroklos's death (18.336–7), but *poinē* is incontestably the spirit that launches his actions in Book 21, which begins with his gathering of those twelve Trojan youths to be *poinē* (21.28) for Patroklos and to be sacrificed on his funeral pyre. The theme of *poinē* continues with his "prayer-boast" (*ep-euchomenos*, 21.121) to all the Trojans over Lykaon's corpse: "Perish, all of you, . . . until you all shall pay [*teisete* 21.134] for the murder of Patroklos and the ruin of the Achaians, whom you killed while

---

[40] Bell 1992: 218.

[41] Bell 1992: 81.

[42] Donna F. Wilson, *Ransom, Revenge, and Heroic Identity in the Iliad* (Cambridge: Cambridge University Press 2002) 20–7, n.b. 23–5, and also 16–17. On the differing Homeric uses of the direct object with *apotinō* and *exapotinō*, see also Huebeck, "Erinus in der archaischen Epic" *Glotta* (1986) 64: 143–65, n.b. 150–51.

I was away" (21.128–35). It continues in his battle with the River Sca-mander, and culminates with the killing and mutilating of Hector, who "will pay back" (*apoteiseis*) for the crowds of Achilles' dead companions (22.271–2). At first glance, there is something rather primeval about *poinē*, which perhaps explains why it should be the paradigm selected to give expression to Achilles' grief and rage when he is so close to death. But a second glance will show that *poinē* has a broad range of significations, from the quite ritualized to the barely so. As an incipient ritual paradigm, *poinē* is uniquely suitable for marking Achilles' reentry to the sphere of human customs.

As the paying of reparations, *poinē*, like *apoina*, sometimes refers to a clearly formalized institution in the *Iliad*, and one expected to repair injuries other than just grief and loss resulting from the death of a loved one. For instance, Agamemnon attaches a clause to his oath with the Trojans in Book 3, justifying *poinē* for the failure to pay him compensation for the slight against his family and the Achaians.

> "If Priam and the sons of Priam do not wish to repay me
> compensation (*timē*), after Alexandros has fallen,
> then at that point I shall fight for the sake of *poinē*,
> staying right here, until I shall reach the end of the conflict."
>
> (3.288–91)

Although the clause is unanticipated before Agamemnon utters it, his claim of the right to seek reparation for dishonor requires little explana-tion at this point: Reparation for dishonor and repayment of debts are the ostensible reasons for the war against the Trojans in the first place, and fundamental principles in the *Iliad* – all too visible in Agamemnon's effort to pacify Achilles with *apoina*.

That such reparation need not be paid in lives is clear from Ajax's reproval of Achilles in Book 9:

> "... For a man has even accepted *poinē*
> from the murderer of his brother, or even his child who has died.
> And the other man stays in the deme, having paid well to him,
> and the heart and manly *thumos* of the first man are restrained,
> having received the *poinē*. But the gods have put a persistent
> and evil *thumos* in your chest, for the sake of a girl,
> only."
>
> (9.632–38)

Nor is *poinē* necessarily paid in lives in Book 13, when a father sheds tears for his son for whom no *poinē* will be forthcoming (13.659), nor when

Zeus gives immortal horses to Tros in exchange (*poinē*) for the company of his son Gannymede (5.265–66). Despite the differing contexts, these examples have the appearance of straightforward bartering along con-ventionalized parameters. *Poinē* seems virtually a synonym for bartering when Zeus exchanges Hector's life for battlefield power by conferring strength to Hector in *poinē* for the fact that Andromache will not receive him back from battle, when Hector dons the arms he stripped from Patroklos (17.206–8).

*Poinē* is more explosive, however, when a wedding is disrupted by an argument over *poinē* for a man who has perished, in a scene portrayed on Achilles' great shield (18.498–502). In that scene, where two men seem to dispute whether a judge has mandated that one accept payment or whether he is permitted lethal vengeance,[43] the violence appears to be just below the threshold, which is significant because of the paradigmatic nature of all the scenes rendered by Hephaestus on the shield.[44] Explosive violence is similarly close to the threshold in Phoinix's tale of his father's wish to harm him because of his trespass in sleeping with the father's concubine (9.453–68), although *poinē* is not precisely mentioned.[45] It has been argued that it is the nature of *poinē* to seek violent expression when appeasement through payment, as in the case of the scene on the shield, or through banishment, as in Phoinix's case, is not forthcoming.[46] But an awareness of the enormous difficulty of surrendering to appeasement seems to lie behind Thetis's urging of Achilles to accept from Priam the *apoina* that, according to Andersen, is meant to end the cycle of revenge at least as much as to ransom Hector's corpse.[47] These examples render

---

[43] See the cogent discussion on different aspects of this scene by Edwards 1991: *A Commentary, Vol. V.* Cambridge: (Cambridge University Press 1991) 214–17.

[44] For a discussion of the shield as an illustration of the facets of everyday life that make one contemplate war and its relation to peace, see Oliver Taplin, "The Shield of Achilles within the *Iliad*," *Greece and Rome* 27 (1980) 1–23, reproduced in Vol. III of *Homer: Critical Assessments*, ed. Irene J. F. De Jong (New York: Routledge 1999) 179–200.

[45] Compare the biblical story of Reuben sleeping with his father Jacob's concubine Bilhah (Gen. 35.22). The story has been seen as portraying an attempt by Reuben to usurp his father's power (see notes by Robert Alter, 1996: 200, and Victor Matthews, *Old Testament Themes* (St. Louis: Chalice Press 2000) 15), but Alter also points out that the Talmud explains Reuben's deed as an attempt to defile the slavegirl of his mother's dead rival, to make her off limits to his father. This makes an interesting comparison to Phoinix.

[46] See discussion by Edwards 1991: 216.

[47] O. Andersen, "Some Thoughts on the Shield of Achilles," *Symbolae Osloenses* LI (1976) 5–18.

*poinē* the barest of ritual formalizations, constraining raw violence by only a thread.

Then there are yet other cases, more germane to Achilles, where *poinē* heralds nothing short of nonspecific revenge killing. For instance, it is not precisely his brother's killer whom Akamas stabs as a way of exacting *poinē* (14.483) for a brother who "was not long unavenged (*atitos*)" (14.484); it was just the man dragging away the corpse. The target is even broader when Patroklos mows down the first Trojan phalanxes, "paying back *poinē* for many" (16:398). Equally broad is Achilles' *poinē* against the 12 Trojan youths collected for human sacrifice on the pyre of Patroklos (21.28) and the implied *poinē* against all the other Trojans who "shall pay" (*teisete*), in Achilles' boast over the corpse of Lykaon (21.134–35). It wouldn't be apt to apply contemporary notions of individualized guilt to the *Iliad*, when the emphasis in these examples seems to be on restitution to the wronged party, not on the culpability of the victim. Nonetheless, the presumption of fairness in Ajax's comment about *poinē* and the legalistic precision expected in the scene on the shield both seem distanced from the wider expression of rage that *poinē* signifies when Akamas, Patroklos, and Achilles exercise it. It would seem that *poinē* runs deep enough in Homeric imagination that it may lend itself to a range of significations, at one end of which is the formalized expression of lethal anger.[48]

In Achilles' case, *poinē* would seem to be precisely a formalized expression of *cholos*, given his vow to cut the throats (*apodeirotomeō*) of Trojan youths in rage (*cholōtheis*) for the death of Patroklos (18.337), and the narrator's later equation of these same "evil" intentions (*kaka de phresi mēdeto erga* (21.19)) with *poinē* for Patroklos (21.28). These equations make Achilles' *poinē* virtually a performance of *cholos*. Any ritualized shape to Achilles' *poinē* is only incipient, however, and ultimately dissolves when Achilles' *poinē* against "you all [who] shall pay [*teisete*] for the death of Patroklos and the ruin of the Achaians" (21.134) culminates in a theomachia-like battle among Achilles, Scamandros, and (later on) Hephaestos. This mini-theomachia as a consequence of unleashed *poinē* is notable because it is similar to the consequence barely checked when Athene stops Ares from exacting payment (*teisasthai*) for the death of his son on the battlefield (15.112–127), a vengeance so violent that it would

---

[48] Dennis D. Hughes interprets the motive for Achilles' funeral sacrifice of the twelve Trojan youths primarily as anger, in *Human Sacrifice in Ancient Greece* (London: Routledge 1991) 54–5. Donna Wilson's use of the notion of symbolic capital would also seem pertinent. (See note 38.)

have aroused *mēnis* and *cholos* among the gods (15.122).[49] *Poinē* in these last cases would seem to suggest a barely constrained expression of rage. Such renderings of exacting payment (*epitinō*) and of *poinē* and the link to *cholos* give the impression of an underlying codification of anger that embraces even the earth-shaking violence of divinities, and confines it within a loose system of ritual logic.

The notion of *poinē* as a formalized expression of anger brings us to the more theoretical question of *poinē* as ritualization. What might be the narrator's point in impressing *poinē* on behavior that doesn't quite need it – that is, on behavior that is tantamount to wartime slaughter? The psychological and sociological aspects of wartime rage are beyond the scope of this book, of course, but in Chapter 1 we hinted at some possible explanations for the formalization of behavior through ritual. Here we may observe that, first, within the model of ritual as communication, ritualization marks out and distinguishes certain behavior, infusing it with a special register, amplifying its communicability and importing a kind of traditional authority to it, which helps to explain why battlefield killing might be formalized in terms of legalized retribution even when its target is indiscriminate.[50] Precisely the paradox of *poinē* is that, as part of its range of expressions in the *Iliad*, it can invoke an established institution with seemingly religious sanction – exactly as Zeus "avenges" (see *apeteisan* at 4.158–62) the violation of oaths; yet it can also stand for the most urgent and uncontainable of human passions, as we have indicated. *Poinē* thus may offer the barest of ritualized configurations to battlefield slaughter while at the same time embracing lethal vengeance as one of its institutional expressions. By investing his battlefield slaughter with *poinē* at 21.28, 21.134, and 22.271–2, Achilles, or the narrator, stamps ritual form on his behavior. There seems to be an intuition that a ritual may distinguish and formalize behavior, may enunciate the messages it communicates, and may cast those messages within a primordial paradigm, which legitimates and elevates them. Because ritual formalizes and traditionalizes behavior, Achilles' enactment of *poinē*

---

[49] On *tinō* with the direct object, see again Huebeck 1986.

[50] As Rappaport sees it, "The formalization of acts and utterances, themselves meaningful, and the organization of those formalized acts and utterances into more or less invariant sequences, imposes ritual form on the substance of those acts and utterances, that is, on their significata. At one and the same time such formalization constitutes the specific forms of *particular* rituals and, reciprocally, *realizes the general* ritual form in specific and substantial instances. . . . In all ritual performances there is a substantiation of form and an informing of substance, . . . " (1999: 29).

in Books 21 and 22, perhaps ironically, would seem to mark his reentry into the sphere of human rituals and customs, even as it also expresses his angry distance from the sphere of compassionate conventions and mutual trust.[51]

In terms of its poetic effect, we might note from the perspective of oral traditional performance that *poinē*, in the array of examples cited thus far, is often ascribed to action by the implied narrator of the poem rather than by the characters themselves. Here we must remember the predicating model of ritual performance, at three levels. For Fernandez, predication is just what ritualization does for performers: It maps metaphorical switches onto previously inchoate ritual participants, endowing performers with more precise formal identities and the traditional authority that comes with those identities. A ritualized utterance – for instance, announcing and establishing that this behavior is *"poinē"* during a performance of it – executes a similar office for ritual performances more generally, according to Rappaport. Eschewing the splitting apart and rejoining talents of ordinary language, ritual utterances invoke paradigmatic, stylized, and often archaic forms, mapping canonical ideals onto behavior.[52] The predication of *poinē* to battlefield slaughter by the implied narrator in ritualized oral-poetic performance, not surprisingly, does the same thing. It invokes paradigmatic, stylized, and archaic forms and maps canonical ideals onto behavior, in harmony with the *telos* of epic poems in the first place, which is to "sing the glorious human deeds, that song whose glory reaches the vast heavens" (Od.8.73–74).

This invoking and mapping of stylized and archaic forms, then, occurs at three levels: that of the ritual performers (such as Achilles); the performances of rituals as a whole (by the implied narrator); and the ritualized oral poetic performance of the *Iliad* (by the presumed poet). For performers and audiences at all levels, *poinē* would seem to behave as a ritual leitmotif, effectively thickening and transforming the spectacle of battlefield slaughter,[53] linking it to a primordial pattern or canonical ideal. Based upon our earlier uses of Valeri and Jacobson, we may envision the configuring of battlefield slaughter as *poinē* as adding a poetic sense to the slaughter, resulting from the projection of the paradigmatic over the syntagmatic axis.[54]

---

[51] I attempted to argue this point, using different terms, in 1999. See Kitts 1999.

[52] See his discussion in Rappaport at pages 151–52.

[53] See Fernandez on ritual leitmotifs (1977: 126).

[54] Valeri 1985: 343.

Examining ritual behavior for its most fundamental properties of signification, we also might observe that, without the flag of *poinē*, Achilles'
battlefield killings might resemble something like unshaped slaughter
with no form. Bateson, Fernandez, and Rappaport have commented on
the form–substance dichotomy as it pertains to myth, and its apparent
analogy with the subject–predicate relationship in language. Except by
inductive extrapolation from the analogy of language, says Bateson, there
is just no other basis for the distinction between form and substance, as
no one has ever seen or experienced formlessness and unsorted matter.[55]
Yet a number of creation myths around the world begin by positing
the preexistence of unformed matter, which comes to be "formed" by
primordial utterances, for instance, "God said, 'Let there by light . . . and
he separated light from darkness" (Genesis 1.3–5), or "God said, 'Let
there be a vault between the waters, to separate water from water' " (Gen.
1.6–7). Rappaport summarizes a number of such myths world round, and
argues that the predicate–subject relationship fundamental to language
is reflected also in the form–substance dichotomy of these myths of
creation.[56] Without precisely equating myth and ritual but envisioning
ritual as a mode of communication, one can envision ritual, too, as a very
basic configuration of "substance," configuring space, bodies, time, and
the world of sound.[57] By a poetic assimilation, the way that ritual motifs
inform substance and the way that figures inform subjects are conjoined
in the *Iliad*'s example of Patroklos's *poinē*: "Patroklos then mowed into
(*epekerse*) the first phalanxes, . . . leaping, he killed them, paying back
*poinē* for many" (16.394–98). Here the figure of Patroklos as a mower
"cuts into" (*epekerse*) the field of Trojans (the first phalanxes) as the figure of *poinē* "cuts into" the shape of battlefield slaughter. In the imposing
of form on a field by mowing it, we have an analogy to the imposing
of form on slaughter by *poinē*, contiguous illustrations of the very basic
form–substance dichotomy in the predicating process of both myth and
ritual.

---

[55] Bateson 1985: xxv. Despite Bateson's assertion, the analogy to clay would seem apt.
[56] Rappaport discusses numerous illustrations (1999: 155–64).
[57] As Rappaport puts it, "The formalization of acts and utterances, themselves meaningful, and the organization of those formalized acts and utterances into more or less
invariant sequences, imposes ritual form on the substance of those acts and utterances,
that is, on their significata. At one and the same time such formalization constitutes
the specific forms of *particular* rituals and, reciprocally, *realizes the general* ritual form in
specific and substantial instances. . . . In all ritual performances there is a substantiation
of form and an informing of substance, . . . " (1999: 29).

Given this pervasive property of ritual to configure substance and behavior into the shape of canonical paradigms, and given the general purpose of oaths to fix commitments and modify preexisting relationships, as defined earlier,[58] it is perhaps not surprising that Homeric oath-making rituals are the kinds of ritual performances that constrain behavior and congeal new configurations of formal relationships. As such, they are the very thing to constrain and stabilize the superhuman exuberance manifest in the examples at the start of this chapter. Oaths therefore may be regarded as one of the antidotes to the exuberant expression of unbridled power that forms such a polyvalent theme in the *Iliad*. Their configuring and constraining effects apply beyond the *Iliad*, however, in that such effects are basic to ritualization itself. As we shall see, some of the formal properties of ritual, as well as their metaperformative properties, apply broadly to oath-making traditions across the Mediterranaean into Biblical and Hittite literature.

## OATH-MAKING PRINCIPLES

The ability to imagine and establish alternative orders ... makes possible, or even constitutes, a quantum leap in adaptive flexibility, the capacity of a system to adjust or transform itself in response to changing conditions. This enhanced flexibility has, however, an unavoidable but dangerous concomitant: increased grounds for disorder.

(Rappaport 1999: 17)

Understanding the premises behind oath-making as portrayed in the *Iliad* should help us to identify the principles of oath-making in the *Iliad*. The principles can be illuminated also by a glance at comparable Near Eastern traditions, as well as by our general understanding of ritual as outlined in Chapter 1. We shall reiterate that understanding before examining the precise principles illustrated in the *Iliad* and in Near Eastern traditions.

We have argued that the constraining and stabilizing effect of oaths is due in part to their formality. We also argued that ritual formality is constituted to some extent by a felt invariance in a ritualized sequence of utterances and acts, and that the invariance amplifies formality, which

---

[58] I am ignoring the fine distinctions between *horkos* and *horkia* that Karavites and Plescia have examined, and for this treatment of ritual I am enlisting Karavites's definition of *horkia*: "The standard case of *horkia* implies an element of reciprocity and mutuality of obligations, the extent of which is defined by the relationship which the *horkia* creates or alters" (1992: 65).

tends to affect participants in the same way that extraordinary registers of speech affect listeners – by compelling attention and deference. We referred to this affective feature as a matter of "ritual register."

Seen in the light of communication theory, the constraining and stabilizing effect of oaths is due also to their nature as metaperformatives. Their metaperformative nature is obliquely related to their nature as iconic reconfigurations of primordial paradigms, and thereby as substantiations of canonical forms within adjusted metaphoric domains (as seen by Tambiah, Rappaport, and others). Primarily, however, oath-making rituals are metaperformatives because their performances instantiate commitments, bringing formalized obligations into existence in a particular time and place.[59] These commitments are made obvious in the course of the poem by the terrible cost presumed to be due those who violate oaths, once oath-making rituals have been performed.

Further, with Roy Rappaport we have dubbed as "liturgical orders" those metaperformative rituals possessing a high degree of punctiliousness and thought to be encoded by authorities other than the performers. Homeric oath-making rituals qualify as liturgical orders because of exactly these features: their high degree of formality and punctiliousness, their reputed encoding by divine figures, and also, as we've stated, because their performances establish commitments, which is precisely what makes them metaperformatives. A liturgical order also has been argued to "preserve the conventions it encodes inviolate in defiance of the vagaries of ordinary practice, thereby providing them with existence independent of, and insulated against, the statistical averages which characterize behavior."[60] The Homeric oath-making ritual does exactly this, establishing and preserving oath-making commitments within the story, just as, at another level, the oath-making scene may be said to preserve the oath-making institution itself, for Homeric audiences. That is, because of the canonical status of the *Iliad* in Classical Greek society, the oath-making scenes might be seen as reifying the conventional ritual procedure of oath-sacrifice, as well as its institutional grounding, for later generations of audiences, thereby securing the institution against the entropy of change.

Another feature shown to adhere to oath-making conventions is their establishment of moral dicta through performance. As explained in Chapter 1, material truth and moral dicta are established through the

[59] Rappaport 1999: 37–8 and 117–18.
[60] Rappaport 1999: 129.

ritual's performance in time and space: Once a ritual has been performed, the participant's behavior will be judged by his or her conformance to the canonical ideal instantiated in the performance, regardless of the performer's insincerity, lack of belief, or any other "interior" state. Acceptance of that ideal is entailed by the performance of the ritual.[61] This is obvious in the *Iliad*, where failure to abide by an oath is expected to subject the oath-violator to cosmic penalties, even if it was a god who caused the violation of the oath in the first place – as when Aphrodite abducts Paris from his duel with Menelaos, or when Athene induces Pandaros to break the Trojan-Achaian truce. Even without cosmic penalties, moral dicta are implicit in the ritual's metaperformative nature: Performance establishes fact,[62] and also, for the performer, acceptance of the fact, which in turn establishes obligation. Breach of obligation, we will remember, is the one act universally held to be immoral, apparently of a higher and more general order of social breach than are murder, rape, and robbery, which vary considerably in the way they are stigmatized across societies. For Rappaport, violating the obligations implicit in the performance of a liturgical order is the basis for immorality: "Since obligation is entailed by acceptance, and the breaking of obligation is per se immoral, the existence, acceptance and morality of conventions are joined together indissolubly in rituals; they are, in fact, virtually one and the same."[63]

There are many oaths in the *Iliad* and also in East Mediterranean literatures that illustrate this cluster of features: formality, metaperformativeness, preservation of commitments, and the moral dicta implied by performance. By far the most portended, detailed, and significant example in the *Iliad* is the oath-sacrifice between the Trojans and Achaians in Book 3. That sacrifice will receive careful treatment in Chapter 3, but let us note in passing that its rhetorical and sacrificial acts are fastidiously performed and are embedded within the tightest of typical scenes, suggesting a punctilious formality. Primordial sources of power (Zeus, Erinyes, and so on) are invoked to guard against its future violation, and its performance establishes a new relationship between the Achaians and the Trojans. The terms of that relationship are sealed into fate by analogy with the killed lambs and by imprecations tying oath-violation to

---

[61] "[Ritual's] social efficacy lies in its very lack of profundity, in the possibility of disparity between the outward act and the inward state." Rappaport 1999: 121.

[62] Rappaport 1999: 132.

[63] Rappaport 1999: 137.

sure death. The moral dicta implied by participation in it are emphasized again and again in Achaian lambasts against the Trojans after they violate the oath, and are addressed also by the Trojans, to wit: Antenor suggests the Trojans return Helen and all her possessions, because "now we fight as liars regarding trusty oaths" (7:351–2), and Hector tries to rectify the Trojan failure by offering to settle the matter with a second duel, invoking Zeus as his witness (7.69–76) and announcing that *philotēs* (alliance or friendship) still might follow strife (7:300–02). Other examples in the *Iliad* illustrate the same oath-making principles, although they enunciate different features of the ritual constellation.

Perhaps the very best illustrations of the punctiliousness and metaperformativeness of oaths are the two oaths sworn by Zeus. One is the oath Hera beguiles Zeus into swearing in the story of *Atē*, ruinous folly, a story offered by Agamemnon to explain his own rash behavior toward Achilles. In the story of *Atē*, Zeus has just boasted that a son of his seed and blood is about to be brought into the light by the labor-inducing Eileithuia, whereupon Hera induces him to swear an oath that such a son will lord it over his neighbors (19.108–11). Zeus swears not just an oath, but a "great oath" (*megan horkon*) (19.113) on the matter, whereupon Hera immediately arrests the birth of Heracles, the preferred seed, and hastens the birth of Eurustheus, a different seed of Zeus's line. Eurustheus then will come to lord it over his neighbors, including Heracles. In fury, Zeus expels *Atē*, Folly, a reputed accomplice to Hera's trick, from heaven to earth to mingle among the mortals and no longer to befuddle the gods. Agamemnon ridiculously makes Zeus's folly serve as an analogy to his own in his mistreatment of Achilles, but the story nonetheless illustrates the punctiliousness of oaths, because the letter of Zeus's oath clearly prevails over its spirit. The story further illustrates an oath's metaperformativeness, albeit based on extreme principles. Once the oath is performed, Zeus cannot take it back, despite his anger. Hera and *Atē* are blamed for exploiting the metaperformative compulsion of the sworn oath.

The same emphasis on punctiliousness and metaperformativeness is illustrated in the "greatest pledge" (*megiston tekmor*) Zeus swears in Book 1, when he promises Thetis to direct the course of war so as to highlight the absence of Achilles. He is hesitant to accept Thetis's supplication that he promote the cause of the Trojans and deprive the Achaians, as he imagines the consequences among the gods. As he explains to her, his words are not barren, and there is no withdrawing of terms once he has nodded his head to them, "for this is the greatest pledge [*megiston tekmor*] among the immortals. It cannot be ameliorated, nor twisted, nor left incomplete" (1.524–7). Clearly this statement is evidence of the sealing power of his commitment – the oblique distinction between a *horkos* and a *tekmor*, an oath and a pledge, can barely be relevant to its commissive force. The consequences of this pledge, too, are obvious, because of the course of the war that follows. The same binding principle can be seen when Nestor attempts to hold Zeus to his earlier nod and promise to defend the Achaians and allow them to return from the war (15.372–76), as if the nod and the promise were quite binding.[64] These examples clearly demonstrate that oath-making performances are understood not only to reenact preestablished conventions, but to instantiate conventions as material truth. Their new instantiations occur in time and stand as public acts against which future acts may be judged. Zeus's oaths actually instantiate more than material truth; they instantiate binding force: Once Zeus nods his divine head to something, he cannot fail to bring it to fruition.

Of course, there is nothing unique about the commissive and enduring consequences of divine oaths in the Mediterranean milieu. Such oaths abound in biblical and Anatolian literature – not among gods, typically, but between gods and humans. Such oaths usually are configured to highlight the beneficence of the deity and the privilege gained by the human, who is usually a ruler. These contrast somewhat with human-to-human oaths, which, although often modeled on the divine–human paradigm, vary in terms of the status between and obligations assumed by the two parties. Moshe Weinfeld analyzes such oaths as part of the treaty-covenant traditions that are robustly evident in the Hittite, Hebrew, Akkadian, Assyrian, Egyptian, and Achaian cultural spheres, and claims that the shapes of such treaty-covenants must have crystallized in the international Near Eastern diplomatic exchanges of the mid-second millennium, although the forms reach back into the third and are manifest in the first.[65] Such divine–human treaties vary in motif from loyalty oaths to unconditional land grants that persist for generations, often entailing adoption metaphors.

---

[64] "Zeus father, if anyone in Argos, rich in wheat, ever prayed to return, burning the fat thighs of oxen or sheep, and you promised and nodded, remember those now, and ward off, Olympie, the pitiless day."

[65] For a synopsis, see Weinfeld 1990: 175–91. The Hittites were the first to crystallize the form, and several aspects are considerably different from the Assyrian manifestations. See Weinfeld 1993 vol. 22: 135–39.

Although Near Eastern divine loyalty oaths often differ in tone from the oaths of Homeric divinities, at least two of their features seem germane to Zeus's oaths: their unbreakable nature and, at least obliquely, their premise of partiality. On the latter theme, consider these biblical examples, "The Lord swore to David / an oath which he will not break" (Psalm 132.11); "I have made a covenant with him I have chosen, / I have sworn to my servant David; / 'I will establish your posterity for ever, / I will make your throne endure for all generations' (Ps. 89.3–4); and "I will establish the throne of his kingdom forever" (II Sam.8.8).[66] Similar themes inform Hittite king Hattusilis's claims of favor from the goddess Ishtar, according to his Apology: "Never in troubled times did you in any way step away from me. In no way did you abandon me to my enemies. Nor did you abandon me to my court-opponents, nor to those who envied me. If it was the plot of the enemy, if it was the plot of the prosecutor, if it was the plot of the king's household, in any way, You, my lady, defended me at every opportunity."[67] "Goddess Ishtar took me as a prince, she allowed me into kingship,"[68] and "[The goddess said:] 'Make me, goddess Ishtar, your special divinity.' Goddess Ishtar stepped behind me. As she would tell me, so it would become."[69] Although Zeus's pledge to Thetis and his oath about his unborn son are not couched as loyalty oaths, it is well

---

[66] Unless otherwise noted, all biblical translations are taken from the *Oxford Study Edition of The New English Bible* (Oxford: 1976).

[67] [All transliterations of cuneiform texts are mine, this one based on the composite text put together by Otten and based on my own work in Hittite courses offered at UC Berkeley. My transliterations are literal, including the scripzio plena. I have varied from Otten only where my notes do. Further, the translations are all mine, derived from my in-class work with Ruggero Stefanini and Gary Holland, who are not responsible for my errors.] Nu-mu DINGER$^{LUM}$ GAŠAN-*JA* $^{[LUV]}$ kuwaĵami meḫuni Ú-UL kuwapíikki šeer tiĵaat. *A-NA* $^{LÚ}$KÚR-mu píraan katta Ú-UL kuwapíiki tarnaaš. Ú-UL-ma-mu *A-NA* EN. *DI-NI-JA* $^{LÚ.MEŠ}$ aršanaattallaaš kuwapíikki píraan katta tarnaaš. Ma-a-na-aš INIM.$^{LÚ}$KÚR ma-a-na-aš INIM EN.*DI-NI*, ma-a-na-aš INIM É.LUGAL kuiški nu-mu $^D$IŠTAR-pát GAŠAN-*JA* ḫuumaandaza $^{[LUV]}$palaaḫšan seir ḫarta. Based on composite text, by Heinrich Otten: *Die Apologie Hattusilis III*, *Studien zu den Bogazkoy-Texten*, Heft 24 (Wiesbaden: Otto Harrassowitz 1981) I. 51–7). Compare this about Athene and Menelaos: "Not you, Menelaos, did the great gods abandon, but first the booty-bringing daughter of Zeus stood before you and warded off the short-pointed missiles. She warded them off from your skin in such a way as a mother wards off flies from her son, when he lies in sweet sleep" (4.127–31).

[68] nu-mu DUMU.LUGAL daaaš, nu-mu-kán $^D$IŠTAR GAŠAN-*JA* LUGAL-iznaanni anda tarniišta (IV.48–49).

[69] nu-mu ziiqqa-ĵa-mu-za $^D$IŠTAR paraaššiin iĵa. nu-mu $^D$IŠTAR GAŠAN-*JA* EGIR-an tiĵaat. Nu-mu memiiškiit, GIM-an kišaatĵaza (IV. 15–17).

known that Zeus cares greatly for Thetis, a matter of legendary concern to Hera, and he is fond enough of his unborn son in the oath to Hera that he swears blindly a "great oath" about the son's future greatness. If the partiality is not obvious, however, the unbreakable aspects of the pledge certainly are. Zeus's pledge, which "cannot be twisted, ameliorated nor left incomplete," is of the same genus as the oath that "The Lord . . . will not break" and as the forceful, perlocutionary words of the goddess Ishtar – "As she would say, so it would become."[70]

The metaperformative and commissive effects of oaths in the *Iliad* are often signaled by "taking by the hand," a polyvalent gesture also in Near Eastern treaties and sacred literature. According to my review of such literature, gestures "by the hand" connote one or more of the following: the exercise of power over ("laying on the hand," also at *Iliad* 1.80, 1.89), the conferring of power, the oath, guidance, and solidarity.[71] Particularly the last two connotations conjoin in numerous examples that are instructive for understanding "taking by the hand" in the *Iliad*. In the Hittite Apology of Hattusilis, for instance, taking by the hand appears to be both a guiding gesture and a gesture of solidarity when Hattusilis claims, "In the hand of Ishtar, my lady, I saw prosperity. My lady Ishtar took me by the hand. She led me along."[72] "So Ishtar my lady appeared to me in a dream. In the dream she told me this: 'Shall I, myself, abandon

---

[70] A curious bit of enhancement of divine promises in Anatolian religion is to be found in magical curses added to the petitions humans send to their gods, as in "Go, Sun God of the Earth. Do and perform everything well. If you do not, may the oath-gods of this ritual seize you, Sun God of the Earth." (Kbo XI 10 III 18 sqq.). Cited in Ahmet Unal's "The Role of Magic in Ancient Anatolian Religion," in *Essays on Anatolian Studies in the Second Millenium BC*, Vol. III, ed. HIH Prince Takahido Mikasa (Wiesbaden: Otto Harrassowitz 1988) 52–85, n.b. 62–3. Also, interestingly, not all sealed oaths or curses must remain that way. So, the Old Woman speaks as follows: "In whatever curses you indulged, let now the Sun-god turn those curses (and) tongues toward the left!" Ritual Against Domestic Quarrel, from Kbo II 3, translation according to A. Goetze, *ANET* (1969 350 sq.), cited by Unal at p. 60. Gary Beckman gives another example of forcing the gods, "Set out, O Sun-Goddess of the Earth! Make everything favorable; attend to it! If you do not attend to it, let the divine oath of this ritual proceed to seize you, O Sun-Goddess of the Earth! [(20). . . . nu-ut-ta ú-id-du ki-i ŠA SISKUR.SISKUR (21) *NI-EŠ* DINGER[LIM] tu-uk ták-na-aš [D]UTU-un e-ip-du.] "Proverbs and Proverbial Allusions in Hittite," *JNES* 45 no.1 (1986), 19–30, n.b. 25–6.

[71] For an interesting analysis of another gesture by the hand – that of slapping the thigh with the flat of one's hand – see Steven Lowenstam, *The Death of Patroklos, A Study in Typology* (Konigstein, Ts: Verlag Anton Hain 1981).

[72] nu-za-kán *A-NA* ŠU [D]IŠTAR GAŠAN-*JA* [LUV] luúlu uuḫḫuun. nu-mu [D] IŠTAR GAŠAN-*JA* ŠU-za *IZ-PAT*. na-aš-mu-kán paraa ḫaantaanteešta (I.20–21).

you to a[nother] god? Fear not.' . . . Since the goddess, my lady, held me by the hand, she did not abandon me in any way to the evil god,"[73] and "the goddess, my lady, held me by the hand away from all [matters], since I myself was the chosen [guided] man."[74] A similar connection between guidance and solidarity might be perceived in biblical Psalm 144: "Reach down your hand from on high; / deliver me and rescue me / from the mighty waters, / from the hands of foreigners / whose mouths are full of lies, / whose right hands are deceitful" (Ps.144:7–8).[75] A conjoining of the motifs of guidance and solidarity through taking by the hand can be seen in the *Iliad* when the gods Poseidon and Athene bind themselves to Achilles by oath, precisely by the gesture of taking him by the hand.

> . . . , so Poseidon and Athene stood,
> going next to him, they took the shape of men, and
> *taking his hand in theirs they bound themselves with words* [*cheiri de cheira*
> *labontes epistōsanto epessi*],
> Poseidon earthshaker began a speech to him,
> 'Peleide, do not fear nor be afraid at all,
> since we are helpers to you from the gods
> with the approval of Zeus, I and Pallas Athene.'
>
> (21.284–90) (Italics mine)

Guidance and solidarity, then, are frequent themes in oaths between divinities and mortals. Their commissive effect is often signaled by the gesture of "taking by the hand."

Also in a number of the *Iliad*'s human-to-human encounters, taking by the hand seems to connote guidance and solidarity, although the arrangement between these themes is sometimes ambiguous and distinctions are elusive. For instance, when the Achaians welcomed back Diomedes and Odysseus from their raid on the Trojan camp, "they rejoiced and greeted them warmly with right hands and sweet words" (10:541–2). Similarly,

---

[73] ᴰIŠTAR-ma-mu GAŠAN-*ĮA* Ù-at. nu-mu Ù-it kii memiišta. DINGIR^LUM-ni-ꭒa-at-ta ammuuk tarnaaḫḫi. nu-ꭒa- lee naaḫti. . . . nu-mu DINGIR^LUM kuit GAŠAN-*ĮA* ŠU-za harta (I.36–39). I have deleted part of line 39: nu DINGIR^LUM-za parkuueeššuum, "I became pure (exorcized?) by/from the [evil] god," but I imagine that the ablative serves similarly here as it does in the expression, *linkiyaz parkui* – to become exempt from oaths (see Vol. 3, Fascicle 1 eds. Gütterbock and Hoffner of *The Hittite Dictionary of the Oriental Institute of Chicago* 1980:67). In other words, "I become exempt from the evil god."

[74] DINGIR^LUM-mu GAŠAN-*ĮA* ḫuumaandaz-pat ŠU-za harta, ammuuk-ma-za paraa ḫaandaaanza kuit UKÙ-aš ešuun (I.46–47).

[75] New International Translation.

Nestor greeted Patroklos, "taking him by the hand," into the hut of Machaon (11:646), and Nestor recalls that Achilles "rose in wonder, taking us by hand, led us inside, and bid us to seat ourselves" (11.777–78) when he came as a guestfriend to the house of Peleus. The commissive connotation in these greeting gestures would seem at least implicit. The kinship between a commissive hand and a greeting hand seems explicit, however, in the more formalized handshake between Glaukos and Diomedes, opponents who meet on the battlefield and discover their paternal bond of guestfriendship: They "leapt from their horses, took each others' hands (*cheiras t'allēlōn labetēn*), and bound each other mutually by oath (*pistōsanto*)" (6.232–3). Note that virtually the same language used to signal the oath between Poseidon, Athene, and Achilles is used to signal the cementing of a tie between Glaukos and Diomedes: They took each other's hands and bound each other mutually by oath.[76]

Grasping hands is often a straightforward gesture of binding commitment between humans in the *Iliad*. The most obvious example is the handshake between Achilles and Priam, who clasp right hands to seal the truce they arrange between Achaians and Trojans for the duration of Hector's funeral (24.70–72). The symbolic weightiness of clasping hands and its connection with oaths is implied also in Agamemnon's imprecation against the Trojans after Menelaos is wounded: "In no way barren is the oath and the blood of lambs, / the unmixed libations and the right hands in which we trusted. / For if the Olympian does not fulfill it at once, / he will fulfill it later, and with might he will avenge it / with their heads and their wives and their children" (4.158–62). Right hands together with unmixed libations are symbols for the enduring force of oaths again in Nestor's rebuke against untrustworthy and too-malleable Achaians who give not a thought to their former commitments: "Whither have gone our treaties and oaths? / Our counsels and the thoughts of men have gone in the fire, / and also our unmixed libations and the right hands in which we trusted" (2.339–41).

Biblical evidence for the same commissive gesture may be drawn from these illustrations: "They all gave their hands in pledge to put away their wives, and for their guilt they each presented a ram from the flock as a guilt offering" (Ezra 10:19);[77] "He despised the oath by breaking the covenant. Because he had given his hand in pledge and yet did all these things, he

---

[76] On the nature of the obligations entailed by *xeinia*, see Herman 1987: 120–28.

[77] New International Translation.

shall not escape" (Ezekiel 18:19);[78] and again the Psalm, "Deliver me and rescue me /.../ from the hands of foreigners / whose mouths are full of lies, / whose right hands are deceitful" (Psalm 144:7–8). An Assyrian example, discussed by Weinfeld and Hermann, is the handshake represented on the monument from Nimrud memorializing the pact between Shalmaneser III and a Marduk-zakir-shumi of Babylon.[79] Slightly more ambiguous for its adoption imagery is the Hittite-Akkadian establishment of relations between King Suppiliuliuma and Mattiwaza, cast from the latter's perspective: "(The Great King) grasped me with [his ha]nd ... and said: when I will conquer the land of Mittani, I shall not reject you, I shall make you my son, and I will stand by (to help in war) and will make you sit on the throne of your father ... the word which comes out of his mouth will not turn back."[80] Overall, these Homeric, biblical, and Hittite examples suggest that hand-clasping between humans or between humans and deities denotes solidarity[81] and the bond of the oath.[82]

To analyze the semantic impact of such gestures in oath-making rituals, we must remember Rappaport's view of the inverse relationship between the weightiness of gestures in a ritual and the weightiness of the words that accompany them. Weighty gestures tend to dramatize what words are insufficient to signify.[83] The commissive gesture of clasping hands illustrates this particularly well in the context of war, where taking the right hand requires one to transfer one's weapons to the left, thereby leaving the (presumably right-handed) parties vulnerable to betrayal and attack. The risk is obvious. Herman notes that on the monument from Nimrud memorializing the pact between Shalmaneser III and a king of

---

[78] New International Translation.

[79] Herman 1987: 51; Weinfeld 1990: 180–81.

[80] Cited by Weinfeld 1970: 184–203, n.b. 191. Text transcribed in E.Weidner, *Politische Dokumente aus Kleinasien Die Staatsvertrage in akkadischer Spruche aus dem Archiv von Baghazkoi*, Bogh. St. Heft 8, 1923 (in No.2, ll. 24ff; pp. 40–41), cited by Weinfeld. Consider also the enduring features of the oath between Tudhaliya IV and Kurunta, King of Tarhuntassa, memorialized on the Bronze Tablet: "What I, my majesty, gave to Mr. Kurunta, king of Tarhuntassa, the boundaries which I made for him, let no one in the future take them away from the seed of Mr. Kurunta. The king does not take them for himself. He does not give them to his son. To another tribe let him not give it" (Bo 86/299 IV.21–24).

[81] See Bickerman 1976: 1–3.

[82] See Karavites 1992: 35, n.30 on hand-clasping as a gesture for an oath.

[83] See also Donald Lateiner, *Sardonic Smile, Nonverbal Behavior in Homeric Epic* (Ann Arbor: University of Michigan Press 1995), especially 14–16.

Babylon, the weapons of the kings are transferred to the left hands while the right hands are clasped. The men behind the kings bear gifts in their right hands, their swords in their left hands.[84] The same transfer to the left must have taken place when Diomedes and Glaukos clasped hands on the battlefield, renewing and reinstantiating their forefathers' pact of guestfriendship.[85]

An even more dramatic situation for its implied vulnerability and trust is their temporary defenselessness when they exchange armor. The exchange itself is of such significance that it astonishes the narrator, who remarks that Zeus took away Glaukos's wits because of the fine armor he traded (6.235). Although puzzling to the narrator-poet, this gesture of exchanging armor is less puzzling when seen in the light of the same gesture by biblical Jonathan to David, famous friends whose intimacy has *therapon*-like associations, such as the battle against the Philistines by Jonathan and his "armor-bearer" (1 Samuel 14), and who "each loved the other as dearly as himself" (1 Samuel 18.3). As a demonstration of their mutual love, Jonathan made a solemn pact with David by exchanging arms as well as clothing in Jonathan's father's house (1 Samuel 18:2–4),[86] and a second vow because "[Jonathan] loved [David] as his own life" (1 Samuel 20:17). The reciprocity in this ritual is recalled when king David later spares Jonathan's son Mephibosheth from execution "because of the oath which had been taken in the Lord's name" (2 Samuel 21:7). The motif of exchanging armor in this story has obvious resonance not only with Glaukos and Diomedes but with Achilles and Patroklos, given the *tarpanalli*-like implications of Achilles lending Patroklos his armor, and given Achilles' claim that he loved Patroklos as his own life (18.81–82), although the cultic identities forged by such gestures may extend beyond the formalization of commitments normally associated with clasping the hand.[87]

---

[84] Herman points this out as proof of the pacific intentions of clasping the hands (1987: 51).

[85] The reinstantiation of their agreement is obvious by its consequences: Because of their renewed guestfriendship, they agree that there are plenty of others they may kill, without killing paternal guestfriends (6.226–31).

[86] "And Jonathan stripped himself of the robe that was on him and gave it to David, and his armor, even his sword, his bow, and his girdle" (1 Samuel 18:3–4).

[87] On the Homeric *therapon* as Hittite *tarpanalli*, see Nadia Van Brock, "Substitution Rituelle," *Revue Hittite et Asianique*, 65 (1959): 117–46, cited by Gregory Nagy, *The Best of the Achaians* (Baltimore: Johns Hopkins University Press 1979) 33. On the cultic implications, see also Dale Sinos, *Achilles, Patroklos and the Meaning of Philos* (Innsbruck: Innsburcker Beitrage zur Sprachwissenschaft 1980).

The clasping of hands and exchange of armor in these examples, then, clearly are meant to symbolize, minimally, a commitment between parties when the words of commitment alone seem insufficient to demonstrate the force of the solemn pact. This is in keeping with Rappaport's observation that ritual gestures convey semantic information and dramatize what words alone may not be sufficient to convey.

There is also a certain logic in these ritual gestures for the making of oaths and pacts, based on the breach of personal space implied in the intimacy of physical touching and of donning someone else's vestments.[88] Irrespective of differing biblical and Homeric views of acceptable bodily proxemics, one may surmise that, in general, welcome bodily contact implies interpersonal trust, which in turn allows for the sealing of an interpersonal bond. The common gestures attached to the oath-making ritual and the enduring consequences of mutual oaths in these stories support the contention that oath-making ritual paradigms crossed cultural and geographical lines in the ancient world and that some oath-making rituals from both sides relied on a similar logic.

A subtheme of the commitment conveyed by Homeric oath-making rituals is *philotēs* – friendship, alliance, and multiple other significations, including *xeinia*. Karavites is impressed with the particular use of the term *philotēs* to designate "an extremely close bond forged in the course of resolving political or military hostilities."[89] The juxtaposed notions of oaths and friendship as a means of resolving strife is evident in a handful of examples in the *Iliad*, some already discussed. It is evident in Hector's anticipation that witnesses to his duel with Ajax will say, "let them both fight in heart-gnawing strife (*eris*) and let them part being bound (*arthmēsante*) in friendship (*philotēti*)" (7.301–02). A similar overcoming is felt, and spurned, when Hector wishes to establish a *harmonion* between himself and Achilles (22.255), to which Achilles responds that neither *philemenai* nor *horkia* are possible for them (22.265–66). It is evident, third, in Hector's contemplation of swearing an oath by elders to appease Achilles, an appeasement he compares to *oarisdō* (sweet talking) (22.110–30). The most developed narrative of overcoming strife by means of oaths and friendship is, however, the oath between the Trojans and Achaians in *Iliad* 3, because of the overcoming of hostilities that must be in place for the duel between Paris and Menelaos to take place and for temporary *philotēs* to be established among everyone else. This overcoming is a

---

[88] For a discussion of bodily proxemics in Homer, see Lateiner 1995: 49–56.
[89] Karavites 1992: 54.

delicate maneuver, as one moment Hector causes the Trojan phalanxes to be seated in the midst of battle, while the Achaians aim their arrows at him (3.78–79); then, just as arrows and rocks are about to fly (3.80), Agamemnon shouts to get the Achaians under control, and the fighting stops (3.81–84). The new relationship of *philotēs* anticipated between both parties in the truce is emphasized four times before the duel is thwarted and the truce fails, and each time *philotēs* is collocated with *horkia pista* – literally, "trusty oaths" (3.73; 3.94; 3.256; 3:323).

*Philotēs kai horkia pista*, "friendship and trusty oaths," in fact represents a hendiadys of international significance, given similar collocations in Hebrew *(bryt šlwm, bryt wsd* – covenant and peace/grace), in Aramaic (*'dy' wbt'* – bond and goodness), in Akkadian *(riksu salïme, adê salïme* – bond and peace)[90] and in Hittite *(išḫiul and lingai-* – bond and the oath[91]) from the second millennium. Moshe Weinfeld explains the interpenetration of these two semantic fields, oaths and friendship, by the fact that a mutual understanding between parties must be in place to conclude an agreement, and that a formal commitment may be necessary to keep the mutual understanding going.[92] Although the hendiadys often is displayed in formal treaties between heads of state, the semantic link behind it is implied also in treaties that consummate personal friendships, as reflected in the story of youthful *aššaues* (loyalty, friendship, goodness) by *lienkias* (oaths) between Hittite prince Tudhaliya IV and his companion Kurunta:: "To us [Tudhaliya IV and Kurunta], at that time we were friends (*aššaues*). To us, we were bound by oath (lit. "of oath," *lienkịas*)."[93] Friendship and oaths of course may combine into diplomatic alliance, as they do when Tudhaliya IV grows up to become king and confers to Kurunta control of Tarhuntassaland for all time, based on their enduring friendship (*aššịiatar*) by oath (*lingai*).[94] The Bronze Tablet elaborates:

> When I, Tudhaliya, Great King, had not yet become king, the god even then brought Kurunta and myself together in friendship, and even then

[90] Moshe Weinfeld, "'Rider of the Clouds' and 'Gatherer of the Clouds.'" *JANES* 5: 421–26 1973: 191–93; 1990: 176–77.

[91] Beckman 1996: 2. The notions of oath and friendship would also seem to be at least collocated in Tudahliya IV's pact with Kurunta: "When my father saw the friendship (aaššijatar) between us (Vs. II. 46), ... he caused us to be bound by oath (lienganuut)" (47). (Bo 86/200).

[92] Weinfeld 1973: 190.

[93] nu-un-na-aš an-ni-ša-an-pát na-ak-ki-e-eš a-aš-ša-u-e-eš e-šu-u-un. nu-un-na-aš li-en-ki-ja-aš e-šu-en (Bo 86/299 Vs.II 33).

[94] Vs II 46–47.

we were ... beloved by one another. We were sworn allies: "Let one protect the other."[95]

[W]hen my father observed the respect and affections (*aššiiatar*) between Kurunta and myself, my father brought us together and had us swear an oath (*lienganut*): "Let one protect the other." Thus my father had us swear an oath, and aside from that we were sworn allies. And Kurunta protected me and in no way broke the oaths which he had sworn to me. I, My Majesty, spoke to him as follows: "If the gods recognize me so that I become king, on my part there will be only good things for you."[96]

For all time no one shall take the kingship of the land of Tarhuntassa away from ... [Kurunta] – if someone does do that, and gives it to another descendant of Muwattalli, taking it away from the progeny of Kurunta, the Storm-god of Hatti and the Sun-goddess of Arinna shall eradicate whoever should commit that deed. For all time only a descendant of Kurunta shall hold the kingship of the land of Tarhuntassa.[97]

The theme of an intimate and binding friendship endorsed by a significant parent is of course widespread in ancient literature. Gilgamesh and Enkidu, David and Jonathan, and Achilles and Patroklos leap to mind.

But the semantic link of friendship and trusty oaths is more typically understood in the diplomatic sphere, wherein it is cemented by ritual, as it is in *Iliad* Book 3. This diplomatic equation is formalized in the collocation *philotē ta kai horkia pista*, friendship and trusty oaths, which is three times the accusative object of the verb *tamnō*, to cut, in the *Iliad* (3.73, 3.94, 3.256). "To cut an oath" is a well-known Near Eastern international idiom, as attested by the Hebrew *krt bryt* – to cut a covenant, Phoenician *krt 'lt* – to cut the oath, and the same in Aramaic (*gzr 'dy'*), Latin (*foedus ferire*),[98] and implicated in the Akkadian/Old Babylonian expression from Mari, to kill an ass (*haram qatalum*), used in the context of concluding a treaty.[99] In the *Iliad* the expression "to cut oaths" occurs without the

---

[95] Translation by Beckman 1996: 112.

[96] (Bo 86/299 ii 45–52). Translation modified slightly from Beckman 1996: 112.

[97] Translated by Beckman, Text 18C (1996: 110, 114).

[98] See Weinfeld 1990: 178–79. It is difficult to imagine that the expression somehow eluded the Hittites, given their participation in the second millennium international scene. That they did practice animal-sacrifice for dramatizing an oath might be inferred from "When we killed a sheep, we put the following words under oath" (Kbo 16:47:15–16, cited in *The Hittite Dictionary* Vol. 3, Fascicle 1 (1980) 65).

[99] See A. Finet, "Le sacrifice de l'ane en Mesopotamie," in J. Quaegebeur, ed., *Ritual and Sacrifice in the Ancient Near East* Orientalia Lovaniensia Analecta 55 (Leuven: Uitgeverij

collocated "friendship" a handful of times, as in Agamemnon's hypothetical oath between the Trojans and Achaians (2.124), twice in the bid to get Priam to cut trusty oaths on behalf of the Trojans with the Achaians (3.105 and 3.252), and once in anticipation of Agamemnon's oath with Achilles (19.197). Bickerman points out that the expression "to cut oaths" would seem to clash semantically with its underlying signification, which is to bind together, not to cut apart. He believes that the expression probably has a ritual origin in the cutting of sacrificial victims in the process of swearing an oath.[100] (Idomeneus's reference to "pouring oaths" (4.269) comes to mind for a similarly apparent semantic clash and ritual origin.) Although the expression "cutting friendship" never appears in the *Iliad*, it is easy to grasp the underlying logic in collocating friendship with trusty oaths in the phrase "let us cut friendship and trusty oaths (*philotēta kai horkia pista tamōmen*)": The same sense of obligation is implicit in friendship as it is in oaths, and that obligation is cemented by ritualized blood-sacrifice. Hence the expression "let us cut friendship and trusty oaths" connotes the general theme of establishing a mutual bond between parties and relies on the overlapping semantic domains of *philotēs* and *horkia*, both of which may be ritually configured when oath-sacrifice takes place.

The overlapping semantic domains of *philotēs* and *horkia* (oaths) may help to shed light also on the link of *xeinia*, or guestfriendship, to *horkia*. While *philotēs* has a variety of significations in the *Iliad*, at least some of them bear on *xeinia*, as is obvious when Menelaus prays that Zeus punish Paris's violation of *philotēs* "so that a person in future generations will shudder before doing evil to a guesthost (*xeinodokos*) who provides friendship (*philotēta*)" (3.351–54).[101] As Karavites points out, the establishment of *xeinia*, or guestfriendship, is tantamount to an oath, or at least a pledge of trust,[102] as both rely on good faith relationships and honor between the parties lasting for generations. We saw this in the renewed pledge of guestfriendship between Diomedes and Glaukos, the

Peeters en Departement Oriëntalistiek 1993) 135–42, Leuven 1993, 135–42, cited by Mauro Giorgieri, "Aspetti magico-religiosi," 421–40.

[100] Bickerman 1976: 1–32.

[101] Compare to 17.582–84, where Apollo rouses Hector in the guise of Phinopse of Asia, the most *philtatos* of all *xeinōn* to him, of those dwelling in Abudos, and 17.576.

[102] Guestfriendship and marriage were the two fundamental devices for the establishment of alliances among nobles and chieftains in the ancient world, Karavites points out, which makes them both tantamount to oaths in the sense that they sealed alliances (1992: 53).

one's father having been a *xeinos philos* to the other's (6.224). The same collocation of notions – guestfriendship and the commitment established by oaths – may be implicit in the young Achilles' gesture of taking Nestor and company by the hands when they arrived at Peleus's house. He took them by the hand, led them inside and "put before us guestgifts, as is the custom for guestfriends" (11.779). Further, both *xeinia* and *horkia* draw religious sanction from Zeus and are endorsed by other gods. With this link between *xeinia* and *horkia* in mind, it is perhaps not surprising that violation of *xeinia*, or guestfriendship – legendarily the very cause of the war (referred to at 3.351–54 and 13.622–27) – bears the same ominous consequences as does oath-violation, which is death. Hence, Menelaos prays that "a person in future generations will shudder before doing evil to a guesthost (*xeinodokos*) who provides friendship (*philotēta*)" (3.351–54) and anticipates Zeus's utter destruction of the steep citadel of Troy because of the Trojan outrage against him and Zeus Xeinios (13.622–27).[103]

Related to the link between formalized commitments and familial bonds is another Near Eastern promising *topos* identified by Moshe Weinfeld as the adoption motif. Weinfeld sees it as relevant for Agamemnon's offer to Achilles in Book 9 and the oath between them in Book 19. According to Weinfeld, the Near Eastern adoption motif functions as a forensic metaphor legitimating the unconditional and multi-generational nature of the promises made by oath. It is hardly surprising to find this motif in descriptions of the rapport between deities and their chosen few, such as "I will establish the throne of his kingdom forever, I will be his father and he shall be my son, when he sins I will chastise him with the rod of men and with human afflictions but my grace will not be removed . . . your house and your kingdom will be steadfast before me forever, your throne shall be established forever" (II Sam. 7:8–16).[104] But it is well-known that this Biblical language borrows from

---

[103] This future shuddering, too, is a traditional motif in Near Eastern curses. See Hillers 1964: 76–7.

[104] Not surprisingly, parental imagery pervades the conceptions of divine-human relationship. Compare Athene's protection of Menelaos: "Standing before him she warded off the sharp missiles, she fenced in this way from your skin, as when a mother fences off flies from her child, when he lies in sweet sleep" (4.129–31), and the goddess Ishtar's protection of Hattusilis, "Since I myself nurtured him (literally "caused him to grow" – šallanunuun wa ra an kuit amuk), I did not abandon him in any way to an evil trial or an evil god" (*Apology of Hattusilis*, IV: 11–12). On the adoption motif in the biblical context, see Weinfeld 1990 and Dennis J. McCarthy, *Der Gottesbund im Alten Testament* (Stuttgart: Verlag Katholisches Bibelwerk 1966) 54–5.

suzerain–vassal treaties common to much of the Near East.[105] For instance, in the Hittite-Akkadian example already mentioned, vassal Mattiwaza says of Hittite king Suppiliuliuma: "(The Great King) grasped me with [his han]d . . . and said: when I will conquer the land of Mittanni I shall not reject you, I shall make you my son, I will stand by (to help in war) and will make you sit on the throne of your father."[106] Brotherhood is another common familial metaphor put up for a treaty-partner,[107] and, unlike the paternal metaphor, may imply a relationship between equals. Some kind of brotherhood would seem to be implied in Hittite king Tudhaliya IV's declaration that Kurunta's father gave Kurunta to Tudhaliya's father to raise (Bo 86/299 Vs.I 12),[108] and that when they were young, he and Kurunta swore by oath to protect one another, even if Tudhaliya's father should never appoint Tudhaliya to kingship (Bo 86/299 Vs.II 34–39). On the other hand, Tudhaliya's treaty also makes Kurunta to have claimed to be Tudhaliya's servant (Bo 86/299 Vs.II 41),[109] thereby endorsing a relationship of hierarchy.

Treaties that specify relationships between treaty parties as those of father and child – while unconditionally binding for both parties – allot different roles to each party, the vassal owing a duty of obedience. If

---

[105] On the Hittite source, see Weinfeld 1993: 135–9. This is not to say that there are not important differences in Near Eastern treaty patterns. The enduring nature of Hittite and biblical covenantal land grants is not the norm in Ugarit or in Alalah, for example. Weinfeld points out that there the property of a condemned man is to be confiscated, whereas in these Hittite and biblical texts, the property of a condemned person is not to be taken away. Weinfeld 1970: 195.

[106] Weidner, *Politische Dokumente*, No. 2 Il.24ff (40–41), cited by Weinfeld 1970: 191, note 60.

[107] For instance, Hittite king Suppiliuliuma swears to Huqqana of Haisa: "Recognize yourself into brotherhood with my sons and brothers. . . . I my majesty will do loyally to your sons, on your account," (*Aus dem Vertrag des Suppiliuliuma mit Huqqana von Haisa*, composite, this from Kbo V 3 I 12, 33), and Hattusilis III complains to Kadashman-Enlil III of Babylon, "When your father and I established friendly relations and became affectionate brothers, we did not become brothers for a single day. Did we not establish brotherhood and friendly relations in perpetuity?" (Kbo 1.10 and KUB 3.72, Text No. 23 in Beckman's *Hittite Diplomatic Texts* (1996: 133) Section 4 [obverse lines 7–24). Weinfeld points out that brotherhood as a term for covenant is already attested in third millennium Sumerian interstate agreements (1990: 177).

[108] An-ni-ša-an-pát-an ¹NIR.GAL-iš LUGAL-uš *A-NA* A.BU-*IA* ¹ḫa-at-tu-ši-li sal-la-nu-um-ma-an-zi pí-ja-an har-ta. Na-an an-ni-ša-an-pát A.BU-*IA* šal-la-nu-uš-ki-it. (Bo 86/299 Vs.I 12–13. "At that time (previously), indeed, Mr. Muwatallis, the king, had given him to my father, Mr. Hattusilis, to be raised. And at that time my father did indeed raise him."

[109] Nu-ja-za tu-el ÌR-iš. (Bo 86/299 Vs.II 41).

Weinfeld is correct to see this suzerain–vassal paradigm in the offer of Agamemnon to confer riches and seven cities to Achilles and to make him a son-in-law equal in status to his biological son Orestes (9.141–43),[110] it is hardly surprising that Achilles rejects the offer. He would not even get the right of primogeniture! As he points out, his own father will find him a wife, and with her he will enjoy his inheritance from Peleus (9.403ff). If Weinfeld is right to see the Near Eastern treaty pattern underlying Agamemnon's offer, Achilles, in making the contrasting inheritances explicit, is rejecting not a generous offer but a personal slight.

It is significant that the same punishment of death is anticipated for violators of *xeinia*, *philotēs*, and *horkia* and also for violated family bonds in the *Iliad*. This can hardly be accidental. As Glueck points out about the biblical world, "Allies had the same rights and obligations as those who were blood relatives."[111] Similarly, Karavites compares the friendly feeling connoted by the term "brotherhood" in ancient Near Eastern treaties with the positive and friendly nuance conveyed by *philotēs* in the *Iliad's* treaty-making contexts,[112] and Weinfeld, McCarthy, and others explore the familial metaphors used in the Near Eastern and Mediterranean diplomatic vocabulary of the second millennium.[113] Rappaport has pointed out that breach of trust is the one violation universally held to be sanctionable, across societies. These four violations, of *xeinia, philotēs, horkia*, and family bonds, would appear to be similarly sanctionable because each signifies a breach of intimate trust.

Notable among the agents of destruction invoked for punishing perjurers in the *Iliad* are the subterranean Erinyes, who also happen to defend familial propriety in the *Iliad*. The Erinyes have been seen generally to aid in the promotion of the cosmic order as it filters into the human judicial–religious sphere,[114] and especially to defend maternal bonds, womb-bonds, and the rights of elders. The breadth of their roles is apparent from the stories in which they appear in the *Iliad*. For instance, Phoinix expects them to punish him for sleeping with his father's concubine (9.454–57), which is apparently related to the role of the Erinyes to defend the prerogatives of elders. Hence, too, Poseidon has to give way to Zeus because, as Iris reminds him, Zeus was born first – "you know that

---

[110] Weinfeld 1990: 185.

[111] *Hesed in the Bible*, 1967, 46, cited by Weinfeld 1970: 194, note 97.

[112] Karavites 1992: 48–53.

[113] Weinfeld 1970. McCarthy 1966: 54–5.

[114] See Hesiod, W&D 803–04, Th. 231–32, and Heubeck 1986: 145–65, n.b. 163.

the Erinyes always follow the elders" (15.204). But their role as advocates of elders is complicated when they hear Meleagros's mother's prayer to punish her son – product of her womb – for killing her brother (9.566–72), a womb-mate, because the Erinyes reputedly defend both kinds of womb-bonds. Given the recurring theme of brother and sister bonds in Greek tragedy (as in *Seven Against Thebes*, *Antigone*), it is just impossible not to ponder the similarity of the sister–brother fidelity of Meleagros's mother and his uncle to, say, Antigone's fidelity to her brother, based on their common womb of origin. The womb-bond of course is given primordial depth in Aeschylus's dramatization of the Erinyes' relinquishment of their primordial role as its defenders.[115] For the relevance of this bond to Homer, one might compare Lykaon's plea to Achilles to spare him because he was not a womb-mate (*homogastrios*) of Hector, the half-brother who killed Achilles' gentle friend (21.95–96) – although this way of thinking is explicitly rejected by Achilles (21:103–5). Curious also in this motherly regard is Athene's excoriation of Ares, "So this is how you repay the Erinyes of your mother" (21.412), which, as Heubeck notes in a discussion of *ex-apotinō*, seems to denote pacifying one's mother's Erinyes.[116] But clearly the Erinyes have other functions beside elder and womb-defense in the *Iliad*, as is apparent when they stop the voice of the immortal horse Xanthus after he advises Achilles (19.417), and when they send *Atē* down to Agamemnon (says he) in order to throw him into a befuddling rage (19.86–89). The last two examples make the Erinyes defenders and avengers of the boundaries established by gods for the human good. It is doubtlessly this role that they perform in the defense and avenging of the oaths in Books 3 and 19, as "[those] who toil underground and punish humans, whoever should swear a false oath" (3.279) and as "Erinyes who punish humans, who ever should swear a false oath" (19.260). Their role as defenders of cultural propriety brings together the matters subsumed under family ties and ritualized commitments, seemingly of a piece in Homeric imagination.[117]

That the Erinyes equally defend commitments sealed by oath and commitments sealed by blood requires some reflection on the tendency for

---

[115] See Jon D. Mikalson for analysis of the transformation of the Erinyes into Semnai in Aeschylus, *Honor Thy Gods* (Chapel Hill: University of North Carolina Press 1991) 214–17.

[116] Heubeck 1986: 150–1. See also Richard Seaford on the ancient function of the Furies to embody the anger of those injured by their kin. *Reciprocity and Ritual* (Oxford: Clarendon Press 1994, 1999) 133.

[117] See Heubeck 1986, n.b. 163.

ritualized commitments to be treated as naturalized. Rappaport points out that similar formative processes and creative agencies often are enlisted to account for the existence of both the natural order and the conventional order. This is partly due to the cultural roles of liturgy and myth, which transform the conventional into the natural by attributing similar creative and defensive agencies, such as the Erinyes, to relationships established by nature and relationships established by convention. But it is also due to the overall tendency of ritual performances to establish factive orders, which, once established, are treated as "natural" facts made in time and thus irreversible.

The factive element is especially striking when the consequences of the ritual are brought into immediate being as facts through the process of physical ordeal, such as circumcision to denote new identity or ritual killing to denote commitments. Such "brute facts" contribute substantiality to the ritual's semantic force by being observable, visceral, and often irreversible. Bodily markings and ritual killings are probably the most dramatic cases in point. However, it also may be difficult to identify precisely when the ritual "magic" takes effect. Rappaport suspects that, for instance, in the Australian ritual of subincision, there may be something especially perlocutionary about pain, and it is difficult to know if the ritual significance derives from the painful ordeal or from the scarred flesh left by the ordeal,[118] the latter being the public fact that everyone can see. The difficulty in identifying the moment of persuasive transformation in Homeric oath-sacrifice is just as complicated. It is unclear whether the dramatic force of the ritual derives precisely from the stated analogy between sacrificial victim and perjurer or from the theatrical spectacle of killing and dying. Although the first surely relies on the latter, an argument also may be made that the theatricality of the killing and dying has more dramatic punch than any independent belief in the punishing power of divine agents. As Pierre Smith noticed during fieldwork in Senegal, the spectacle of the ritual may impress its own "truth" on participants, independent of their outward "belief" in the ritual.[119] In the oath-sacrifice of Book 3, such truth is highlighted by a narrative focus on each fine step of the ritual process, which culminates in slitting the throats of the lambs and placing them on the ground, where they

---

[118] Rappaport 1999: 147.
[119] A point observed in passing, in "Aspects of the Organization of Rites," in *Between Belief and Transgression*, trans. John Leavitt, eds. M. Izard and P. Smith (Chicago: University of Chicago Press 1979), 103–28, n.b. 104 and 126.

lie, gasping and deprived of *menos* and *thumos*. The power of the ritual as a theatrical display may be due in part to the participants' tendency to identify with the victim, an identification cultivated by the high drama of the death more than by any explicit equation of them with the victim. We will return to this subject when we discuss Ricoeur and "ritual fictions" in Chapter 3. For now, however, let us observe simply that the death brought into being by the ritual convention of oath-sacrifice becomes perfectly "natural" to the extent that the death, highlighted by the elevated register of the ritual performance, becomes an irreversible fact, just as if it had occurred by accident or by nature. Further, the semantic force of the killing in the ritual is seemingly palpable, more real than words could possibly say. Thus, the oath-making ritual establishes an irreversible fact that is linked with the participant's commitment to its terms. Breach against that commitment is regarded as a breach against a brute fact and punishable by the same agencies who punish violations of natural relationships (or facts), such as the Erinyes. At least to some extent, this ritual logic helps to explain why relationships made by ritual are defended and avenged in the same way as are relationships made by blood.

As for the divine forces invoked "to witness and to protect" (3.280) an oath, it is notable that not only the Erinyes but a variety of divine figures may stand up to the task. As the head of the pantheon, "Zeus greatest and best" is the chief canonizer of oaths (see 2. 412, 3.276, 3.298, 3.320, 19.258), and oaths invoking many gods may be referred to in brief as the "oath of Zeus" (3.107, 7.69, 7.411). Zeus leads the pantheon invoked by Agamemnon in his two oath-sacrifices, the prayer for which begins when Agamemnon holds up his hands to Zeus (3.275–76; 19.254–255). It is also to Zeus, presumably Zeus Xeinios, that he prays for the total destruction of the house of Priam because of the violation of guestfriendship by Priam's son (2.412–18). Hector invokes Zeus as a witness in his challenge to the Achaians for a second duel to remedy the broken oath of Book 3 (7.76), and invokes him as consort of Hera in his "false oath" (*epiorkon* 10.332) to Dolon that Dolon may have the divine horses of Peleus (10.329) after Hector gets them. Zeus is also invoked as the "consort of Hera" by both sides during the burial truce (7.411), and Hera invokes him, or at least his "head," as well as their marriage bed, Gaia, Ouranos, and the River Styx in an oath regarding her role in Poseidon's exploits while she seduced Zeus (15:36–40). In Book 23 Achilles swears by Zeus not to bathe before burying Patroklos (23.43–44), and holds laws to be generally matters "before Zeus" during his second oath in Book 1 (1.239). Further, Athene and Poseidon bind themselves in oath with Achilles "with the approval of Zeus" (21.290). Yet again, it is Zeus, alone or along with other immortals, who is called upon four times precisely to avenge the violated oaths of the Trojans (3.298–301, 3.319–22, 4.234–39, 4.155–65), and in dire language, such as:

> "Argives, do not let go of your rushing courage.
> For Zeus father will not be a helper to liars,
> but to those who were the first to violate oaths,
> indeed vultures will feast upon their own tender skins
> and we, in turn, will lead their wives and little children
> to the ships, after we take the citadel."
>
> (4.234–39)

Finally, it is in his persona as Zeus Katachthonios that Zeus, along with dread Persephone, fulfills Phoinix's father's petition to the Erinyes (9.454) to retaliate against Phoinix by depriving him of offspring (9:456–7). The significant substitution of Zeus and Persephone for the Erinyes as punishers of familial impropriety is testament to the long-held supposition that Zeus wields power from chthonic as well as celestial spheres. His Erinyes-like persona overlaps with that of Hades as well, considering that Hades and dread Persephone are the gods Meleagros's mother invokes, beating on the ground, to avenge her brother against her son. Although Hades and dread Persephone are called, it is the mist-flitting Erinyes who reply, from underneath the ground in Erebus (9:567–62). The boundary of performance between Zeus Horkos, Zeus Chthonios, and other deities of the chthonic realm is clearly fluid when it comes to oaths.

The reason that some oath-sanctioning bodies tend to reside in the ground has its own logic, which extends beyond the requirement that liturgical orders be encoded by forces other than the human participants. One aspect of the logic is surely analogical: As the earth endures, so should the oath, and also the earthly figures who protect the oath.[120] It does not require a great leap of imagination to grasp the sense in measuring the endurance of an oath by the longevity of its sanctioning element. The same logic is behind Achilles' oath to Kalchas that "Not while I am living and seeing on earth will anyone by the hollow ships lay a heavy hand against you . . . not even Agamemnon" (1.88–90). As long as Achilles lives and there is anyone by the ships, his oath to protect Kalchas will hold.

---

[120] Hence, even the god of the Hebrew Bible summons heaven and earth to witness against potential transgressors of the covenant he establishes with Israel, in Deuteronomy 20:19.

The oath's compulsion is as real as the forces to which it is ritually tied. Hence Hera touches the earth in a conspicuous ritual gesture during her oath with Hypnos (14.272). The gesture formalizes her commitment and enunciates that the commitment will endure as the earth endures.

However, the earth surely has a different nuance as an oath-guarantor for mortals than it does for immortals. After Zeus, the earth is the most commonly invoked sanctioning element in formal oath ceremonies in the *Iliad*. Hera invokes the "all-nourishing earth" (14.272) in her oath to Hypnos, and the earth again in her oath to Zeus (15.36). Agamemnon invokes the earth in his oath with the Trojans (3.278) and again among the Achaians (19.259). The invocation of the earth, in various guises, has an established history also across the Near East.[121] However, the invocation of the earth to sanction oaths for mortals is complicated in the *Iliad* by the Homeric vision of the earth as not only a benefactor but a devourer of human life as well. Hence the earth frequently is invoked to "yawn around," or swallow, the targets of curses: Agamemnon curses himself, "May the wide earth yawn around me" (4.182); Hector says of Paris, "So may the earth yawn around him" (6.282); and Diomedes says to Nestor, "Then may the wide earth yawn around me" (8.150). The "yawning earth" is apparently a *topos* in Hittite curses as well, given the curse of the midwife: "Whoever should prepare evil for this child, let him see the broad heaven! Let him see the yawning earth!"[122] There must be a dozen ironic references in the *Iliad* to the fertile earth as the receiver of the dead, as when "[Teukros] drove them all, one after the other, into the all-nourishing earth" (8.277), or when "in quick succession [Patroklos] drove them into the fertile earth" (16.418).[123] The association of "mother earth" with death is surely pan-Mediterranean, as in "Hard work is the lot of every man / . . . from the day when they come from their mother's womb / until the day of their return to the mother of all" (Ecclesiasticus 40:1). An immortal god's oath by the "all-nourishing earth," therefore, must be less ironic than a similar oath for mortals, who can expect to return to the earth in death. The fact of death and the earthly home for

---

[121] See Karavites 1992: 103.

[122] KI-an genuwandan(an) aušdu – "let him see the lapped earth" would be the literal translation (KUB XLIV 4 + KBo XIII 241 Rv.31). These birthing rituals are collected and translated by Gary Beckman (*Hittite Birth Rituals* [Wiesbaden: Otto Harrassowitz 1983], n.b. 179).

[123] See Erwin Floyd, "Homer and the Life-Producing Earth," *Classical World* 2 (1989) 1ff. See also Kitts 2000: 105–08.

it would seem to give more bite to the mortal over the immortal oath. Thus mortals invoke the earth as an enduring source of life but also of death (such as Menelaos's "May you all be water and earth" [7.99]). For immortals, in contrast, swearing by the earth would seem tantamount to swearing by the current order, and one's place in it into perpetuity. Hera's invocation of the earth, the seas, the River Styx, and the Titans below in her oath to Hypnos (14.270–80), and her invocation of the earth, the sky, Styx, Zeus himself, and their marriage bed in her oath to Zeus (156.36–40), rely on a fixed reality and her own place in it. They may also rely, implicitly, on certain legends of primal conflict and the establishment of subsequent stability, as mirrored in the works of Hesiod.[124]

Divine oaths especially, but also many human oaths, invoke divine figures whose natural manifestations are conspicuous: Hera is bidden to swear by the River Styx, the earth and sea, and all the gods under Tartaros, who are called Titans (14.279), that she will give the nymph Pasithees to the god Hypnos as a consort (14.271–74). So, too, she invokes the River Styx, the sky (Ouranos), the earth (Gaia), Zeus's head, as well as her marriage bed, when she swears to Zeus that she did not concretely abet Poseidon while Zeus slept (15:36–40). Similarly, Agamemnon invokes the earth and sun (Ge and Helios), as well as Zeus and the Erinyes in his oath with Achilles, and Helios "who sees and hears everything" (3.277), the rivers and earth, Zeus, and the Erinyes (3.276–79) in his oath with the Trojans. A similar panoply of deified natural elements, some named, some generic, are frequently invoked in Hittite oaths. For instance, the sun-god of heaven, the sun-goddess of Arinna, a dozen different storm gods, a moon-god, a god of the oath, mountain-dwelling gods, as well as mountains, winds, rivers, springs, the great sea, and clouds are invoked as witnesses to the oath between Hittite king Muwatalli II and Alaksandu of Wilusa,[125] and in other oaths, the witness list may begin by summoning the Thousand Gods of Hatti to assembly before they are named.[126] Sometimes there is a perceivable logic in the choice of gods – celestial deities, for instance, are known to look down and supervise the practice of justice in Mesopotamia as well as in Anatolia, which may account

---

[124] On this theme, see Daniel R. Blickman, "Styx and the Justice of Zeus in Hesiod's Theogony," *Phoenix* 41 (1987) 341–55.

[125] #13 in Beckman 1996: Vol I, 86–7. On the prominence of sun-deities in Hittite treaty oaths, see also O. R. Gurney, *Some Aspects of Hittite Religion* (Oxford: Oxford University Press 1976) 4.

[126] #18B in Beckman 1996: Vol. I, 106, treaty between Hattusili III of Hatti and Ulmi-Teshshup of Tarhuntassa.

for the invocation of Helios in the Achaian oath with the Trojans. Presumably the deified natural elements are felt to embody at least staying power, if not also power of a more personalized sort, such as we glimpse in many Hittite ritual fragments involving ritual personae (for instance, bear-men, wolf-men, an archeress, cooks, and priests) offering meat to natural elements, such as springs.[127]

The ultimate embodiment of punishing power for divine perjury is of course the primeval River Styx. That oath-sanctifying water – "the greatest and most terrible source of oaths for the great gods" (15.37) – is purported to inspire awe and fear among the gods. Hence, according to Janko, there exists the cognate verb *stugeō*, to shiver with fear.[128] Its fearsome aspect seems to involve its under-earth connection with a primeval ocean and the ability of its waters to send a perjuring god into a temporary, coma-like deep sleep, the equivalent of death for gods (Hesiod's *Theogony* 789–806).[129] In the *Theogony* the abode of Styx is set apart from the other gods, and even in the *Iliad*, the river Tartaressos, an offshoot of Styx, does not mingle with other waters, "but runs down from there like oil, for it is an offshoot of the terrible oath-making water of Styx" (2.753–55). The historical role of Styx in supporting the current celestial order is given in Hesiod's account of Zeus's defeat of the other Titans (*Th.* 389–403). For supporting Zeus against her siblings, Styx was rewarded with the power to punish divine transgressions. Styx would seem to function as a veritable Erinus for gods, alongside the Erinyes themselves.

At the same time, there are a handful of oaths in the *Iliad* that invoke no god at all, or that at least rely on some other force for effect. There may be a semantic distinction between an oath and a curse, but the ritual distinction is slight when one considers that both appear to be formalized by special speaking registers, both utilize a restricted vocabulary with a traditional scope, and both rely at least to some degree on what Austin called "illocutionary" force for effect. That is, their utterances are illocutionary speech-acts intended to have perlocutionary effects. Achilles is responsible for three of these illocutionary speech acts that have the appearance of swearing without invoking gods. The first one is to the

---

[127] KUB LVIII 14 1–34.

[128] Richard Janko, *The Iliad: A Commentary*, Vol. IV (Cambridge: Cambridge University Press 1992) 245.

[129] Ironically, it also is alleged to confer immortality – hence Thetis bathes Achilles in it, all but his heel, and Demeter is in the process of immortalizing the infant Demophon with its waters when she is discovered by the child's mother. For Styx as an elixir of immortality, see Nagy 1979: 187–89.

seer of Apollo, in Achilles' promise to defend Kalchas in Book 1. Despite the invocation of the god Apollo, the force of his oath is also by his own life, and for the duration of the Trojan expedition:

> "Be brave and speak the prophecy as you know it.
> For not by the god Apollo dear to Zeus, to whom you, Kalchas,
> pray and show prophecies to the Danaans,
> not while I am living and seeing on earth
> will anyone of quite all the Danaans, not even Agamemnon,
> lay a heavy hand against you by the hollow ships."
>
> (1.85–90)

The two sources invoked to back this oath, Apollo and the life of Achilles, appear to be parallel, and not necessarily co-dependent. The double source illustrates the features of redundancy and condensation of meaning that intensify the message communicated by ritual, according to Tambiah,[130] as touched upon in Chapter 1.

Differently, Achilles' famous oath by the scepter that the Achaians will regret their mistreatment of him invokes only the "dead" scepter, and no gods. This example will be discussed shortly, for the complexity of its gestures, symbols, and repercussions.

Third Achilles doesn't call it an oath, precisely, but his exhortation that the Achaians postpone eating until the battle has been won (19.205–08[131]) and his emphatic vow that "before that time in no way will food nor drink be sent down my gullet, while my dead companion lies cut asunder by the sharp bronze" (19.209–11) is so similar to "A curse be on the man who eats any food before nightfall until I have taken vengeance on my enemies" (1 Samuel 14:24), that one must ponder the possibility of a cross-Mediterranean tradition of swearing to fast for vengeance.[132] No gods are invoked, however – just the deadly intent of the speaker. In a similar vein, Odysseus curses Thersites, swearing only by his own "head" and his fatherhood of Telemachos (2.258–60) that he will smite him if he sees him, and Poseidon invokes no sanctioning source in his oath to Hera "never to ward off the evil day for the Trojans" (21.373–74).

---

[130] Tambiah 1979.

[131] "You urge me to food. But I would emphatically now bid the sons of the Achaians to fight, unfed and without food, and with the setting of the sun to prepare a great feast, after we might repay the outrage."

[132] I have found no other instances of this tradition to use for further analysis.

It is these kinds of utterances that lead one to ponder the persuasive force behind words spoken in charged registers, lacking the invocation of gods but apparently attributed lethal force.

As for whence the force presumed to lie behind such ritualized utterances, I wholeheartedly agree with Christopher Faraone in bemoaning the Frazerian distinction between "primitive magic" and "prayer." Faraone finds the absence of gods in self-curses to be of little apparent consequence for meaning and impact.[133] Clearly, ritual utterances, with or without invoking gods, are felt to wield some kind of power, whether it is the self-referencing power of the speaker's intent or some power "out there" to be harnessed to the task the utterances explicate.[134] This force harks back to our earlier discussion of the archaic Greek admiration for the power of the spoken word to reveal or conceal, as well as to the power of ritualization to configure commitments, as seen by various anthropologists. Considering the duplicitous potential of spoken words, Rappaport points out the simple fact that inherent in speaking is the possibility that words may be uttered in the absence of the referents they signify. This enables discourse to separate from what it is about, and enlarges exponentially the scope of what humans can say and mean, but also enlarges the capacity for duplicity.[135] It is precisely this capacity for duplicity, aroused by the separation of discourse from what it is about, that the formalization of utterances – ritualization of speech – attempts to overcome. By formalizing what can be said, ritualization impresses upon participants a conformity to preestablished and often archaic ideals of behavior, and helps to guard against deviance from traditional norms.[136] These norms include, among other things, confining utterances to the restricted sphere of material truth or commissive pledges and avoiding duplicity of speech.

A keen awareness of the underlying duplicity of language and of perception may be discerned in the works of Hesiod and Homer. Of the many examples that could be cited, most conspicuous are Hesiod's whimsical and sometimes lying muses, the seductive voices of the Odyssean sirens, and, indeed, lying Odysseus himself, as well as his famous relative,

---

[133] Faraone 1993: 60–80, n.b. 77.

[134] Joseph Plescia also points out that sometimes a religious oath refers only to the curse on oneself, one's relatives, or one's property in the case of perjury, relying for force on the magical power of words (Plescia 1970: 6).

[135] Rappaport 1999: 11.

[136] On this topic, see Bloch 1975: 1–28.

Autolycus. A certain awareness and also wariness of the power of spoken words to befuddle and persuade is evident in much ancient Near Eastern literature as well (see Proverbs 2:16, 5:3, 7:5, 22:24). The power of ritual to manipulate a seemingly palpable bond between utterances and what they signify (Tambiah's "magical missiles") is conspicuous in numerous Hittite rituals. It is indisputable in some Hittite midwifery rituals, where in one example the midwife ritually endeavors to thwart (turn back) the sorcerous tongue of evil that might target the newborn child.[137] The same theme is demonstrated when the Old Woman, a frequent Hittite ritual persona, ritually reverses curses already pronounced by cutting off wax tongues and pronouncing various undoing phrases, such as "In whatever curses you indulged, let now the Sun-god turn those curses (and) tongues toward the left!", "Spit ye out those evil curses!", "Be ye cleansed of mouth and tongue!", "Let the evil words of mouth (and) tongue be rubbed away from you!", and "As this dough does not get into a sacrificial loaf for the gods, even so let the evil tongue not get to the body of the two sacrificers!"[138] One may find many Near Eastern examples of the ritual "undoings" of powerful words. That such words are felt to be cosmically forceful is apparent because the gods themselves may be ritually constrained by them: "Set out, O Sun-Goddess of the Earth! Make everything favorable; attend to it! If you do not attend to it, let the divine oath of this ritual proceed to seize you, O Sun-Goddess of the Earth!"[139] This spread of examples suggests an acute East Mediterranean awareness of some basic problems in communication consisting, first, of the notion of a slipperiness of connection between words and the matters they signify and, second, of a felt, palpable connection between ritualized utterances and the things they signify. Both problems are addressed by the formalization of ritual speech, because ritualization tends to give formal weight to utterances and to constrain their signification in line with the ritualist's intent.

Considering the power of ritualization to configure commitments and perceptions, we find in the *Iliad* an impressive array of both verbal and gestural reinforcements that secure the commitments made with words,

---

[137] KUB XLIV 4 + Kbo XIII 241 obv. 10–16 and rev. 1–6 . Analyzed by Gary Beckman in *Hittite Birth Rituals*, 192–93.

[138] See the Ritual Against Domestic Quarrel, given as an illustration by Ahmet Unal in "The Role of Magic in the Ancient Anatolian Religions," 66–70. (Text Kbo II 3 and its duplicates translated by A. Goetze (ANET II 350sq.).)

[139] Kbo XI 10 iii 18–21, discussed for its use of the expression "The tongue is a bridge!" by Beckman 1986: 19–30, n.b. 25.

as if the ritual gestures could impress into hard reality the meanings the words denote. These paralinguistic features are usually matters of bodily display, and often include manipulation of ritual objects. Similarly to the gesture of clasping hands, such physical displays make verbal commitments "heavy" by acts, as Rappaport would see it. The communicative logic behind this relies on the metaphor of matter. As Rappaport suggests, matter is palpable. Notions so abstract that words can barely represent them are rendered more palpable by gestures using manipulatable sacra – scepters, libations, sacrificial victims, and so forth. Further, bodily manipulations – such as raising hands, bowing, the grasping of objects, the pouring of libations – are inseparable from the being of the performer. Even as they may be symbolic, they are also immediately sensory to the performer, and a matter of physical display the audience can see. As Rappaport would see it, ritual gestures make the commitments they signify as real as flesh and blood.[140]

There are many physical gestures that accompany oaths in the *Iliad*. We have already discussed the gesture of taking by the hand as a symbol for the making of pacts, but using the hand in other gestures also dramatizes an oath. Hera touches the "all-nourishing earth by one hand and the glittering sea by the other" (14.272–73) in her oath by Styx and all the gods below that she will give one of the Graces to Hypnos. Menelaos bids Antilochos to swear to Poseidon by standing before the horses and chariot, holding the slender whip in his hand and clasping the Earthshaker, that he did not cheat during the chariot race at Patroklos's funeral games (23.581–85). Meleager's mother smites the ground, presumably with her hands, when she curses her son and calls upon the gods to punish him (9:568–72). Zeus hurls *Atē* to the earth, whirling her with his hand (19.131), while he swears a great oath that she should not return to Olympos (19.126–31). A most significant gesture by the hands is the hand-washing and holding of hair from the oath-sacrifice victims in Book 3 (3.269–73), as is the holding up of hands in the prayers that begin the formal oaths to Zeus in the oath-sacrificing rituals (3.275–76, 19.254–255).

Another significant gesture is the symbolic disarming that initiates the truce in *Iliad* 3, wherein the participants lay down their weapons in the plain (3.77 and 3.114–15), making themselves vulnerable to attack but surely also concretely symbolizing their good faith. The same disarming is contemplated by Hector in his self-query about the oath by senators, wherein he imagines putting down his shield and his helmet and

---

[140] While his examples are different, his discussion is on theme, at 1999: 146–47.

leaning his spear against a wall (22.111–12) to negotiate with Achilles. We have discussed the implied disarmament in the hand-shaking gestures of Glaukos and Diomedes earlier in this chapter.

The act of libating – "pouring oaths" as Idomeneus calls it (3.300–01) – is similarly significant as a ritual act, and is virtually equated with the making of oaths in Nestor's admonition to the Achaians: "Whither have gone our treaties and oaths? Our counsels and the thoughts of men have gone in the fire, and also our unmixed libations and the right hands in which we trusted" (2.339–41). Of course the ultimate ritual gesture for an oath is the slitting of an animal victim's throat and the display of its death: In Book 3 the victims are laid on the ground, "gasping and emptied of life" (3.293) and in Book 19 the boar is hurled, spinning, into the sea (19.267–68) (compare Zeus hurling *Atē*, whirling, to the earth [19.131]). In all of these cases, the ritual gesture would seem to add to the ritual's force, enunciate its significance, heighten its formal register, and in many cases bring the oath to final completion.

One conspicuous ritual gesture for oath-making is the grasping of the scepter. Achilles does this in his oath of separation in Book 1; Hector does it in his "false oath" to Dolon in Book 11; and Idaios does the same in invoking Zeus, consort of Hera, during the truce for burial of the dead in Book 7. The scepter is used emphatically for dramatic impact also when Odysseus curses himself regarding his intentions toward Thersites, whom he strikes with it. As a symbol of authority the scepter requires little explanation.[141] Yet Achilles' oath by the scepter in Book 1 is a famous manipulation of it as a symbol of perverted justice. His dramatic performance with the scepter demonstrates once again the way that meaning may be encoded and also subverted in ritual performances.

To understand Achilles' oath by the scepter, we should glance again at his preceding oath, which sets the stage for the second. Achilles' first oath is in response to the request of the seer Kalchas, who fears to say what he knows because of the likely wrath of king Agamemnon (1:73–83). The forbidden knowledge is that Apollo has released a plague upon the Achaians because Agamemnon has seized the daughter of Apollo's priest. Achilles vows to defend Kalchas against those who would prohibit his prophecy by threatening harm: "Not while I am living and

---

[141] For comparison, see Weinfeld's discussion of swearing while holding a blazing torch in biblical and Shurpu documents (1970: 196).

seeing on earth will anyone of quite all the Danaans by the hollow ships, not even Agamemnon, lay a heavy hand against you" (1.88–90). Although his oath implies a threat of deadly force against Agamemnon and all the Danaans, the significant death in Achilles' oath to defend Kalchas is that of Achilles himself, because he swears by his life, albeit in an oblique way. "While I am living and seeing on earth" (1.90) means no less than "as long as I live," modified by the circumstance of there being "anyone by the hollow ships" to threaten Kalchas. Despite the preliminary invocation of Apollo, to whom Kalchas prays (1.86), the force of Achilles' oath to defend the seer of Apollo against Agamemnon relies on the living and breathing of Achilles, at least as long as the ships are at Troy.

It is against a life already spent that Achilles swears the second oath. In that one, he swears by the scepter "which no longer bears leaves nor shoots." This context emerges directly from the first. As a result of the prophecy of Kalchas, Agamemnon returns his own concubine to her father, and seizes the one who belongs to Achilles. In outrage Achilles swears to himself, but also before all of the Achaians, that the consequences will be dire.

> "But I will speak out now and swear a great oath on it.
> That is that by this very scepter, which no longer bears leaves nor
>     shoots,
> since it first left its tree stump in the mountains,
> and it will not bloom again, for the bronze has peeled
> its leaves and its bark; and now the sons of the Achaians
> hold it in their hands as judges, who defend the laws
> before Zeus. And a great oath it will be.
> There will come a time when a longing shall overcome the sons of
>     the Achaians,
> quite all of you, for Achilles. And the grieving of heart will be
> unbearable, when many fall and die under man-slaying Hector.
> You will rend your heart inside, vexed that you did not honor the
>     best of the Achaians."
>
> (1:233–244)

Following these words Achilles flings down the scepter in a passionate rejection of all the judgments and laws and other cultural institutions with which the scepter is associated. There seems to be a scholarly consensus that Achilles' discarding of the scepter gives a kind of symbolic finality to his oath, yet scholars disagree regarding precisely how the scepter figures into the content of this oath.[142] We will discuss the scepter first as a poetic symbol and then as a ritual implement.

We have pointed out that Achilles appears to swear by the scepter's life, already lost. No longer will it bloom leaves or shoots in the mountains because it has been cut and peeled by bronze, a killing substance acting in the service of human culture. Although there is in this oath a parallel between the finality of the tree shoot's death and the finality of Achilles' intention, the symbol would appear richer than that. By its death, the tree's shoot has become an artifact of culture, essentially a once-living victim whose life was taken to support human institutions. Now the dead victim has become a symbol for the oaths and legal dispensations of men – human institutions that, in Achilles' eyes, have become perverted, stripped of both legitimacy and vitality. The symbolism in the flinging of the scepter is partly in the flinging away of the death-perpetrating culture the scepter represents. In connecting the death of the scepter with the imminent death of many Achaians, Achilles also extends the cost of the scepter's life, taken to serve human institutions, to human beings who likewise "will not bloom again" because of the perversion of justice that Agamemnon has manipulated through corrupt leadership. The symbol of the scepter that has lost its life in the service of culture thus richly connotes the threat of death to human beings who are *not* served by the rituals and institutions the scepter is supposed to represent.

As a ritual tool, however, the scepter is more ambiguous. The "dead" scepter is pointed out for all to see essentially as a swearer might point to an oath-victim, with whom the swearer is supposed to identify for all to see. The identity between a swearer and the victim by whose death the oath is sworn was recognized early in the last century by Stengel: "Zweck und Sinn des Opfers sind klar: der Schwörende verflucht sich für den Fall des Meineids und ruft die Götter an, ihn das Schicksal des Tieres erleiden zu lassen, wenn er den Schwur nicht halte."[143] Just as one swears by the life of a boar or ram in oath-sacrifice and then the victim's life is taken, here the life of the victim (the wooden scepter) has also been taken. The death of the scepter is, in fact, the first thing Achilles points out in his "great oath": "by this scepter, which no longer bears leaves nor shoots ever since it left its tree stump in the mountains, nor will it bloom

---

[142] See, among others, Nagy 1979: 47, Griffin (*Homer on Life and Death* [Oxford: Clarendon Press 1980, 1990] 11–12), Kirk 1985: 77, Michael Lynn-George, "Aspects of the Epic Vocabulary of Vulnerability," *Colby Quarterly* XXIX:3 (1993) 201–02.

[143] Stengel 1920: 136.

again, for bronze has peeled its leaves and its bark." Achilles would appear to be likening his death in the event of perjury to that of the scepter, emphasized by the relatively long account of its death.

Yet, complexly, by ritual identification, Achilles' oath by the scepter extends the fact of death in two directions – not just to himself, but also to the Achaians, for whom "the grieving of heart will be unbearable when many fall and die under man-slaying Hector. You will rend your heart inside, vexed that you did not honor the best of the Achaians." Notably, Achilles' great oath (*megan horkon*) is as deadly in consequence as the greatest oath (*megiston tekmor*) Zeus will swear to Achilles' mother (1524–7), although Zeus may not swear by his life. Rather, in both cases, Achaian lives are at stake. The fact of death to the Achaians is implied in Achilles' analogy between the "dead" scepter and the "great long-ing [that] will overcome the sons of the Achaians for Achilles, all of you . . . when many fall and die under man-slaying Hector." By the logic of Achilles' oath, the anticipated yearnings and deaths of those Achaians, to which Achilles verbally points, is to be measured by his gesture of holding up the "killed" scepter, which dramatizes the equation between them, as well as his commitment to the oath. Their future regret of their treatment of him will be the fruition of his oath. There appears to be a kind of three-way identification between the two spectacles against which Achilles swears and Achilles himself. As we have already seen, ges-tures such as holding up the scepter and verbally identifying its seman-tic import are ways of adding dramatic weight to a vow and specifying its content. Thus both the many dying Achaians and the dead scepter become the implements of ritual display for Achilles, measuring the force of Achilles' vow, which is that the Achaians will regret their actions and will die.

But there is also a more basic ritual equation between the scepter and the Achaians who will regret and die. They are linked because the Achaians at Troy, too, have taken an oath, at least implicitly, to support the institutions that the scepter represents just by joining together in the collective military enterprise against the Trojans. Yet, in Achilles' eyes, they have failed to uphold their oaths, as discussed earlier in terms of perverted justice. To swear by a perverted symbol – a dead scepter – is to undertake a perverted justice, here manifest as the corruption of fairness and good faith among the combined force of the Achaian armies. Perversions of justice are known to invite lethal punishment, such as the thunderstorms and devastating floods by which Zeus diminishes the works of men because of crooked law judges who refuse to heed the voice of the gods (16.384–93). Thus the deaths of the Achaians are implicated in this oath by ritual analogy to the dead scepter because of their implied oath-violation in failing to uphold a righteous scheme of justice. The reported death of the scepter thus ritually invites the death of the corrupt Achaians.

But the oath of Achilles by the scepter would be little more than a curse on others were he not also swearing by his own life. Given the dramatized analogy between the oath-victim and the swearer, both the scepter and the many imprecated to "fall and die under man-slaying Hector," held up by Achilles as ritual flags for his oath, stand as hypothetical ritual substitutes for Achilles himself, in the case of perjury. They are the killed rams, so to speak, by which Achilles swears. Yet Achilles does not commit perjury – he is sorely missed, just as he swore. Despite this, he shall die. Achilles' oncoming death does not fit within the strict constraints of ritual logic; it is a more subtle matter of cultic themes.[144] There appears to be an insinuation in the *Iliad* that Achilles has violated some profound social bond, beyond the prewar oath, just by removing himself from the war. In so doing he has created a ritualized identification of himself with the dead victims.

The penetration of cultic themes into the *Iliad* has been observed by a number of scholars, as in the famous connection of the Homeric *therapon* and the Hittite *tarpanalli*, the ritual substitute who assumes the burden of the king's misdoing and is sacrificed in place of the king. Such themes have been argued to implicate Achilles in some grievous sin, if only implied.[145] By Book 18, Achilles clearly feels that he has committed some fatal error, if not outright perjury, in staying away from battle. Consequently he determines to die rather than to return home, explicitly because he was no beacon to Patroklos nor to his other companions (18:101–02), and because he instead sat by the ships, "a useless burden on the cultivated ground" (18:104). The irony is, of course, that by joining in battle and cementing a most basic bond between comrades in battle, Achilles's fate is sealed. As he explains at 19.98, removing himself from the war would have been his only way to survive it. Similarly to the scepter, he will be a symbolic victim to the bonds that define human culture.

Of course, the ultimate ritual substitute identified with Achilles, and who will die while Achilles is away, is Patroklos, the *therapon* who dies

[144] See Nagy 1979.
[145] Sinos 1980.

suited out in Achilles' armor and pretending to be Achilles, fighting the battle that Achilles refuses to fight. The nuance of ritual substitution to the Homeric presentation of the death of Patroklos has been researched by, among others, Nadia Van Brock, Gregory Nagy, and Steven Lowenstam,[146] who point out different aspects of the figurative and possibly implicit cultic identification of the two heroes. Within the text, the close identification of Achilles with Patroklos is emphasized by Achilles when he tells his mother that he honored his companion "as his own life" (18:81–82), and when he refers to the shade of Patroklos as his "dear life" or "head" (*ētheiē kephalē*, 23:94). It is supported further by the decision to mix the bones of Patroklos with those of Achilles in a single funerary urn (23:91–92). Dale Sinos has argued for the cultic implications in the two heroes' bones in a common funeral urn.[147] The cultic and epic identity between Patroklos and Achilles infers not only that Achilles essentially has sacrificed himself in his oath by the scepter, but also that Achilles has sacrificed Patroklos, who is so closely identified with Achilles and who is also one of the Achaians who will "fall and die under man-slaying Hector" while Achilles is away from the battleground.[148] The three-way identification between Patroklos, Achilles, and the other Achaians who have died is notable.

With the cultic identification of Achilles and Patroklos in mind, we might note also some earlier arguments about the sacrificial features of the death of Patroklos, to the extent that these arguments bear on the significance of Achilles' oath by the scepter. Stephen Lowenstam has reviewed each facet of the funeral of Patroklos for its sacrificial features, such as the layering of fat around the body before cremation (23.166–169). This feature is often explained by comparative Indic and Hittite funerary

---

[146] van Brock 65 (1959) 227–46, G. Nagy (1979) 33, 292–3, Lowenstam 1981: n.b. 126–77.

[147] Sinos, 1980: 55ff.

[148] According to Sinos, "Achilles and Patroklos are two aspects of the same character; the identification within the narrative is that close" (1980: 55). On a related theme, the notion of a status distinction between the hero and his *therapon* – a poetic and possibly cultic motif formerly thought to hold across Near Eastern literatures – has been challenged implicitly by Andrew George in his recent translation and analysis of the extant tablets of the Babylonian version of the Epic of Gilgamesh. Insofar as the intimacy of the Achilles-Patroklos relationship is deemed to be based upon the Mesopotamian paradigm, it is significant that George denies any such status distinction as a compelling motif in the Babylonian epic. See Andrew R. George, *The Babylonian Gilgamesh Epic, Vols. I and II* (Oxford: Oxford University Press) 2003, and also his *The Epic of Gilgamesh, A New Translation* (Oxford: Oxford University Press 1999).

evidence; the practical purpose for the fat has been suspected to be as an aid in getting the body to burn.[149] Nonetheless the feature is ignored in the other funeral rituals in the *Iliad* and, given the sacrificial features of the *tarpanalli*'s relationship to the king, as the Hittite paradigm tends to get applied to Patroklos and Achilles, the sacrificial feature in the funeral rite conjures up the layers of fat surrounding offerings to the gods during commensal sacrifices (as in 1.460–461 and 2:423–24). More precisely on point, however, is the double layer of fat in which Patroklos's bones are encased within the golden urn, once his body is burned and his companions lovingly collect the bones (23.252–254; per Achilles' instructions at 23:243). As Lowenstam points out, the collocation of "white bones" (*ostea leuka*) and "double layer of fat" (*diplaka dēmon*) and "hidden" (*kaluptein*) in those lines is reminiscent of Hesiod's description of the prototypical sacrifice of an ox at Mycenae, where the white bones (*ostea leuka*) of an ox are hidden in double layers of fat (*diplaka dēmon . . . kalupsan*) to become the gods' portion (Th. 540–541).[150] Whether or not Patroklos's bones are to be seen as ultimately a god's sacrificial portion, they are to be mixed with those of Achilles (23.90, 23.244), thereby strengthening the ritual identification in the *tarpanalli* sacrifice. Moreover, Lowenstam shows that Patroklos is situated within a sacrificial scheme also in Book 11, where he heals Eurypylos before the altars of the gods, operating on his thigh – which gushes dark blood – with a *machaira*, the sacrificial knife (see Chapter 3), and speaks in what might be considered sacrificial double entendres, such as his query, *ti rheksomen?* (What shall we do? Or What shall we sacrifice?) at 11.838; and his quip that the Achaian fat will be a feast for the dogs. Lastly, Patroklos's death in Book 16 as the *therapon* of Achilles, suited in his armor and dying in his place, essentially renders the priest of Book 11 as the sacrificial victim in Book 16. As Lowenstam sees it, all of these features, plus others of which space prohibits discussion, combine to support a distinctly sacrificial theme surrounding the figure and the death of Patroklos. This theme seems to be at least obliquely anticipated in Achilles' oath by the scepter, which will be fulfilled by the death of *therapon* Patroklos, and thereafter by that of king Achilles.

That there may have existed a known sacrificial theme in connection with Patroklos also outside of the *Iliad* is further supported by the Triptolemos painter's stamnos ARV² 361.7 and the Attic rf calyx-krater

---

[149] Lowenstam 1981: 152. N.b. note 71.
[150] Lowenstam 1981: 154–5.

fragment 86.AE.213 from the J. Paul Getty Museum.[151] Alan Griffiths has introduced the two as presenting different facets of the theme of Patroklos as a sacrificed ram. In the first, Ajax and Hector prepare to fight over the body of a ram named Pat[roklos] whose neck unmistakably has been slit, while in the higher register Achilles is shrouded in misery and surrounded by the solicitous Phoinix, Diomedes, and Odysseus. Griffiths takes the two registers as representing the fight over Patroklos's body in Book 17, set as a tragic consequence of Achilles' obduracy in response to the embassy in Book 9, the ram being the puzzling symbol for Patroklos. Griffiths speculates on the possibility that one tradition may hold Patroklos's body to have been spirited away by Thetis, with the ram offered as a substitute, similarly to Euripides' version of the Iphigenia story, for instance, wherein a deer is substituted for the girl. The second representation is more difficult, but its higher register is interpreted by Griffiths as a duel by Ajax and Hector over the body of Patroklos. The body is not shown, but a ram's neck is being cut just to the left of the fight. In the bottom register two fighters are dragging a shrouded body to Achilles, who, distraught, is tearing his hair. The body appears to be that of the sheep. For Griffiths this appearance is not clearly perceived by either the fighters nor by Achilles, who are apparently under the illusion that the body is that of Patroklos. From these two representations, Griffiths speculates that there may have been a known theme in Classical times about Patroklos as not actually dying, but being spirited away and his body substituted by that of a sacrificial ram. Here too, the theme of sacrificial substitutes is prominent, although what stories lie behind it we can only guess.

Although Griffiths's interpretation of these vases does not support my point about Achilles' oath of separation anticipating the death of Patroklos, another interpretation might. In this second way of thinking, the stamnos with the sacrificed ram named Patroklos might reference indeed Achilles' decision to stay out of the war, which explains the upper register where he sits with hands to face in obvious misery over what has taken place in the lower register, which is the fight over the substitute's

---

[151] Identified as ARV² 361.7, the stamnos is now in the Basel Antikenmuseum as Inv. BS 477. The vase is shown (Plate 4) and discussed by Alan Griffiths in "A Ram Called Patroklos," *Bulletin of the Institute of Classical Studies* 32: 49–50 (1985). His argument is supplemented in "Patroklos the Ram (Again)," *Bulletin of the Institute of Classical Studies* 36:139 (1989), in which he introduces an Attic rf calyx-krater fragment (86.AE.213) from the J. Paul Getty Museum, in which a ram's throat is being cut as Hector and Ajax prepare to fight for possession of Patroklos's body.

corpse. But the source for this misery and for the depiction of Patroklos as a sacrificial ram might be ultimately Achilles' oath of separation, and the various levels of symbolic substitution implied in the death of the scepter (the death of the Achaians, Achilles, and Patroklos, all implicated by the death of the sacrificial scepter-victim). Unlike the explanation about the body being stolen away, this explanation has at least the benefit of a reference in the text. In this case the depiction of Patroklos as a ram would be figurative, and would explain the question that Griffiths asks in note 8: Why a ram? Rams are known as traditional animal victims for oath-sacrifice, as we saw in Book 3's oath-sacrifice and in Agamemnon's imprecation on the Trojans for failing to honor "the blood of lambs" (4.158–9), at least one of which was male. With the ram commonly recognized as an oath-sacrificing victim, the ram here would represent Patroklos as an oath-victim, a ram, still the cost of Achilles' absence from the war and a consequence, ultimately, of his oath by the scepter, a figuratively killed oath-victim. In this interpretation, Achilles would not be unaware of the figurative significance of Patroklos as ram: the death of Patroklos is the cost of his oath of separation, with the ram representing the "killed" scepter, and ultimately Patroklos.

As for the krater depicting a fight between Ajax and Hector, with the sacrificed ram on the left, one fairly straightforward reference for this scene might be the duel between Ajax and Hector in Book 7. The duel is stated by Hector explicitly to be an attempt to rectify the Trojan failure in the first duel between Paris and Menelaos, the terms of which were established over sacrificed lambs. But, as Hector sees it, those terms were thwarted by Zeus: "The oaths of the high-throned son of Kronos have not been fulfilled / rather he has planned and decreed evil for both sides" (7.69–70) Hence Hector challenges the Achaians to a second duel to rectify the first, invoking Zeus as his witness (7.76), and announcing that *philotēs* (alliance or friendship) still might follow strife (7:300–02). The specter of the ram on the left then would be a reminder that this second duel invokes the same terms as were set over the sacrificed lambs in the first duel. As we know from the text of the *Iliad*, this duel resolves nothing, and the war resumes. Hence the lower register, which depicts a corpse being carried by two fighters and obscured by the tunic of the leading fighter, may still depict Patroklos, or for that matter, his substitute, to the same effect. Achilles is distraught, and Patroklos's death is a consequence of the failure of the duel to end the conflict. Ultimately, then, if the corpse is that of a sacrificial animal, figuratively Patroklos, or actually Patroklos, the point is the same: The cost of the war is the death of Patroklos as a sacrificial victim. This, too, might be anticipated, at least obliquely, by Achilles' oath of separation.

This brings us, finally, to the theme of death as punishment for mortal oath-violation. We have already discussed the ritual logic in death's finality, but here we will glance at the evidence for death as punishment for oath-violating. It should be noted right off that painful death is not the only punishment for oath-violators in the ancient world. An array of punishments specifying either total humiliation (such as rape and naked exposure), banishment, and other terrible deprivations are conveyed by biblical curses.[152] Assyrian campaign boasts make the vengeance for oath-violation result in horrifying spectacles such as starvation and cannibalism, including the devouring of one's own children.[153] Hittite treaty-oaths promise annihilation of the families of oath-breakers, and complaints to the gods invite plague, hunger, discord, and fever to nation-states who violate oaths of fidelity to Hatti.[154] Although

---

[152] The best summary is Delbert Hillers's *Treaty Curses*. See also F. Rachel Magdalene's "Ancient Near Eastern Treaty-Curses and the Ultimate Texts of Terror: A Study of the Language of Divine Sexual Abuse in the Prophetic Corpus," in *A Feminist Companion to the Latter Prophets*, ed. Athalya Brenner (Sheffield Academic Press 1995) 326–52.

[153] See Luckenbill 1968: section 831.

[154] When the oath is between individuals, it is the curse on the family that is explicit, as we see in his agreement with Haggana.

> Behold to you these words under oath I put: If you men of Haisha and Mr. Mariasha do not protect it, these sacred oaths of yours, your lives, together with your wives, your children, your brothers, your sisters, your families, your houses, your fields, your cities, your vineyards, your threshing floors, your cattle, your sheep, together with your possessions, let them be completely destroyed! May the [oath-gods] seize you from the dark earth!

> [nu-uš-ma-aš kaaša kie k[ue u]ddaaar *ŠA-PAL NI-IŠ* DINGER-*LIM* teeḫḫuum na-at-ma-a-an [šumeeš LÚ.MEŠ ᵁᴿᵁh]aiaša 1 maarijašša *Ú-UL* paaḫḫaašteni. nu-uš-ma-[aš kie] *NI-IŠ* DINGIR-*LIM* šumeenzaan SAG.DU. MEŠ-*KU-NU QA-DU* DAM.MEŠ-*KU-NU* DUMU.MEŠ[-*KU-NU* ŠEŠ]. MEŠ-*KU-NU* NIN.MEŠ-*KU-NU* MÁŠ.HI.A-*KU-NU* É.MES-*KU-NU* A.ŠÀ.HI.A-*KU-NU* URU.DIDLI.HI.A-*KU-NU* ᴳᴵˢSAR.GEŠTIN-*KU-NU* KISLAḪ.HI.A-*KU-NU* GUD.HIA-*KU-NU* UDU.*HI.A* -KU-NU [*QA-DU MIM-MU-KU-NU*-I a] kataan arha [harganut] daankuṷaiaaz-ma-aš-k[án tagna]az seir arḫa niniinkandu (Kbo V 3 IV 34–46).]

> When it is vassals who are revolting from their oaths, Hittite king Mursilis prays for vengeance by plague:

> They do not extol (sara iṷanzi) the gods. They violate the oath of the gods.... They keep despoiling the houses of the gods. Let them become a cause for vengeance again. Allow in plague, enmity, and fever to Kizzuwatna (Mittani) and Arzawa.

the bereaving of parents, the ravishing of wives, the orphaning of children, and the rending of bodies by dogs and birds are common enough battle curses in the *Iliad*, the primary punishment for oath-violators is more straightforwardly painful death and destruction, with all other punishments hinging upon the first. Hence the swearers in the oath-sacrifice of Book 3 pray, "Whoever is first to violate the oaths, so may their brains pour onto the ground, as does the wine, and the brains of their children, and may their wives be subdued by others'" (3.300–01), and Agamemnon prays a bit less precisely in Book 19, "'If I have sworn any of these things falsely, may the gods give to me pains, exceedingly many, as many as they give to anyone who transgresses against them in swearing'" (19.265–67). The overwhelming evidence in the *Iliad* is that oath-violation is to be punished by nothing less than painful death, at least for the swearer, and then by either painful death or humiliation for his family.

After the oath of Book 3 is violated, the threat of death for oath-violation becomes a pronounced theme, and one etiology for the destruction of Troy. Death and oath-violation are explicitly equated in Agamemnon's lament and threat over the wound of Menelaos after he is struck by Pandaros:

"Oh my brother, the oaths I cut for you were your death,
putting you alone before the Achaians to fight the Trojans,
since the Trojans struck you, and trampled [*patesan*] upon the trusty
  oaths.
But in no way barren is the oath, the blood of rams,
the unmixed libations and the right hands in which we trusted.
For indeed, if the Olympian does not fulfill it at once,
he certainly will fulfill it later, and with might he will avenge it,
with their heads and their women and their children.
For well I know this in my head and in my heart,
there will be a day when sacred Ilion will be destroyed,
and also Priam and the host of Priam of the ashen lance."

(4:155–165)

[nu-za-kán DINGIR.MES saraa *Ú-UL* iịaanzi. na-aš-ta *NI-EŠ* šarriir....
É.HI.A DINGER-MEŠ-ma lauaarruna šaanhiiškanzi. na-at *A-NA* DINGIR.
MEŠ-aš kattaaatar nam-ma kisaru. nu-uš-ša-kán hiinkan kuruur gaaštaan
idaaluun tapaaššan *A-NA* KUR.URU miittani Ù *A-NA* KUR.URU ar-za-u-ụa.
tarnaatten.

(Composite of three texts from KUB XXIV – prayers of Mursilis).]

Aside from the equation of the oath cut by Agamemnon with Menelaos's wounding and possible death,[155] the most conspicuous death in this utterance is that due those who trampled the oaths sworn – the Trojans. The same threat of death is implicit in the frequently intoned formulae "the first who trample on oaths sworn" (*oppoteroi proteroi hyper horkia pēmēneian* (3.299), and first to violate / who violated the oath (*proteroi hyper horkia dēlēsasthai / dēlēsanto* (4.67, 4.72, 4.271, variation at 3.107). Such menacing refrains occur at least six times (at 3:107; 3:299; 4:67; 4:72; 4:236; 4:271) and constitute a relatively tight formula by Parryan standards. As Richard Martin might see it, the phrase can be considered to function essentially as a theme fragment, which the story will fill out.[156]

Although Trojan unreliability in regard to oaths is pronounced before the oath ceremony begins (3.106–07) and once again during the ceremony itself (3.300), the cost to pay for oath-violation, intoned through this repeated formula, becomes emphatic after the duel between Paris and Menelaos is thwarted. Then Hera urges Zeus to orchestrate Trojan culpability and thereby eventual devastation by ordering Athene to establish that the Trojans lead the Achaians as "the first to violate oaths" (*proteroi hyper horkia dēlēsasthai*) (4:65–67). Zeus obliges, repeating the formula again in his instructions to Athene (4.71–72). The theme is continued when Agamemnon rouses the Achaians to fight, now that they can claim Zeus to avenge them against the Trojans,

> "Argives, in no way let go of your rushing courage.
> For Zeus father will not be a helper to liars,
> rather, those who were *the first who violated oaths*,
> vultures indeed will feast upon their tender skins
> while we, in turn, will lead their own wives and little
> children to the ships, after we take the citadel."
>
> (4:234–39)

Idomeneus supports Agamemnon's imprecation:

> "So rouse up the other flowing haired Achaians,
> so that we quickly may fight, since the Trojans poured oaths

---

[155] Kirk understands the double accusatives in this expression as implying an identity between the oaths and the death, the two accusatives he makes the object of "cut": "The oaths I cut were death to you" (1985: 347). Conceivably the accusative for death could also be an accusative of respect: "The oath I cut for you in respect to the death [of oath-violators, in the guise of animal victims]."

[156] Richard Martin, "Telemachus and the Last Hero Song" *Colby Quarterly* XXIX:3 231 (1993).

with us. To them now shall be death and destruction,
since they were *the first who violated oaths*."

(4:269–71) (my italics)

The menacing aspect of the formula "the first who violated oaths" may
be seen to function not only in the way of a nominal sentence,[157] but also
as a protasis for an actual or implied curse. At the very least, its repetition
helps to heighten anticipation of cosmic punishment in Books 3 and 4,
serving to create a continuum of increasing anticipation from the point
of Hera's crafting of imminent disaster for the Trojans in Book 3, right
through Idomeneus's speech in Book 4 and reverberating into Book 7.
There Hector blames the unfulfillment of the oaths on Zeus (7:69), and
wiser Trojans such as Antenor acknowledge that the Trojans are culpa-
ble, because "now we are fighting as ones who have lied regarding trusty
oaths" (7:351–52). Interestingly, the terms of the oath of Book 3 are introduced again as Hector faces his demise at the hands of Achilles in Book
22. There, in his contemplated "oath by senators," Hector muses over
the unlikely possibility that Achilles might be mollified should Hector
promise to give over to the Atreides Helen and all of her possessions,
plus to divide up whatever is left inside Troy, swearing an oath by the
elders not to hide anything (22.119–121). This stream of references to the
failed oath of Book 3 suggests at least a supplemental poetic and possibly
a cultic etiology of oath-violation for the fall of Troy.

In this chapter I have attempted to uncover some premises and principles
of oath-making in the *Iliad* and to demonstrate how they fit into the ritual
patterns discussed in Chapter 1. I have also attempted to demonstrate
that Homeric oath-making principles share features with oath-making
principles of the Near East. It has not been my intention to uncover
identical parallels between Near Eastern and Homeric rituals, but rather
to demonstrate shared principles of ritual logic. At the same time, I hope
to have demonstrated also the Homeric premises that temper this shared
ritual logic and give Homeric oath-making its unique cast. This unique
cast is surely an epic cast. The most compelling evidence for that, however,
is yet to come.

---

[157] Martin sees the formula in this way, 1993: n.b. 231.

# CHAPTER THREE

# RITUAL SCENES AND EPIC THEMES OF OATH-SACRIFICE

T HE THEORIES OUTLINED IN CHAPTER I AND THE CULTURAL PRIN-
ciples and premises described in Chapter 2 provide us with lenses
through which we now can examine the *Iliad*'s two complete oath sacrifices of Books 3 and 19. In the first part of this chapter, we shall examine
each element of the oath-sacrificing ritual scene, as well as the cohesion
of its elements into a liturgical order, as defined in Chapter 1. As part
of this examination, we shall weigh each element in the oath-sacrificing
scene against other instances of that same element as displayed in other
ritual events in the *Iliad*, and also against a handful of conspicuously similar events referred to in Near Eastern texts. To explore the cohesion
of the ritual's various elements we shall attempt to trace the intertextual
tensions between the apparent performance pattern of the ritual and the
typical poetic scene of oath-sacrifice, relying on theories introduced in
Chapter 1.

The second part of this chapter has a more elusive aim, which is to
gauge the extent to which a resonance between ritual slaughter and
battlefield slaughter, if any, could have been intuited by ancient audiences
to the *Iliad*. To establish that there was such a resonance, we first shall
explore some shared lexical features between the oath-sacrificing ritual
scene and certain killing and dying scenes, to illuminate some common
narrative shapes and themes. Next, using Fernandez and other ritual
theorists, we shall outline the metaphorical transformation promoted
for ritual actors by the oath-sacrificing performance, and show how a
transformation of identities from swearers to avengers is portrayed in the
narrative surrounding the oath-sacrifice in Book 3. A transformation is
implied also for oath-violators, as sacrificial lambs. To show the way an
audience might have perceived these metaphorical transformations, we
shall conclude with a brief summary and application of Paul Ricoeur's

theory of metaphor. His theory will be joined with the theories of ritual outlined in Chapter 1, to illuminate the "ritual fiction" created by oath-sacrifices in the *Iliad*.

## RITUAL PATTERNS AND NARRATIVE FIXITY IN HOMERIC OATH-SACRIFICES

[S]anctity is a product of ritual's form rather than of its substance.

Rappaport 1999: 328

As we alluded in Chapter 1, the two examples of the typical scene of oath-sacrifice in the *Iliad* share a number of ritualized gestures and speech acts, rendered with similar and occasionally identical verses, although the sequential order varies slightly and the scene in Book 3 is more elaborate than the one in Book 19. The two events are comprised of the following ritual steps, represented by the following verses (in columns).

(1) The participants stop all other activity, come to order, and attend to the ritual.

Hector causes the Trojans to be seated and proposes the oath-sacrifice to the Achaians (3.78ff). When the oath is about to occur, "The Achaians and Trojans rejoiced, hoping to stop the piteous war. And they pulled their horses into rows, they dismounted, and took off their weapons. They laid them on the ground, clustered together, and little was the earth on both sides" (3.113–15).

"The Argives all sat right where they were, in silence, as was proper (*kata moiran*), listening to their king" (19.255–56).

(2) The animal victims are led into the scene by heralds, wine libations are prepared, and hands are ritually cleansed.

"Then the wondrous heralds led up the trusty oath-victims of the gods" (3.268–9). "They mixed wine in cups, then poured water over the hands of the kings" (3.269–70).

"Talthybios, resembling the gods in voice, held a boar in his hands, and stood next to the shepherd of hosts" (19: 250–51).

(3) The king draws his sacrificial knife.

Agamemnon "drew with his hands his *machaira*, which always hung by the great sheath of his sword" (3.271–72).

Agamemnon "drew with his hands his *machaira*, which always hung by the great sheath of his sword" (19.252–53).

(4) He cuts hair from the victim[s] with the *machaira*.

"[H]e cut hairs from the heads of the lambs" (3.273). "And next the heralds distributed them to best of the Achaians and Trojans" (3.274).

"Cutting the hairs from the boar" (19.254).

(5) The king prays, holding up his hands to Zeus.

"Before them Atreides prayed, holding up his great hands" (3.275–76).

"Holding up his hands up to Zeus, he prayed" (19.254–255).

(6) He invokes a series of divine witnesses, concluding with the Erinyes, either by function or by name.

"Zeus father, ruler from Ida, greatest and best, and Helios, who watches over all and hears all things, and rivers and earth, and those toiling underneath who punish humans, whoever should swear a false oath, you be witnesses, and guard the trusty oaths" (3.276–80).

"Now let Zeus see first, highest and best of gods, and Ge and also Helios and the Erinyes who from underground punish humans whosoever should swear a false oath" (19: 259–60).

(7) He gives the terms of the oath.

"If Alexandros should kill Menelaos, then let him take Helen and all her possessions, while we return home in our sea-going ships. And if fair Menelaos should kill Alexandros, then the Trojans are to give back Helen and all her

"... that I have not laid a hand on the girl Briseis, not desiring her under the pretext of bed, nor for any other reason. She has been untouched by me in my hut" (19.261–3).

possessions, and we shall exact *timē* for the Argives as may be fitting, which shall be for future humans [to remember]. If Priam and the sons of Priam do not wish to pay *timē* to me, in the case of Alexandros having fallen, then I at that point shall fight for the sake of the *poinē*, staying here until I reach the end of the war" (3.281–291).

(8) There is a curse on oath-violators, either just before or just after the oath-sacrifice. In Book 3 it is after the sacrifice and the libation of wine; in Book 19, it is before the sacrifice.

"Drawing wine in cups from the bowl, they poured it out, and prayed to the gods who always are. And so each of the Achaians and Trojans would say,[1] 'Zeus greatest and best, and all the other immortal gods, whoever is first to violate the oaths, so may their brains fall to the ground as does this wine, and those of their children, and may their wives be subdued by others'" (3.297–301).

"Praying, . . . 'if I have sworn any of these things falsely, may the gods give to me pains, exceedingly many, as many as they give to anyone who transgresses against them in swearing'" (19.264–66).

(9) He cuts the throat of the victim(s) with the *machaira*:

"And so he said, and he cut [*tame*] the throats of the lambs with the pitiless bronze" (3.292).

"And so he said, and he cut [*tame*] the throat of the boar with the pitiless bronze" (19.266).

---

[1] I am taking the iterative *eipesken* in its distributive sense.

(10) The fate of the victim is observed.

"And he put them on the ground, gasping and emptied of life (*thumos*), for the bronze had taken away their might (*menos*)" (3.293–94).

"Talthybios hurled him, setting him whirling, into the great abyss of the sea, to be food for fish" (19.267–68).[2]

One might be struck by both the similarity and the variability in the substance of these scenes. The ritual pattern is undeniably similar, while the oral traditional pattern as portrayed in the scenes permits at least some flexibility. Conspicuous for their seeming lack of flexibility, however, are the three identical phrases configured around the most lethal of ritual acts: drawing the *machaira*, invoking the formidable Erinyes, and cutting the throat of the victim(s) "with the pitiless bronze." Other acts, while not rendered in identical phrasing, are at least close. For instance, the word order varies, but Agamemnon's prayer-act is rendered similarly in both scenes as holding up his hands, with the participle, and praying in the indicative (*eucheto cheiras anaschōn* 3:275; *Dii cheiras anaschōn / eucheto* 19.254–5). Such lexical parallels will command our attention presently. In contrast to these, the king's cutting of the hair of the victim(s) is represented with two different verbs, and the curses on oath-violators are differently phrased, despite a similarity in menacing tone. Other features of the ritual, such as presenting the animal victims and the assembling of witnesses in respectful silence around the king, have different renderings based on context, but seem to conform to the same underlying performance pattern. The slight variety in the choice of gods, as we discussed in Chapter 2, is contextual: That a wider group of oath-defending deities is invited to sanction the oath with the Trojans in Book 3 demonstrates that oaths between parties of differing nationalities are likely to invoke deities from both sides. That Zeus, Helios, and Ge are the three deities of choice is evident not only because these are invoked in the oath among the Greeks alone, in Book 19, but also because these three deities are referred to by name in the planning for the oath in Book 3, before it actually takes place – "You [Trojans] bring lambs, one light, the other dark, for Gē and for Helios, and we will bring another for Zeus" (3.103–4).[3]

---

[2] I have used this sequence before (Kitts 2003: 1–18).

[3] The abbreviated list for Book 19, in contrast, is just Zeus and Helios: "Let Talthybios swiftly prepare the boar for me, to cut for Zeus and Helios, down through the wide army of the Achaians" (19.195–95).

The concluding lines of the two scenes, wherein the last moments of the victims are described, also vary in their overt drama – the lambs' gasping and being deprived of *thumos* and *menos* is clearly a more graphic portrayal of death than is the whirling and hurling of the boar. Yet, as we will show, there are at least resonances between the language describing the disposal of the boar in Book 19 and that describing the disposals of corpses in nearby killing scenes, which may bear on the dramatic impact of the rendering of the boar's death.

Regardless of the specific lexical similarities and differences, it is notable that both oral traditional scenes are rendered with precise detail, ritually significant vocabulary (for instance, the sacrificial "*machaira*," a knife never mentioned in the *Iliad*'s commensal sacrifices), and a series of finite action verbs signifying a series of finite acts. This is consistent with Leonard Muellner's description of the typical ritual scenes containing the verb *euchomai*, to pray, plus the dative of god, ritual scenes being a subgenre of the typical scene. According to Muellner, the series of finite action verbs represents a series of behavioral microadjustments, a ritual feature whose significance Muellner draws from Lévi-Strauss.[4] Here, the series of microadjustments includes the concrete ritual acts of presenting victims, drawing the *machaira*, cutting hair, uttering prayers, pouring wine, slicing necks, disposing of corpses, cursing oath-violators, and so on, rendered with a series of finite verbs, as well as a few participles. It is notable that figurative speech, although not entirely absent from the oath-sacrificing ritual sequence (for instance, the *machaira* when it cuts throats is referred to as a "pitiless bronze"), is relatively scarce in the two scenes, seemingly eclipsed by the emphasis on precise detail signifying concrete ritual acts. This lack of figurative speech and emphasis on precision would seem to support the claim of a close correspondence between ritual scenes and ritual performances, and of a tension between them.

At the same time it is also worth noting, with Dale Launderville and many others, that poetic resonance with actual religious experience in ancient Near Eastern and Greek texts may be measured not just in terms of narrative coherence – as when whole ritual narratives resonate with whole ritual sequences in the lives of audiences – but also in terms of symbols and metaphors that may denote ritual personae, tools, circumstances, and "point beyond the surface of the narrative to ways in which the world of

---

[4] Muellner 1976: 33.

the narrative relates to a world beyond it."[5] As Muellner also points out, the detailed precision may denote sacral actions with symbolic meaning and intent.[6] Specifically, the recognition of ritual significance, as argued in Chapter 1, may involve the recognition of deeply rooted ritual paradigms cast within newer metaphoric domains, even as those paradigms may be skewed, contracted, or expanded to serve the larger story. As we stated in our discussion of Nagler, such scenes may reflect underlying Gestalts emerging in new allomorphs, in accord with narrative and performance exigencies. The underlying Gestalts may be recognized through the text in the way that Tambiah attributes to the recognition of "truth"in rituals: their manifestations trigger iconic recognitions of primordial events, or – in Nagler's generative view – a bursting forth (the *sphut*) of meaning upon the mind, a bursting that may be triggered in part by a linguistic symbol or by independent linguistic elements occurring "in the happy synergism of a meaningful pattern" and generating "an artistic entity (a *sphota*), which is somehow greater than the sum of its parts."[7] The communicative function of both ritual performances and ritual scenes was established in Chapter 1.

Needless to say, viewing a ritual scene as a way of communicating primordial paradigms or originary Gestalts within newer iconic arrangements vastly expands the dimensions of an audience's potential recognition of ritual events. Rather than identify precise ritual actions with precise phrases in epic poetry, then, an audience may recognize ritual significance as a deep theme, corresponding to a ritual or metaphoric domain lying beneath the array of precise ritual figures and events. Given the epic and ancient nature of our evidence, that deep theme may have resonated with the lived ritual traditions of ancient audiences in a way and to a degree that eludes contemporary grasp.

Notwithstanding the potentially deep levels of ritual recognition on the part of an audience, the superficial sequence of actions that constitute the ritual appears to be more fixed than loose. Given this fixity and the fact that the performance of the ritual is what establishes the oath, oath-making sacrifices in the *Iliad* indeed seem to qualify as "liturgical orders" in the sense Rappaport gives them: "more or less invariant sequences

---

[5] Dale Launderville, *Piety and Politics, The Dynamics of Royal Authority in Homeric Greece, Biblical Israel, and Old Babylonian Mesopotamia* (Grand Rapids, MI: Eerdmans 2003) 29.

[6] Muellner 1976: 36.

[7] Nagler 1974: 85.

of formal acts and utterances not entirely encoded by the performers,"[8] which are "enlivened, realized, or established only when those acts are performed and those utterances voiced."[9] Considering the second half of this definition, it is obvious on the surface of the narrative that oath-making ritual performances establish a compulsion regarding future acts because the Trojans are berated repeatedly for violating the terms of the oath-sacrifice of Book 3, and the consequences are anticipated to be dire. As for the first half of the definition, there is obviously a formal quality to these ritual procedures – hence the attention to precise detail and the invariance of elements, performance to performance. As we argued in Chapter 1, the set features of the ritual may not be explained away entirely as a product of poetic composition by typical scenes. Rather, the invariant detail and sequence of the ritual events support the contention that the sequences are felt to be "not entirely encoded by the performers," or even by the poets, but instead are imagined to reflect, at least to some extent, ritual sequences hallowed by religious tradition. The cohesion of the performed ritual acts, further, would appear to be tight – just as tight as the tension that exists between the various elements in the oath-making typical scene, which is the most fixed configuration of verses of virtually any typical scene in the *Iliad*. Given its relatively fixed character, the configuration itself surely communicates a greater or different significance than its individual parts taken as a sum.

As argued also in Chapter 1, the fixity of elements in the oath-sacrificing ritual would seem to denote not only a whole performance Gestalt, but performance in a highly formalized ritual register, which is somber, sacred, and resistant to challenge. The tension between the elements may be correlated with the degree of ritual formality that, as Rappaport observed, reflects the degree of constraint required for individuals entering into the convention established by the ritual. The fixity of elements in a ritual would reflect a bulwark against violation, given the predictable proportionality between the most formalized, least variant ritual structures in a society and a felt likelihood they might be violated. Oath-making surely qualifies as one of the most precarious cultural structures in Homeric society, hence the emphatic ritual formality, a bulwark against violation.

The fixity of liturgical features may be explained also in terms of Bloch's view of ritual oratory (see Chapter 1). The stressed and formal

---

[8] Rappaport 1999: 24.
[9] Rappaport 1996: 432.

qualities of ritual oratory, says Bloch, protect the contents of particular orations from challenge by anyone who would break with tradition. The oratorical formality of the oath-making rituals is clear from the emphasis on the speech acts in oath-making scenes. The speech acts, performed with a formal sequence of predictable phrases and marked vocabulary, reflect a heightened communicational register that helps to enunciate the commitment of the speakers to the substance of the oath. At the same time, the speech acts are not necessarily more ritually weighty than the physical gestures that accompany them, such as the cutting of animal throats, a polyvalent gesture that, among other things, seems to seal the substance of the illocution into time.[10]

So, in the light of (a) the specialized phrasing and vocabulary in the oath-making ritual scene, (b) the relative fixity in the pattern of verses for the typical scene and presumably also in the features of the ritual performance, and (c) the hypothetical proportionality between a ritual's formality and a ritual's conventional force, let us now glance at each feature of the oath-making ritual scene to examine the way each feature helps to shape the whole, and to examine those features against other examples in the *Iliad* and occasionally in other Near Eastern literatures. The simple features of the ritual may be summarized as coming to solemn order, introducing victims, drawing the *machaira*, cutting the victim(s)'s hair, praying with arms raised, invoking witnesses, pronouncing terms, cursing perjurers, killing victim(s), and disposing of the corpse(s). Examining these features will help us to gauge the heightened register of the ritual performance, argued already to be communicated by the formality and fixity of the ritual performance, and will help us to piece together some possible dimensions of audience recognition of the ritual event denoted by the typical scene.

---

[10] Rappaport points out that not all elements of a ritual performance must be equally invariant to communicate its liturgical quality:

> [A] higher degree of punctiliousness (care, decorum, or reverence) is likely to be required in the performance of some elements of canon than of others. Some expressions may have to be enunciated more precisely than others, or a higher degree of solemnity may be required in the performance of some portions of the liturgy than of others, stricter limitations may be placed upon where or when or by whom they may be performed, or the act of performance may be subject to special stylistic constraints – particular postures must be assumed, or gestures executed, or objects manipulated, or particular modes of expression such as chanting required. Some elements, finally, may be indispensable and therefore invariably present while others are not. Illustrations abound. (1999: 330)

## COMING TO ORDER

Perhaps the most striking thing about the first feature – coming to order –
is how it stands in contrast with the battle scenes either just before or just
after the ritual. In Book 3, for instance, the Trojans and Achaians are in the
very heat of battle when Hector goes up the Trojan phalanxes holding his
sword by the middle, a signal all the Trojans recognize and that convinces
them to be seated right then and there (3.78). The Achaians are about to
exploit their advantage over the Trojans when Agamemnon halts them
by a great shout (3.80–81). They fall immediately silent (*hoi d'éschonto
machēs áneǫ t'égenonto essumenōs* – 3.84–85). The leadership on both sides
is striking, as is the responsiveness of the warriors. The Trojan gesture of
sitting is also striking, given the vulnerability it implies in a battle with
spears, swords, and arrows. Nothing explicit is said about the Achaians and
Trojans continuing to sit as they await the oath-sacrifice, but the sitting
right through to the duel can be presumed, based on Paris's expectation
that the sitting of the troops would be customary while he and Menelaos
engage in a duel (*nun au't' ei' m' étheleis polemizdein ēde machesthai, /
allous men kathison Trōas kai pantas 'Achaious*, 3.67–68). The vulnerability
implied by sitting is similar to that implied when the two sides disarm and
put their armor on the ground, seemingly in a pile (*teuchea t'éxeduonto; ta
men katethent' épi gaiǫ plēsion allēlōn* 3.114–115).[11] The significance of this
vulnerability is of course the mutual trust it suggests, given that the two
sides were in such close proximity that, for their armor, "little was the
earth on both sides" (*oligē d'ên amphis aroura* 3.115). This phrase has been
interpreted in a few different ways,[12] but it seems to denote at the very
least the lack of separation between the armor of each side there on the
plain. The collective pile of armor might be correlated with their collective hope at 3.111–112: "So he said, and they rejoiced, the Achaians and
Trojans, hoping to stop the wretched war" (*hōs éphath', hoi d'écharēsan
Achaoi te Trōes te / élpomenoi pausasthai oïzdurou polemoio*). The mutuality of this hope and the close proximity of the weapons (and possibly
also the men) would seem to point ahead to the prospective new social
configuration of *philotēs* sought by the "cutting of trusty oaths" as we
discussed in Chapter 2. *Philotēs* by itself is exactly the opposite social status heretofore presupposed, so this moment indeed marks the beginning
of a new social arrangement ritually configured by oath-sacrifice.

[11] It is interesting to compare the Platean oath, wherein shields are piled atop the sacrificial
victim. See Faraone 1993.
[12] See Kirk 1985: 279 on the possibilities for lines 114–15.

The poet and his characters appear to take for granted that the ritual assembly is staged inclusively to promote cooperation. This is in keeping with a ritual feature noted by a number of anthropologists, which is that ritual performances tend to be demarcated from other cultural activities in the interests of the harmony of the participants.[13] The demarcation promotes social cohesion: This is a special occasion and former enmities are to be forgotten. Yet it is notable that when Priam and Antenor arrive on the field, any informal atmosphere that may have been indicated by the Trojan and Achaian sitting and mutual hoping is eclipsed by an emphasis on rank and order. Hence they arrive among the Trojans and Achaians, dismount from the horses, and take their places between both sides (3.264–66). Agamemnon and Odysseus arise, presumably from sitting, to assume matching positions from the Achaian side (3.267–68). After the ritual takes place, there is another collective indicator, when each of the Achaians and Trojans prays (note the distributive nuance to the iterative *eipesken*, at 3.319) that Zeus will let one man perish into Hades and let friendship and trusty oaths be to everyone else ("*Zeu pater, Idēthen medeōn, kudiste megiste, oppoteros tade erga met' amphoteroisin ethēke, ton dos apophthimenon dunai domon Aidos eisō, hēmin d'au philotēta kai horkia pista genesthai*" 3.320–23). But then the men sit in rows (*hisdonto kata stichas* 3.326), each with his horse and armor nearby, to watch the duel, presumably moving into positions appropriate for such precarious circumstances. Clearly, the initial mood of cooperation does not eclipse the sense of danger and the tension between sides.

The collective hope for *philotēs* is dampened further by references to the unreliability and fluttery hearts of Priam's children when it comes to conventions such as oaths (3.106, 3.205–10), and it must have been proverbial knowledge among Greek audiences that the Trojans would violate the oath, just as Paris had violated guestfriendship. Thus the references to Trojan unreliability would have been somewhat ominous. Narratively speaking, these references lessen the dramatic separation of the ritual sphere from the battle sphere. Although one might expect that formal ritual would be distinguished from battlefield melee in a poem of war, the cultural spheres of oath-sacrificing and war ultimately will interpenetrate in the *Iliad*, when the violation of the oath will result in punitive violence on the battlefield.

The orderliness of the oath-sacrifice in Book 19 contrasts not with the battle before it but with the battle passion that will succeed it. As has been

---

[13] See, for instance, Tambiah 1979: 117 and Burkert 1985: 56–8.

argued, the oath-making ceremony in Book 19 inducts Achilles back into the Achaian army and, superficially at least, dissolves his alienation from Agamemnon and the rest of the troops. They, of course, are delighted that he has put away his *mēnis* (*"hos ephath', hoi d'echarēsan euknēmides Achaioi / mēnin apeipontos megathumou Pēleiōnos"* 19.74–75). Nonetheless, he is not eager to participate in the ritual nor to receive gifts, but claims instead to be hungry for battle-lust (*charmē*) (19.147–49) and concerned not with a conciliatory meal but with "killing and blood and the hard groaning of men" (19.214). He is forced to endure the ritual anyway, but his subsequent slaughter of Trojans is presented as breaching the very line between mortal and immortal levels of destructiveness, inviting nothing short of a theomachy in response (21.304ff), and thereby destabilizing the cosmos. Against Achilles' lust for battle, the social containment in the oath-sacrificing scene is a significant contrast.

This is not to say that the atmosphere of the oath in Book 19 is not solemn or menacing in any way. One is a bit pressed to take Agamemnon's excursus on the delusional power of *Atē* and the punishing power of Zeus, Moira, and the Erinyes (19.87) as particularly menacing in tone,[14] but the solemnity of the entire oath is enhanced by the desperate need of the Achaians for Achilles and by the fact that so many have died while he was removed from fighting. Also, during the feast that follows the oath-sacrifice, the convivial atmosphere that usually prevails at feasts is dampened by Achilles' refusal to partake of it (19.203–214, 19.304–308, 19.314–321). Similarly to the oath-sacrifice of Book 3, then, the oath-sacrifice in Book 19 occurs under the specter of battlefield slaughter.

The orderliness of the ritual in Book 19 nonetheless is represented succinctly in the behavior stated to be proper for human witnesses. Just when Agamemnon begins the prayer that constitutes his oath, the Argives are to sit in order and show respect: "The Argives sat right there in silence, as was customary (*kata moiran*), listening to their king" (19.255–56). It has been argued persuasively that the ritual roles of the king in the *Iliad* mirror the ritual roles of the king in the ancient Near East, where he is expected to intercede between heavenly and earthly spheres and to represent his flock on earth before the gods.[15] Hence, in Book 3 we see Agamemnon taking a pose as the principal spokesperson for the Achaians to the gods who witness oaths, and during the oath of Book 19, where he is swearing only for himself, he is actually referred to as the "shepherd of hosts"

[14] But compare the kings deluded by *Atē* at 8.237.
[15] Launderville 2003: 38–56.

(19: 250–51), a title with obvious Near Eastern resonance.[16] To observe that Homer employs the Near Eastern king-as-shepherd paradigm for ritual authority is not to say that he accepts unquestioned monarchic privilege, because clearly he does not. The *Iliad* demonstrates the weakness of Agamemnon's authority frequently, and one of the central dramas of the story is built precisely around the tug of war between the competing interests of rival kings Achilles and Agamemnon. The same kind of rivalry plagues the heavenly order, it would seem, given the tensions between Zeus and Poseidon. Apparently Homer accepts royal friction as part of life, on earth as it is in the heavens.[17] Nonetheless, the paradigmatic role of the good king as good shepherd and as mediator between divine and human realms is a long-standing model in ancient Near Eastern notions of leadership, going back all the way to the Sumerians.[18] That model appears a stronger influence on these ritual scenes than the narrative fact of Agamemnon's failure of leadership in other situations. The rapport between a shepherd king and his flock during oath-making rituals is evident in the way the "flock" here sits in silence, according to custom, listening to the "shepherd of hosts."

## PRESENTING OF THE VICTIM

The second feature is the presenting of the victim, which in Book 3 is followed by the ritual gestures of washing hands and mixing wine. In both scenes, heralds present the victim(s) to the king: "The illustrious heralds led up the trusty oath-victims (*horkia pista*[19]) of the gods, mixed wine in bowls, and they poured water over the hands of the kings" (3.268–70); "Talthybios, resembling a god in voice, stood by the shepherd of hosts, holding the boar in his hands" (19.250–51). Heralds, of course, mark ceremonious occasions with their pronouncements and actions, and here seem to function in positions that join diplomatic and religious authority, assisting the king in his roles as chief diplomat and as priest before the gods.

As for the choice of the victims, there appears to be a scholarly consensus that animal victims in oath-sacrifice must be male, because they

---

[16] Launderville 2003.

[17] Launderville 2003.

[18] I am thinking of stelae that depict the presentation of kings before the gods.

[19] See Bickerman 1976 for a discussion of the identification of the trusty oath victims and the trusty oaths. See also the discussion in Karavites 1992: 62–76 on the multiple significations of *horkia* and its differentiation from *horkos*.

supposedly are castrated in the process of oath-sacrifice.[20] Yet in the *Iliad* there is no mention of castration, and one of the lambs sacrificed in Book 3 is actually female.[21] Whereas the boar that Agamemnon sacrifices in Book 19 is obviously male, the lambs sacrificed in Book 3 are said to be a white male and black female, for the sun and the earth,[22] and another male of unspecified color for Zeus (3.103–04). Nor are they cut into pieces for standing upon, another custom that has received scholarly attention.[23] Rather they are simply cut at the throat, and then either placed on the ground (Book 3) or hurled into the sea (Book 19). Further, despite the claim the victims are for the gods, when actually sacrificed the victims are not directed toward nor apparently expected to be received by any gods, as pointed out by both Burkert and Stengel (citing the Scholion on 19: 310),[24] who claim that the animals slaughtered are rarely the ones suitable for offering to the particular gods anyway.

Yet it should also be pointed out that the *Iliad* is ambiguous on both the purpose and the suitability of animal victims. In Book 19 the preparation for the sacrifice includes making ready the victim "to cut for Zeus and Helios" (19.197), with the gods precisely in the dative, just as in Book 3 Menelaos tells the Trojans, "you bring lambs, one white and one black, for Earth and for Helios. We will bring another for Zeus" (3.103–05), also with the deities in the dative. But when the animals are killed, nothing at all is said about them being for any gods, which gives the earlier match of victims to gods the feel of a cultic reflex. Further, regardless of any later Classical schemes for matching sacrificial victims to gods,[25] the *Iliad* provides no clear guidelines for the suitability of a match, other than an occasional reference to various male victims being sacrificed to male

---

[20] Burkert 1985: 251; Paul Stengel, *Opferbrauch Der Griechen* (Darmstadt: Wissenschaftliche Buchgesellschaft 1972: 81).

[21] As for the gradually firming principle of appropriateness in the choice of a victim to match the god, see Jameson, "Sacrifice and Ritual, 959–79, n.b. 973, and A. M. Bowie, "Greek Sacrifice: Forms and Functions," in *The Greek World*, ed. Anton Powell (London: Routledge 1995) 463–82, n.b. 475. The *Iliad*, however, gives little evidence for any such scheme.

[22] Presumably on the basis of later literature, Kirk claims that the white male lamb was designated for the sun, the black female for the earth, and that the order is reversed by chiasmus (1985: 277–78).

[23] Stengel 1920.

[24] Burkert 1985: 251; Stengel 1920: 138.

[25] See Bowie 1995 for the wide range of sacrificial occasions and kinds of sacrifices in later periods. See Bruit Zaidman and Schmitt Pantel on the appropriateness of certain victims for certain cults in Classical times 1989, 30.

gods (as at 4.101–103; 11.728–29; 15.373–76), while heifers are offered to Athene (at 10.291–95; 11.727–29). Even so, this gender specification is not steadfast in the *Iliad*. At 24.33, for instance, both goddesses and gods are expected to appreciate Hector's rather generic offerings of the thighs of blemishless goats and oxen. When Zeus's animal of choice is specified at all (c.f. 11.727), it tends to be an ox (11.772, 15.372–73), lamb (3.103–05), or goat (15.372–73), and only in this one occasion (in Book 19) is it a boar. Yet it is conceivable that Zeus does have at least an oblique affinity for boars, given his chthonic impersonation in matters of oaths and curses (see Chapter 2) and the general association of swine with other chthonic cults in Greece.[26] Ultimately, one may surmise that the choice of victim for divine offerings of any kind during a long war probably would have as much to do with availability as with suitability, with domestic cattle, sheep, goats, and an occasional boar being the norm in the *Iliad*. That the choice is not limited to these domesticated animals is apparent when the Achaians are said to sacrifice to Zeus the wild fawn that an eagle drops over his altar (8.250).

Grasping the purpose for sacrificing an oath-victim in the *Iliad* is complicated by a documented tradition of Near Eastern treaty sacrifices extending back to the third millennium, as evidenced by the animal sacrifices that accompany the treaty between Naram–Sin and the Elamites of 2300–2250 BCE.[27] According to Weinfeld, it is not until the first millennium that the bonding feast in the context of treaties (which may illuminate the purpose of the feast in Book 19) gives way to ritual killing of an animal victim as a dramatic act intended to symbolize and impress upon participants the dire consequences of failing to abide by the treaty's terms. First millennium Assyrian examples include, for instance, the treaty between Assyrian king Ashurnirari V and Mati'-ilu of Bit-Agusi, which makes the dramatic act explicit: "Just as the head of this spring lamb is cut off and its knuckle placed in its mouth, [so shall] the head of Mati'-ilu be cut off."[28] Similarly, in Jeremiah 34, the god of Israel threatens to punish those who violated a covenant to free their slaves by fulfilling the curse symbolized in the ritual act of promising: "I will make you like the calf of the covenant when they cut it into two and passed between

[26] W. K. C. Guthrie, *The Greeks and Their Gods* (Boston: Beacon Press 1955) 221.

[27] Weinfeld discusses this and other examples (1970: 197–98).

[28] *State Archives of Assyria, Volume* II, *Neo-Assyrian Treaties and Loyalty Oaths*, eds. Simo Parpola nd Kazuko Watanabe (Helsinki: The Neo-Assyrian Text Corpus Project and the Helsinki Press, 1988), 9. Also cited by Weinfeld 1970: 198.

the pieces" (Jer.34.18). Greek sacrifice has been argued to serve a wider variety of theological and social functions than Biblical sacrifice,[29] but it is intriguing nonetheless that the *Iliad* at one moment appears to endorse the notion of oath-victims as being somehow for gods and at another moment as being illustrations of the fate awaiting oath-violators, with the gods looking on as witnesses.

An interesting scheme for the ritual logic has been argued by Bickerman, who relies on Dictys's version of the three different moments to the oath-ceremony performed by Agamemnon at Troy. Dictys describes a ceremony in which the Achaian chiefs prepare for the alliance with Priam by bloodying the tips of their swords in the blood of a sacrificial victim, thereby, according to Bickerman, invigorating the power of the bond as well as the power of the oath against the perjuring Trojans: "Il semble que par le contact avec la force vitale de la victime on renforce la concorde entre les allies tandis que le serment, selon Dictyes, porte sur la guerre sans merci contre Ilion."[30] Next, the pact between parties is solemnized by invoking the gods as witnesses, and third, by passing between the pieces of two victims, which Bickerman compares to the Near Eastern tradition of passing between the cut halves of a victim in order to seal an oath, exemplified by the illustration in Jeremiah.[31] According to Bickerman this last ritual gesture, if accompanied by an explicit formula identifying the swearer with the cut-up animal, shifts the focus of the rite to the animal's death, away from the focus on its former vitality.[32] Rather than precisely invigorating the treaty-bond, then, the animal's death serves to exemplify the fate awaiting perjurers.

Although the purpose of the animal killing is insinuated only obliquely in both oath-sacrificing narratives in the *Iliad*, scholars usually assume that the killing of the animal there serves the same kind of symbolic purpose the pouring of wine does in Book 3. The pouring of wine is stated explicitly to mirror the pouring of the brains of the perjurers and their families.[33] If this symbolic purpose is the primary purpose, the focus on the animal's death during the oath-ritual in Book 3 would exemplify not

---

[29] See, for instance, A. M. Bowie 1995: 463–64.

[30] Bickerman 1976: 14.

[31] See also the overview of types of Hittite sacrifice by René Lebrun, "Aspects Particuliers du sacrifice dans le monde Hittite," in *Ritual and Sacrifice in the Ancient Near East*, ed. J. Quaegebeur (Leuven: Uitgeverij Peeters en Departement Orientalistiek 1993) 225–33, n.b. 229.

[32] Bickerman 1976: 14–15.

[33] Faraone 1993.

the principle that the animal's slaying invigorates the bond, but that its death dramatizes the punishment in store for oath-violators, by analogy. However, because the analogy for the sacrifice is not explicitly stated, neither there nor in Book 19, it should be admitted that the *Iliad* gives more than one clue as to the purpose of the victims. The purpose may even be forgotten. At the very least, given the evolution of the poem, it is possible that more than one ritual principle may be reflected in the text.

Considering this possibility, one may find intriguing two recently analyzed oath-fragments from the southwestern (Arzawan) and southeastern (Kizzuwatnan) regions of Hittite Anatolia. Both regions are known for Luvian cultural influences, although to different extents (Kizzuwatna bearing Hurrian and Syrian influences as well[34]), which makes their oath-ceremonies of interest for possible relevance to Ahhiyawan (Achaian) traditions.[35] The oath-ceremonies reflected in these fragments are substantially different from the oaths in the Hittite diplomatic treaties collected by Gary Beckman, for instance, which are sealed by curses and lists of witnessing gods rather than by symbolic acts.

The Arzawan fragment, from a treaty between a certain Huhazalma of Arzawa and a Hittite king, reads simply: "When we killed a sheep, we put the following words under oath" (*anda-ma-kán UDU-un kuwapi kuewen nu linkiya [ka]ttan kiššan daiwen*),[36] which seems to equate the fixing of an oath with the killing of a sheep, as if the dramatic act of killing were to give the oath a kind of irreversible finality. In contrast, the more complicated Kizzuwatnan fragment exorcizes an epidemic from the land by persuading the god Shanta (a deity associated with war and pestilence) and the Innarawantes demons to swear an oath never again to approach the door of the house. In that ritual, a goat is presented and the god Shanta is libated with wine. Then Shanta and the Innarawantes deities are invited to come and eat, as the master of the house and the invited gods are to make an oath (*likuwanni*).[37] Next the goat is slaughtered with a bronze ax and its raw liver and heart are presented to the gods along with blood and

---

[34] See Alfonso Archi, "Kizzuwatna Amid Anatolian and Syrian Cults," in *Anatolia Antica, Studi in memoria di Fiorella Imparati, Vol. I*, eds Stefano de Martino e Franca Pecchioli Daddi (Florence: LoGisma 2002) 47–54.

[35] For the link, see Gutterbock 1996: 33–44.

[36] KBo 16.47 Ro. 15′–16′, MH/MS. Discussed in "Aspetti magico-religiosi" by Mauro Giorgieri 2001: 436–37. See also *The Hittite Dictionary, Vol. I* (Chicago: University of Chicago 1980) under *lingai*, p. 65, 2b.

[37] Giorgieri translates *likuwanni* as first person plural of *li(n)k* – "*giurare*." 2001: 438 foonote 61.

a straw, whereupon the master of the house takes up a piece of the liver
and imitates the sucking up of blood from the straw, saying, in relevant
part: "Here, Shanta and the Innarawantes, we have sanctified an oath
(*lengawen*). We have eaten a piece of the raw liver, and drunk from one
straw. O Shanta and you Innarawantes, do not again approach my door."[38]
As Giorgieri sees it, the contact with the vital organs and blood – in
this human-to-divinity oath as probably among human-to-human oaths
serves to fortify and sanctify the oath,[39] along the lines of Bickerman's first
hypothesis, wherein contact with the blood is understood to strengthen
the bond created between parties to the oath. This is in contrast to
the Arzawan oath, where the dramatic killing of a victim in an oath
seems rather to seal the oath into time, the act being significant for its
finality. Or perhaps, as Stengel and the majority of Classical religionists
might see it, the killing in the Arzawan oath may serve to identify the
perjurer's fate with the sheep's, by analogy. Before one accepts that the
distinctions between the Arzawan and Kizzuwatnan oaths are far-reaching
in significance, however, one must recognize that the Kizzuwatnan ritual
also exudes the air of a ruse, based on the pretense of commensality and
hospitality toward deities whose presence is not desired, as if they could
be appeased and then dismissed by a common meal. The ritual might be
considered a version of the treaty-meal discussed in brief by Weinfeld. In
fact, after the raw liver and heart are mouthed and the blood is sucked
up through a straw by the host, the rest of the goat is cooked and then
is enjoyed by the human host, the gods Shanta and the Innarawantes,
and also by the sun-god and the other thousand gods of Hatti, who are
summoned to be witnesses (*kutruenes̆ es̆ten*) to the oath and to join in the
meal. One has the impression that the meal and oath function to join
all these deities together in a diplomatic effort to pacify Shanta and the
Innarawantes, and to promote common goodwill and cooperation with
the terms of the oath.[40]

---

[38] Giorgieri discusses this entire ritual (HT I lines 26–60) on 437–40.

[39] Giorgieri 2001: 440.

[40] A similar logic may be discerned in prayers by Mursilis II to the vanished god Telepinu.
For instance, in KUB XXIV 2 Mursilis instructs the priest to entreat Telepinu to
return to dine in his temple, as follows: "Go! Entreat Telipinu, our lord, god of our
person. . . . Now, let the sublime refreshment of cedar and oil summon you. Come
back into your temple. Behold, I am entreating you with regular bread and libations.
Be fully nourished" (lines 5–13). The devastation caused by the absence of Telipinu is
thus to be solved by encouraging the god to return to his dining table. This suggests
food is his source of empowerment and goodwill.

Both rituals, from Arzawa and Kizzuwatna, are intriguing for possible affinities with Homeric oaths. The dramatic killing and dying of the victim in the oath of Book 3 can be seen in the light of the Arzawan oath, "when we killed a sheep, we put the following words under oath," while the communal meal that follows the oath in Book 19 might be compared to the Kizzuwatnan oath, wherein a meal both confirms and follows the oath to exorcize the Innarawantes demons. Overall, these two rituals demonstrate that populations of Luvian regions of Anatolia during the period roughly contemporaneous with the peoples usually associated with the Homeric Achaians,[41] may have practiced sacrificial killing in oath-ceremonies under the umbrella of more than one apparent ritual logic. This opens up the possibility that the dramatic gesture of killing an animal in Homeric oath-sacrifice may not be as simply analogical as many scholars have tended to assume, and that the two Homeric oath-sacrificing scenes may correspond to different ritual logics.

On the other hand, the poetic focus on the victims' gasping and dying in Book 3 certainly provides a punishing nuance to the scene, and highlights the analogical explanation for killing an animal in oath-sacrifice. The punishing nuance also infects the rhetoric surrounding that ritual, particularly the curses on oath-violators.[42] Consequently, intriguing as the Anatolian comparisons may be, one must recognize that ritual purpose and poetic stress may be conflated in the poems of Homer, thereby eclipsing any clues to the ritual logic.

## WASHING OF HANDS

As for the washing of hands in Book 3 but not in Book 19, there is arguably some practicality to the gesture in Book 3, as chiefs Agamemnon and Odysseus have come straight from battle, and presumably are soiled with battle gore. In Book 19, on the other hand, Agamemnon has been out of battle for some time because of his wounds and is not likely to have soiled hands.

Nonetheless, given the brevity of the narrative in Book 19 and the coincidence elsewhere in the *Iliad* of washing hands with libating gods and uttering prayers, it would seem that the ritual in Book 3 may illustrate a persistent association of lustral rituals with libations and prayers to the gods. For instance, Nestor commands the ambassadors to allow water to

[41] See, for instance, Gutterbock 1996: 33–44.
[42] See my "Not Barren" (Kitts 2003: 1–18) and also my contribution to the *Journal of Ritual Studies* 13: 2 (1999) 42–57 and to *Metis* 7(1–2) (1992): 161–176.

be poured over their hands and to observe a holy silence while he prays on their behalf in Book 9; at the same time the heralds mix wine in cups for libating and also for drinking (9: 171–72). Achilles, too, washes his hands before prayer in Book 16 and purifies a cup given him by his mother, using sulfur first and then washing it with water, before he libates the gods with wine (16.228–30). Priam also combines handwashing with prayer and libating before his embassy to Achilles (24: 302–05). Given the widespread practice of sprinkling lustral waters over the hands in ritual contexts during Classical times,[43] it seems probable that these Homeric handwashings also are preliminary purifying rites, with the hands deemed instruments for sacred acts[44] – that is, hands often are held up during prayers, as if transporting the prayer upwards and summoning divine attention downwards. That washing is not always correlated with libations and prayers is apparent when the Achaians wash before sacrificing to Apollo in Book 1 (1.449), not only to show respect, surely, but also to wash off the debris of plague. Similarly, although Diomedes and Odysseus bathe and libate the gods after the Doloneia (10: 577–79), their bathing is arguably due to the accumulated filth of their nighttime slaughtering escapade as much as due to honor for the gods. In short, one might assume that washing, then as now, may have symbolic or purely profane significance, and also both.

The mixing of wine in Book 3 is explained by Kirk as signifying the mixing of wine from both sides into one bowl, symbolizing unity.[45] Unlike wine for human consumption, wine-libations technically remain "unmixed" with water. Libations are made of a number of different liquids in Greek religious life, particularly of water, wine, honey and oil, all enlisted at various times and to various ends.[46] Amphoras of honey are placed on the funeral pyre of Patroklos (23.170), possibly implying honey libations, but most libations in the *Iliad* are of wine. Wine libations are made to Apollo during the feast in his honor at the return of Chryses' daughter, in Book 1 (1.462, 1.470). They are made by the Trojans to appease Zeus when he resounds in thunder in Book 7

---

[43] Louise Bruitt Zaidman and Pauline Schmitt Pantel (1989, 1992: 33, 35, 56).

[44] So, too, is ritual purity a matter of concern for royal personnel in Hittite sacrifices. See Rene Lebrun, "Aspects particuliers du sacrifice," 1993: 255–33, n.b. 231.

[45] Kirk, *Commentary*, Vol. I.

[46] Funerary contexts appear the most inclusive of these substances, the sequence of which arguably mimics a kind of ontology of being. See my "Two Expressions for Human Mortality," 132–51, and Fritz Graf, "Milch, Honig und Wein," in *Perennitas, Studi in Onore di Angelo Brelich*, ed. Giulia Piccaluga (Rome: Edizione dell'Ateneo 1980) 210.

(7.480–81). Wine libations are made as a ritual gesture – no god is named, but Zeus Xeinios seems probable – by the ambassadors as they leave the hut of Achilles (9.656–67) and once again when they leave the Achaian assembly to return to their own huts for the night (9.712–13). They are made by Diomedes and Odysseus to Athene after the Doloneia (10.579). They are made by Peleus to Zeus in an offering of thanksgiving, according to Nestor's story of his visit to the house of Peleus (11.774–75). They are made famously by Achilles to the winds, in his attempt to light the pyre for Patroklos (23.219–20). Then they are made by Priam to Zeus at the start of his embassy to Achilles (24.305). Wine libations thus appear in a broad range of contexts. They appear to be gestures of religious propriety, serving frequently to solicit divine favor or to demonstrate gratitude in a variety of occasions. Hence Zeus measures the piety of Hector precisely by his consistency in offering Zeus libations and fats (24.70–71). One may surmise from these examples that libations accompanied many of the rituals that punctuated daily life for the ancient Greeks[47] and served different ends under the well-known principle that the same precise act may bear a different significance depending on the ritual situation.[48]

Yet it is notable in the context of Homeric oath-making that "unmixed libations" is several times virtually a figurative expression for oaths. It is in fact one of three in Agamemnon's warning that "in no way barren shall be the oath, the blood of lambs, the unmixed libations, and the right hands in which we trusted" (4.158–59) when he refers to the dire consequences of the Trojan violation of the truce. "Unmixed libations" along with "right hands" has the same figurative significance in Nestor's rebuke on the Achaians for disregarding "our unmixed libations and the right hands in which we trusted" (2.339–41), which is apparently a reference to the pre-war oath of the Greek troops. As used in these examples, "unmixed libations" clearly draws into its semantic sphere the compulsory nature of oath-making, suggesting that the pouring of unmixed libations is regarded as a powerful ritual act signifying an oath. As Bruitt Zaidman and Schmitt Pantel see it, the ritual wastage of wine poured into the ground serves to establish a connection between the world of men and the world of infernal powers, who are ever ready to break into the world of men to chastise perjurers.[49]

---

[47] For a summary see Bruitt Zaidman and Schmitt Pantel 1994: 39–41.

[48] Giorgieri 2001: 425.

[49] Bruitt Zaidman and Schmitt Pantel 1994: 41.

More ritually precise is the expression "pouring oaths" in Idomeneus's imprecation toward the Trojans:

> "Since the Trojans poured oaths
> with us, to them now shall be death and destruction,
> since they were the first who violated oaths"
>
> (4.269–71).

Our earlier discussion of the ritual origin for the expression "to cut an oath" comes to mind for comparison with "pouring oaths" here (see Chapter 2). Similar ritually based shorthand is evident in a number of expressions for making oaths in the ancient Near East, ranging from, for instance, "eating an oath" at Mari – based apparently on the poisonous consequences of an herbaceous "oath" swallowed and then betrayed[50] – to uttering "the three words" (the words sadly lost) while making hand gestures before symbols of different Old Assyrian deities of the oath (often Ashur for men, who make oaths before his dagger, and Ishtar for women, who make oaths before her tympanum).[51] Each expression – eating an oath, uttering the three words, and pouring an oath – appears to denote the precise act of swearing to, or committing to, an oath. That oath-making rituals in the *Iliad* may be figured as "pouring oaths" suggests that libations were not just supplements to oath-sacrifice, but as ritual acts wielded their own force.

---

[50] See Charpin 1996: 85–96. On the relevance of ingesting liquids as a dramatic gesture for oath-making among the Hittites, see "Birra, acqua ed olio: paralleli sirianni e neo-assiri ad un giuramento ittita" by Mauro Giorgieri, in *Anatolia Antica, Studi in memoria di Fiorella Imparati, Vol. I*, eds. Stefano de Martino e Franca Pecchioli Daddi (Florence: LoGisma 2002) 299–320. For an Assyrian comparison, see the succession treaty of Esarhaddon, section 72: "Just as bread and wine enter into the intestines, [so] may they (= the gods) make this oath enter into [your] intestines and into those of [your] so[ns] and your [daught]ers." See Parpola and Watanabe 1988: 52.

[51] See Cecile Michel, "Hommes et femmes pretent serment a l'epoque paleo-assyrienne," in *Jurer et Maudire* (Paris 1996) 109. The variety of ritual gestures for Neo-Assyrian oaths might be gauged by the list given in the succession oath of Esarhaddon, which names Ashurbanipal as the crown prince: "You shall not take a mutually binding oath with (anyone) who installs (statutes of) gods in order to conclude a treaty before gods, (be it) by set(ting) a table, by drinking from a cup, by kindling a fire, by water, by oil, or by holding breasts, but you shall come and report to Ashurbanipal, the great crown prince designate, son of Esarhaddon, king of Assyria, your lord, and shall seize and put to death the perpetrators of insurrection and the traitorous troops, and destroy their name and seed from the land," Parpola and Watanabe 1988: section 13, p. 35.

In the oath of Book 3, the expression "pouring oaths" is of course consistent with the actual curse that accompanies the libation of wine, wherein the pouring-out of wine is equated with the pouring-out of the brains of the perjurers and their families: "Whoever is first to violate the oaths, so may their brains fall to the ground as does this wine, and those of their children, and may their wives be subdued by others" (3.297–301).[52] The symbolic link between poured-out wine and poured-out life seems clear enough, and happens to be articulated in a Hittite military oath that precisely equates poured-out wine with poured-out blood: "This is not your wine, it is your blood. As the earth swallows it, so shall it swallow your blood."[53] The underlying association is clearly that blood is life, and one's life is symbolically poured out when the red wine, as blood, is poured out. In the Homeric oath, poured-out wine (as brains) has a parallel significance to the Hittite poured-out wine (as blood), but the Homeric expression is more graphic. "Poured out brains" is entirely in keeping with the semantic sphere of the battlefield in the *Iliad*,[54] where there is no shortage of detail in the carnage. Whether the wine stands for blood or for brains, then, ancient wine-libations from Hittite Anatolia and from the *Iliad* apparently dramatize perjury's dreadful consequence, which is the dissipation of life.[55]

## DRAWING THE *MACHAIRA*

The third feature is the drawing of the sacrificial knife: Agamemnon "drew with his hands his *machaira*, which always hung by the great sheath of his sword" (3.271–72; 19.252–53). Much ado has been made about the *machaira* as the killing knife hidden in the *kanoun* in commensal sacrifices, and about its traditional confinement to sacrificial use, not battlefield use.[56] In the *Iliad*'s commensal sacrifices, though, the *machaira* is never

---

[52] On the bashing of the enemies' children's heads in warfare, compare Psalm 137: 9.

[53] "wa UL GE[STIN] sumenzan. Wa eshar nu. Wa ki [mahhan] [tag]anzipa kit[ta] pastha [sumen]zann. [a eshar] . . . -ya taganzipas katt[a QATA]MMA [] pashu." (KUB 32.38 Vo. 13–16, NH; ed. Oettinger, StBoT22, cit. p. 210 s.) Discussed in brief by M. Giorgieri, 2001: 430.

[54] Giorgieri makes this point, in 2001: 431.

[55] As for the notion of the earth or infernal powers drinking the blood, compare *Seven Against Thebes* 42–56, and the discussion of this oath by the blood in the shield in Giulio Guidorizzi's "Uno scudo pieno di sangue," in *I Sette A Tebe. Dal mito alla letteratura* (Bologna: Patron Editore 2002) 63–72.

[56] See, for instance, Bruitt Zaidman and Schmitt Pantel 1989, 1994 33, and Detienne 1989: 1–20.

named at all, while in oath-sacrifices it is the ritual implement par excellence. Nor, in the *Iliad*, is it ever concealed in a basket, as it is famously in some later rituals.[57] Instead it is drawn from the sacrificer's side, from its place next to the sheath of the sword, apparently lodged in the belt (compare with 18.597). Further, as Richard Martin has pointed out, in the *Iliad* the *machaira* is not confined to sacrificial use in a strict sense, but has other semantic shadings, particularly in association with the healing of *amēchania* (helplessness). He establishes this link by examining cognate words and narratives, as he sees it, such as *machomai* (to fight), *mēchanē* (craft), and *mēchos* (healing), whose meanings are tied to, for example, the work of healer *Machaōn*, who would perform a *mēchos* by operating with the *machaira*, or the work of Patroklos, who effects a healing (*mēchos*) of the wound of Eurypolos by using his *machaira* and some healing herbs (11: 844), and who is the ritual substitute whose death effects a healing of the rift between Achilles and the rest of the troops.[58] As Martin argues, such healing roles and healing tools support the complex theme of ritual killing (sacrifice) as ritual healing in the *Iliad*. In the context of oath-making in the *Iliad*, however, the *machaira* is conspicuous as a killing tool whose drawing initiates the most lethal of ritual acts, which is the killing of the animal victim whose death is dramatically on display for all to see. The *machaira* also concludes that most lethal act when, as "the pitiless bronze" (*nēlei chalkō*; 3.292, 19.266), it cuts the throat of the victim. Although one may argue, as I did in Chapter 2, that in a broad sense ritual oath-sacrifices do indeed mend rifts in society,[59] the *machaira*'s most conspicuous work in oath-making rituals is to slice the neck of oath-victims.

In light of its serious work, the *machaira* is also of interest in regard to who wields it. In the *Iliad*'s oath-sacrifices, it is the king. In Book 3 it is wielded as a symbol of his authority to make oaths for the Achaians, whereas in Book 19 it is wielded as a symbol of his authority to make oaths for himself. Either way, drawing the *machaira* from one's belt seems to signal a readiness to assume social responsibility of some weight. This is consistent with the depiction of the *machaira* in a scene rendered on

---

[57] But is it always hidden in the basket? For an analysis of the evidence, see Pierre Bonnechere, " 'La machaira etá dissimulee dans le kanoun': quelques interrogations," *Revue des etudes anciennes* 101: 1–2 (1999) 21–35.

[58] Richard Martin, *Healing, Sacrifice, and Battle* (Innsbruck: Innsbrucker Beitrage zur Sprachwissenschaft #41 1983) 85ff.

[59] Kitts 1999: 42–57.

the shield of Achilles, where young men and dowry-earning maidens dance, the girls wearing fine garments and garlands, the boys wearing oil-glistening tunics and bearing *machairas* in their belts (18.593–98).[60] Given the symbolization of potential marriage in this scene, it is significant that the boys wearing *machairas* in their belts are on the verge of adulthood, and that having a *machaira* in one's belt, along with wearing glistening tunics, is made to correspond to the wearing of adornments by dowry-earning maidens. Both sets of adornments, male and female, appear to denote a readiness to assume adult responsibilities in society. Bearing the *machaira*, then, would seem to be a mark of manhood, which apparently includes a readiness to conduct oath-sacrifices. It shows a readiness to become "a man of one's word," as we say today.

It is significant that the drawing of the *machaira* is referred to with identical phrasing in both oath-making scenes: "[Agamemnon] drew with his hands his *machaira*, which always hung by the great sheath of his sword." As suggested in Chapter 1, the fixity of a verse in a typical ritual scene may signify not a bard's rote memorization, but rather the verse's semantic weight as an indicator of a key ritual act. In this case, drawing the *machaira* is the first fixed verse leading toward what seems to be the dramatic high point of the ritual, which is the ritual killing of the victims, a step also rendered in virtually identical verses in both oath-making scenes: "And so he said, and he cut the throats of the [lambs, boar] with the pitiless bronze" (3.292; 19.266). Thus, the introduction of the killing tool, as rendered in this verse, introduces also the ritual's core symbolic act: the killing of the victim. One may surmise from its fixed versification that, at the very least, the gesture of drawing the *machaira* marks a meaningful step into a very somber ritual realm.

More profoundly, as I argued earlier with my use of Rappaport, the fixity of the phrasing that describes the drawing and using of the *machaira* may indicate not only formality in the ritual performance – as opposed to merely in the poetic scene – but equally may indicate the resistence of the gesture to omission or alteration in ritual performance. I already have argued that ritual fixity and formality represent a kind of bulwark against a violation of the convention put into effect by the ritual performance, with the most unstable of human conventions tending to be represented

---

[60] O. Taplin points out that fine dress here, as in Phaecia, Troy, and on Olympus, is symbolic of a prosperous and civilized society in Homer. 1980: 1–21.

with the greatest formality and fixity.[61] Oath-making surely qualifies as a foundational institution in Homeric society, and one fraught with problems of instability. As argued in Chapter 1, the very workings of a society depend upon the reliability of oaths, even archaic Greek society, despite the poetic fanfare about clever deceivers such as Odysseus, Hermes, and Autolycus. Hence Homeric oath-making rituals are represented as formal ritual sequences with fixed liturgical components, their fixity a seeming fence against violation and deceit. That the *machaira* is a central instrument in this fence against deceit may explain why references to it in both the initiating and the concluding verses of the ritual are rendered almost identically in the two oath-making scenes of Books 3 and 19. The verse fixity denotes ritual formality.

## CUTTING THE VICTIM'S HAIRS

The next ritual step is the cutting of hair from the victims, also with the *machaira*: "Cutting (*arsxamenos*) hairs from the boar, . . ." (19.254); "he cut [*tamne*] hairs from the heads of the lambs. And next the heralds distributed them to the best of the Achaians and Trojans" (3.273–4). The distribution of the victim's hairs in Book 3 usually is considered to establish a collective identity among the swearing parties and a collective responsibility for upholding the terms represented in the oath-sacrifice.[62] This is in keeping with Bickerman's analysis of Dictys's account of the military leaders wetting the tips of their spears with the blood of a sacrificial victim. Just as the blood invigorates and binds their oath and their collective promise to punish whoever violates the oath, the touching and sharing of cut hair among the leaders in the oath may be interpreted as a bonding ritual among the parties swearing, with all parties committed not only to upholding the oath but also to helping to punish whoever should violate it. The collective responsibility implied by the distribution of hairs seems straightforward enough.

But what of the relationship between the parties holding the hairs and the victim from whom the hair is cut? According to Stengel, the cutting of a victim's hair is analogic for cutting off his head, which is to say, cutting off his life.[63] For Burkert, the act of cutting the animal's hair is

---

[61] In a similar vein, Burkert regards oaths as "attempts at imprinting by construing a common cosmos of meaning, with anxiety lurking at the fringe," in *Creation of the Sacred*, 175.

[62] See, for instance, Kirk 1985: 304.

[63] Stengel 1920: 136.

the beginning of the victim becoming no longer inviolate, implying a first act of aggression that will lead to the animal's death.[64] Both theories are plausible, but they emphasize the aggressive aspects of the gesture at the expense of the end of it, which is where the hairs wind up. But surely there is implied some relationship – beyond the immediate intention of harm – between the animal victim and those who hold its hair. Why hold the cut hairs of the victim if the relationship between swearer and victim has no bearing on the ritual? At least three different explanations come to mind.

Although the same gesture may have different meanings in different ritual contexts, the comparable gestures of cutting and handling hair in oath-sacrifices and in funeral sacrifices is striking – Achilles' hair as held in Patroklos's hands during his funeral (23.151–152), for example, and the other Achaians's hair as thrown upon Patroklos's body (23.135–53). The gesture of hair-offering in Patroklos's funeral rites has been interpreted in various ways over the years, as a mark of hero cult, for instance, or as a substitution for the offerer himself, in a kind of symbolic self-sacrifice to accompany the deceased.[65] The evidence for hero cult is beyond the surface of the Homeric text, but the idea of symbolic substitution is not. Let us attempt to get a glimpse of the ritual logic by examining Achilles' vow not to bathe nor cut his hair until the time for cremating Patroklos:

> "No, by Zeus, who is last and best of the gods,
> it is not customary (*themis*) for a bath to come nearer to my head
> before I put Patroklos on a pyre and pour a funeral mound
> and cut my hair, since a second such grief will not come
> upon me again while I go among the living.
> But now let us be persuaded to the hateful feast."
>
> (23.43–48)

Along with the refusal to bathe and the pouring of a funeral mound, cutting hair is cast by Achilles as a customary component of the grieving ritual, which he waits to fulfill, according to his vow. He also notes that he is cutting his hair now, "since a second such grief will not come upon me while I go among the living," intimating, of course, his proximity to his own death, a theme tied to the well-known *therapon/tarpanalli*-like

---

[64] Burkert 1985: 56; 1983: 5.
[65] These are summarized by Lowenstam 1981: 150–1.

relationship – a matter of possible ritual substitution – between Patroklos and Achilles.[66] A few lines later, in fact, Achilles explicitly equates his gift of hair to his dead companion with his expectation to die in Troy, when he announces to the River Sperchios that he had been growing his hair long so that his father could offer it to the river, along with a sacrificial hecatomb, when Achilles returned home (23.120–149). But now he will not be returning to his fatherland, and "I should like to give [*opasaimi*] my hair to the hero Patroklos to carry" (23.150–51).[67] Without entering into the complex subject of Hittite cultic borrowings, for now, let us observe Christiane Sourvinou-Inwood's seemingly more anthropological point about the identification between mourner and mourned in Greek funeral rituals. Following Aristotle, she points out that self-abuse and refusing to bathe in early Greek death rituals entails a partial identification with the dead: "The embracing of pollution and death entails also a partial identification with the deceased and it is acted out in the pre-burial part of the death-ritual."[68] If cutting the hair is part of these pre-burial death-rituals, constituting a form of self-abuse for purposes of identification with the dead, that Achilles cuts his to give to Patroklos may be assumed to establish a sympathetic link between Achilles and the dead Patroklos.

The coincidence of the ritualized act of cutting and holding hair in both funeral and oath-making rituals does not make for an identical purpose for the act between the two types of ritual, of course. For one thing, the parties holding and cutting the hair in oath-sacrifice and in funeral sacrifice are reversed: It is the living who hold the hair in oath-sacrifice, while they await the victim's death. In funeral sacrifice, the dead hold the hair of the living. Despite this reversal, and although the ritual gesture permits many interpretations, the identical acts of cutting and holding hair in both contexts does at least suggest the probability

---

[66] See, for instance, Sinos 1980, Nagy 1979: 33, et alia, and Lowenstam 1981: 144–59 n.b. 158). The first work advancing the possibility of this identification was, of course, by Van Brock 1959: 227–46.

[67] For an intriguing parallel to dedicating one's hair and cutting it off when abandoning that dedication, see Jeremiah's prophecy against Jerusalem:

> O Jerusalem, cut off your hair,
> the symbol of your dedication,
> and throw it away;
> raise up a lament on the high bare places.
> (Jer. 7: 29)

[68] Christine Sourvinou-Inwood, *Reading Greek Death* (Oxford: Clarendon Press 1995) 111. See also Seaford 1994: 86–92.

that underlying both acts is a similar principle, most likely that of an identification between the holder of hair and the one whose hair has been cut. In the oath-sacrifice, this may be explained most simply as being due to the same fate awaiting the perjurer that was met by the animal victim. This analogical explanation has been touched upon many times thus far in this book.

But the holding of hair is also consistent with Bickerman's notion of strengthening bonds by contact with symbols of the victim's vitality. Within his scheme, contact with the victim's hair, symbolizing his essence, would appear to vitalize the oath. As we argued in the discussion of the purpose of cutting victims in oath-sacrifice, contact with the victim's living substance adds force to the compulsion of the oath, at least in the cases where no other clearly stated principle is attributed to the symbolic act. Hence the handling of the victim's hair would serve to help unite the parties to the oath, as well as to vitalize their oath.[69]

A third interpretation for the hair-cutting in oath-sacrifice might emphasize the act of cutting rather than the substance cut. This indeed is the emphasis of Burkert and Stengel, and also of Fritz Graf. Fritz Graf proposes the notion of persuasive analogy to explain such symbolic actions within the field of Greek magic. Relying upon a facet of Tambiah's theory of ritual communication, Graf argues that the message communicated by certain rituals can be demonstrated by a plethora of symbolic acts, so that the message is repeated at various frequencies or registers,[70] and that it is the various acts rather than the substances acted upon that are key to deciphering the core meaning. In other words, the message is overdetermined. Notably, audiences to the Homeric ritual are given ample opportunity to decipher the metaphors enacted by these symbolic acts in the oath-sacrificing ritual. Poured out wine, cut hair, the sliced necks of victims, and precise curses threatening death to perjurers leave little room for doubt as to the consequence of violating an oath. Each ritual act convincingly dramatizes the consequences of perjury and also identifies

---

[69] One might consider, again, the treatment of Patroklos' corpse, which is made to be in contact with the mourner's hair. Does the contact vitalize the corpse or deaden the mourners? Lowenstam has pointed out the sacrificial aspects to the treatment of Patroklos' corpse, which he deems to be due to the poet's figurative aim to show Patroklos as a sacrificial victim. Lowenstam 1981: 127–57, n.b. 155. The coincidence of the cut hair and the sacrificial connotation in the funeral ritual as well as the oath-making ritual is suggestive.

[70] Fritz Graf, *Magic in the Ancient World*, trans. Franklin Philip (Cambridge, MA: Harvard University Press 1996) 209, building on Tambiah 1979: 132–4.

the fate of the perjurer with the fate of the particular substance manipulated. As Graf might see it in the case of the cut hair, the analogy is in the cutting, with the cutting off of hair representing the cutting off of life, just as the poured libation in Book 3 was tied to the pouring out of life.

For explaining the ritual significance of cutting and holding hair in oath-sacrifices, then, all three possibilities appear to have their merits, and one must admit that a single ritual feature may be polyvalent. In sum, the cutting of the hair may serve to underline the analogy between cutting off hair and cutting off life – linking the fates of oath-swearer and oath-victim – while holding the hair may serve both to create an identity between the victim and swearer and also to add vital force to the oath sworn, based on the principle that hair represents the vital force of the victim.

## HOLDING UP THE HANDS IN PRAYER

Next is the gesture of prayer: "Before them Atreides prayed, holding up his great hands" (3.275–76); "Holding up his hands up to Zeus, he prayed.... Praying he spoke, looking up to the wide heavens" (19.254–257). Holding up the hands as a gesture of prayer is frequently discussed as a typical Homeric prayer feature, but in the *Iliad* it is also an optional one,[71] omitted either because it is presumed, or because it is unessential praying.

The gesture figures conspicuously in formalized petitions to the gods, as when Chriseis prays for the lifting of sanctions against the Achaians, holding up his hands to Apollo (1.450), or when the Trojan women hold up their hands with a ritual cry (*oluluge*) to Athene (6.301). Holding up the hands is a component of the prayers Nestor remembers from the battles in his youth, when he would raise his hands many times to the immortals (7.130–31). It is certainly part of his performance on the battlefield in Book 15, when all of the warriors and he most of all hold up their hands to pray that Zeus should uphold his promise to allow them to return home (15.367–78). The armies on both sides hold up their hands, looking skyward, while praying over the casting of lots before the duel of Ajax and Hector (7.177–180). Holding the hands skyward is also a component of Priam's prayer before his embassy to Achilles, when he tells Hecuba that it is always good to hold up ones hands to Zeus, "if he

---

[71] See outline by J. V. Morrison, "The Function and Context of Homeric Prayers: A Narrative Perspective," *Hermes* 139 (1991) 145–57, in I.M.F. deJonq, ed., *Homer: Critical Assessments Vol.* III, 284–97, n.b. 286.

will show pity" (24.300–01). In each case, the raising of the hands toward the heavens appears to reflect a formal plea to the gods.

On the other hand, a number of prayers in which gods are beseeched for protection or for other favors, lack an explicit reference to the hand gesture. The praying gesture may be only the upward look (as in 7.201–05), or there may be no reported gesture at all (such as in 12.163–73, 16.512–27, 17.46). For instance, there is no mention of hands raised during Agamemnon's pre-sacrificial prayer to Zeus that he be allowed to effect a total demolition of Troy (2.410–32). Diomedes' prayer to Athene for assistance in Book 5 is fully successful, but he is not said to lift his hands (5.113–32). Achilles never lifts his hands in prayer to Zeus, but performs other gestures, such as libating, while looking upward (see 16.231–32, 21.272). Odysseus, on another hand still, prays to Athene "in his heart" without making any obvious gesture at all (23.768–69). Hand gestures thus appear an arbitrary feature of prayers, broadly conceived. When the hand gestures are reported as occurring, the context tends to be at the formal end of the praying spectrum. It is as if, as Rappaport has observed, the prayer is "made heavy" by the accompanying ritual act.

Significantly, hand gestures appear to be part and parcel of the oath-prayers of Books 3 and 19. They are reported with nearly identical phrasing: "Holding up his hands to Zeus, he prayed" (19.254–255); "Before them Atreides prayed, holding up his great hands" (3.275–76). The nearly identical phrasing suggests that raising the hands is an expected feature of the ritual sequence that constitutes oath-sacrifices. To explain the essentiality of the hand-raising gesture in oath-sacrifices, as opposed to in other kinds of prayer, we may enlist Rappaport's invocation of Abrahams (1973) to argue that, for heuristic purposes, there is a correspondence between increasing formality and decreasing spontaneity in cultural ceremonies, with the most formal and least spontaneous end of the cultural spectrum being constituted by "liturgical orders," those "more or less invariant sequences of formal acts and utterances of some duration repeated in specified contexts."[72] The physical gestures may be argued to add formality to the ritual and to cause oaths to weigh in at the least spontaneous end of the ritual spectrum.[73]

[72] Rappaport 1999: 34.

[73] With the correspondence between greater formality and lesser spontaneity in mind, we might characterize the prayers accompanied by hand gestures in oath-sacrifices as *muthoi*, in the sense that Martin describes *muthoi*, as the authoritative speech acts of heroes, which I would have to distinguish from the softer *epos* that Martin sees in prayers generally (Richard P. Martin, *The Language of Heroes* [Ithaca, NY: Cornell

## INVOKING OF WITNESSES

Next is the invoking of witnesses, usually Zeus and the Erinyes, with other divine figures in Book 3, who are to look upon, and witness, the oath. The particular deities invoked and their roles in enforcing prayers were discussed in Chapter 2. It is the act of witnessing and the calling of witnesses that will be of interest here.

It has been suggested that divine witnesses are necessary in the absence of the legal institutions that would impose sanctions on perjurers.[74] True as this may be, it does not take a psychologist to recognize that the invoking of powerful gods heightens the register of the ritual performance and that this heightening of register may serve to imprint the oaths sworn on the minds and memories of the participants, as well as (from their perspective) on the cosmos itself. Indeed, the summoning of the gods as witnesses is a crucial act that identifies formalized oath-rituals on both sides of the Mediterranean in the ancient world. The commonality of this ritual phenomenon points to the shared expectations that gods will respond to ritual acts, will affix power to oaths performed, and will punish violators of those oaths, oftentimes with personal zeal, a matter to be discussed further in our chapter on battlefield theophanies. Hence there is the common Mediterranean swearing feature of affixing curses to oaths: The curses effectively bind both swearers and gods to protect the oaths sworn.

Notably, the speech acts that summon the gods are surrounded with significant ritual acts and are uttered in the special register that characterizes performative illocutions, as described in Chapter 1. Yet the subpoenaing of gods is also more than an illocutionary speech act. Besides establishing its perlocutionary consequences on earth, the oath-prayer is felt also to magically reconfigure the cosmos, by harnessing divine powers to witness and to defend the oaths sworn. The speech acts thus deepen ritual effects to the cosmic sphere and elevate the ritual register to an extraordinary dimension, with Zeus and the Erinyes, usually, understood to respond

University Press 1989] 37–42). This is despite the particular verbs used to denote the speech in prayers. I see these oath-making speech acts as formal prayers with sacral force, that force accentuated by the gesture of raising the hands. I have to disagree with Martin on the small point about the lexicon of praying when it comes to the oath-making sphere. I see no hard and fast line between an *epos* and a *muthos* there, but varying degrees of formality may be discerned by the praying context and by the gestures that accompany the prayers, with oath-prayers standing at the most formal and performative end of the praying spectrum.

[74] Karavites 1992.

to the spoken words of humans.[75] The oath-prayer is ritual gravity at its most profound, a dramatic actualization of a primordial articulation understood to have resounding effects on the universe.

For this reason, the particular features of ritual speech are of interest. Tambiah has discussed some of these features of ritual speech and precisely where they overlap with oral traditional speech. He lists common elements as redundancy and stereotypy, parallelism and formulae, the adaptation of metrical patterns, melodies, and the frequent use of word-clusters, metaphors, and metonyms.[76] The actual ritual utterance Tambiah characterizes as a "stereotyped stream of repeated words intoned with modulations of speed, loudness, and rhythm, thereby foregrounding them as well as telescoping or fusing them into an amalgam that is given motion and direction by compelling illocutionary words of command and persuasion or declaration," whose ultimate purpose is to produce "a sense of heightened and intensified and fused communication."[77] Although we are not privileged to hear the way the bard may have vocalized Agamemnon's prayer, the content of the prayers and the language describing their making give us some sense of it. Agamemnon "prayed, raising his hands to Zeus" – *eucheto cheiras anaschōn*" (3.275); *Dii cheiras anaschōn eucheto* (19.254–55) – *euchomai* being the verb denoting sacral speech when accompanied by the dative of god, according to Muellner's study of *euchomai* in Homeric formulae.[78] The high formality in raising the hands during prayer has already been discussed. The actual content of the prayers consists of "Zeus father, ruler from Ida, greatest and best, and Helios, who watches over all and hears all things, and rivers and earth, and those toiling underneath who punish humans, whoever should swear a false oath. You be witnesses (*humeis marturoi este*), and guard the trusty oaths (*phulassete d'horkia pista*)" (3.276–80); and "Now let Zeus see first (*istō nun Zeus prōta*), highest and best of gods, and Ge and also Helios and the Erinyes who from underground punish humans whosoever should swear a false oath" (19: 258–60). Clearly the honorary titles and defined spheres of influence by which the gods are addressed speak to the stereotypy, formulae, parallelism, and word clusters Tambiah has identified as typical of ritual speech. The gods who are invoked

---

[75] As Aineas puts it, "Zeus helps the prayers of men, even if just a little, when he wishes" (20.242–43).

[76] See also his "The Magical Power of Words," 175–208, n.b. 189–90, and 193.

[77] Tambiah 1979: 131–42.

[78] Muellner 1976: 32–3.

are traditional, have traditional eponyms, and have traditional spheres of interest.

Further, the formality of these titles as well as the use of the second and third person imperatives – "see," "be witness," "defend" – which impel the gods to their witnessing task, speak to Tambiah's sense of "compelling illocutionary words of command and persuasion or declaration" whose ultimate purpose is to produce "a sense of heightened and intensified and fused communication." Note that, unlike in other petitions to the gods, there is no personalized begging of favors based on past history between the petitioner and the god. Instead of negotiating favors or delivering an exposition of some kind, these utterances act essentially to conscript the gods. The very uttering of imperative verbs and honorary titles in a heightened register is understood to draw the gods into the human sphere. These are extraordinary speech acts. Further, I see no reason to suppose that every verse in the bard's performance would be sung with exactly the same intonation and register. One well might imagine that the Homeric bard as well as Agamemnon himself would have vocalized the prayers in a special register, most probably using a somber intonation with a heaviness of rhythm and pace to match the gravity of the oath-claims and the curses that police them. With Tambiah, one might expect that these ways of vocalization would serve to heighten the ritual performance and to intensify the participatory effect on human witnesses, especially when Agamemnon invokes the fearsome Erinyes "toiling underneath who punish humans, whoever should swear a false oath" to witness his speech. Similarly to the speech of a masterful bard, who is expected to awaken audiences from their private, quotidian concerns to larger ones – to "that song whose glory reaches the vast heavens" (Od.8.74) – the speech of the oath-maker may be expected to awaken both human and divine witnesses to the gravity of his promises and to the lethal punishment due perjurers from forces residing in the very earth.

Ritual utterances not only conscript gods, of course, but accomplish other things. For instance, they also establish semantic horizons for the substance of the oath sworn, which they do by verbal act. As Tambiah sees it, all ritual acts have their symbolic capabilities, but verbal acts especially have "the power to invoke images and comparisons, refer to time past and future and relate events which cannot be represented in action."[79] Thus, besides bringing the primordial into the present by invoking traditional ritual paradigms and summoning the gods known to be witnesses

[79] Tambiah 1968: 202.

and defenders of oaths, Agamemnon's speech also constructs a semantic stage for the particular issues tied to the oath. In Book 3, for instance, Agamemnon not only invokes divine punishment in the case of perjury, but also announces his intention to exact from the Trojans *timē* or *poinē*, as the case may be, as part of the outcome of the duel. In Book 19, he builds a semantic stage for the oath both by what he mentions – that he did not touch Briseis – and by what he does not mention – his earlier offer to adopt Achilles into his own family by marrying him to one of his daughters, an offer Achilles explicitly has rejected. The unmentioned offer may linger in the memory of the audience, but the focus of the ritual speech is away from it, and tilts the semantic plane to the quarrel over Briseis, the symbolic heart of the struggle between rival kings.

Further, oaths may be supplemented or embellished by expository stories, such as Agamemnon's preritual lecture on the befuddling power of *Atē*, dangerous even to Zeus, in Book 19. Such expository stories and the contexts in which they are recited mold the narrative significance of the ritual and illuminate larger societal frameworks. Notable by the story of *Atē* is Agamemnon's purposeful diminishing of his own responsibility for the quarrel with Achilles, which reflects Tambiah's point that a ritual performance may not only symbolically or iconically represent the cosmos, but also may serve to indexically legitimate and realize social hierarchies.[80] We discussed the potential for duplicity and the manipulation of social realities through ritual schemes in Chapter 1. Odysseus, Nestor, and Achilles are especially discerning in this kind of ritual savvy, whereas Agamemnon's attempts to use it are undisguised and obtuse.

## CURSING OATH-VIOLATORS

Perhaps the most ominous speech in oath-sacrificing scenes is the curses that conclude the prayers. We have already discussed the symbolic significance of the act of pouring wine that accompanies the curse in Book 3. Let us now examine the precise curse:

> Drawing wine in cups from the bowl,
> they poured it out, and prayed to the gods who always are.
> And so each of the Achaians and Trojans would say,
> "Zeus greatest and best, and all the other immortal gods,
> whoever is first to violate the oaths,
> so may their brains fall to the ground as does this wine,

---

[80] Tambiah 1979: 153. See also Bell 1992.

> and those of their children, and may their wives be subdued
>     by others."
>
> (3.295–301)

The deadly substance of this curse is tantamount to the vaguer curse that
ends Agamemnon's oath in Book 19:

> "If I have sworn any of these things falsely, may the gods give
>     to me pains,
> exceedingly many, as many as they give to anyone who
>     transgresses against them in swearing."
>
> (19.264–65)

Both curses are representations of the "magical missiles" discussed by
Tambiah, and, with their third person imperatives, essentially attempt to
harness punitive forces to harm perjurers.[81] They are equally as forceful,
if not more so, as the summoning of the gods to be witnesses to the oath.
As performative illocutions, curses too manipulate forces felt to reside
in the cosmos, but they invoke those forces directly to inflict punishment
on the perjurer, such as "may their brains fall onto the ground," and
"may the gods give me pains."

Notable in Book 3 is the distributive nuance to the iterative verb
denoting the making of the curse. The verb is common, just *eipesken* –
"each of the Achaians and Trojans would say" (*hōde de tis eipesken Achaiōn
te Trōōn te*) – but in the ritual context its illocutionary force would appear
to be amplified by the distributive nuance. It must have been perceived to
be similar to a chant intoned collectively by a crowd. The stressed, performed, and collective qualities of the curse promote a kind of sacrosanct
register, which grants the curse authority and power.

Arguably, the curse wields power both within the ritual and right
through it beyond the oral poetic scene, effecting a kind of shiver of
recognition, one might expect, in ancient audiences familiar with cursing customs. We have already observed that performative speech-acts
within the oath-sacrificing ritual are, in effect, doubly inscribed, essentially ritual speech within the ritually performed speech of the poem.
Based on the audience's familiarity with the particular ritual traditions
depicted in the poem, it is conceivable that reverberations from curses
within the ritual scene would reverberate right out of it into the audience's recognition of the power behind an actual curse. Considering the
participatory dimension of oral poetic performance and the audience's

---

[81] For a summary of the ritual logic, see Chapter 2.

recognition of primordial paradigms in performed rituals, the audience's recognition of the power behind the oath-curse in the ritual scene would seem to be a matter of recognizing and identifying the curse's effects. This level of recognition is dependent upon our earlier argument about the intertextuality between ritual performances and epic depictions of rituals, and the communicational efficacy of both. By this logic, audiences to the poem are invited to a kind of double witnessing, as witnesses to the poetic scene representing the oath-making ritual and also as witnesses to the performance of the oath-making ritual itself. All of this hinges upon the participatory experience of the listening audience, whose involvement presumably would be excited by the heightened register of the performative speech-acts in cursing verses, similarly to the presumed participation of ritual actors within the ritual scene.

## RITUALIZED KILLING OF A VICTIM

The same kind of chill that emanates from the formalized and collective cursing illocutions might be thought to emanate also from the depiction of the sacrificial death of the oath-victim. This, too, presumably works at interpenetrating levels. That is, the symbolic actions that result in death might be expected to resonate with the ancient audience who hears of the ritual scene, as well as with the witnesses to the oath-victim's death within the epic, at least as the audience would imagine it. Notably, the verses for sacrifice in the killing scenes in Books 3 and 19 are somber and, in effect, identical: "And so he said, and he cut [*tame*] the throats of the [lambs, boar] with the pitiless bronze" (3.292; 19.266). As argued in Chapter 1, The fixity of a ritual scene is likely to be a reflection of ritual formality, and precisely fixed verses are likely to represent ritual notions or gestures that are identified as key elements within the ritual performance. The identical versification in the two scenes highlights the killing act. The audience presumably would recognize in this verse fixity a meaningful signal of ritual formality and gravity.

In light of the fixity of the verse for killing, we also may appreciate the localization of the one obviously figurative expression within this series of finite ritual acts. It is the depiction of the *machaira* as "the pitiless bronze" (*nēlei chalkō*), an expression that occurs at the end of the killing verse in both scenes. The combination of the adjective "pitiless" and the abstract "bronze" is already striking for the deadliness attributed to the *machaira*, as if it were a tool of war rather than of ritual. The assignation of deadliness here contrasts with the knife's role in the *Iliad*'s commensal scenes, where, as pointed out earlier, the *machaira* is never mentioned at all, nor is the animal's death. Yet in oath-sacrificing, the *machaira* is prominent and given the epithet of a killing tool, not once but twice (3: 292; 19.266).

To appreciate the significance of the localization of *nēlei chalkō* at the end of the verse, one must contrast the versification of typical ritual scenes with the versification of typical battlefield scenes. It has been argued on the basis of a study of battlefield killing scenes that the lexical units at the beginning of killing verses tend to bear the greatest semantic weight, while peripheral expressions describing the killing tool, such as "by a spear" – which is semantically redundant because most battlefield killings are by a spear – tend to be localized toward the end of the line and permit a variety of metrical and lexical substitutions that fit the end of the hexameter verse. The semantic weight of such peripheral expressions in killing scenes is deemed secondary to the nuclear element of killing, which is the verse's essential message.[82] It should be noted, however, that the lexical flexibility of battlefield scenes is much greater than the flexibility of ritual scenes. The versification of wartime killings has to be flexible in order to suit the fast-moving pace of battle and the shifting narrative contents, whereas ritual scenes tend to be rendered in relatively fixed phrasing because they reflect paradigms that are regarded as primordially set (see Chapter 1). Hence the verse "And so he said, and he cut the throat of the [lambs, boar] with the pitiless bronze" is in essence identical in both scenes. As argued in our discussion of methodology, the fixity of ritual verses does not empty them of significance; rather, the fixity of ritual verses and of ritual scenes in general may reflect a poetic gravity resulting from the projection of the paradigmatic over the syntagmatic axis. This poetic gravity invites a different aesthetic scale for weighing the so-called peripheral elements. "With the pitiless bronze" at the verse end in scenes that depict rituals may therefore retain a different semantic weight than "by a spear" at the end of a killing verse in the context of the battlefield. Simply, because of the relatively stiff sequence of ritual acts (and the fixity of the verses expressing those acts in the ritual scenes) localization patterns count. Localization patterns in ritual scenes bear different significations than they do in battlefield killing scenes.

---

[82] See Egbert Bakker and Florence Fabbricotti, "Peripheral and Nuclear Semantics in Homeric Diction," *Mnemosyne* XLIV: 1–2 (1991) 63–84, and Edzard Visser, "Formulae or Single Words?" *Warzburger Jahrbucher fur die Altertumswissenschaft* 14 (1988) 21–37.

Further, because ritual scenes are characterized by concrete detail and a series of precise, finite, microadjusting verbs that reflect a series of ritualized acts (see Muellner's analysis of praying scenes), figurative expressions are both rare and significant. "With the pitiless bronze" as a figurative expression for the *machaira* at the end of the killing verse in a ritual scene is conspicuous. It is impossible not to notice this figurative phrase, given that it follows a cluster of finite verbs representing concrete behavioral microadjustments and ritual detail. Based on this contrast, the localization of this lone figurative expression is arguably significant and may even be argued to effect a kind of semantic tilt toward the end of the line. The idea of an end-of-line semantic tilt for purposes of emphasis might be supported by the reputed expectation of oral-traditional audiences that the end of a hexameter verse would mark the end of a semantic unit. Milman Parry once noted that the tendency for a verse end to reflect the end of the semantic unit occurs more than twice as often for Homer as it does for the literate poets,[83] and many others have argued that patterns of lexical localization may be a significant factor for the communication of verse nuance.[84] John Miles Foley, for instance, discusses the consistent tendency (99 percent consistent, according to Foley) for sense units in a line of hexameter to break into two unequal hemistiches at masculine or feminine caesura. Foley has even discerned a tendency he calls "right justification," wherein the texture of a metrical unit consists of a clustering of dactyls at the unit's end (this applies to both lines and half-lines). He also notes a tendency for metrically larger compositional units to be located to the right of the line.[85] He further observes that certain noun-epithet phrases, such as the well-known "winged words," tend to have a favored location in a line and that localization tendencies persist when the noun-epithet phrase is combined with other verse constituents to form a whole line formula, such as the familiar "and to him [speaking, pleading, or some other participle] he spoke winged words."[86] This may be correlated with Gregory Nagy's finding that favorite phrases

[83] Milman Parry, "Enjambemenst in Homeric Verse," in *The Making of Homeric Verse*, ed. Adam Parry (New York: Oxford University Press 1987) 251–65, n.b. 265. See also Carolyn Higbie, *Measure and Music: Enjambement and Sentence Structure in the Iliad* (Oxford: Clarendon Press 1990) 8–9.

[84] See particularly Higbie 1990: n.b. 8–9; Mark Edwards, *Homer, Poet of the Iliad* (Baltimore: Johns Hopkins University Press 1987) 11; and Foley 1991.

[85] Foley 1991: 73–85.

[86] Foley 1991: 129–37, 155–7.

may generate favorite rhythms, around which larger verses may be built.[87] These arguments support the claim that meter and localization patterns may be significant factors for texturing individual verses and that localization patterns may affect verse nuance. Hence, end-of-line formulae in the verses that comprise ritual scenes may bear significant, if traditional, connotations, and may even tilt the emphasis toward the end of the verse.

The semantic weight of "with the pitiless bronze," *nēlei chalkō*, at the end of the line might be gauged also by examining a few metrically and aurally similar expressions that happen to fall at the end of the line elsewhere. Perhaps the most spectacular comparison with *nēlei chalkō* is *nēlees hemar*, pitiless day, a match for verse position and meter that occurs at least three times. One occurrence is at 11.484 – "Darting with his spear, [Odysseus] warded off the pitiless day." "Pitiless day" is obviously a synonymous expression for fate, or pitiless death, in this verse, as it is again when Achilles reflects upon the survival of Lykaon, who has come before Achilles a second time – "fleeing his pitiless day" (21.57). In both cases a similar deadliness is implied for "pitiless day" as for "pitiless bronze," and both occur as end-of-verse formulae. The same emphasis is apparent in Nestor's remonstration to Zeus that he remember his earlier nod and promise to the Argives to ward off "the pitiless day" (15.375). This "pitiless day" also falls at the same slot in the line and is parallel for meter and verse position with *nēlei chalkō*, pitiless bronze.[88] Aurally and metrically similar pairs with similar patterns of verse localization, such as *nēlei chalkō* and *nēlees hēmar*, are examples of the phenomenon Milman Parry, and after him Michael Nagler, referred to as "calembour," a notion that has been bandied about by Homeric scholars for generations. Although mine is surely not the concluding word, allow me to suggest that the expression "with the pitiless bronze" – because it is the only figurative expression in the whole ritual scene, because of the pitilessness it ascribes to the abstracted "bronze," and because of the ritual gravity of the act the "bronze" performs – weights the verse nuance toward the line end and enhances the gravity of the ritual killing. Similar-sounding verse-ending formulae, such as *nēlees hēmar* and *nēlei chalkō*, support the idea that in certain circumstances, particularly ritual circumstances, an audience might expect a certain dramatic weight at the end of the verse.

---

[87] Nagy 1990: 18–35.

[88] A different kind of formulaic resonance might be felt in the formula *nēlees ētor* (9.497), pitiless heart, which falls at the beginning of the line in Book 9, when Phoinix admonishes Achilles that is it not necessary to have such a pitiless heart.

As for the significance of animal killing in oath-sacrifice, I have already argued for a mixture of the different interpretations usually given, the analogical threat to perjurers being one of those and the invigorating of the promise being another. Yet it is also apparent that the killing of the animal is, if not absolutely the final moment, then at least the clinching moment of the ritual performance. In addition to dramatizing the oath-bond and the consequences for its breaking, the killing of the animal is essentially the final effect, a mirror of the irreversible facticity established by the ritual and proportional in theatrical depth to the drama in the victim's dying. The theatrical force of the ritual act is reflected in the fixity of the verse depicting the killing, by the subsequent depiction of the victim's last moments, and by the high register of the whole performance. We discussed the matter of the irreversible facticity established by rituals earlier when we discussed the appearance of ritual orders as natural orders and discussed the brute facts that rituals may bring into existence. As pointed out in Chapter 1, brute facts such as ritual scarring or killing contribute substantiality to the ritual's semantic force by being observable, often visceral, and irreversible. Their apparent effects may be more persuasive than any words describing them and may deliver their own dramatic punch. That dramatic punch may impress its own truth on participants independent of any outward belief in the stated analogies or ritual traditions involved,[89] due in part to the difficulty of resisting the persuasiveness of the elevated ritual register and symbolic acts, and due in part to the participants' natural tendency to identify with the victim on the ritual stage.

The identification of the participant with the victim is suggested here in substance by the focus on the animal's last moments after its throat is slit: "And he put [the lambs] on the ground, gasping and emptied of life (*thumos*), for the bronze had taken away their might (*menos*)" (3.293–94); "Talthybios hurled [the boar], setting him whirling into the great abyss of the sea, to be food for fish" (19.267–68). Many scholars have observed the humanized depiction of the dying lambs in book 3, and I myself have argued for an echo of the sacrificial killing of the boar in Book 19 in Achilles' stabbing the neck of Lykaon and hurling his corpse into the wide bosom of the sea, where fish shall nibble at it, in Book 21.[90] The boar's fate as "food for fish" echoes similar fates for Achilles' other

[89] A point observed of ritual performances in Senegal by Smith 1979: 103–28, n.b. 104 and 126.
[90] Kitts 2000: 103–24, and 1999: 42–57.

victims by the river in Book 21, and the death of the lambs in Book 3 seems clearly to be prophetic for the fate of the Trojans, similarly to the spilling of wine, which is stated explicitly to anticipate the spilling of the perjurers' brains.

Unlike the wine, however, the plight of the lambs in Book 3 is focalized with an ear for the victim's painful last gasps. The association of gasping and exhaling (*aspairontas, asthmainontas*) with dying is notable when breathing verbs are ascribed to victims in a handful of dying scenes on the battlefield. For instance, Asteropaios exhaled (*asthmainonta*) his *thumos* when Achilles killed him at the beginning of his fight with the rivergod (21.182). Also killed by Achilles, Hippodamas exhaled (*aisthe*) his *thumos* like a bull being sacrificed for Poseidon (20.403). Thracians gasped (*aspairontas*) when Diomedes and Odysseus slaughtered them in the night (10.521). While dying, Adamas gasped (*ēspair'*) like an ox dying by human blows (13.571). Medon exhaled (*aisthmainon*) as he was struck in the temple and fell from the chariot (5.585). Asios's charioteer did the very same thing (13.399).[91] These gasping and panting verbs in verses for dying on the battlefield clearly give the audience a relentless view of the victim's last moments, to full dramatic effect. It is intriguing that the victims who die gasping and panting like sacrificial lambs are on the Trojan side, given the Trojan culpability as perjurers of the oath in Book 3. Yet there also appears to be a bigger comment here. When lambs dying in oath-sacrifice are ascribed the characteristics of men dying on the battlefield, a metaphorical transference is implied between dying in oath-sacrifice and dying in battle.

This last step brings us to the larger picture of ritual as promoting metaphorical transformation for participants.

## RITUAL PERFORMANCE AS METAPHORICAL TRANSFORMATION

He lay there stretched out, and his dark blood ran from him and moistened the earth.                                                                     (13.655; 21.119)

To explore this metaphorical transference further, let us examine a few features of the oath-sacrificing spectacle for its resonance with killings and dyings on the battlefield. This will take us into an analysis of the oath-making ritual as negotiating a metaphorical transformation of the

---

[91] See Kitts 2003.

participants, which in turn will help us to apply Ricoeur's theory of metaphor to the "ritual fictions" communicated by ritual performances.

It is significant that the verb for cutting the throat in oath-sacrifice is the simple *tamnō*, "I cut," as opposed to the verb *sphazdō*, "I slaughter" or ostensibly "I cut the throat" that one finds in commensal sacrifices in the *Iliad*. *Tamnō* as used in the *Iliad*'s oath-sacrifices is at once more concrete and also more deadly than *sphazdō*. In fact, the verb *sphazdō* in the commensal sacrifices may seem relatively abstract, containing, as it reputedly does (per Liddell and Scott), the notion of cutting the throat, considering that no throats are mentioned and, with the exception of the funeral feast of Patroklos – which elicits its own *topos* – the very death of the victim is totally ignored. Instead, typically in commensal sacrifice, the victim is restrained, its head is bent back, and it is simply *"esphaxan."* Not a single word, not even a killing tool is mentioned to describe its death. Immediately after the verb *esphaxan*, the victim is flayed and its thighs are cut out, wrapped in fat, braised with wine libations, and tasted, after which the rest of the animal is cut into bits, skewered, cooked over fire, then drawn off and eaten (1.459–470; 2.410–432). There is a conspicuous silence in this procedure regarding not only the victim's death, but also its blood.[92] The bloodlessness is remarkable, first, considering the fastidious detail in the sacrificial description: Why should the blood be left out? Second, it is remarkable considering the undoubtedly bloody work of butchering a large animal. Third, it is remarkable considering the Classical procedure of draining the animal's blood so that its meat can be cooked and eaten.[93] No such draining is mentioned in the *Iliad*. Nor, admittedly, is blood mentioned in the exact ritual sequence of oath-sacrifice in the *Iliad*, but it is inferred to be one of three identifying features of the ritual when Agamemnon curses the perjuring Trojans with punishment linked to "the blood of lambs, the unmixed libations and the right hands in which we trusted," all of which are "in no way barren" (4.158–9). Further, scholars since at least Guthrie have noted that blood tends to be a core feature of Greek chthonic sacrifices,[94] in which the animal's blood dains into the earth. Oaths are usually, and rightfully, deemed chthonic sacrifices.

As for the portrayal of the victim's dying – in contrast to the oblique killing of the victim of commensal sacrifice – the victim in oath-sacrifice explicitly is cut: "and he cut the throat[s] ... with the pitiless bronze"

---

[92] But see for comparison Od. 3.417–72.
[93] Bruitt Zaidman and Schmitt Pantel, 1996: 28–36.
[94] See Guthrie 1955: 221.

(*stomachon . . . tame nēlei chalkō* 3.292, 19.266). Although in Book 19 the animal's dying moments are eclipsed by the dramatic gesture of disposing of its corpse ("Talthybios hurled him, whirling, into the great abyss of the sea, to be food for fish" [19 267–268], in Book 3, the gash in the lambs' throats precipitates a gasping that leads to a very vivid dying: "And he put [the lambs] on the ground, gasping (*aspairontas*) and emptied of life (*thumos*), for the bronze had taken away their might (*menos*)" (3.293–94). The killing effect is triply reenforced in these lines by the variously conjugated verbs for gasping, emptying, and depriving. In effect, the lambs gasp out their lives, they are emptied of *thumos*, as the "bronze" deprives them of *menos*. In comparing the *Iliad*'s commensal and oath-sacrificing rituals, then, there could be no greater contrast than that denoted by *sphazdō* and by *tamnō* for representing the killing feature of animal sacrifice.

We might learn more about some connotations of the verb *tamnō* by examining the *Iliad*'s uses of the compound verb, *deirotomeō*, a relative of *tamnō* combined with a word for throat or neck (*deire*). *Deirotomeō*, to cut the throat or neck, is used five times in the *Iliad*, each time to describe a killing, or planned killing, by Achilles after learning of the death of Patroklos. Each use is conspicuous for its sacrificial nuance. The first use is in Achilles' lament for Patroklos in Book 18, when he promises to *appodeirotomeō*, to cut the throats clear through, of twelve Trojans youths as a demonstration of his anger (*cholōtheis*) over Patroklos' death (18.336–37), a promise he fulfills during the funeral sacrifice, where he is described as having cut the throats (*deirotemēsas*) of "two table dogs, and twelve good sons of the greathearted Trojans, destroying them with the bronze" (23.174–76). I discussed the *cholos* of Achilles in my treatment of *poinē* as a ritual leitmotif, in Chapter 2.

Given the fulfillment of this promise to cut the throats of the 12 Trojan youths at the funeral of Patroklos, it is worth noting that *appodeirotomeō* in both instances signals nothing short of human sacrifice. Scholars and particularly archeologists have studied the possible customs behind this report of human sacrifices at the pyre of Patroklos, and have argued about the historical implications for ancient funereal rituals. While the debate is ongoing regarding the historicity and cultural reasoning behind such a custom, the poet's thinking is less debatable. Homer makes Achilles' killing of the boys appear as a premeditated act of ritualized revenge. This is the way that Hughes interprets the killings,[95] and it is also in

---

[95] D. Hughes 1991: 54. He discusses the preeminent literature on Patroklos's funeral ritual at 49–70.

keeping with my earlier argument about *poinē* as a ritual leitmotif that configures Achilles' behavior along the line of a paradigmatic axis. The killing is granted an explicit revenge motive by Achilles in Book 18, as we have noted, and again in Book 23, when he reports to dead Patroklos that he has the twelve good Trojan youths ready to *apodeirotomēsein* before his pyre, in anger (*cholos*) for his death. Notably, he uses there virtually the same words he used in Book 18: *dōdeka de proparoithe purēs apodeiro-tomēsein Trōōn aglaa tekna, sethen ktamenoio cholōtheis* (23.22–23). The same basic verb, *deirotomeō*, is used again when they actually are sacrificed: "*deirotomēsas* them [cutting their throats] he threw two [dogs] on the fire and twelve good sons of the greathearted Trojans, destroying them with the bronze" (23.174–76)[96] which is followed by a statement of his mood, "vile were the deeds he devised in his mind" (23.176).[97] Whether Achilles cuts their throats before (*proparoithe* [18.336]) or on (*eneballe* [23.174]) the pyre of Patroklos,[98] that the poet makes Achilles cut human throats in deliberate revenge for Patroklos's death seems indisputable based on these passages.

Before discussing the other passages with *deirotomeō*, it is worth pointing out that the sacrificial connotation to revenge killing is amply attested in Near Eastern rhetoric, especially from Mesopotamia in the first millennium before the common era. Just a few examples will make the point. Assyrian king Ashurbanipal (668–626 BCE) explicitly invokes the motif of revenge to explain his slaughter of humans to his grandfather's shade during his sixth campaign against Babylonia:

"As for those men (and) their vulgar mouths, who uttered vulgarity against Ashur, my god, and plotted evil against me, the prince who fears him, – I slit their mouths [v. Tongues] and brought them low. The rest of the people, alive, by the colossi, between which they had cut down Sennacherib, the father of the father who begot me, . . . at that time I cut down those people there, as an offering to his shade. Their dismembered bodies [lit. flesh] I fed to the dogs, swine, wolves, and eagles, to the birds of heaven and the fish of the deep."[99]

---

[96] Presumably the *machaira* is meant by "the bronze."

[97] Obviously, I disagree with Hughes in his dismissal of any ritual significance in the use of the verbs *appodeirotomeo* and *deirotomeo* (Hughes 1991 at 52).

[98] A matter of possible significance for understanding funeral sacrifice, according to Hughes 1991.

[99] Section 795 in Luckenbill 1968.

More generalized sacrificial connotations are attested in this Assyrian battle boast by Sennarcharib (705–681 BCE) against the sons and nobles of Merodachbaladan of Elam:

> Like fat steers who have hobbles put on them, – speedily I cut them down and established their defeat. I cut their throats like lambs. I cut off their precious lives [as one cuts] a string. Like the many waters of a storm, I made [the contents of] their gullets and entrails run down upon the wide earth. My prancing steeds, harnessed for my riding, plunged into the streams of their blood as [into] a river. The wheels of my war chariot, which brings low the wicked and the evil, were bespattered with blood filth. With the bodies of their warriors I filled the plain, like grass. [Their] testicles I cut off, and tore out their privates like the seeds of cucumbers of Simanu [June]. . . . "I overpowered them like a bull."[100]

Elsewhere Esarhaddon (680–669 BCE) relies on the same motif: "The people of Hilakku, who dwell in the high mountains, I slaughtered like lambs,"[101] and "In the anger of my heart I made an assault upon Kutha; the troops about its walls I slaughtered like lambs, and took the city."[102] Nor is the Bible exempt from using sacrificial motifs for battlefield vengeance:

> For the sword of the Lord appears in heaven.
> See how it descends in judgment on Edom,
> on people whom he dooms to destruction.
> The Lord has a sword steeped in blood,
> it is gorged in fat,
> the fat of ram's kidneys, and the blood of lambs and goats;
> for he has a sacrifice in Bozrah,
> a great slaughter in Edom
> Wild oxen shall come down and buffaloes with them,
> bull and bison together
> and the land shall drink deep of blood
> and the soil be sated with fat.
> For the Lord has a day of vengeance,
> the champion of Zion has a year when he will requite
> (Isaiah 34.5–8).[103]

---

[100] Section 254 in Luckenbill 1968.
[101] Section 329 in Luckenbill 1968.
[102] Section 259 in Luckenbill 1968.
[103] On these themes in the Bible, see Niditch 1993.

Notably, the sacrificial motif for slaughter on the battlefield is often explained by reference to oaths made and broken. Hence this by Ashurbanipal:

"Every curse, written down in the oath which they took, was instantly visited upon them by Ashur, Sin, Shamash, Adad, Bel, Nabu, Ishtar of Nineveh, the queen of Kidmuri, Ishtar of Arbela, Urta, Nergal [and Nusku]. The young of camels, asses, cattle and sheep, sucked at seven udders and could not satisfy their bellies with the milk. The people of Arabia asked questions, the one of the other, saying: "Why is it that such evil has befallen Arabia?"... saying "Because we did not keep the solemn oaths sworn to Ashur."[104]

Many dozens of actual treaty curses make the same equation, such as this threat to perjurers in the succession treaty of Esarhaddon: "Just as [thi]s ewe has been cut open and the flesh of [her] young has been placed in her mouth, may they make you eat in your hunger the flesh of your brothers, your sons and your daughters,"[105] and "Just as young sheep and ewes and male and female spring lambs are slit open and their entrails rolled down over their feet, so may (your entrails and) the entrails of your sons and your daughters roll down over your feet."[106]

It is perhaps not surprising that the rhetoric of oath-sacrificing and cursing would lend itself to figurative expressions for battlefield killing in the ancient world. As explained above, the ritual killing in oath-sacrifice is presented as high drama and in unmistakably symbolic terms. Agamemnon promises that the symbolic terms will be fulfilled by Zeus with vengeance when Agamemnon curses the Trojans for their failure to honor the terms sealed by blood-sacrifice in Book 3:

"Not barren is the oath, the blood of lambs,
the unmixed libations and the right hands in which we trusted.
For indeed, if the Olympian does not fulfill it at once,
he certainly will fulfill it later, and with might he will avenge it,
with their lives and their wives and also their children."

(4.158–162)

---

[104] Section 828 in Luckenbill 1968.
[105] From Parpola and Watanabe 1988: Section 69 (p. 52).
[106] Parpola and Watanabe 1988: 52. Section 70. A similar quid pro quo is implied by Saul when "the spirit of God seized him" and he enacted an implicit treaty-curse: "In his anger he took a pair of oxen and cut them in pieces, and sent messengers with the pieces all through Israel to proclaim that the same would be done to the oxen of any man who did not follow Saul and Samuel into battle" (I Sam 11: 7).

Based on these examples, it would not be adventurous to assert that battlefield killing is occasionally cast as sacrificial killing in first millennium Near Eastern and Mediterranean literature, and that the sacrificial motif seems to impose ritual gravity on the reports of battlefield killing. By making Achilles sacrifice the Trojan youths on the pyre of Patroklos, the poet exploits the overlapping semantic domains among killing in revenge, killing in battle, and killing in sacrifice.

A more subtle exploitation of this sacrificial motif occurs in the account of Achilles' killing of Lykaon in the first part of Book 21, where the verb *deirotomeō* appears again. The significance of the verb in this scene is illuminated partly by the setting and partly by the sequence of gestures Achilles performs when killing Lykaon, which mirrors the sequence of gestures in oath-sacrifice. The stage is set in the first ten lines, whose aural rumblings foreshadow the upcoming theomachia. Men fall into the river with the *megalō patagō*, the streams bray (*brache*), and the riverbanks shriek (*iachon*) (21.9–10), which anticipates the forthcoming *megalō patagō* of gods falling together in battle, the braying (*brache*) of the wide earth, and the quaking (*salpingxen*) of the great heavens later in the book (21.387–88). The cacophony is unmistakable, as is the surreal tinge to the first killings, when Achilles leaps "resembling a daimon" (21.18) upon his victims in the river, stabbing and cutting until an unseemly groan arose (21.20) and the river's waters ran with blood (21.21). Then, wearying of that, he collects the twelve Trojan youths, "stunned like fawns," to be living *poinē* for Patroklos (21.26–32), essentially to become victims of *deirotomia*.

This leads directly to his encounter with the young unarmed Lykaon, a half-brother to Hector. Lykaon is no stranger to Achilles, having benefitted from Achilles' relative generosity the first time they met, when Achilles abducted the boy from the orchard near his home and, rather than kill him, took him to Lemnos and sold him as a slave. Lykaon was ransomed by a family friend and sent home to his mother just eleven days prior (21.35–45). Lykaon's new encounter with Achilles is a piteous and relatively long narrative of 99 lines, with Lykaon supplicating Achilles at his knees and begging for pity based on their once-shared "meal of Demeter,"[107] on the fact that Lykaon is not a "womb-mate" (*homogastrios*) of Hector "who killed your gentle and strong companion" (21.96), and on the plight of his mother, who bore him to be but brief (21.84–85[108]).

---

[107] On the maternal, agricultural, and sacrificial imagery in this scene, see my "Wide Bosom of the Sea," 103–24.

[108] As did Achilles' own mother at 1.352.

She is in fact soon to be bereaved of both of her sons. Her younger son Polydoros was already stabbed in the back by Achilles as the boy was running away (20.407–18), but Lykaon doesn't report the killing as it happened in Book 20. Instead he says, "we two sons were born to her, and you will *deirotomēseis* us both" (21.89). The use of the verb *deirotomeō* in this setting helps to construct Lykaon's pitiable circumstance as an ill-fated and vulnerable victim.

Achilles kills Lykaon with what appears to be a mock ritual for oath-sacrifice. The killing is initiated by a clear statement of Achilles' implacability, when he responds to Lykaon's petition for suppliance. First, Achilles rejects the logic of Lykaon's appeal based on the boy's maternal identity as a non-*homogastrios* of Hector – no son of Priam is to escape (21.99–105), no matter who his mother. Second, he will refuse to pity Lykaon's mother – she will not be allowed to place him on a bier and wail for him, but eddying Scamander will bear him into the wide bosom of the sea (21.123–125). Achilles does, however, seems to recognize that Lykaon's plea based on their past "meal of Demeter" has some merit. Although earlier personified as a daimon (21.18[109]), Achilles now is perfectly lucid in calling Lykaon a "*philos*," already argued to bear affinities with *hiketēs* and *xeinos*, and in explaining the pointlessness of resistence. There was a time when Achilles was likely to spare suppliants, and export them for sale rather than kill them (he says) but that was before Patroklos met his fate. Now, both Achilles and Lykaon must die:

> "Nonetheless, *philos*, you too must die. Why mourn in this way?
> Even Patroklos has died, and he was far better than you.
> And do you not see the sort of man I am, fine and great?
> I am of a good father, and the mother who bore me was a goddess.
> Even so, death and strong fate are on me too, you know.
> It may be during dawn or the afternoon or the middle of the day.
> When someone in battle will take my life from me,
> Either striking me with a spear or with an arrow from a bow."
> (21.106–113)

Hearing Achilles' implicit comparison of their mothers – both shall suffer the loss of sons – and explicit comparison of their fates, Lykaon realizes that Achilles will not pity him. Then his limbs and "dear heart" give way, he releases his grip on Achilles' spear, and he sits, his arms outstretched on both sides (21.114–16). Drawing his sharp sword, Achilles strikes down

---

[109] (And again at 21.228.)

on Lykaon's collar bone along the neck (*kata klēida par'auchena*), and the sword penetrates all the way through. Then, "prone on the earth, stretched out, / he lay, and his dark blood ran from him and wet the earth" (21.118–119). Note the three indicative verbs in the dying verse of 119.

Before examining the disposal of the corpse, let us scrutinize this killing and manner of death. Achilles has cut Lykaon at, or at least very near, the throat, just as Lykaon anticipated when he predicted that his mother would see his death as a second *deirotomia* ("two sons were born to her and you will cut the throats of us both"). Lykaon's status as an unprotesting victim – reminiscent of some excurses on the Bouphonia[110] – is all too apparent. As a suppliant, he had been clinging to Achilles' knees and spear, one hand to each. Now he releases his grips, as well as his personal hold on his own limbs and his *philon ētor*, seemingly his very will to live. He sits back, arms outstretched, awaiting death. After he is stabbed in the neck, he falls face down on the earth and his blood runs out and wets the earth, similarly to the wine in the oath of Book 3, or presumably to the blood of lambs, as insinuated in Agamemnon's curse "no way barren is the blood of lambs, the unmixed libations" (4.158–59). Wetting the earth with blood is of course a common feature of chthonic sacrifices (such as the *nekyia* of the *Odyssey*), where, similarly to wine libations (see 23: 220–221), the blood establishes a link between humans and the world of infernal powers.[111] Lastly, the clustering of three indicative verbs in the dying verse is reminiscent of the clustering of finite verbs Muellner sees as characteristic of ritual scenes.[112] The cluster of indicative verbs not only makes the dying vivid, but gives it a ritualized nuance.

What happens next particularizes this ritualized nuance. Achilles takes Lykaon by the foot and hurls him into the river to be borne into the sea, at which point Achilles boasts (*epeuchomenos*) to Lykaon,

> "Lie there now with the unpitying fishes, who will nip
> at your bloody wound. Your mother will not lay you on a bier
> and wail for you, but eddying Scamandrous
> will bear you in to the wide bosom of the sea.
> Leaping, a fish will dart up from the ripples along the dark waves,
> and eat the white fat of Lykaon."
>
> (21.122–127)

---

[110] See Marcel Detienne, "The Spice Ox," in *The Gardens of Adonis* (Chicago: Princeton: Princeton University Press 1994) 37–59.

[111] Bruitt-Zaidman and Schmitt-Pantel 1994: 41.

[112] Muellner 1976.

Similarly to the boar in Book 19, Lykaon is hurled into the water. He is hurled not quite into "the great abyss of the sea," as is the boar (19.267), but to be borne into "the wide bosom of the sea" (21.125). The two expressions are parallel for verse position and meter, as well as for general meaning. Similarly to the boar, who will become "food for fish," Lykaon will be devoured by fish – "leaping, a fish will dart up from the ripples along the dark waves and eat the white fat of Lykaon." Perhaps most ironically, Achilles' death boast over Lykaon is rendered as an *ep*-prayer (*ep-euchomenos*) plus the dative. As Muellner established in his study of Homeric prayer formulae, the Homeric use of *euchomai* plus the dative of god is an elliptical way to report a prayer. Hence we have the *eucheto* plus the dative of god in the prayer that accompanies the oath-sacrifice in Book 19 (*Dii cheiras anaschōn/eucheto* 19.254–5), and in a number of other prayers we have outlined. In the killing of Lykaon, however, the dative object of the prayer is not a god, but a victim, which suits the macabre tone of this sacrifice. The *ep*-prefix with *euchomai*, together usually constituting "boast," arguably signals here the same kind of contemptuous oath as the *epi-orkon* Agamemnon swears not to have made, when he pronounces a hypothetical self-curse at the end of the oath-sacrifice in Book 19. The *ep*-prefix appears to be the narrator's way of signaling a mock-prayer, consistent with the macabre tone of this mock-sacrifice.

Hence the mapping of oath-sacrificing features onto the slaughter of Lykaon in Book 21 is subtle but perceivable, marked especially by the assignment of *deirotomia* to the killing and colored surreally by the theomachia-like imagery at the start of the book to the *ep*-prayer over the corpse when it is hurled into the sea. The particular features combine to create a distorted facsimile of an oath-sacrifice. Those features include (a) the anticipation of Lykaon's death as a *deirotomia*, (b) the pitiable vision of Lykaon as an unprotesting and unarmed victim (c) his death by a wound at the neck, comparable to the boar's and the lambs' deaths by cutting the throat, (d) the seeping of his blood into the earth, a common feature of chthonic sacrifice[113] and a match with the wine libation in Book 3, (e) the disposal of his corpse by hurling into the sea–going waters, as the boar in Book 19 is hurled, whirling, into the "great abyss of the sea," (f) the fate of both corpses as food for fish, and (g) the conclusion of the ritual by a prayer-curse based on *euchomai*, not with the dative of god as in the Homeric praying formula (per Muellner), but with the *ep*-prefix and the dative of Lykaon. The whole narrative is darkly cast and the sacrificial

---

[113] See Guthrie 1955: 221.

features help to shape the killing of the boy into a skewed and sinister human sacrifice.

The last use of *deirotomeō* is also in Book 21, although any obvious sacrificial features are missing. Instead it is used when Agenor ponders at length his various options for surviving a fight with Achilles. This, too, is a relatively long narrative. Agenor considers joining the others who have been put to rout by Achilles toward the city, or else running to seek shelter in the pastures and mountain valleys of Ida. Then he dismisses running away because, "even so, he will seize me as a coward and cut my throat" (*analkida deirotomēsei*; 21.555). Because fleeing is guaranteed such a pitiable end, Agenor does eventually fight with Achilles, but is spared death because Apollo intervenes to save him. This narrative is similar to that of Lykaon primarily in the pitiableness it ascribes to the prospect of being killed without a fight. Achilles would *deirotomēsei* Agenor in his cowardice, as he did Lykaon in his. Indeed, all of these narratives with *deirotomeō* imply being killed as an unprotesting victim, and all of the killings are conducted by Achilles.

The notion of battlefield victims as sacrificial victims and of warriors as sacrificers brings us back to the theory of ritual performance as fostering metaphorical transformation, which relies in turn on the model of ritual as communication and, regarding ritual scenes, of typical scenes as particular hypostases of underlying Gestalts. We shall apply these in reverse order.

First, regarding typical scenes and their underlying Gestalts, one might observe right off that the verb *deirotomeō* in Lykaon's anticipation of his mother's view of his death is a veritable flag for the sacrificial scene to come, given the connotation of victimization we have seen tied to the word in all of its occurrences and given the cutting of throats that occurs in actual oath-sacrifices. The imposition of a series of oath-sacrificing markers on Lykaon's slaughter has already been established. Using Nagler's analysis, the net effect might be compared to the bursting forth (the *sphuṭ*) of meaning, triggered by independent linguistic elements occurring "in the happy synergism of a meaningful pattern" and generating "an artistic entity (a *sphoṭa*), which is somehow greater than the sum of its parts."[114] In this case, the artistic entity generated is the rendering of a battle-field killing as a human sacrifice. One of its independent but constituent linguistic elements would be, for instance, the hurling of Lykaon's corpse into the "wide bosom of the sea," which might be grasped by audiences as an iconic analogue to the swinging of the boar's corpse into

[114] Nagler 1974: 85.

"the abyss of the grey sea" in the oath-sacrificing ritual two books earlier. As we have said, the phrases happen to be equivalent for meter and verse position. The fate of the corpse might also arouse images tied to more general chthonic sacrificial patterns: The seeping of blood into the earth, in Lykaon's case from his wound at the neck, is not attested in the oath-sacrifice of Book 19, but is part of a general pattern for Greek chthonic sacrifices, wherein an animal is cut at the neck and its blood pours into the earth.[115] By the theory discussed in Chapter 1, the whole scene might be considered to represent a skewed hypostasis of the oath-sacrificing Gestalt, drawing the bulk of its sacrificial shape from the sacrifice of the boar in Book 19, while its pathetic connotation takes shape in that intermediate sphere between the preverbal template for oath-sacrifice and the exigencies of the immediate narrative situation, which happens to describe Achilles' waging of a pitiless war of vengeance. As we may recall, Nagler characterized that intermediate sphere as consisting of patterns of phonological and syntactic norms and a multidimensional network of sounds, sense, and even rhythm, but I see no reason to exclude inchoate ritual patterns from this intermediate sphere of sense. They seem particularly relevant here, where the crystallization of the scene into a combination of details reminiscent of an oath-sacrificing performance might lend itself to a flash of recognition by audiences already familiar with oath-making practices, as well as with oath-making scenes in epic poetry.

Second, given our earlier argument that a ritual form is not empty but instead communicates actual semantic content, one might expect that the shaping of the slaughter of a young, unarmed boy along the lines of an oath-sacrifice would inject a hallowed quality into the killing. Remembering our earlier discussion of Jakobson and Valeri, the killing would seem to communicate the fact of death along the lines of a paradigmatic axis, conferring a primordial nuance to the death, similarly to the way that *poinē* confers a primordial nuance to certain other battlefield killings, which was discussed in Chapter 2. In our discussion of Jakobson in Chapter 1, we allowed that ritual communication, because it is shaped along the lines of a paradigmatic rather than syntagmatic axis, confers a poetic sense, even more so when the ritual performance is embedded in a poem already, and initially probably in an oral-poetic performance. The shaping of a battlefield killing as a ritualized killing thus expands the significance of the scene with Lykaon beyond its particular syntagmatic content relative

[115] Guthrie 1954: 221.

to the larger story. Configuring a battlefield killing along the lines of a sacrificial paradigm injects a primordial connotation that may not be evident from the gist of the killing on its face. This connotation, further, might very well escape the notice of an audience not thoroughly familiar with that oath-sacrificing paradigm, an audience such as us in the 21st century. An additional influence on keeping the sacrificial paradigm in the ancient audience's imagination might be the proximity of the oath-sacrifice of the boar two books earlier. The repetition of the fate that befalls both the boar's and Lykaon's corpses must have been felt: Both are cast into "the wide bosom/great abyss of the sea" (the verse location and metrical shape of the two expressions being identical) and both become food for fish. In sum, the shaping of the killing of Lykaon along the lines of a paradigmatic ritual axis deepens the poetic aim to a more profound level than one might expect if one were to envision the killing of Lykaon as a battlefield death like any other. For an audience already familiar with the oath-sacrificing ritual pattern, this killing would be cast as high drama and would stimulate recognition of a primordial ritual paradigm.

None of this answers the basic question of why Achilles would be attributed these killings by *deirotomeō* at this point in the epic. I have argued elsewhere that by highlighting the killing of the suppliant Lykaon in this way, the poet inversely prefigures Achilles' acceptance of Priam's suppliance in Book 24, and that Achilles' inchoate ritual performance of oath-sacrifice in Book 21 provides a gauge for Achilles' incipient reentry to the sphere of human customs.[116] That is, despite the macabre tone in the accounts of Achilles' killings and in his collection of Trojan boys for funeral sacrifice, this inchoate ritual performance of an oath-sacrifice does seem to signify that he has begun, however obliquely and paradoxically, to rejoin the collective cultural sphere of the Achaians. This is so if not from his own perspective, then at least from the narrator's. Just by impressing a ritual shape onto Achilles' killing of Lykaon, the narrator implies that Achilles is participating, albeit in a skewed way, in the sphere of human customs, a switch from his former defiant disengagement from them. Presumably, this reengagement began with the oath-sacrifice with Agamemnon, although Achilles only reluctantly and half-heartedly participated in it. We have already discussed his refusal to join in the post-sacrificial commensal meal and his preference to postpone the oath-making ritual until vengeance for the death of Patroklos had been paid.

---

[116] Kitts 1999.

As for why this killing performance imitates an oath-sacrifice and not some other ritual, we must consider a few facts about oath-making. First, oath-sacrifice is one of the few cultural conventions that prescribe ritual killing. Indeed, the death of the victim is central to the ritual experience, as we have seen. Further, oath-sacrifice imposes a hallowed sanction on killing not just animal victims, but anyone who violates oaths. We have seen that the oath-sacrificing ritual performance may be essentially a symbolic enactment of the consequences invited upon perjurers, for instance in Book 3, where the dying of the lambs and the spilling of wine anticipate dying and brain-spilling by perjurers. Oath-sacrifice's sanction on killing perjurers arguably runs just as deep as *poinē* in the *Iliad*, and, significantly, overlaps with *poinē*, considering that Zeus and the Erinyes are expected precisely to pay back oath-breakers (for instance, Zeus' *apeteisan* at 4.161 and the Erinyes' *tinuschon* at 3.279), just as relatives of homicide victims might pay back offenders in *poinē* (as in Agamemnon's threat to *apotinemen* his family's honor to a fitting extent, at 3.286). We saw the overlap of the semantic spheres of *poinē* and *tinō* in Chapter 2. Now we see the overlap of *poinē* and oath-sacrifice, ritual performances whose semantic spheres intertwine.

Although *poinē* is not always configured as a ritual, once ritualized both *poinē* and oath-making do share an important feature in that they both articulate profound levels of cultural response to aspects of human existence that are felt to be precarious and difficult to control. Achilles, faced with the unexpected death of Patroklos and now his own death, might be imagined to respond to this challenge at the level of *poinē* or of oath-sacrifice, precisely because both conventions allow and also shape human responses to significant feelings of violation, in the one case a violation of life and family integrity, in the other a violation of promises. We have discussed Rappaport's argument that certain rituals defend against the violation of commitments and thereby effect security for the very foundations of human society, and that violation of commitments is the one trespass that appears to be universally sanctionable (see Chapter 1). The oath is one of these defensive rituals against violation. Although, narratively speaking, the Trojans have made no clear oath with Achilles that would require him to punish them as perjurers, they *are* implied to have committed a violation of life, if one takes into consideration Achilles' horror and rather remarkable surprise that Patroklos could be killed at all, as if the possibility had never occurred to him when he sent Patroklos out, almost casually, to fight in his stead. Hence Achilles claims to be launching *poinē* against all the Trojans in

Book 21, as we see at the moment he has hurled Lykaon's corpse into the river:

> "Perish! Until we overtake the city of sacred Ilion,
> you fleeing, and I destroying you from behind.
> You will not be protected by the well-running,
> silver-eddying river, to whom, doubtless, you have sacrificed many
> living
> bulls, and in whose waves you have released single-hoofed horses.
> Even so, you shall meet your evil fate, until you all shall
> pay [*teisete*] for the death of Patroklos and the ruin of the Achaians
> whom you killed by the swift ships, while I was away."
>
> (21.128–135)

In short, Achilles kills Lykaon by way of a mock oath-sacrifice and then swears that the Trojans shall pay for the death of Patroklos, imputing *poinē* to the substance of his oath. But this seems to work at two levels: By oath-sacrificing Lykaon, he is paying back the Trojans and also pledging to pay back the Trojans for the death of Patroklos. The use of the oath-sacrificing motif sequence to shape Achilles' killing of Lykaon and the attribution of *poinē* to Achilles' motive for it by the implied narrator of this episode, attest to the close association of the two ritual spheres in Homeric imagination.

On the other hand, one might also see the oath-making performance as dimly reflective of Achilles' earlier oath that he would sit out the war until the Achaians should regret their refusal to support their earlier gift to him of Briseis. He does occasionally imply that his removal from the war was the cause of Patroklos's death, as at 18.104 – "I sat by the ships, a useless burden on the cultivated ground" – and again at 21.134–5 – "You all shall pay, for the death of Patroklos and ruin of the Achaians whom you killed while I was away in the swift ships." But the logic of his failure to abide by the oath of separation would not imply that the Trojans should die, but rather that he should die, as of course he will.

The link between *poinē* and punishment for violated oaths in Homeric imagination is key to understanding the metaphorical switches conferred by participation in oath-sacrifices. We have already seen that divine vengeance is anticipated punishment for the violation of basic social contracts such as oath-making and guestfriendship. Just as Zeus is expected to witness and to guard the trusty oaths of Book 3 (3.280) and to cause perjurers to perish into Hades (3.322), he is expected to avenge other violations of presumed human contracts, such as bad lawmaking by judges in the agora (16: 384–393) or the violation of guestfriendship perpe-trated by the Trojans against the Greeks (13.622–627). His avenging may occur now or later, says Agamemnon (4.160–165), but avenge them he will. This avenging appears to be based on the notion that violations of ritualized commitments are essentially violations of primordial realities, given the fixing of those commitments into time and nature through rit-ual performance, and given the cosmic nature of the forces called down to protect the commitments made. We touched on this in Chapter 2 when we discussed ritual commitments as natural commitments avenged by Erinyes: Conventional or not, the "facts" brought into effect by rit-ual are treated as natural facts to be protected by divinities who protect and avenge relationships based on blood. As violated natural commit-ments, violations of oaths and other such contracts compel response by the divinities who witness and defend them. Punishment for perjury may be characterized as *poinē* conducted by the gods.

Violations of oaths also compel response for the humans who wit-ness oaths. The metaphorical transformation of witnesses into poten-tially avenging warriors through the ritual performance of oath-sacrifice was implied in our discussion of Fernandez in Chapter 1. As discussed there, Fernandez's metaphorical transformation theory of ritual allows that rituals do not just dramatize static social or cosmological configura-tions, but rather accomplish movement for the ritual actors by bringing into effect certain transformations guided by underlying metaphors. A ritual's semantic movement tends to be from the obscure and inchoate in the subject (often coined the "tenor") to the concrete and ostensive in the metaphoric predicate (the "vehicle"),[117] but however increasingly concrete, each "predicate" may also attract a mix of symbols and cross-penetrating cultural themes to the ritual stage, so that the actors' perfor-mances may radiate a variety of contingent metaphors. This attraction and radiation of metaphors and cultural assumptions through ritual per-formance is implicit in Fernandez's notion of ritual leitmotifs, which "fill out this universe of religious experience giving it resonance, a thick com-plexity and potency, which the discussion of the paradigm of metaphors – however basic – does not fully capture."[118] Ritual performance thus secures for the ritual actor not only a metaphorical identity configured

---

[117] Fernandez 1977: 104. As George Lakoff and Mark Johnson see it, less concrete expe-riences tend to be understood in terms of more concrete ones. See *Metaphors We Live By*, and "Conceptual Metaphor in Everyday Language," in *Philosophical Perspectives on Metaphor*, ed. Mark Johnson (Minneapolis: University of Minnesota Press 1981) 321.
[118] Fernandez 1977: 126.

by the ritual tradition, but also engages the individual in a level of cultural experience that is taken to be profound, fecund, and based on paradigms that interpenetrate at the deepest layers of reality.

Ritual actors are susceptible to these metaphorical transformations because of three rather elementary features of human psychology summarized by Fernandez. One is the inchoateness of the pronomial subject: "In the privacy of our experience we are usually not sure who we really are."[119] The second is our temporal suspension between past and future: We are "framed between the remembered past and the imagined future with the need to fill the inchoate present with activity . . . and to bind the past and the future together."[120] The third is our receptivity to social definition as the remedy that narrows and temporalizes our inchoateness and indeterminacy. These three psychosocial features are simple enough, and foundational for our earlier discussions of Tambiah, Bell, Valeri, and Rappaport. Rather than analyze those features further, we shall illustrate them in the context of Book 3.

The oath-sacrificing narrative in Book 3 is a perfect illustration of the metaphorical transformation put into place by ritual performance, particularly because the ritual fails – a failure provided for by the ritual institution and a failure that brings into effect an unmistakable metaphorical switch. The narrative begins with the Achaians and Trojans in the raw heat of battle. The battle comes to a standstill when Hector causes the Trojans to be seated with a single gesture (3.77–78) and when Agamemnon stops the Achaians from aiming at Hector (3.80–83). Both sides are bid to lay down their weapons in the plain (3.87–90) and to "cut 'friendship' and trusty oaths" (*philotēta kai horkia pista tamōmen*) (3.94, cf. 3.73, 3.256),[121] while Paris and Menelaos fight a duel for Helen and her possessions. Hence, for everyone but Paris and Menelaos, the ten-year-long fighting identity as the foe of the other is momentarily suspended. This establishes the "inchoateness of the pronomial subject" and its suspension in time. Penetrating this liminal moment is the prospective new social configuration of *philotēs* – "friendship," or here possibly "alliance" – for both sides. Most straightforwardly, this forecasts a structural metaphorical switch, from foe to ally.

[119] Fernandez 1972: 54.
[120] Fernandez 1977: 118.
[121] An expression with pan-Mediterranean applications. See Weinfeld 1970: 175–91; and "Covenant Terminology in the Ancient Near East and Its Influence on the West," *Journal of the American Oriental Society* 93.2. (1973b) 190–99.

Yet this new relationship of *philotēs* is also informed by a "network of associations" that adds texture and fecundity to the "ritual leitmotif." As already established, *philotēs* is associated by Homer with *xeinia*, or guest-friendship, a rich tradition sanctioned by the gods and precious to mortals. The sanctioning by gods of *xeinia* and *philotēs* together is apparent at 3.351–54, where Menelaos prays that Zeus will punish Paris's violation of *philotēs* "so that a person in future generations will shudder before doing evil to a guesthost (*xeinodokos*) who provides friendship (*philotēta*)." This violation of *xeinia*, or guestfriendship, – legendarily the very cause of the war (see 3.351–54 and 13.622–27) – invites the punishment of death, the same punishment invited by oath-violation. For reasons we have already examined, relationships by oaths, *xeinia*, and *philotēs* are treated as near-blood bonds in the *Iliad*, and their effects are cemented by ritual performances understood to have ramifications at profound levels of reality.

As for the preciousness of *xeinia* and *philotēs* to mortal humans, it is obvious that *philotēs* or *xeinia* affect the pace and direction of a handful of the *Iliad*'s battlefield narratives, wherein guestfriends attempt to protect and avenge each other. This is especially true of guestfriends on the Trojan side, wherein the deaths or woundings of *xeinoi* affect the hearts and also the fates of other Trojan warriors in battle (such as at 13.661, 17.576–77, 17.582–84, and 21.41–42). The divine sanction of *philotēs* and the preciousness of *philotēs* to mortals demonstrate that the prospective social configuration of *philotēs* secured by the oath-making ritual performance in Book 3 involves more than a simple structural switch.

Yet, as it turns out, *philotēs* is not the transformation effected by the oath-sacrificing ritual anyway, especially for the Achaians. Instead, the duel between Menelaos and Paris fails, and so does the prospective Achaian–Trojan alliance. The duel fails when Aphrodite sweeps Paris away from it, in effect taking with her the "friendship and trusty oaths." The violation of the oath then brings into fruition a transformation of the Achaian warriors, not from foes to allies of the Trojans, or even from allies to foes, but more weightily from profane warriors to sacred ones. Based on references between Books 3 and Book 7, the Achaians appear to take it upon themselves to avenge Trojan infringements upon the cosmic order established by oath-sacrifice.

Let us glance now at the precise ritual steps in order to illustrate this transformation. The Achaians start the oath-making ritual in Book 3 united behind their king. Although it is conceivable that they may think of themselves as having entered the war to be avengers of the institution of guestfriendship, or perhaps even as legendary witnesses and protectors of the marriage between Helen and Menelaos, a more likely assessment, based on the rare mention of such etiologies in the *Iliad* (at 3.351–354 and 13.622–627 primarily, and possibly at 5.348–351, with hints at Alexander's culpability at 7.374 and 7.388), and based on the obvious Achaian disharmony insinuated in the first book, is that they are now in Troy as warriors of the most profane sort, seeking booty and fame, and also as allies to the great king Agamemnon. Yet once they are drawn into the oath-making circle in Book 3, a transformation begins. The change is marked when the "best of the Trojans and Achaians" are induced by the heralds to accept cut hairs from the lambs (3.373–74), signifying, at the very least, that "the best of the Trojans and Achaians" pledge commitment to the oath's terms, as they accept the lambs' hair. The transformation continues when the Trojans and Achaians stand as witnesses to the oaths. True, they are not quite on a par with "Zeus, Helios, the rivers and earth, and those who toiling underneath punish men, whoever swears false oath" (3.276–79). These forces explicitly are invoked to be witnesses (*marturoi*) and to defend the trusty oaths (3.280). Yet the men pledge themselves to the same ends. They do so through a series of finite ritual acts, or ritualized microadjustments, as Muellner has called them. First they witness the presenting of the lambs, who are symbolic substitutes for potential perjurers. Next they witness the sworn testimony of Agamemnon and the commitment of the other chiefs, and they take note of the invocation of divine witnesses. Then they witness the throat-cutting and conspicuous dying of the lambs, which is clearly prophetic of the deaths of perjurers. But their active involvement is cemented when they ritually draw and pour the wine (3.295–96) while praying to the "gods who always are" (3.296). At this time they say, each of them (*eipesken*, at 3.297), "Zeus most glorious and greatest, and the other immortal gods: whoever first shall violate the oaths, may their brains pour to the ground as does this wine, and also the brains of their children, and may their wives be subdued by others" (3.298–301). Besides invoking cosmic sanction on potential perjurers, these ritual gestures and speech acts facilitate a transformation in metaphorical identity for the participants, from onlookers to potential avengers should the oath be violated. Their involvement in the performance of the ritual has become successively deeper with each ritual step, from their acceptance of the cut hairs up through the witnessing of death, the pouring of wine, and the collective curse on whoever breaks the oath. In their potentiality as perjurers, the men of course identify with the oath-victims – earlier we discussed the solemnity of the killing of the animals on the ritual stage and the way that ritual formality commands involvement by enunciating a ritual "register" whose persuasiveness is difficult to resist. Yet the moment of probable commitment for the men is the curse, which they each enunciate: "Zeus most glorious and greatest, and the other immortal gods: whoever first shall violate the oaths, may their brains pour to the ground as does this wine, and also the brains of their children, and may their wives be subdued by others" (3.298–301).

The wording of this curse may be interpreted in two ways. One is as an invitation to the gods to seek vengeance on perjurers, but the other is as an invitation to the gods to witness the collective pledge of the warriors to avenge perjurers themselves. The personalized commitment is evident in the promise that the brains of perjurers and their families shall fall to the ground as does the wine. More than simply inviting the gods to seek vengeance on perjurers, then, the curse also appears to pledge the men, as punishing agents, to avenge the perjury. The ritual performance has effected a transformation of identities for the men from profane warriors to cosmic avengers who will fight to bring fruition the divinely sanctioned curses levied against oath-violators.

The assumption that the battle will be tilted in favor of the Achaians is touted frequently after the Trojans violate the oath, demonstrating that oath-making and oath-violating are indeed expected to precipitate consequences on the battlefield. Hence, after the duel between Paris and Menelaos is thwarted and after Pandaros violates the truce, the Achaians consolidate their forces to fight with renewed zeal, because Zeus would never support oath-violators. As Agamemnon puts it,

> "Argives, do not surrender your rushing courage.
> For Zeus father will not be a helper to liars,
> Rather those who first violated the oaths,
> vultures will indeed devour their tender skin
> while we lead their wives and little children
> to the ships, when we take the citadel."
>
> (4.234–39)

Idomeneus, too, presumes that the Achaians are assured victory, given the Trojan status as oath-breakers:

> "But rouse the other flowing haired Achaians
> so that quickly we may fight. Since the Trojans poured oaths
> with us, to them death and destruction shall follow,
> since they first violated the oaths."
>
> (4.267–71)

175

As discussed in Chapter 2, the formula "the first who violated oaths" or "the first to violate oaths" is repeated during the mustering scenes in Books 3 and 4 (at 3.107, 4.67, 4.72, 4.155–165, 4.236, 4.271), functioning as a veritable flag for the oath-avenging motif. The repetition spurs on the oath-avenging Achaians, and deepens the war etiology to a cosmic plane. In contrast to their fighting status before the oath-sacrifice, now the Achaians fight as avengers of promises made before the gods.

This avenging motif is supported by the pervasive assumption in the *Iliad* that human perjurers will die. As we have noted, there are no fewer than 25 references to oaths in the *Iliad*, and each reference insinuates that perjury shall be punished by death.[122] It starts with Achilles' oath by his own life to defend the seer Kalchas (1.74–91) and ends with Achilles' promise to Priam to allow time for the funeral of Hector before besieging Troy. As we have seen, both gods and humans are unremittingly bound by oaths in the *Iliad*, and gods are bound even to the point of word-magic. Oaths are one of the supports of the Homeric universe.

The pervasive assumption that oath-violations invite death helps to inform the metaphorical identity not only of the avengers of perjury, who act as agents for the gods, but also of the perjurers themselves, who can expect to die like sacrificial lambs. Thus Antenor ominously recognizes in the oath-violation's aftermath, "Now we are fighting as those who have lied regarding trusty oaths" (7.351–52). Although Antenor doesn't explicitly state the equation, the audience will remember that perjurers are expected to experience the same fate as the lambs, which is to suffer slit throats by the "pitiless bronze" and to lie on the ground, gasping (*aspairontas*), deprived of *thumos* and *menos* (3.293–4).

To grasp the persuasiveness of this metaphorical switch of perjurers to oath-sacrificing victims in Homeric rituals and, for that matter, in Homeric poetry, we glance now at Paul Ricoeur's very intricate theory of metaphor. Although a full account of Ricoeur's philosophy is far beyond the scope of this book, at least three features of his inquiry into metaphor are germane to understanding "ritual fictions" in the *Iliad*.[123] These features occur at what he deems an intersection between

---

[122] On this theme, see Stengel 1920: 136–38, and 1972: 78–85; and Walter Burkert 1985: 251.

[123] The bulk of my observations about Paul Ricoeur's theory derive from my reading of his "The Metaphorical Process as Cognition, Imagination, and Feeling," 228–47. A much more elaborate argument, responsive to his contemporaries' philosophies of metaphor, may be found in Ricoeur's *The Rule of Metaphor* (Toronto: University of Toronto Press 1977).

a semantic theory, involving "an inquiry into the capacity of metaphor to provide untranslatable information and, accordingly, into metaphor's claim to yield some true insight about reality,"[124] and a psychological theory of the imagination, involving figurability, a split reference, and poetic feeling.

Ricoeur begins from a position established since Aristotle, that metaphorical movement involves a figuration, "as though the trope gives to discourse a quasi-bodily externalization. By providing a kind of figurability to the message, the tropes make discourse appear."[125] But he rejects the classical theory of metaphor to the extent that it deems the rhetorical deviance in metaphor to be a mere matter of substituting figures, as in "bull" substituted for "Hippodamas" when

> ... [Achilles] stabbed him in the upper back with his spear.
> Then Hippodamas exhaled (*aisthe*) his *thumos* and belched, as a bull
> belches when he is being dragged for the Helikonian lord
> by young men, and the Earthshaker is happy with them.
> So as Hippodamas was belching, the manly *thumos* left his bones.
>
> (20.402–06)

The metaphorical deviance in the classical substitution model would stem from the ordinary assumption that people are not bulls, so we don't die like them. Ricoeur sees metaphorical deviance as occurring not at the level of denominations, but at the level of the sentence as a whole – or, more precisely, in the paradoxical character of the predicative ascription to a logical subject (in other words, seeing the belching of slain Hippodamas as the belching of a sacrificed bull). For Ricoeur, the semantic innovation in a metaphor lies in a mutation of the relationship between subject and predicate, wherein a new predicative meaning emerges suddenly from the collapse of the literal meaning. In the case of Hippodamas and the bull, it is as if the figure of the sacrificed bull intercepts the subject of the dying man and precipitates a sudden awareness of the like features (such as belching) of sacrificed bulls and slain men, essentially schematizing their similarities. Yet an awareness of their unlike features also remains, so that there is simultaneously a semantic clash: "The insight into likeness is the perception of the conflict between the previous incompatibility and the new compatibility. 'Remoteness' is preserved within 'proximity.'"[126] In

---

[124] Ricoeur 1981: 228.
[125] Ricoeur 1981: 229.
[126] Ricoeur 1981: 234.

effect, a semantic proximity has been created between the preexisting and the new semantic fields: dying Hippodamus and dying bulls. As Ricoeur sees it, metaphor generates this *rapprochement* wherein literal incongruence (men are not bulls) yields to metaphorical congruence (men may be envisioned as bulls) and establishes a kinship between semantic fields (dying men and sacrificed bulls, war and sacrifice); but that kinship obtains only as long as there remains a tension between the two heterogeneous fields:

> All new rapprochement runs against a previous categorization which resists, or rather which yields while resisting, as Nelson Goodman says. This is what the idea of a semantic impertinence or incongruence preserves. In order that a metaphor obtains, one must continue to identify the previous incompatibility through the new compatibility.[127]

This tension established in metaphor between the new semantic compatibility and the previous semantic incompatibility is tied to a second point we shall draw from Ricoeur. It involves the split reference, or the phenomenologist's *epochē*, a suspending pose both the reader and the maker of metaphor must assume in order to grasp the fiction established by metaphor. Ricoeur sees this split reference illustrated in the preambles to fairy tales, such as "It was and it was not" ("*Aixo era y no era*") from the Majorca storytellers.[128] To grasp a metaphor, one must *suspend* literal reference ("it was not") in order to allow a metaphorical reference ("it was") to emerge from a figurative use of language. Yet one must also preserve the literal reference, so as to maintain the ordinary vision in tension with the new one suggested by the metaphor.[129] The *epochē* in "reading" an oath-making ritual must work similarly. As hinted by Johan Huizinga,[130] Adolf Jensen,[131] and Pierre Smith,[132] among others, one must cultivate a *ludic* appreciation of the events on the ritual stage, whereby one suspends one's ordinary perspective on the ritual actors in order to allow the ritual drama to emerge and to flourish.[133] But, applying Ricoeur and Fernandez, we see that in order for the ritual not to become

---

[127] Ricoeur 1981: 234.
[128] Ricoeur 1981: 239.
[129] Ricoeur 1981: 241.
[130] Huizinga 1950.
[131] Jensen 1951.
[132] Smith 1979.
[133] See Smith 1979: 103–28, n.b. 104 and 126; Adolf E. Jensen on "*Ergriffenheit*," in 1951: 53, 55, 173; and Huizinga 1950.

comic, one must also recall the preexisting, even if "inchoate," identities of the actors and the commissive purpose of the ritual, so that the actors' actions and the consequences to which they pledge are not dissolved into pure theater. That is, the ludic dimension of the ritual must coexist with its real purpose. The parallel with the fiction created by poetry would seem obvious. Appreciation of both poetic fiction and ritual fiction requires a suspension of ordinary reference, at the same time as it requires sustaining ordinary reference in tension with the fiction in order for the full paradoxical effect of the fiction to be felt. Yet it is the suspension of ordinary reference that allows for the more radical way of seeing things, and that more radical way is what the ritual (and the poetry) attempts to project. The suspension of ordinary reference allows for a projection of new possibilities, of seeing reality in the new way suggested by the metaphorical shift. Relying on Sartre, Ricoeur points out that to imagine is to make oneself absent to the whole of things. It is to address oneself to what is not.[134] The fictional possibilities that emerge from addressing "what is not" are rooted in our most intrinsic potentialities for imagining and for feeling.[135]

Most radically, Ricoeur says that this kind of "feeling" requires a kind of *epochē* of bodily emotions. Poetic feelings are not to be confused with bodily emotions, for Ricoeur. In reading, for instance, the urgent emotions of every day life are suspended in order for poetic feeling to occur. "When we read, we do not literally feel fear or anger. Just as poetic language denies the first-order reference of descriptive discourse to ordinary objects of our concern, feelings deny the first-order feelings which tie us to these first-order objects of reference."[136] Nor is this poetic feeling to be construed as anything like a purely interior state. Instead, when we encounter a metaphor, our feelings participate in the metaphor by predicative assimilation. Says Ricoeur, when we read, "we are assimilated, that is, made similar, to what is seen as similar. This self-assimilation is a part of the commitment proper to the 'illocutionary' force of the metaphor as

---

[134] Ricoeur 1981: 241.

[135] I believe I am "translating" Ricoeur's observation from page 242:

> The poet is this genius who generates split references *by* creating fictions. It is in fiction that the "absence" proper to the power of suspending what we call "reality" in ordinary language concretely coalesces and fuses with the *positive insight* into the potentialities of our being in the world which our everyday transactions with manipulable objects tend to conceal.

[136] Ricoeur 1981: 245.

speech act. We feel like what we see like."[137] In other words, feeling is a kind of intentional structure, in the way a phenomenologist might see it. It is essentially participatory, with poetic illocution as the provocateur for our feeling response, wherein we succumb to the sense of the metaphor.

An outstanding aspect of feeling intentionality is our particular feeling response to a particular string of words. Relying on Northrop Frye's description of the "mood" generated by a poem, Ricoeur proposes that each string of words emits for the hearer a kind of verbal texture specific to that string and in fact "co-extensive to the verbal structure itself."[138] This emitted verbal texture and our participation in it might be compared to Bloch's description of our response to formal oratory in ritual, although for Bloch the formality is more significant than the content of the formal oration. Nonetheless, as argued in Chapter 1, we tend to respond in kind to ritual oratory, by assuming a matching "register" in order to receive it. For instance, we have seen that the register and degree of formality in ritual oratory are proportional to the difficulty in resisting the ritual's authority and truth claims, hence "one cannot argue with a song."[139] Instead of resisting, we are assimilated, often uncritically, into the oratorical mood.

Considering the specificity of what is orated, we now may assert that participants in ritual, just as hearers of poems, are assimilated into the melody, rhythm, and "texture" of the ritual performance. On regarding rituals as poems that generate a poetic texture co-extensive to the particular ritual structure, we might also remember our earlier arguments, based on Jakobson, Tambiah, and Valeri, that audiences to ritual performances are expected to recognize primordial paradigms right through the performance, because rituals, similarly to poems, communicate along a paradigmatic rather than a syntagmatic axis. To the extent that rituals do communicate along a paradigmatic axis, our response to a ritual may be likened to a response to a poem. Similarly to the way a poetic illocution generates a verbal texture and our response to it, the particular features of a ritual may generate a particular texture co-extensive to the ritual structure itself. The particular ritual performance, then, generates a particular poetic texture, which, due to feeling intentionality, elicits a corresponding audience response.

In applying Ricoeur's inquiries about metaphor to oath-sacrificing rituals in the *Iliad*, we first might consider the ascription of gasping (*aspaironta*) and being deprived of *thumos* and *menos* to the lambs in Book 3

[137] Ricoeur 1981: 243.
[138] Ricoeur 1981: 244.
[139] Bloch 1975.

in its paradoxical relationship to the same features of human dying in some battle scenes. Gasping (*aspair-* to pant, gasp, struggle[140]) and other breathing verbs (such as *aisthe*, exhaled) are not very common features of dying scenes in the *Iliad*, but are notable in a handful of sacrificial similes, such as in the killing of Hippodamas, discussed above. A conspicuous parallel with the oath-victims' *aspaironta* and being deprived of *menos* and *thumos* occurs in the killing of Adamas in Book 13. His spear has just been deprived of *menos* (*amenēnōsen*) by Poseidon (13: 563–64) and Adamas dies gasping like an ox:

> As Adamas was leaving Meriones followed after him and struck him with
>     the spear
> between his private parts and his navel, where most of all
> Ares made hard pain for miserable mortals.
> There he planted the spear firmly, and Adamas doubled around the spear
> and gasped (*ēspair'*), as when an ox, whom oxherds in the mountains
> drive in, he being unwilling and they bind and lead him by force.
> So being struck, Adamas gasped (*ēspaire*) just a little, not for very long,
> until the hero Meriones, having come near, drew back the
> spear from his skin and darkness covered his eyes.
>
> (13: 567–75)

The paradoxical ascription of ox-like features to the dying of Adamas is elaborate in this simile. We have Adamas being struck and gasping similarly to the unwilling ox who is bound and driven forcefully by oxherds in the mountains. Both the striking and the gasping are mentioned twice, and the gasping is made more vivid by the adverbial "just a little, not for very long," followed by the focalization on a victim's last moments, "darkness covered his eyes." The figure of the unwilling and gasping ox clearly intercepts the subject of the unwilling and gasping Adamas – already noted to be stripped of *menos* – and to highlight the paradoxical picture of a warrior, just after a coup in battle, now as an animal resisting but forced to surrender to binding, abuse, and capture, presumably for purpose of slaughter. His deprivation of *menos* and his gasping (*ēspair'*) are notably similar to the loss of *menos* and the gasping of the slaughtered lambs in Book 3.

A similar helplessness and gasping (*aspairontas*) is attributed also to the sleeping Thracians in Book 10, who die as victims of Diomedes and Odysseus during their nighttime raid (10.521). These gasping deaths,

---

[140] Liddell and Scott, *A Greek-English Lexicon* (Oxford: Clarendon Press 1968).

plus a handful of other, exhaling deaths – Asteropaios (*asthmainonta*) at 21.182; Hippodamas (*aisthe*) at 20.403; Medon (*aisthmainon*) at 5.585; the Thracian king (*asthmainonta*) at 10.496); and Asios's charioteer (*aisthmainon*) at 13.399 – seem to focalize the pitiable and helpless status we have seen depicted of the victims of Achilles' various *deirotomia*s. Notably, Hippodamas, Adamas, the Thracians, and the Thracian king are all unable to resist, being stabbed either in the back or while sleeping, which supports the attribution of helplessness to these dyings.

As for the lambs' breathing out of *thumos*, this is a well-known Homeric expression for the breathing out of life (such as the Thracian king at 10.495, the sons of Merops at 11.334, the horse Pedasos at 16.468, and Asteropaios at 21.178–81). The word is much discussed in Homeric literature, and who exactly possesses a *thumos* in the *Iliad* is usually presumed to extend beyond humans, unlike those who usually possesses the *psuchē*. This extension does not, however, diminish the personalized aspect to possessing and exhaling a *thumos*. That possessing a *thumos* in the *Iliad* indicates more than just having breath or life is obvious in the numerous scenes where a character converses with his *thumos* as if conversing with his innermost, passionate self. We see this, for instance, at 21.552, when Agenor converses with his *thumos* while facing Achilles; at 22.122 and 22.152, when Hector converses with his *thumos*, also facing Achilles; at 22.475, when Andromache restrains her *thumos* in order to speak to the other Trojan women; at 9.458, when Phoinix cannot restrain his *thumos* in his father's house; at 11.792, when Patroklos is called upon to speak to Achilles privately, and to stir his *thumos*, and conceivably at 9.1–8, when the pan-Achaian *thumos* is rent in two with panic and fear. All of these scenes suggest a personalized aspect to the possession of a *thumos*, as if a *thumos* implies a kind of self-awareness, or at least a life-passion.

That such an assertion is not an anachronistic projection of modern consciousness into Homeric heroes is apparent from a glance at the problems with the reverse assumption: Why should we presume that ancient self-awareness was so vastly different from our own? Clearly, participants in other so-called shame cultures ponder matters privately within themselves, as Genji does frequently in the Japanese 10th-century classic, *Tale of Genji*.[141] Further, why should we presume that *thumos* in one context – death – has a vastly different meaning than in another – internal conversation? But we needn't force the word any further. The point is that possessing a *thumos* in the *Iliad* appears to be used more broadly than just

---

[141] Lady Murasaki, *The Tale of Genji*, from tenth-century Japan.

to denote possessing a life, for animals as for humans. That Hippodamas belches out his *thumos* as a bull does and that a sacrificial lamb may breathe out his *thumos* while substituting for an oath-violator does not make the giving up of *thumos* paradoxically animal-like; rather the opposite is true. It makes the animals human-like, and even hints at a common life-awareness for the animal and human possessors of a *thumos*. Perhaps the most poignant illustration of this is the depiction of the death of Pedasos, the mortal trace horse who ran beside the immortal horses who themselves will weep, so humanly, at the death of Patroklos (17.426–428, 23.280–284).[142] Sarpedon stabbed Pedasos in the right shoulder, at which point the horse exhaled (*aisthōn*) his *thumos*, brayed (*brache*), and fell in the sand "mooing" (*makōn*), while his *thumos* flew from him (16.467–9). Note the vividness in the cluster of verbs. Similarly to the loss of *menos* and the panting features of sacrificial victims and dying men, then, these various cross-attributions of human-like and animal-like losses of *thumos* suggest a metaphorical tension between human dying and animal dying in the *Iliad*.

These symbolizations of animals as humans and humans as animals are rendered denser in the *Iliad* by a plethora of striking hunter/prey and predator/prey similes, all casting humans in battle as animals (for instance, at 5.541–60; 13.471–77; 16.352–56; 17.540–42; 21.22–26; 21.29; 22.94–97; 22.139–42). In addition to such battle similes, we have some famous focalizations on grieving humans as grieving animals, such as Achilles as a bearded lioness grieving her lost cub (18.316–23), or Menelaus as a wailing, first-time-mother cow circling the fallen Patroklos (17.4–5).[143] In Ricoeur's thinking, such images would be "bound" to the metaphorical switch between animal victims of sacrifice and human victims of battle. As Ricoeur sees it, unlike those images in daydreams that sometimes arise and distract us when we read fiction, "bound" images are tied to the fiction. They are "concrete representations aroused by the verbal element and controlled by it."[144] Bound images attach themselves to the imaginative

---

[142] Compare this with the concern of Pandaros for his horses and the reasons he left them at home (5.202).

[143] Compare the protectiveness of Ajax, hiding the fallen Patroklos with his great shield:

> "[Aias] stood like a lion stands around its cubs,
> whom hunters encounter in the woods, having taken her cubs,
> and she raves in her great strength."
>
> (17: 134–35)

[144] Ricoeur 1981: 237. He is relying on Marcus B. Hester (*The Meaning of Poetic Metaphor*, The Hague, 1967).

process when we read metaphorical language, and help to enhance the paradoxical figuration by providing a spectrum of images that get absorbed into our grasp of the metaphor. These images of humans as animals and animals as humans in the *Iliad*, then, are bound to the perception of dying lambs in sacrifice as dying humans in battle and vice versa. Yet, at the same time, there is a semantic clash in the metaphor of animal sacrifice applied to men who fall in battle, deriving from a perceived violation of the men's humanity. By normal Greek custom, humans are not supposed to be sacrificial victims, whereas animals are.

As for the split reference one must assume in order to perceive the paradoxicality in metaphor, this is no different for Homeric oath-sacrifice than it is for the *eucharist* or any other ritual performance. There is a tension between the symbolic event and the real event the ritual symbolizes, but for most of us, they are not exactly the same except, perhaps, as fleeting perceptions. Both the aptness and the paradoxicality of the symbolic enactment in ritual permeate the Homeric oath-sacrifice in Book 3 as well as the narratives that follow it. We might perceive a split reference as implicit in the tension between the symbolizations enacted in oath-sacrifice and the handful of references to the impending actualizations of those symbolizations on the battlefield, wherein the Trojans are cast as imminently sacrificial victims. We already have reviewed numerous references to the impending catastrophe due the Trojans because of oath-violation. The tension starts within the oath-making ritual itself, at 3.299 – "Whoever first would trample on the oaths, so let their brains pour to the ground as does this wine, and those of their children, and let their wives be subdued by others" (3.299–301). It continues with various threats and reminders about the "first who violated oaths" (at, for instance, 3.320–322; 4.158–162; 4.236; 4.269–271), until ultimately it is brought to the attention of the Trojans themselves, when Antenor admonishes them:

> "Hearken to me, Trojans and allied Dardanians
> while I speak what my heart (*thumos*) in my chest commands me.
> Lead here Argive Helen, her and all her possessions with her
> let us give to Atreides to lead. For now we are fighting as liars regarding
> trusty oaths. Thus it is no longer profitable for us
> to wish to prevail, as we will not succeed this way."
>
> (7.348–353)

Antenor doesn't commit himself to the expectation that the Trojans are to be sacrificed as lambs, but implicit in his comment is an awareness of the chilling potentiality embedded in the symbolic actions of the oath-making ritual, "for now we are fighting as liars regarding the trusty oaths."

Rappaport points out that ritualization can bring into comprehensibility notions so abstract that words can barely grasp them, by making them material and thus substantial.[145] By this thinking, the sacrificed lambs would be a material substantiation of the fate that Antenor comprehends as due and owing the Trojans for their oath-violation. He comprehends metaphorically the same thing Agamemnon does when he promises Menelaos that Zeus will make the Trojans pay:

> " . . . since the Trojans struck you and trampled on the trusty
>    oaths.
> Yet in no way barren shall be the oath and the blood of lambs,
> the unmixed libations, and the right hands in which we trusted.
> For if quite at once the Olympian does not fulfill it,
> indeed later it shall be done, and with might he shall avenge it
>    [*apeteisan*],
> With their heads and their women and children.
> For well I know this in my mind and my heart:
> There shall come a day when sacred Ilion will be destroyed
> and also Priam and host of Priam of the ashen lance."
>
> (4.157–65)

Whether or not he shares Agamemnon's total vision of the approaching disaster, Antenor comprehends the impending danger because he was a witness to the symbolic drama of the oath-sacrificing performance. Antenor's comprehension might seem reminiscent of the lesson which Pierre Smith took from the Bedik of Eastern Senegal: The theatricality of the rite seems to have its own truth; the rite has more effect than any independent belief in it.[146] Another way of putting this is that the focalization on the animal's death in the ritual drama is effective in imprinting on the participants a measure of "fascination and tremendum," as Rudolf Otto might say, regardless of their precise beliefs in the existence of oath-avenging deities.[147] On the same matter of "ritual fiction," Adolf Jensen, relying on Kerenyi and Frobenius, points out that a ritual drama may precipitate a sudden *Ergriffenheit*, a seizure by one aspect of reality that

---

[145] Rappaport 1999: 149.

[146] Smith 1979: 104, 106, 126.

[147] Rudolf Otto, *The Idea of the Holy: An Inquiry into the Non-Rational Factor in the Idea of the Divine and Its Relation to the Rational.* Trans. John Harve (London: Oxford University Press 1958).

obliterates others.[148] This is not simply a matter of being beguiled by the actors on the ritual stage, but rather of acquiring a sudden creative insight in response to the "fiction" dramatized by the ritual: "To be seized means to experience a psychological state that lifts man out of the customary. It is a festive sense which is to a certain extent characteristic of man in the creative moments of his life."[149] This might be compared to Tambiah's notion that audiences to ritual performances recognize certain iconic reconfigurations of primordial paradigms that permeate the new reality created by the ritual event. Antenor knows in an immediate way what all of these thinkers know, that the "fiction" generated by the ritual event is compelling in its "truth," and that such truth effectively shortens the distance between the specters of sacrificed lambs and of men who will die as perjurers, lying on the ground, gasping, deprived of *menos* and *thumos*.

Perception of that ritual "truth" also shortens the distance between the spectators to the ritual drama and the drama itself. By Ricoeur's scheme, spectators are assimilated into the spectacle of the dying lambs by the same process that readers are assimilated at the level of feeling into the fiction created by metaphorical thinking: "We feel like what we see like." This assimilation is due to the aforementioned feeling intentionality presumed to lie at the heart of our responsiveness to fiction. I have insinuated this intentionality on another level in my earlier attempt to describe the way that ritual formality, illustrated by the high register and fixity of features in a ritual performance, draws an audience beyond the spectators' seat into the formal sphere of the ritual itself. Both ritual participants and audiences to the performance respond in kind to the ritual "register." In keeping with our paradigm of ritual as communication, the response of the audience to the ritual performance at the level of register might be comparable to the response of the hearer to the illocution of the metaphor, as Ricoeur sees it. The illocution itself elicits the feeling response as well as, indeed, the self-assimilation into the metaphor.

On top of this level of ritual register, however, there is also the matter of ritual texture, to which audiences respond not at the level of formality, but at the level of particularity. Ritualized hospitality, for instance, will draw a different response than ritualized oath-making, because each ritual emits its own peculiar ritual texture. We have already seen that oath-making articulates profound levels of cultural response to aspects of human existence that are felt to be precarious and difficult to control.

[148] Jensen 1951: 53, 55, 173.
[149] Jensen 1951: 53.

The feeling response to the ritual texture of an oath-sacrifice might be deemed a most hallowed response, because of oath-making's profound role in establishing the reliability of human promises, and because the stability of those promises relies on avenging forces felt to be embedded in the cosmos itself. It relies on nothing less than the expectation of sanctified violence.

In sum, as a focalizing event for narration and a vehicle for conferring metaphorical identity, the oath-sacrificing ritual creates the persuasive fiction that dying lambs are similar to dying humans. This is despite the fact that the audience seems blind to that similarity when lambs are sacrificed for food. The self-assimilation of the audience into the experience of the gasping lambs is a response to the poetic "illocution" of ritual performance, a response possible because of what Ricoeur refers to as "feeling intentionality." That is, "we feel *like* what we see *like*": dying lambs.

In this chapter I have explored the various features of the oath-sacrificing rituals in Books 3 and 19 for their similarities and contrasts with ritual features elsewhere in the epic. I have attempted to show that the fixity in the ritual scene and the fixity in ritual performance outside of the text probably are in tension, and I have argued that the fixity of features in a ritual scene bears a different significance than one might assign to a fixity of phrasing in battlefield scenes. This is because oath-sacrifice qualifies as a "liturgical order" for which a certain fixity and formality of elements is definitive, as I discussed in Chapter 1. Further, I have attempted to trace certain lexical features of the oath-making ritual matrix into battlefield scenes, and to demonstrate a sacrificial theme as permeating the killings of Lykaon and other victims of *deirotomia*, as well as, more subtly, the killings of victims who explicitly lose *thumos* and *menos* and who die gasping like sacrificial lambs. In addition, I have attempted to explain the poetic and ritual logic behind the attribution of sacrificial images to battlefield killings by examining the implications of oath-violation in the Homeric world. Lastly, I have attempted to demonstrate the metaphorical transformation effected for the participants in oath-sacrificing rituals and have harvested three aspects of Paul Ricoeur's very intricate theory of metaphor to explain the "ritual fictions" created by the ritual performance. These ritual fictions are supported by various similes "bound" to sacrificial imagery. This effort presumes the theory of ritual communication offered by Tambiah, Rappaport, Valeri, Fernandez, and the other theorists discussed in Chapter 1.

CHAPTER FOUR

# HOMERIC BATTLEFIELD THEOPHANIES, IN THE LIGHT OF THE ANCIENT NEAR EAST

E XTRAVAGANT DESTRUCTION BY GODS ON THE BATTLEFIELD IS NOT an unusual theme in religious texts. Across the spectrum of world religions, such destruction is cast in many guises – protective, punitive, inspiring, even illustrative of divine play. The *Iliad* has its share of these guises. The protective guise might be seen when Athene wards off missiles from Menelaos on the battlefield as a mother swats flies from her sleeping babe (4.128–31); a punishing guise is evident when Zeus, Poseidon, and Apollo storm the Achaian wall with crashing waves after the war, because the Achaians built it without divine permission (12.8–36); it is specifically to inspire the Achaians that Athene enters into the throng of warriors so that she might be seen (4.515–16); and, as for play, Zeus laughs in his heart with joy when he sees the gods coming together in strife on the battlefield (21.389–91). In this chapter, I will trace out some guises for battlefield theophanies in the *Iliad*, exploring their apparent effects on the humans who witness them and concluding with an examination of cosmic destruction represented as a response to oath-violation. Such images in the *Iliad* will be set against similar Hittite, Assyrian, and biblical images, which will help to demonstrate some cross-Mediterranean poetic patterns for the expression of divine power on the battlefield. The evidence will show that the images used in oath-making curses are not rigidly fenced off from those used in poetic representations of battlefield theophanies, or even in the battle narratives of kings. Instead there are demonstrably common themes between the genres, due probably to a shared Mediterranean and Near Eastern stock of images associated with divine participation in human affairs.

It first should be pointed out that there are very few battlefield skirmishes in the *Iliad* that have nothing at all to do with gods. Deities frequently impersonate human advisors or guestfriends on the battlefield in explicit efforts to direct the course of battle, and the feats of mortal heroes often mimic divine effects while being attributed divine backing. There is thus a thin line in the *Iliad* between mortal and immortal battlefield epiphanies, which may be reported with identical phrasing. This identical phrasing may include lexical items from a specialized vocabulary for fighting frenzy, such as *mēnis* and *cholos*, ascribed to both men and gods (as at 15.122 and 15.217). Such vocabulary is well discussed by Homeric scholars, and is part and parcel of the language of battlefield theophanies. Similarly complex lexical items appear in biblical war literature – *herem*, for instance[1] – and kindred notions possibly underlie Assyrian and Hittite literature.[2] Rather than discuss every instance of divine epiphany on the battlefield and the explicit vocabulary for it, here we shall limit ourselves to a discussion of battlefield spectacles of arousal, protection, and punishment. These categories are not entirely distinct, but rather they overlap, as we shall see.

That visions of gods on the battlefield are intended to arouse fighting passions and protect favorites seems obvious from a glance at Homeric, Hittite, biblical, and Assyrian reports that describe gods leading and sometimes following the battle fray. Across ancient Mediterranean and Near Eastern literatures, gods are noted to move in front, behind, beside, and sometimes among warriors in order to provide succor, instill confidence, and enhance the fervor of battle. The theme of running in front is especially striking. Often deities run in front while displaying a terrible weapon. In Book 14, for instance, the god Poseidon brandishes a terrible thin-edged sword while he leads Odysseus and Agamemnon, who in turn lead the Achaians:

> . . . And before Odysseus and Agamemnon went Poseidon Earthshaker
> holding in his stout hand a terrible thin-edged sword,
> which resembled a star. It was not the custom for him to mingle
> in mournful destruction, and fear held back the men.
>
> (14.384–387)

"It was not the custom for him to mingle in mournful destruction," says the poet, but when Zeus is sleeping, it is indeed Poseidon's custom, as he mingles in destruction repeatedly in Books 13 and 14 (for instance, at 13.345–55, 13.434–45, 13.554–56, 13.563–64, and 14.388–401). That "fear held back the men" may be attributed to the same logic that Hera uses

---

[1] See Niditch 1993.

[2] For instance, for a conceptual parallel with Homeric *lyssa*, wolfish rage, see Weitenberg 1991.

when she urges that Achilles be told that it is for his sake that the gods are active in battle; otherwise, "he will fear that a god goes against him in war / and it is a terrible thing for gods to manifest in appearance" (20.130–131). When the actions of the gods do become manifest, spectators may experience both fear and horror. Diomedes experiences horror when Athene opens his eyes so that he can see Ares flitting both before and behind Hector.

> Hector . . . rose up after them
> screaming. The strong Trojan phalanxes followed
> after him, and Ares led him, and also queenly Enyo,
> she holding battlefield melee [Kudomos], shameless of conflict,
> while Ares handled a monstrous spear in his hand,
> and flitted one minute before Hector, the next minute after.
>
> (5.590–95)

At the spectacle of Hector, Ares with his monstrous spear, and Enyo, battle deified, brandishing battlefield melee as if brandishing a spear, Diomedes urges the Achaians to give way, "lest we desire to fight with force against the gods" (5.606).

The same theme of flitting in front and then behind is applied to Hector, who mimics divine behavior and stirs up the fervor of his men.

> Hector bore his perfectly round shield among the front fighters,
> He shone like a deadly star shining all around
> from the clouds, then he sinks again into the misty clouds.
> So Hector one moment would shine among the firsts,
> and next would be calling out orders among the lasts. He shone
> all around with bronze like the lightning of Zeus father, aegis bearer.
>
> (11.61–64)

Apparently, Hector flits both before and among his men, holding a shield and shining all around in the same way that the lightning shines from Zeus's shield, the aegis. In Book 15, it is Apollo who bears that protective aegis of Zeus, as he leads Hector and the flanks:

> The Trojans struck forward altogether, and Hector led,
> taking great strides. Before Hector went Phoibos Apollo,
> wearing a cloud on his shoulders and holding the rushing Aegis,
> conspicuous in its terrible tassels, which bronzesmith Hephaestus gave
> to Zeus to carry into the flight of men.
> Holding it in his hands Apollo led the hosts.
>
> (15.306–11)

That Apollo leads the hosts bearing the shield of Zeus bespeaks divine protection, as well as battlefield arousal and leadership. Similarly arousing and also protecting is the spectacle of Athene leading Achilles in Book 20, although she is described as brandishing not an explicit weapon, but a light for protection. Aineas describes this and a past encounter:

> "[Had Zeus not saved me], I surely would have been subdued
>   under the hands of Achilles and of Athene,
> who runs before him, lights the way, and instructs him
> to kill the Lelegans and Trojans with his bronze spear.
> So it is not possible for a man to fight against Achilles.
> For always one of the gods is nearby and wards off ruin from him."
>                                                          (20.94–98)

As Aineas sees it, Achilles is impossible to defeat, with gods running before him, standing near by him, and protecting him from ruin.

This paradigm of running in front and also behind has clear Near Eastern parallels, which I will illustrate with just a handful of examples. Hittite king Mursilis, for instance, reports that "The sun goddess of Arinna my lady, Teshup the mighty, my lord, the goddess Mezzulas, and all the gods ran in front of me" when he conquers the district of Arzawa.[3] Similarly, Hittite king Hattusilis reports that Goddess Ishtar ran in front and sometimes behind him, ensuring his success:

> At that time also Goddess Ishtar ran in front of me.[4] . . .
> And so while the Goddess Ishtar, my lady, formerly promised kingship to me continuously, at this time Goddess Ishtar, my lady, appeared in a dream to my wife: "I will run in front of your husband. All Hatti will turn to the side of your husband. Since I myself raised him, and I did not abandon him in any way to an evil judgment or an evil god, now I will take him up. I will set him into priesthood for the Sungoddess of Arinna. Make me, Goddess Ishtar, your special divinity." Goddess Ishtar stepped behind me. As she told me, so it became.[5]

---

[3]  20.–22 . . . *I-NA* MU.2..KAM-ma-mu $^D$UTU $^{URU}$TUL$_4$-na GAŠAN-*IA* $^D$U NIR. GAL EN-*IA* $^D$me-ez-zu-ul-la-aš DINGIR.MEŠ-ia ḫu-ma-an-te-eš pí-ra-an ḫu-u-i-e-ir.

[4]  Nu-mu-apia-ia $^D$Ištar GAŠAN.*IA* píran ḫuwais. *Annals of Hattusilis III*, composite, at III:37–38.

[5]  Amukka-ma LUGAL-*UT-TA* $^D$Ištar GAŠAN-*IA* anišaan-pát kuit memiškit nu apedani meḫuni $^D$Ištar GAŠAN-*IA A-NA* DAM-*IA* Ù-at. A-NA $^{LÚ}$MU-DI-KA-ya ammuk piran $^{LÚV}$ḫuiiami nu-ya-za-kán $^{URU}$KUBARBAR-aš ḫumanza *IŠ-TU*

Similarly, Assyrian king Esarhaddon reports to have had a long history with Goddess Ishtar of Arbela, who promises him in an oracle that she will go before and behind him, to protect him and to deliver his foes into his hands.

> The great Lady am I. I am Ishtar of Arbela, who has destroyed thy foes before thee. What words of mine which I spoke to thee could thou not rely upon? I am Ishtar of Arbela, thy foes I will flay and give to thee. I, Ishtar of Arbela, before thee, behind thee, I will go; fear not.[6]

In the same vein, Ashurbanipal received a dream from Ishtar of Arbela during his eighth campaign against Elam. She promises to go before him, to ensure his safety:

> The troops saw the Idide, a raging torrent, and were afraid to cross. Ishtar, who dwells in Arbela, in the night time revealed a dream to my armies, thus she addressed them: 'I will go before Ashurbanipal, the king whom my hands have formed.' My armies put their trust in that dream, and crossed the Idide in safety.[7]

Elsewhere Sargon learns that Shamash will go into battle at his side

> At the most precious nod of Shamash, the warrior, who wrote upon the entrails [of sacrificial animals] the favorable omens [which indicated] that he would go at my side, – with a single one of my battle-chariots and 1000 fierce horsemen, bearers of bow, shield and lance, my brave warriors, trained for battle, I set out and took the road to Musasir.[8]

Esarhaddon points out that Ishtar fought at his side against an insurrection by his own people.

> I rent [my garments] and raised the cry of [lamentation]. I roared like a lion, my passion [lit. liver] was aroused. For [permission] to assume the kingship belonging to my father's house and to exercise my priestly office, I raised my hands [in prayer] to Ashur, Sin, Shamash, Bel Nabu and Nergal, to Ishtar of Nineveh [and] Ishtar of Arbela, and they

---

ŠA ᴸᵁMU-DI-KA neiari. šalanunun-uar-an kuit amuk nu-uar-an ḫuuappi DI-ešni huuapi ᴰUTU-ni Ú-UL kuuapiki tarnaḫun kinuna-ia-uar-an karapmi nu-uar-an A-NA ᴰUTU ᵁᴿᵁTÚL-na AŠ-ŠUM ᴸᵁSANGA-UT-TIM titanumi zikka-wa-mu-za ᴰIštar paraššin iia. Nu-mu memiškit, GIM-an kišatiaz. Annals of Hattusilis III, composite text, IV 7–16.

[6] Luckenbill 1968, section 618.
[7] Luckenbill, section 807.
[8] Luckenbill, section 170.

received my words with favor [gave him a trustworthy oracle to not give up].... "I made my way to Nineveh painfully but quickly. Before me, in the land of Hanigalbat, all of their mighty warriors blocked my path, offering battle. The terror of the great gods, my lords, overwhelmed them. They saw the fierce onset of my battle [-array] and became as insane [men]. Ishtar, queen of war and battle, lover of my priesthood, stood at my side, broke their bows, shattered their battle line.... Following [after me like lambs] they employed my majesty's [favor]. The people of Assyria, who had sworn allegiance before me by the great gods, came into my presence and kissed my feet.[9]

The Bible is not exempt from the theme of its protective god going at its head and caring for his warriors:

The Lord your God who goes at your head will fight for you and he will do again what you saw him do for you in Egypt and in the wilderness. You saw there how the Lord your God carried you all the way to this place, as a father carries his son.       (Deut. 1:30–31)

Sometimes, the deity's "going in front" in battle signals going before in time. When Deborah musters an army in Judges, the victory is already accomplished.[10]

Then Deborah said to Barak: "Up! This day the Lord gives Sisera into your hands. Already the Lord has gone out to battle before you." So Barak came charging down from Mount Tabor with ten thousand men at his back. The Lord put Sisera to rout with all of his chariots and his army before Barak's onslaught.       (Judges 4:14–15)

The same theme may take on added nuances when the god provides his favorites with auspicious signs that he has already launched an attack on the enemy, and with strategic instructions. In 2 Samuel, the deity acts as a commanding officer.

David inquired of the Lord, who said, "Do not attack now but wheel round and take them in the rear opposite the aspens. As soon as you hear a rustling sound in the tree-tops, then act at once; for the Lord will have gone out before you to defeat the Philistine army."
       (2 Sam. 5:23–24)

---

[9] Luckenbill, sections 503 and 504.
[10] For a list of passages demonstrating this precise topos of the enemy already given into Israel's hand, see Gerhard von Rad, "The Theory of Holy War," in his *Holy War in Ancient Israel*, trans. Marva J. Dawn (Grand Rapids, MI: Eerdmans, 1958, 1991) 41–51.

It remains for David to engage the enemy from the rear. Going in front, behind, and beside, then, is an established rhetorical theme for divine participation, leadership, and protection in battle, from both sides of the Mediterranean sea.

In the *Iliad*, the excitement and confusion of the gods' participation in battle may be perceived at a handful of different sensory levels – aural, visual, visceral. A number of passages imply a world of aroused senses and crossed sensory divides. Befitting an oral traditional text, the most conspicuous sense is aural, as when Achilles fights apart from the armies with Athene as his fighting companion. They scream back and forth, and right then twelve of the best men perish.

> There he stood and called out loud, across from him Pallas Athene
> shrieked, while she stirred up an unending uproar among the Trojans.
> As the conspicuous voice which the trumpet screams
> around a town under life-destroying fire,
> just as conspicuous was the voice of Aiakides. . . .
> Three times over the ditch godlike Achilles screamed greatly,
> three times the illustrious Trojans and their helpers were stirred up,
> and right there twelve best men perished.
>
> (18.219–230)

Notably, screaming in battle also may be inspiring rather than destructive. So it is when Zeus sends Eris to raise a battle cry among the Achaians:

> Zeus sent forth to the ships of the Achaians the goddess Eris,
> a hard goddess, bearing in her hands the signs of war.
> She stood before the wide-bellied dark ship of Odysseus,
> her shout was sounded in both directions . . .
> Standing there the goddess sounded, raised a cry, great and terrible,
> shrill, and she instilled a great strength into each heart of the
> Achaians, to make war unceasingly and to fight.
>
> (11:3–14)

Similarly stirring but also cacophonous is the screaming of gods and the braying of earth in the theomachia of Book 21, where the goddess Eris blows confusion into the battle of the gods and yells her resounding yell (her *megalō patagō*).

> Among the other gods fell Eris, heavy
> and hard, and she blew the *thumos* in their minds in two directions.

> She fell in with a resounding yell (*megalō patagō*), and the wide
>   earth clattered (*brache*).
> On both sides the great heavens resounded. And Zeus heard,
> sitting on Olympos, and he laughed in his *philos* heart
> in joy, when he saw the gods coming together in *eris*.
>
> (21.385–390)

That earthly shaking and uproar reflect cosmic instability is obvious in such examples. The world is apparently felt to be coming apart. This earth-shaking cacophony is mirrored at the human level when Achilles meets Aineas in Book 20:

> Quite all of them, men and horses, filled the plain
> and shone with bronze. And the earth, being roused at once,
> quaked with their feet. Then two men, outstanding among the best,
> came together in the middle from both sides, desiring to fight
>
> (20.156–159)

The tone of this particular duel soon will be amplified by the clanging and "mooing" (*muke*) of armor (20.260) and the terrible screaming (*smerdalea iachōn*) of Achilles (20.285), who is just beginning to display his "*mēnis* of the gods" (21.523).

Not all of these noisy reports are intended to inspire fury or fear. There are dozens of shorter references to the aural and other effects of battle that seem designed to generate different sensitivities and to focalize different aspects of war. Such a variety of focalizations seems unique to Homer and the Bible and rare in both Assyrian and Hittite literature, for many possible reasons.[11] An important aspect of this difference is that Hittite and Assyrian literatures tend to report primarily the victor's perspectives, whereas some biblical and Homeric passages, in contrast, are focalized at least partially for the plight of the victims. In Homer, for instance, the victims' perspectives are poignantly and aurally represented when "a great din (*horumagdos*) arose" (as at 8.59 and 8.63) and the air was filled with "cries of distress and the prayers [*oimōgē te kai euchōlē* – note the assonance] of men perishing and causing to perish, and the earth ran with blood" (8.63–65). Other passages may focalize divine battle-lust, as when "Eris rejoiced in looking over the great groaning. She alone of the gods happened to be present at the fighting" (11:73). Still others illustrate

---

[11] These include, perhaps, the exigencies of cuneiform writing and its possible lack of pliability in reflecting Assyrian and Hittite oral traditions.

a possible ambivalence on the part of gods who destroy sometimes with zest, sometimes with remorse.

> . . . Among them Kronides
> raised an evil uproar, sending down from above teardrops
> dripping wet with blood from the aether, because he was about
> to send many mighty heads (*kephalas*) to Hades.
>
> (11.52–55)

And later,

> . . . Greatly rattled (*ebrache*) the arms of men,
> as Zeus stretched out the destructive night of strong battle,
> so that there might be a ruinous labor of fighting around Sarpedon,
> his own son.
>
> (16.566–568)

Similarly, in the Bible there is no dearth of divinely inspired battlefield terror and confusion, focalized from both victors' and losers' perspectives and depicted with conspicuous sound-effects.[12] Typical is the deity's response to Samuel's offering of a lamb while the Philistines were approaching for battle: "The Lord thundered loud and long over the Philistines and threw them into confusion. They fled in panic before the Israelites" (1 Samuel 7:10). A mirror of this effect is apparent in the response to Jonathan's and David's dispatch of the Philistines: "Terror spread through the army in the field and through the whole people; the men at the post and the raiding parties were terrified; the very earth quaked, and there was panic" (1 Sam 14.15). More elaborate for its focalization on fear is this passage from the song of Moses and the Israelites:

> Nations heard and trembled,
> agony seized the dwellers in Philistia.
> Then the chieftains of Edom were dismayed,
> trembling seized the leaders of Moab,
> all the inhabitants of Canaan were in turmoil;
> terror and dread fell upon them:
> through the might of Thy arm they stayed still as stone.
>
> (Exodus 15:14–16)

---

[12] See von Rad for a list of passages describing the enemy's loss of courage and the striking of divine terror into enemy hearts (1991: 46–49).

The fear and trembling of Israel's enemies is a particularly prominent theme with prophets such as 1st Isaiah:

> Wail, for the day of the Lord is near;
> it will come like destruction from the Almighty.
> Because of this, all hands will go limp,
> every man's heart will melt.
> Terror will seize them,
> pain and anguish will grip them;
> they will writhe like a woman in labor.
> They will look aghast at each other,
> their faces aflame
>
> (Isaiah 13:6–8)

Conversely, Israel too, when she is disobedient, may experience a divinely inspired panic. In Leviticus she is warned of a punishing hypersensitivity and extreme fear:

> And I will make those of you who are left in the lands of your enemies so ridden with fear that, when a leaf flutters behind them in the wind, they shall run as if it were a sword behind them; they shall fall with no one in pursuit. Though no one pursues them, they shall stumble over one another, as if the sword were behind them, and there shall be no stand made against the enemy. (Leviticus 26:36–38)

As von Rad points out about biblical war traditions, "Yahweh's intervention in the form of a confusing divine terror was an indispensable element of the tradition."[13] It clearly instills confidence or fear, and the effects of the deity's anger may be focalized from either the victims' or the victors' perspectives.

While Assyrian battle narratives also emphasize the victorious feats of gods and men – human and divine feats often are rendered as parallel in grandeur and equally bloody – only rarely are those feats portrayed with aural metaphors, and rarely is there a focalization on the plight of the victims. I know of only a few possible exceptions to this generalization, two from the annals of Sargon II (ruled 725–704 BCE). In one, Sargon celebrates the contrast between the wailing of the defeated Manneans and the victory songs of their Assyrian conquerors.

> . . . Over all of his mountains, every one of them, I spread [lit. poured out] terror; wailing and lamentation I laid on the enemy peoples. With

---

[13] von Rad 1958, 1991: 49.

joyful heart and jubilation, accompanied by players [on] the harp and tambourine, I entered my camp. To Nergal, Adad, and Ishtar, lords of battle, to the gods who inhabit heaven and earth and to the gods who dwell in Assyria, I offered enormous numbers of pure sacrificial animals, I came before them with prostrations and prayers, I extolled their divinity"[14]

In the other, the rendering of the victim's wails is more laconic.

... Over Urartu, to its farthest border, I spread mourning, and cast eternal weeping over Nairi.[15]

Although the focalization on the victims' plight is oblique in Sargon's campaign boasts, there is at least a hint of awareness of that plight in reports of the wailing and weeping of the mourners.

More usually, however, and as befits what we know of the fine arts as well as the martial arts traditions particularly of the Neo-Assyrians,[16] battle with an enemy is described with an eye for visual spectacle, and not particularly with an ear for the aural liveliness of the landscape or for vocalizations by losers or victors. The spectacle is usually one of complete devastation, and the similes for it tend to be vivid. Hence Sennacharib (705–681 BCE) describes his eighth campaign against Elam:

At the word of Ashur, the great lord, my lord, on flank and front I pressed upon the enemy like the onset of a raging storm. With the weapons of Ashur, my lord, and the terrible onset of my attack, I stopped their advance, I succeeded in surrounding them [or, turning them back], I decimated the enemy host with arrow and spear. All of their bodies I bored through like a sieve [?] ... like fat steers who have hobbles put on them, – speedily I cut them down and established their defeat. I cut their throats like lambs. I cut off their precious lives [as one cuts] a string. Like the many waters of a storm, I made [the contents of] their gullets and entrails run down upon the wide earth. My prancing steeds, harnessed for my riding, plunged into the streams of their blood as [into] a river. The wheels of my war chariot, which brings low the wicked and the evil, were bespattered with blood filth.

---

[14] Luckenbill 1968, section 156.
[15] Luckenbill, section 175.
[16] See, for instance, Steven W. Holloway, *Ashur Is King! Ashur Is King! Religion in the Exercise of Power in the Neo-Assyrian Empire* (Leiden: E. J. Brill 2002). See also Ann Gunter 1990 on Neo-Assyrian royal imagery and the narrative traditions depicted in Assyrian art.

With the bodies of their warriors I filled the plain, like grass. [Their] testicles I cut off, and tore out their privates like the seeds of cucumbers of Simanu (June). . . . I overpowered them like a bull."[17]

The graphic nature of these similes is inescapable.

In the light of the *Iliad*, one might notice particularly Sennacharib's image of blood-splattered chariot wheels – "The wheels of my war chariot, which brings low the wicked and the evil, were bespattered with blood filth." This makes an interesting comparison with Hector's chariot wheels, which tread on bodies and shields so that "the axle below was completely splattered with blood and the rails which went along the carriage threw up drops of blood" (11.534–36). On the one hand, the similarity between these two images might be explained as common imagination for warring and chariot-driving peoples. On the other hand, the blood-splattered chariot wheels is so specific a reference that it is at least conceivable that the Homeric tradition inadvertently has preserved the same *topos* we see in Sennacharib's boast, which presumably reflects the same *topos* found in shorthand in numerous Assyrian oaths "by the chariot."[18] The precise meaning of swearing "by the chariot" may be illuminated by a glance at the fuller oath-curse of Esarhaddon: "Just as this chariot is drenched with blood up to its baseboard, so may your chariots be drenched with your own blood in the midst of your enemy."[19] Notably, Esarhaddon's curse reverses the image. Sennacharib's boast makes it the victor's chariot wheels that are drenched in the victim's blood, as does Homer in the description of the chariot wheels of Hector, whereas Esarhaddon's curse makes it the victim's chariot wheels drenched in the victim's own blood. Nonetheless, the repeated feature of bloody chariot wheels is striking. Given repeated boasts by Assyrian kings that the destruction of the enemy corresponds to their violation of the oaths sworn to Ashur,[20] and given the explicit reference to blood-splattered

---

[17] Luckenbill, section.254 (8th campaign against Elam, battle of Halule (Col V, l.17–Col.VI, hl.35).

[18] Hillers (1964 in *Treaty Curses*) lists some examples of the oath of the chariot on page 22.

[19] This is from the succession treaty of Esarhaddon (ruled 680–669) designating Ashurbanipal as crown prince. Parpola and Watanabe 1988: 55 (section 90). We may observe, with Delbert Hillers, that "in general, ancient curses and prophetic oracles of doom describe evils and calamities which were part of common human experience. . . . There is little of the fantastic or unheard of, since these threats were meant to be taken seriously" (1964: 43).

[20] See, for instance, Holloway 2002, and Hillers 1964: 81–2.

wheels in treaty curses, the persistence of the theme of bloodsplattered wheels here and in Homer may suggest a common theme in the rhetoric both of victory on the battlefield and of punishment for oath-violation. In any case, the image of bloody chariot wheels, along with the cut throats of humans as lambs and castrated testicles as cut out cucumber seeds in summer, does at least typify an apparent relish for graphic representation in Assyrian treaty curses and royal annals.

Equally vivid, but perhaps a bit ironic, are the war boasts based on similes derived from everyday activities such as harvesting and sacrificing. Note this by Sargon II:

> . . . I plunged into his midst like a swift [lit. frightful] javelin, I defeated him. I turned back his advance; I killed large numbers of his [troops], the bodies of his warriors I cut down like millet [?], filling the mountain valleys [with them]. I made their blood run down the ravines and precipices like a river, dyeing plain, countryside and highlands red like a royal robe [?]. His warriors, the mainstay of his army, bearers of bow and lance, I slaughtered about his feet like lambs, I cut off their heads.[21]

The horrible irony in these similes of agriculture and sacrifice is based of course on their misapplication to the sphere of battle. The *Iliad* has its share of sacrificial similes and inferences, as we explored in Chapter 3. There are plenty of Homeric agricultural similes as well, as when Patroklos mows down the first phalanxes of the Trojans (16.394), the Trojans and Achaians cut each other down as farmers cutting grain (11.67–77), or the two Ajaxes push into battle as oxen pulling a plow over a field left fallow (13.701–708). On the face of it, there is nothing so surprising about agricultural similes used by agricultural populations; the irony is in the parallel between cutting up grain and fields and cutting down humans. Humans as short-lived plants or trees is of course a frequent image in Homeric poetics (for instance, 6.142–143, 13.178–181, 21.462–467).

Another recurring theme for depicting divine arousal on the battlefield is natural disaster. We have already seen the earth quaking under the weight of battle in the theomachia of the *Iliad* and with divine terror in the Bible, and we just saw the war prowess of Assyrian Sennacharib compared to a raging storm. Similarly, in *Iliad* 14, the clash of the hero

---

[21] Luckenbill 1968, section 154.

Hector with the god Poseidon resounds through the earth and precipitates a terrible and loud marine storm:

> Shining Hector, in turn, set the Trojans in order on the other side.
> And then darkhaired Poseidon and shining Hector
> stretched out the most terrible strife of battle.
> with one helping the Trojans, and the other helping the Argives.
> The sea splashed toward the huts and ships of the
> Argives, and the others slammed together with a great war cry (*alalētō*).
> No wave of the sea ever shouted as this toward the shore,
> being roused from the sea by the hard breath of Boreas,
> never was there as great a roar of crackling fire
> in the ravines of mountains, when fire rises to burn the forest,
> no wind which roars, raging, most greatly of all,
> blows as hard around the lofty trees,
> so great was the sounding of the Trojans and Achaians
> calling terribly, when they rose up against each other."
>
> (14.388–401)

Famously, too, the river Scamander is roused to torrential anger by Achilles' overkilling in Book 21.

> . . . And the river rushed upon him, raging with swells,
> rolling, he stirred up all his streams, and he thrust the many
> corpses which were clustered together beneath him, those whom
>     Achilles had killed.
> Bellowing as a bull, he threw them out
> to dry land. The living he saved in his fine streams,
> hiding them in the deep and great eddies.
> Terribly he set his waves around Achilles, who was twirled
>     around,
> he pushed in at his shield, dropping a swell upon him, and
>     Achilles could not
> resist enough to plant his feet. He grasped with his hand an elm
>     tree,
> flourishing and great. It ripped away by the roots
> and pushed away completely from the overhang, holding up the
>     fine currents
> with its thick shoots, and it bridged him inside there,
> falling completely around him. But Achilles arose from the
>     eddies and
> darted toward the plain to fly on swift feet,
> in fear. But the great god did not release him, but rose up on top
>     of him

foaming darkly, so that he might stop the labor
of godlike Achilles, and ward off the ruin for the Trojans.

(21.233–250)

No other examples are as vivid as these, but elsewhere it is raging humans
who are compared to raging rivers. Thus Diomedes

> . . . wove through the plain similarly to a swollen,
>     winter-flowing
> river, which, running swiftly, scatters the gates
> and the holding gates don't contain it,
> nor does the fence hold it back from the fertile threshing
>     floor,
> but it goes suddenly, when the thunder of Zeus weights down
> . . . .
> So under Tydeides the stout phalanxes were put to the rout.

(5.87–94)

Likewise, Ajax is compared to a river in winter:

> As when a full river goes down toward the plain
> from the mountains under a winter snowstorm, joined with the
>     thunder of Zeus,
> and carries along with it many dry oak trees, and many pines
> and much mud, it goes toward the sea
> so, then, shining Ajax followed after and put to rout
> horses and men, destroying them.

(11:492–96)

Similarly, Assyrian kings in their royal annals often model reports of
their destruction on paradigms of natural storms, which in turn reflect
the destructiveness of the gods. Thus the boundary between the king
and the deities who back him is porous in Sargon's report of his attack
on Urartu.

> Adad, the violent, the powerful son of Anu, let loose his fierce tempest
> against them and, with bursting cloud and thunderbolt [lit. Stone of
> heaven], totally annihilated them. Ursa, their prince, who had trans-
> gressed against Shamash and Marduk, and had not kept sacred the oath
> [sworn by] Ashur, king of the gods, became alarmed at the roar of my
> mighty weapons, his heart palpitating [being torn] like [that of] an owl
> [or bat; lit. bird of the cave], fleeing before an eagle. Like a man whose
> blood is pouring from him, he left Turushpa, his royal city; like [an
> animal] fleeing before the hunter, he trod the slope of his mountain;
> like a woman in travail he lay stretched on his bed, his mouth refusing

food and drink [water], a fatal injury [lit. Disease without escape] he inflected upon himself. I established the might of Ashur, my lord, upon Urartu for all time to come, leaving there for future days his never-to-be-forgotten fear. The surpassing power of my might and the fury [lit. Onset] of my all-powerful weapons, which are without rival in the four regions [of the earth] and cannot be turned back, I let loose [lit. Made bitter] against Urartu in a bitter fight. The people of Zikirtu and Andia I bespattered with the venom of death.[22]

In the same vein, Odysseus blurs the boundary between mortal fury and divine power in his match of Hector's *lyssa*, his "wolfish rage," with Zeus's auspicious thunderbolt:

> Zeus Kronides hurls lightning, showing auspicious signs
> to them. And Hector raves in his great strength,
> raging terribly, trusting in Zeus, he honors
> neither men nor gods. A wolfish rage [*lyssa*] has entered him
> (9.236–239).[23]

We have already seen the battle fury of both Hector and Achilles depicted as godlike, and also backed by the gods. All of these examples represent divine power as auspicious and natural and radiating through or against mortals on earth. The very vividness of these images suggests that divine power is felt to be fully present in nature and expressive in the heat of battle.

Another occasion for the demonstration of divine power in Homer's battlefield scenes is the stunning and bewitching of warriors, who are directly affected, similarly to victims of the divine panic we have seen thrown into enemies of Yahweh in the Bible. We have seen that mortals

---

[22] Luckenbill, section 155. The boundary between rulers and gods is equally porous when Assyrian king Sennacharib has himself represented in art as stationed in Ashur's chariot, with the other gods following behind him.

> [This is] the image of Ashur as he advances to battle into the midst of Tiamat, the image of Sennacherib, king of Assyria, of Shar-ur, Shar-gaz, Gag, Nusku, Daianu, Tishpak, Mash of the Wall, Kubu, Hani, Sibitti – these gods who were advancing in front of Ashur; Ninlil, Sheru'a, Sin, Ningal, Shamash, Aia, Gamlat, Anu, Antum, Adad, Shala, Ea, Damkina, the mistress of the gods, Mash, – these gods who are behind Ashur. I am the one who conquers, stationed in Ashur's chariot. Tiamat and the creatures inside her.      (Luckenbill section 447)

[23] Teukros reports a similar indomitability of Hector: "I am unable to hit him, the raging [*lyssetera*] dog" (8.299), and of course Achilles bears a matching *lyssa* when he pursues the Trojans (21.544).

who witness Poseidon, Ares, or Eris on the battlefield experience dramatic responses, whether of inspiration or of terror. Further, Zeus is said to stun warriors at 11.545–557 and 12.252–255, Poseidon bewitches Alkathos under Idomeneus (13.435), Apollo famously deceives Hector in order to make him vulnerable to Achilles in Book 22, and Athene memorably deceives the minds of the Trojans who applaud Hector for planning to wear the armor of Patroklos, which is really that of Achilles, "fools, for Pallas Athene had taken away their wits" (18.311). But it is Poseidon whose bewitching work receives the longest and most elaborate treatment in the *Iliad*. His victims are the two Ajaxes in Book 13, who discover themselves infused with an overwhelming appetite for battle:

> ... and the earthholding Earthshaker smote both
> with this scepter, filling them with a great strength.
> He made their limbs nimble, as well as their feet and hands above.
> Then he rose up to fly as a swift-flying hawk
> who, separating from a precipitous and very high cliff,
> impels himself across the plain in pursuit of another bird,
> so Poseidon Earthshaker darted away from them.
> Swift Ajax Oileos recognized him first.
> At once he spoke to Ajax son of Telamon,
> "Ajax, just now one of the gods who holds Olympos
> has shown himself to us as a sign, and calls us to fight by the ships.
> It couldn't possibly have been Kalchas, the inspired bird-interpreter.
> For I would have recognized easily the footprints of his feet and shins
> as he was leaving. Instead, the gods are conspicuous.
> And my *thumos* inside me and in my own chest
> is roused greatly to make war and fight,
> my feet are infused with power, as are my hands above them."
> Answering him Telamon Ajax said,
> "In the same way now to me, my invincible hands are raging
> around my spears, and my spirit is stirred, I feel impelled
> in both of my feet below. And I intend quite alone,
> without incitement, in eagerness, to fight with Hector Priamide.
> So they spoke these things to each other,
> rejoicing in *charmē*, which the god had thrust into their *thumos*.
>
> (13.59–82)

The process of self-discovery for the Ajaxes is remarkable for their suspicion of divine cause. They rejoice in the lust for battle (*charmē*), which the god has injected into their spirits.

I know of nothing precisely comparable to this in Hittite or Assyrian stories, although the overlap between the might of gods and the might of Assyrian kings might approach it. For instance, Ashurbanipal reports that after he and the gods defeated the armies of a certain Tarku, king of Egypt and Ethiopia, "the terrible splendor of Ashur and Ishtar overcame him and he went mad."[24] Inversely comparable might be the loss of vigor in the land and its inhabitants construed as a result of the disappearance of the god Telepinu in Hittite myths.[25] A similar inverted comparison might be the failure to thrive implied by the loss of appetite of goddess Ishtar of Nineveh, as she describes to the other gods her frightening encounter with the monster Hedammu.[26] Generally speaking, in Hurrian and Hattic myths from Hittite Anatolia, disaster seems to be portended when gods lose the courage or the desire to exercise their powers, often symbolized by their refusal to eat. In the *Iliad*, the direct influence of Poseidon for the positive speaks to the same underlying logic. Essentially, all is well when divine powers are ebullient. This ebullience is represented in the encounter with Poseidon when the two Ajaxes experience a surge of power.

There is one other occasion for reports of divine passion on the battlefield in the *Iliad*, already alluded to in our discussion of the bloody chariot wheels: the imposition of vengeance on oath-violators who violate covenants made in the name of the gods. Although the battlefield spectacles of punishment may not always correspond precisely to the curses that finalize oaths, there is an indisputable pattern of expectation that oath-violators will suffer divinely abetted defeat. In the case of the failed truce of *Iliad* Book 3, for instance, the curse has promised the annihilation of the family of the oath-breaker – " 'Zeus greatest and best, and all the other immortal gods, whoever is first to violate the oaths, so may their brains fall to the ground as does this wine, and those of their children, and may their wives be subdued by others' " (3.297–301) – which mirrors closely what Agamemnon tells the Argives is about to occur.

> "Argives, do not give up on your rushing courage.
> For Zeus father will not be a advocate for liars,
> but those who were first in violating oaths,
> vultures surely will devour their own tender skins,
> while we lead their wives and little children
> to the ships, after we take the citadel."
>
> (4.234–39)

---

[24] Luckenbill 1968, section 771.
[25] For a translation, see *Hittite Myths* by Harry A. Hoffner, Jr. 1973: 14–20.
[26] Kbo XIX 112, lines 1–12.

Although the wives and children survive in Agamemnon's promise here, they might not in another of his promises, wherein the entire family is apparently to be wiped out.

> "In no way barren is the oath and the blood of lambs,
> the unmixed libations and the right hands in which we trusted.
> For if the Olympian does not fulfill it at once,
> he will fulfill it later, and with might he will avenge (*apeteisan*) it
> with their heads and their wives and also their children.[27]
> For well I know this in my mind and my heart:
> There shall come a day when sacred Ilion will be destroyed
> and also Priam and the host of Priam of the ashen lance."
>
> (4.158–165)

That the family of a covenant-violator is doomed to extinction is implicit also in Agamemnon's promise of terrible vengeance against the Trojan child carried in the womb of the Trojan mother:

> "Let none of them escape sheer ruin
> in our hands, not even the child a mother carries
> in her womb, let him not escape, but all of them together
> shall be utterly destroyed in Ilion, uncared for and left without a trace."
>
> (6.57–60)

It is simply indisputable that the expectation that the perjurer and his family shall be annihilated is pan-Mediterranean. As noted, Assyrian royal annals repeatedly blame an enemy's demise on failures to honor the oath of Ashur, although the means of demise vary. In this boast by Ashurbanipal, the demise of an entire population is due to oath-violation, and the means of its demise are famine and the cannibalism of one's children:

> Uaite', together with his armies, who had not kept the oath [sworn] to me, who had fled before the weapons of Ashur, my lord, and had escaped before them, – the warrior Irra [the pest god] brought them low. Famine broke out among them. To [satisfy] their hunger they ate the flesh of their children. Every curse, written down in the oath which they took, was instantly visited [lit. fated] upon them by Ashur, Sin, Shamash, Adad, Bel, Nabu, Ishtar of Nineveh, the queen of Kidmuri, Ishtar of Arbela, Urta, Nergal [and Nusku]. The young of camels, assess, cattle and sheep, sucked at seven udders [lit. suckling mothers]

---

[27] True, the text does not say with the heads of his wives and his children, but the implication could be argued to exist.

and could not satisfy their bellies with the milk. The people of Arabia asked questions, the one of the other, saying: "Why is it that such evil has befallen Arabia?" [And answered], saying: "Because we did not keep the solemn [lit. great] oaths sworn to Ashur; [because] we have sinned against the kindness [shown us by] Ashurbanipal, the king beloved of Enlil's heart."[28]

Such cannibalism of one's children is explicitly predicted in some treaty curses of Esarhaddon, in the case of disloyalty to his son Ashurbanipal:

(Ditto, ditto;) just as [thi]s ewe has been cut open and the flesh of [her] young has been placed in her mouth, may they make you eat in your hunger the flesh of your brothers, your sons and your daughters."[29]

(Ditto, ditto) just as honey is sweet, so may the blood of your women, your sons and your daughters be sweet in your mouth.[30]

The horrors of cannibalism are also called upon Judah in the prophetic book of Jeremiah, precisely because of her betrayal of Yahweh in favor of the god Baal (Jer. 19.5–9).

For they have forsaken me, and treated this place as if it were not mine, burning sacrifices to other gods, whom neither they nor their fathers nor the kings of Judah have known, and filling this place with the blood of the innocent. They have built shrines to Baal, where they burn their sons as whole offerings to Baal. . . . In this place I will shatter the plans of Judah and Jerusalem as a jar is shattered; I will make the people fall by the sword before their enemies at the hands of those who would kill them, and I will give their corpses to the birds and beasts to devour. I will make this city a scene of horror and contempt, so that every passer-by will be horror-struck and jeer in contempt at the sight of its wounds. I will compel men to eat the flesh of their sons and their daughters, they shall devour one another's flesh in the dire straits to which their enemies and those who would kill them will reduce them in the siege.                                        (Jer. 19:4–10)

However, there appears to be no case in our extant version of the *Iliad* that acknowledges cannibalism as a punishment for oath-violation.

In other ancient Near Eastern curses, the means of demise is not specified, but the expectation that the gods will administer punishment is

---

[28] S.828 in Luckenbill 1968.
[29] Luckenbill 52, section 69.
[30] Luckenbill 52, section 75.

clear. The foundation deposits and *kudurru* (boundary stone) curses of Sargon II use language that is clearly formulaic:

> Whosoever destroys the work of my hands, injures my statue [lit.features], brings to naught the law which I have established, – may Ashur, Ningal, Adad, and the great gods, who dwell therein, destroy his name and seed from the land, may they set him in chains under [the heel] of his foe.[31]

> Whoever destroys the work of my hands, who obliterates [the evidence of] my noble deeds, may Ashur, the great lord, destroy his name and his seed from the land.[32]

Ashurbanipal expects much the same for violation of his work:

> But whoever blots out [my memorial] or changes its location, does not [set it up] beside 'his memorial', may Ishtar of Erech, the great lady, look upon him in anger, his name and his seed may she destroy from the lands.[33]

> But whoever blots out my written name, destroys my royal image, or changes its location, and does not set it up beside his [own] image, – may Nabu, the mighty lord, look upon him in anger, may he overthrow his royal throne, may he make his rule gloomy [or "eclipse" his rule], may he destroy his name and his seed in the lands, and have no mercy upon him.[34]

The succession treaty of Esarhaddon to Ashurbanipal pronounces a similar curse for straying by oath, listing an array of apparently binding rituals. However, in this case the enforcing power is not divine, but human:

> You shall not take a mutually binding oath with [anyone] who installs [statutes of] gods in order to conclude a treaty before gods, [be it] by set[ting] a table, by drinking from a cup, by kindling a fire, by water, by oil, or by holding breasts, but you shall come and report to Ashurbanipal, the great crown prince designate, son of Esarhaddon, king of Assyria, your lord, and shall seize and put to death the perpetrators of insurrection and the traitorous troops, and destroy their name and seed from the land.[35]

---

[31] Luckenbill, section 109.
[32] Luckenbill, section 111.
[33] Luckenbill, section 973.
[34] Luckenbill, section 977.
[35] Section 13 of Parpola and Watanabe 1988: 35.

Later curses in the same treaty use different analogies, but to the same effect, should a party to the oath violate it:

> Just as the *Cursers* sinned against Bel and he cut off their hands and feet and blinded their eyes, so may they annihilate you, and make you sway like reeds in water; may your enemy pull you out like reeds from a bundle.

> May [the gods] [slaughter] you, your women, your brothers, your sons, and your daughters like a spring lamb and a kid.[36]

> "Just as young sheep and ewes and male and female spring lambs are slit open and their entrails rolled down over their feet, so may [your entrails and] the entrails of you sons and your daughters roll down over your feet."[37]

Although the means are not specified in Hittite Anatolia, the net effect for oath-violation is the same. Hittite king Mursilis promises that Haggana and his family will be annihilated to the last trace, should he violate their oath:

> Behold to you these words under oath I put: If you . . . do not protect them, these sacred oaths of yours, your lives, together with your wives, your children, your brothers, your sisters, your families, your houses, your fields, your cities, your vineyards, your threshing floors, together with your possessions, let them be destroyed! May the oath-gods seize you from the dark earth![38]

Likewise, Hittite king Tudhaliya IV invites divinely inflicted death upon anyone who violates his promise of Tarhuntassaland to Kurunta, for all time:

> The one who brings trouble to Mr. Kurunta concerning this country, or who takes it away from him, or who takes it away from the progeny of Kurunta afterwards, if he diminishes his boundary or that which I have given to him, if he takes away anything whatsoever, or twists even one word of this tablet, may the oath-gods completely destroy him.

> What I, my majesty, gave to Mr. Kurunta, king of Tarhuntassa, the boundaries which I made for him, let no one in the future take them away from the progeny of Mr. Kurunta. The king does not take them for himself. He does not give them to his son. To another

---

[36] Sections 95 and 96A of Parpola and Watanabe 1988: 57.
[37] Ibid., 52, section 70.
[38] Kbo V3 IV 36–40.

tribe / descendants, let him in no way give it. Let no one take it away from him. In the future, let only the progeny of Mr. Kurunta hold the kingship of Tarhuntassaland. But the one who brings woe to him, indeed, if he takes anything from him, let the oath-gods destroy him completely along with his offspring (Bo. 86/299 RS IV: 16–21).

In the same vein, the deity in Deuteronomy promises that the name of one who transgresses his covenant shall be wiped out under the heavens.

[If a man willfully transgresses the covenant] Yahweh will refuse to forgive him, because then the anger and jealousy of Yahweh would smoke against that man, and all the curses written in this book would descend upon him, and Yahweh would wipe out his name from under the heavens.                                         (Deut. 29:19–20)[39]

And later, in Jeremiah, the devastation for the people is made explicitly to correspond to a ritualized covenant (to free its slaves) that the people failed to uphold:

You have disregarded my covenant and have not fulfilled the terms to which you yourselves had agreed; so I will make you like the calf of the covenant when they cut it into two and passed between the pieces. . . . I will give them up to their enemies who seek their lives and their bodies shall be food for birds of prey and wild beasts. . . . They shall attack [your city] and take it and burn it down, and I will make the cities of Judah desolate and unpeopled.                              (Jer. 34:18–22)

Similarly menacing, although perhaps not as complete, is the curse Joshua pronounces on the father who lays anew a foundation stone for Jericho, after the Israelites have practiced *herem* (divinely commanded war) upon it. The father will lose both his first-born and youngest sons.

"At that time Joshua pronounced this solemn oath: "Cursed before the LORD is the man who undertakes to rebuild this city, Jericho:

"At the cost of his firstborn son
will he lay its foundations;

---

[39] Translation by Hillers 1964: 74. Later in the same speech by Moses there is a similar, concluding curse:

But if your heart turns away and you do not listen and you are led on to bow down to other gods and worship them, I tell you this day that you will perish; you will not live long in the land which you will enter to occupy after crossing the Jordan. I summon heaven and earth to witness against you this day.
(Deut. 30:17–20). [Trans. Oxford English Study Edition]

> at the cost of his youngest
> will he set up its gates"
>
> (Joshua 5.26)

Yet, interestingly, the deity of the Bible usually is made to stop short of annihilating the family line of any whole tribe of Israel, instead driving him and his family off into distant countries beset by dire circumstances (as in Deut. 29:22–23).

A related theme that appears in the *Iliad*, the Bible, and Assyrian literature is the rendering of cities into vacant mounds. We have seen Agamemnon promise that the city of Priam should one day be empty, and all of Priam's family gone from the earth (4.158–165), and we have seen that Jeremiah prophecies that Judah shall be made desolate and unpopulated (Jer. 34:22). That this curse is traditional in the ancient Near East is apparent from Isaiah's blast against Babylon, which shall be uninhabited for all generations:

> Therefore I will make the heavens tremble;
> and the earth will shake from its place
> at the wrath of the LORD Almighty,
> in the day of his burning anger.
>
> Like a hunted gazelle,
> like sheep without a shepherd,
> each will return to his own people,
> each will flee to his native land.
> Whoever is captured will be thrust through;
> all who are caught will fall by the sword.
> Their infants will be dashed to pieces before their eyes; their houses
>     will be looted and their wives ravished.
> See, I will stir up against them the Medes,
> who do not care for silver and have no delight in gold.
> Their bows will strike down the young men;
> they will have no mercy on infants
> nor will they look with compassion on children.
> Babylon, the jewel of kingdoms,
> the glory of the Babylonians' pride,
> will be overthrown by God
> like Sodom and Gomorrah.
> She will never be inhabited
> or lived in through all generations.
>
> (Isaiah 13:13–20)

Elsewhere in Isaiah it is Israel who shall become an uninhabited tell, desolate for all but wild animals (Is.34:11–17), as was Judah in Jeremiah (Jer. 19:7–9). There are many Assyrian examples of the same theme.[40] Assyrian king Sennacharib boasts of destroying the city of Babylon so that its temples might not ever be remembered.

> Adad and Shala, the gods of the city of Ekallate, whom Marduk-nadin-ahe, king of Babylon, in the reign of Tiglath Pileser, king of Assyria, had seized and carried off to Babylon, after 418 years I brought them to their place in Ekallate. The city and [its] houses I destroyed, I devastated, I burned with fire. The wall and outer wall, temples and gods, temple towers of brick and earth, as many as there were, I razed and dumped them into the Arahtu Canal. Through the midst of that city I dug canals, I flooded its site [lit. ground] with water, and the very foundations thereof [lit. the structure of the foundation] I destroyed. I made its destruction more complete than by a flood. That in days to come the site of that city, and [its] temples and gods, might not be remembered, I completely blotted it out with [floods] of water and made it like a meadow."[41]

In his battle against the Manneans, Sargon goes so far as to fell the enemy's orchards and set the tree trunks on fire,[42] an act of violence so severe that it actually is prohibited in the rules for war as presented in Deuteronomy.[43]

---

[40] For instance, Tiglath Pileser I: "The lands of Saraush and Ammaush, which had never before known defeat, I overwhelmed, (so that they were) like a heap of ruins left by a flood" (Section 231, Luckenbill 1968: Vol. I).

[41] Luckenbill, section 341.

[42] At district of Uaiais: "I took that fortress from the rear, its warriors I slaughtered in front of its gate like lambs. Its orchards I cut down, its forests I felled, all of its severed tree trunks I gathered together and set them on fire" (Luckenbill, section 167); likewise Shalmaneser III against the king of the city of Gannanate, "I defeated him, I slew his people, . . . I carried off the grain of his fields, I cut down his orchards, I turned aside his river" (section 622, Luckenbill 1968: Vol. I).

[43] "When you besiege a city for a long time . . . you shall not destroy its trees by wielding an axe against them; for you may eat of them, but you shall not cut them down. Are the trees in the field men that they should be besieged by you? Only the trees which you know are not trees for food you may destroy and cut down that you may build siegeworks against the city that makes war with you, until it falls" (Deut. 20: 19–20).

Relatedly, that divine protection and kingly beneficence is measured at least in part by the flowering of orchards, vines, and fields is obvious in numerous boasts such as Sennacharib's: "By the command of the god, within the orchards, more than in their native habitat, the vine, every fruitbearing tree, and herbs throve luxuriously" (Luckenbill, section 402), or Ashurbanipal's: "After Ashur, Sin, Shamash, Adad, Bel,

The reasoning behind the exhortation that an enemy's city may become a desolate tell seems apparent. In nearly all cases, a major violation before the gods is said to have been committed, and the cost is extermination of the violator, his family, and his city. The wish to annihilate the enemy and all trace of him corresponds to the biblical practice of *herem* (the ban)[44] and arguably corresponds to aspects of religious warfare across the Mediterranean and Near East.[45] Given the crimes of oath-violation and hospitality-violation attributed to Troy, Agamemnon's wish to annihilate the people and city of Priam falls within traditional parameters for the rhetoric of religious warfare in the ancient Mediterranean and Near East.

That not only Troy but the bodies of the slain should be reduced to natural elements is of course a familiar theme in the *Iliad*, beginning with its opening eulogy to those whose bodies have become carrion for wild dogs and birds, and continuing through Book 22, when Achilles threatens to make Hector's body food for dogs (23.182–183). The Homeric theme of the mutilated corpse is familiar to students of the *Iliad*.[46] Part of its traditional horror lies in the lack of burial rites. This theme is not absent from some books of the Bible, particularly from the prophetic book of Jeremiah, which frequently relies on the tropes of bodily rending by animals and rent bodies becoming dung on the ground. For instance, the deity is made to avenge the practice of child-sacrifice by causing the bodies of the guilty to become "food for the birds of the air and the wild beasts, and there will be no one to scare them away . . . for the land will become desert" (Jer. 7:30–34). For the sin of denying the terms of the covenant with the one god, the people shall witness an enemy bringing the bones of the old kings, officers, and priests of Judah out of their graves and "they shall expose them to the sun, the moon, and all the host of heaven, . . . . Those bones shall not be gathered up nor buried but shall become dung on the ground" (Jer.8:1–3). In the same vein, "the corpses of men shall fall and lie like dung in the fields, / like swathes behind the

---

Nabu, Ishtar of Nineveh, queen of Kidmuri, Ishtar of Arbela, Urta, Nergal and Nusku, had caused me to take my seat, . . . Adad sent his rains, Ea opened his fountains, the grain grew 5 cubits tall in the stalk, the ear was 5/8 of a cubit long, heavy crops and a plenteous yield made the fields continuously luxuriant, the orchards yielded a rich harvest, the cattle successfully brought forth their young, – in my reign there was fulness to overflowing, in my years there was plenteous abundance" (Luckenbill, section 769).

[44] See Niditch 1993.
[45] See von Rad 1958, 1991.
[46] The classic treatment is Segal 1971.

reaper, but no one shall gather them" (Jer.9:22); "when men die, struck down by deadly ulcers, there shall be no wailing for them and no burial; they shall be like dung lying upon the ground. When men perish by sword or famine, their corpses shall become food for birds and for beasts" (Jer.16:4). For following false prophets, similarly, "the people to whom they prophesy shall be flung out into the streets of Jerusalem, victims of famine and sword; they, their wives, their sons, and their daughters, with no one to bury them: I will pour down upon them the evil they deserve" (Jer.14:16), and "four kinds of doom do I ordain for them, says the Lord: the sword to kill, dogs to tear, birds of prey from the skies, and beasts from their lairs to devour and destroy" (Jer.15:3–4).

Yet in Assyrian literature, perhaps surprisingly, the theme of a corpse mutilated by wild animals is eclipsed by the theme of the mutilation imposed on corpses by the warriors themselves. I found no Assyrian, or for that matter Hittite, battle boasts of casting bodies to wild animals. Rather, from Tiglath Pileser on down, the Assyrian kings themselves make pyramids of enemy heads,[47] scatter enemy corpses over the mountain sides,[48] and dye the plain with enemy blood. Occasionally a Near Eastern king does compare his destruction to that of a wild bull (for instance. Sennacharib) or a swarm of locusts (like Sargon[49]), or more simply compares his country to an indomitable animal (old Hittite king Anitta: "The countries are like a lion!"[50]); but a much more common theme is devastation by a king and his armies in the persona of a deluge or storm. Sennacharib, for instance, pressed on against Elam as a storm: "At the word of Ashur, the great lord, my lord, on flank and front I pressed upon the enemy like the onset of a raging storm."[51] He advanced swiftly upon Babylon like a hurricane: "Like the onset of a storm I broke loose, and overwhelmed it like a hurricane."[52] As we have seen, the language of natural disaster is not uncommon in battlefield theophanies.

---

[47] For example, Tiglath Pileser I against the Mushki, "I cut off their heads and outside their cities, like heaps of grain, I piled them up" (section 221, Luckenbill, Vol. I); Shalmaneser III against Aridi, the royal city of Ninni, "A pyramid (pillar) of heads I reared in front of his city" (section 598, Luckenbill, Vol. I)

[48] See, section 236 of Luckenbill, Tiglath Pileser I against the 23 kings of the land of Nairi: "The bodies of their warriors I scattered upon the high places of the mountains and alongside their cities like ____"; section 599, Shalmaneser III: "with the corpses of their warriors I filled the wide plain."

[49] Luckenbill, section 163.

[50] Bo 447, No.22 VAT 7479 (Forrer BoTU 2.7) Vs. line 26. (my translation)

[51] Luckenbill, section 254.

[52] Luckenbill, section 339.

Whether by storm or by rending by wild animals, the desired end is clearly the reduction of cities to the most elemental nature. This corresponds, again, to a pan-Mediterranean tradition of cursing violators of covenants. We have seen numerous accounts of oath-violating cities and individuals being reduced to nothingness. In the *Iliad*, that nothingness is occasionally earth. The theme that the accursed should be reduced to earth is implicit in a handful of curses, such as Menelaos' curse on the Achaians who refuse to fight Hector, "May you all be water and earth" (7.98), Hector's curse on Paris, "So may the earth swallow him" (6.282–283), and Diomedes' and Agamemnon's identical self-curses, "May the wide earth swallow me" (8.150, 4.182).

In sum, many of the *Iliad*'s battlefield theophanies fall into traditional Near Eastern patterns. Gods on the field of battle tend to be depicted as leading or marching with the fray, as inciting the warriors to a fighting frenzy, as stunning and bewitching them, and as punishing them for violations of oaths and other sacred covenants. Reports of such punishments tend to fall within some pan-Mediterranean poetic motifs, such as annihilation of whole families, reduction of cities to vacant mounds, rending of corpses by wild animals, and the reduction of perjurers to mere earth.

# CONCLUSION

To summarize, in the *Iliad* and seemingly throughout early Mediterranean and Near Eastern cultures, divine vengeance may be expected for oath-violation because the covenants forged by rituals are performed in a high register, according to canonical paradigms regarded as initiated and fixed by supernatural forces, and are regarded as on a par with bonds made of blood. Bonds forged by ritual are deemed irreversible, and as if inscribed on the cosmos itself. In Homeric tradition, such bonds are defended by the same forces that defend blood ties, suggesting equal standing between ritual bonds and blood bonds in the eyes of the gods. In Near Eastern traditions, the same equivalency is implied in treaty language awarding to treaty-partners various titles drawn from the sphere of family relations. These and other features of oath-making rituals in the *Iliad* have been found to correspond to features of oath-making as depicted in the traditional literatures of the ancient Near East.

Exploring the means by which the high register of certain ritual performances establishes authority and compulsion has been one of the aims of this book. Envisioning that register, authority, and compulsion through ritual narratives in the *Iliad* has been another. The structure of the oath-sacrificing typical scene has been demonstrated to be relatively fixed, and has been argued to correspond to the ritual item named a liturgical order by anthropologist Roy Rappaport. Liturgical orders confer a special degree of sanctity to ritual performances, based on the relative fixity of their utterances and gestures and on the relatively high register in which they communicate. Rituals have been argued to function essentially as means of communication, but they communicate in a different way than ordinary speech, by virtue of their highly paradigmatic nature. Based on their projection of the paradigmatic over the syntagmatic communicational axis, rituals may be said to generate a poetic "text" that, especially in the *Iliad*'s ritual scenes but also in some killing scenes, may be exploited by the poet, who weaves the poetic text produced by the ritual performance into the larger poetic text of the *Iliad*.

Further, the dynamic aspects of the oath-making ritual performance have been outlined in the terms of Fernandez's theory of ritual as effecting a metaphorical transformation for participants. The poetic use of ritual leitmotifs in the *Iliad* has been shown to shape expectations and interpretations of behavior on the battlefield, particularly in the case of Achilles' *poinē* and the case of the subtle oath-sacrificing ritual paradigm that underlies the killing of Lykaon and other victims of Achilles' *deirotomia*. The theory of ritual performance as metaphorical transformation opens up an intricate view of what happens in Homeric oath-sacrifice and certain battlefield killings by, among other things, highlighting the fictional capacity of human imagination and its response to ritualized speech acts and gestures. This fictional capacity of imagination is responsive not only to ritual practice but to oral poetry representing ritual practice, both of which may be understood as symbolic modes of communication, and which interpenetrate in Homer's *Iliad*. Because the interactive poetic practice thought to constitute oral traditional composition allows the symbolic language of ritual practice to emerge through the text, one may expect to find "ritual fictions" not only in ritual narratives but in other kinds of narratives whose semantic spheres overlap with rituals. Hence, oath-sacrifice generates its own ritual fictions that may be exploited in Homeric narratives of ritual killing and also battlefield killing. These ritual fictions are supported by symbolic acts as well as utterances within the oath-sacrificing narratives, and are enriched by a network of poetic images that effectively impress animal figures on human figures and vice versa.

That such ritual fictions are not unique to Homer but are part of a pan-Mediterranean imagination might be discerned in the recurring motifs for battlefield slaughter as animal sacrifice, for curses stressing the annihilation of families, towns, and bodies as a punishment for oath-violation, and for spectacles of divinities marching amidst armies to arouse their favorites in battle and to punish the violators of oaths.

Needless to say, understanding ritualized violence as an attempt at communication in a very high poetic register and as an attempt to dramatize the lethal consequences of violating sacred covenants, speaks to acts of religious violence beyond the *Iliad* and into the contemporary world. The contemporary implications of such a theory must await further reflection, but I hope that my audience will grasp the potential for a broader application.

# APPENDIX A

# HOMERIC TEXTS FOR THE PRINCIPAL OATHS DISCUSSED[1]

Achilles' oath to defend Kalchas (1.85–91).

"θαρσήσας μάλα εἰπὲ θεοπρόπιον ὅ τι οἶσθα·
οὐ μὰ γὰρ Ἀπόλλωνα Διὶ φίλον, ᾧ τε σὺ, Κάλχαν,
εὐχόμενος Δαναοῖσι θεοπροπίας ἀναφαίνεις,
οὔ τις ἐμεῦ ζῶντος καὶ ἐπὶ χθονὶ δερκομένοιο
σοὶ κοίλης παρὰ νηυσὶ βαρείας χεῖρας ἐποίσει
συμπάντων Δαναῶν, οὐδ' ἢν Ἀγαμέμνονα εἴπης,
ὅς νῦν πολλὸν ἄριστος Ἀχαιῶν εὔχεται εἶναι."

Achilles' oath by the scepter (1.233–244).

"'ἀλλ' ἔκ τοι ἐρέω καὶ ἐπὶ μέγαν ὅρκον ὀμοῦμαι·
ναὶ μὰ τόδε σκῆπτρον, τὸ μὲν οὔ ποτε φύλλα καὶ ὄζους
φύσει, ἐπὶ δὴ πρῶτα τομὴν ἐν ὄρεσσι λέλοιπεν,
οὐδ' ἀναθηλήσει· περὶ γάρ ῥά ἑ χαλκὸς ἔλεψε
φύλλα τε καὶ φλοιόν· νῦν αὖτέ μιν υἷες Ἀχαιῶν
ἐν παλάμῃς φορέουσι δικασπόλοι, οἵ τε θέμιστας
πρὸς Διὸς εἰρύαται· ὁ δέ τοι μέγας ἔσσεται ὅρκος·
ἦ ποτ' Ἀχιλλῆος ποθὴ ἵξεται υἷας Ἀχαιῶν
σύμπαντας· τότε δ' οὔ τι δυνήσεαι ἀχνύμενός περ
χραισμεῖν, εὖτ' ἂν πολλοὶ ὑφ' Ἕκτορος ἀνδροφόνοιο
θνήσκοντες πίπτωσι· σὺ δ' ἔνδοθι θυμὸν ἀμύξεις
χωόμενος ὅ τ' ἄριστον Ἀχαιῶν οὐδὲν ἔτεισας."

Thetis begs Zeus for a great oath to punish the Achaians for dishonoring Achilles (1.503–530).

[1] Greek passages reproduced by permission of Oxford University Press. Based on the Monroe and Allen edition of the *Iliad* (Oxford: Oxford University Press), Volume I (1982) and Volume II (1978).

"Ζεῦ πάτερ, εἴ ποτε δή σε μετ' ἀθανάτοισιν ὄνησα
ἢ ἔπει ἢ ἔργῳ, τόδε μοι κρήηνον ἐέλδωρ·
τίμησόν μοι υἱόν, ὃς ὠκυμορώτατος ἄλλων
ἔπλετ'· ἀτάρ μιν νῦν γε ἄναξ ἀνδρῶν Ἀγαμέμνων
ἠτίμησεν· ἑλὼν γὰρ ἔχει γέρας. αὐτὸς ἀπούρας.
ἀλλὰ σύ πέρ μιν τεῖσον, Ὀλύμπιε μητίετα Ζεῦ·
τόφρα δ' ἐπὶ Τρώεσσι τίθει κράτος, ὄφρ' ἂν Ἀχαιοὶ
υἱὸν ἐμὸν τείσωσιν ὀφελλωσίν τέ ἑ τιμῇ."
"Ὣς φάτο· τὴν δ' οὔ τι προσέφη νεφεληγερέτα Ζεύς,
ἀλλ' ἀκέων δὴν ἧστο· Θέτις δ' ὡς ἥψατο γούνων,
ὣς ἔχετ' ἐμπεφυυῖα, καὶ εἴρυτο δεύτερον αὖτις·
"νημερτὲς μὲν δή μοι ὑπόσχεο καὶ κατάνευσον,
ἢ ἀπόειπ', ἐπεὶ οὔ τοι ἔπι δέος, ὄφρ' ἐῢ εἰδέω
ὅσσον ἐγὼ μετὰ πᾶσιν ἀτιμοτάτη θεός εἰμι."
Τὴν δὲ μέγ' ὀχθήσας προσέφη νεφεληγερέτα Ζεύς·
"ἦ δὴ λοίγια ἔργ' ὅ τέ μ' ἐχθοδοπῆσαι ἐφήσεις
Ἥρῃ, ὅτ' ἄν μ' ἐρέθῃσιν ὀνειδείοις ἐπέεσσιν·
ἡ δὲ καὶ αὔτως μ' αἰεὶ ἐν ἀθανάτοισι θεοῖσι
νεικεῖ, καί τέ μέ φησι μάχῃ Τρώεσσιν ἀρήγειν.
ἀλλὰ σὺ μὲν νῦν αὖτις ἀπόστιχε, μή τι νοήσῃ
Ἥρη· ἐμοὶ δέ κε ταῦτα μελήσεται, ὄφρα τελέσσω·
εἰ δ' ἄγε τοι κεφαλῇ κατανεύσομαι, ὄφρα πεποίθῃς·
τοῦτα γὰρ ἐξ ἐμέθεν γε μετ' ἀθανάτοισι μέγιστον
τέκμωρ· οὐ γὰρ ἐμὸν παλινάγρετον οὐδ' ἀπατηλὸν
οὐδ' ἀτελεύτητον, ὅ τί κεν κεφαλῇ κατανεύσω."
Ἦ καὶ κυανέῃσιν ἐπ' ὀφρύσι νεῦσε Κρονίων·
ἀμβρόσιαι δ' ἄρα χαῖται ἐπερρώσαντο ἄνακτος
κρατὸς ἀπ' ἀθανάτοιο· μέγαν δ' ἐλέλιξεν Ὄλυμπον.

Hypothetical oath for purpose of census (2.123–130).

εἴ περ γάρ κ' ἐθέλοιμεν Ἀχαιοί τε Τρῶές τε,
ὅρκια πιστὰ ταμόντες, ἀριθμηθήμεναι ἄμφω,
Τρῶας μὲν λέξασθαι ἐφέστιοι ὅσσοι ἔασιν,
ἡμεῖς δ' ἐς δεκάδας διακοσμηθεῖμεν Ἀχαιοί,
Τρώων δ' ἄνδρα ἕκαστοι ἑλοίμεθα οἰνοχοεύειν,
πολλαί κεν δεκάδες δευοίατο οἰνοχόοιο.
τόσσον ἐγώ φημι πλέας ἔμμεναι υἷας Ἀχαιῶν
Τρώων, οἳ ναίουσι κατὰ πτόλιν·. . .

Odysseus swears by his own head, against Thersites (2.257–264).

ἀλλ' ἔκ τοι ἐρέω, τὸ δὲ καὶ τετελεσμένον ἔσται·
εἰ κ' ἔτι σ' ἀφραίνοντα κιχήσομαι ὥς νύ περ ὧδε,
μηκέτ' ἔπειτ' Ὀδυσῆϊ κάρη ὤμοισιν ἐπείη,

μηδ' ἔτι Τηλεμάχοιο πατὴρ κεκλημένος εἴην,
εἰ μὴ ἐγώ σε λαβὼν ἀπὸ μὲν φίλα εἵματα δύσω,
χλαῖνάν τ' ἠδὲ χιτῶνα, τά τ' αἰδῶ ἀμφικαλύπτει,
αὐτὸν δὲ κλαίοντα θοὰς ἐπὶ νῆας ἀφήσω
πεπλήγων ἀγορῆθεν ἀεικέσσι πληγῇσιν.

Nestor's complaint about the forgotten oaths of the Achaians (2.337–341).

"ὢ πόποι, ἦ δὴ παισὶν ἐοικότες ἀγοράασθε
νηπιάχοις, οἷς οὔ τι μέλει πολεμήϊα ἔργα.
πῇ δὴ συνθεσίαι τε καὶ ὅρκια βήσεται ἧμιν;
ἐν πυρὶ δὴ βουλαί τε γενοίατο μήδεά τ' ἀνδρῶν,
σπονδαί τ' ἄκρητοι καὶ δεξιαί, ἧς ἐπέπιθμεν·

Preparations for the oath-sacrifice of Book 3 (3.245–258).

Κήρυκες δ' ἀνὰ ἄστυ θεῶν φέρον ὅρκια πιστά,
ἄρνε δύω καὶ οἶνον ἐΰφρονα, καρπὸν ἀρούρης,
ἀσκῷ ἐν αἰγείῳ· φέρε δὲ κρητῆρα φαεινὸν
κῆρυξ Ἰδαῖος ἠδὲ χρύσεια κύπελλα·
ὄτρυνεν δὲ γέροντα παριστάμενος ἐπέεσσιν·
"ὄρσεο, Λαομεδοντιάδη, καλέουσιν ἄριστοι
Τρώων θ' ἱπποδάμων καὶ Ἀχαιῶν χαλκοχιτώνων
ἐς πεδίον καταβῆναι, ἵν' ὅρκια πιστὰ τάμητε·
αὐτὰρ Ἀλέξανδρος καὶ ἀρηΐφιλος Μενέλαος
μακρῆς ἐγχείῃσι μαχήσοντ' ἀμφὶ γυναικί·
τῷ δέ κε νικήσαντι γυνὴ καὶ κτήμαθ' ἕποιτο
οἱ δ' ἄλλοι φιλότητα καὶ ὅρκια πιστὰ ταμόντες
ναίοιμεν Τροίην ἐριβώλακα, τοὶ δὲ νέονται
Ἄργος ἐς ἱππόβοτον καὶ Ἀχαιΐδα καλλιγύναικα."

Oath-sacrifice of Book 3 (3.268–301).

. . .          ἀτὰρ κήρυκες ἀγαυοὶ
ὅρκια πιστὰ θεῶν σύναγον, κρητῆρι δὲ οἶνον
μίσγον, ἀτὰρ βασιλεῦσιν ὕδωρ ἐπὶ χεῖρας ἔχευαν.
Ἀτρεΐδης δὲ ἐρυσσάμενος χείρεσσι μάχαιραν,
ἥ οἱ πὰρ ξίφεος μέγα κουλεὸν αἰὲν ἄωρτο,
ἀρνῶν ἐκ κεφαλέων τάμνε τρίχας· αὐτὰρ ἔπειτα
κήρυκες Τρώων καὶ Ἀχαιῶν νεῖμαν ἀρίστοις.
τοῖσιν δ' Ἀτρεΐδης μεγάλ' εὔχετο χεῖρας ἀνασχών·
"Ζεῦ πάτερ, Ἴδηθεν μεδέων, κύδιστε μέγιστε,
Ἠέλιός θ', ὃς πάντ' ἐφορᾷς καὶ πάντ' ἐπακούεις,
καὶ ποταμοὶ καὶ γαῖα, καὶ οἳ ὑπένερθε καμόντας
ἀνθρώπους τίνυσθον, ὅτις κ' ἐπίορκον ὀμόσσῃ,
ὑμεῖς μάρτυροι ἔστε, φυλάσσετε δ' ὅρκια πιστά·

εἰ μὲν κεν Μενέλαον Ἀλέξανδρος καταπέφνῃ,
αὐτὸς ἔπειθ' Ἑλένην ἐχέτω καὶ κτήματα πάντα·
ἡμεῖς δ' ἐν νήεσσι νεώμεθα ποντοποροισιν·
εἰ δέ κ' Ἀλέξανδρον κτείνῃ ξανθὸς Μενέλαος,
Τρῶας ἔπειθ' Ἑλένην καὶ κτήματα πάντ' ἀποδοῦναι,
τιμὴν δ' Ἀργείοις ἀποτινέμεν ἥν τιν' ἔοικεν,
ἥ τε καὶ ἐσσομένοισι μετ' ἀνθρώποισι πέληται.
εἰ δ' ἂν ἐμοὶ τιμὴν Πρίαμος Πριάμοιό τε παῖδες
τίνειν οὐκ ἐθέλωσιν Ἀλεξάνδροιο πεσόντος,
αὐτὰρ ἐγὼ καὶ ἔπειτα μαχήσομαι εἵνεκα ποινῆς
αὐθι μένων, ἧός κε τέλος πολέμοιο κιχείω."
Ἦ, καὶ ἀπὸ στομάχους ἀρνῶν τάμε νηλέϊ χαλκῷ·
καὶ τοὺς μὲν κατέθηκεν ἐπὶ χθονὸς ἀσπαίροντας,
θυμοῦ δευομένους· ἀπὸ γὰρ μένος εἵλετο χαλκός.
οἶνον δ' ἐκ κρητῆρος ἀφυσσόμενοι δεπάεσσιν·
ἔκχεον, ἠδ' εὔχοντο θεοῖς αἰειγενέτῃσιν·
ὧδε δέ τις εἴπεσκεν Ἀχαιῶν τε Τρώων τε·
"Ζεῦ κύδιστε μέγιστε, καὶ ἀθάνατοι θεοὶ ἄλλοι,
ὁππότεροι πρότεροι ὑπὲρ ὅρκια πημήνειαν,
ὧδέ σφ' ἐγκέφαλος χαμάδις ῥέοι ὡς ὅδε οἶνος,
αὐτῶν καὶ τεκέων, ἄλοχοι δ' ἄλλοισι δαμεῖεν."

Agamemnon's lament over the wound of Menelaos (4.155–168).

"φίλε κασίγνητε, θάνατόν νύ τοι ὅρκι' ἔταμνον,
οἶον προστήσας πρὸ Ἀχαιῶν Τρωσὶ μάχεσθαι,
ὥς σ' ἔβαλον Τρῶες, κατὰ δ' ὅρκια πιστὰ πάτησαν.
οὐ μέν πως ἅλιον πέλει ὅρκιον αἷμά τε ἀρνῶν
σπονδαί τ' ἄκρητοι καὶ δεξιαί, ᾗς ἐπέπιθμεν·
εἴ περ γάρ τε καὶ αὐτίκ' Ὀλύμπιος οὐκ ἐτέλεσσεν,
ἔκ τε καὶ ὀψὲ τελεῖ, σύν τε μεγάλῳ ἀπέτεισαν,
σὺν σφῇσιν κεφαλῇσι γυναιξί τε καὶ τεκέσσιν.
εὖ γὰρ ἐγὼ τόδε οἶδα κατὰ φρένα καὶ κατὰ θυμόν·
ἔσσεται ἦμαρ ὅτ' ἄν ποτ' ὀλώλῃ Ἴλιος ἱρὴ
καὶ Πρίαμος καὶ λαὸς ἐϋμμελίω Πριάμοιο,
Ζεὺς δέ σφι Κρονίδης ὑψίζυγος, αἰθέρι ναίων,
αὐτὸς ἐπισσείῃσιν ἐρεμνὴν αἰγίδα πᾶσι
τῆσδ' ἀπάτης κοτέων· τὰ μὲν ἔσσεται οὐκ ἀτέλεστα."

Agamemnon's declaration that Zeus will avenge the violated oaths of the Trojans (4.234–239).

" Ἀργεῖοι, μή πώ τι μεθίετε θούριδος ἀλκῆς·
οὐ γὰρ ἐπὶ ψευδέσσι πατὴρ Ζεὺς ἔσσετ' ἀρωγός,
ἀλλ' οἵ περ πρότεροι ὑπὲρ ὅρκια δηλήσαντο,

τῶν ἤτοι αὐτῶν τέρενα χρόα γῦπες ἔδονται,
ἡμεῖς αὖτ᾽ ἀλόχους τε φίλας καὶ νήπια τέκνα
ἄξομεν ἐν νήεσσι, επὴν πτολίεθρον ἕλωμεν."

Idomeneus agrees with Agamemnon that the Trojans should be punished for oath-violation (4.265–270).

Τὸν δ᾽ αὖτ᾽ Ἰδομενεὺς Κρητῶν ἀγὸς ἀντίον ηὔδα·
" Ἀτρεΐδη, μάλα μέν τοι ἐγὼν ἐρίηρος ἐταῖρος
ἔσσομαι, ὡς τὸ πρῶτον ὑπέστην καὶ κατένευσα·
ἀλλ᾽ ἄλλους ὄτρυνε κάρη κομόωτας Ἀχαιούς,
ὄφρα τάχιστα μαχώμεθ᾽, ἐπεὶ σὺν γ᾽ ὅρκι᾽ ἔχευαν
Τρῶες· τοῖσιν δ᾽ αὖ θάνατος καὶ κήδε᾽ ὀπίσσω
ἔσσετ᾽, ἐπεὶ πρότεροι ὑπὲρ ὅρκια δηλήσαντο."

Hector's reaffirmation of the oath of Book 3, and invitation to a second duel (7.67–86).

"κέκλυτέ μευ, Τρῶες καὶ ἐϋκνήιδες Ἀχαιοί,
ὄφρ᾽ εἴπω τά με θυμὸς ἐνὶ στήθεσσι κελεύει.
ὅρκια μὲ Κρονίδης ὑψίζυγος οὐκ ἐτέλεσσεν,
ἀλλὰ κακὰ φρονέων τεκμαίρεται ἀμφοτέροισιν,
εἰς ὅ κεν ἢ ὑμεῖς Τροίην εὔπυργον ἕλητε,
ἢ αὐτοὶ παρὰ νηυσὶ δαμήετε ποντοπόροισιν.
ὑμῖν δ᾽ ἐν γὰρ ἔασιν ἀριστῆες Παναχαιῶν·
τῶν νῦν ὅν τινα θυμὸς ἐμοὶ μαχέσασθαι ἀνώγει,
δεῦρ᾽ ἴτω ἐκ πάντων πρόμος ἔμμεναι Ἕκτορι δίῳ.
ὧδε δὲ μυθέομαι, Ζεὺς δ᾽ ἄμμ᾽ ἐπιμάρτυρος ἔστω·
εἰ μέν κεν ἐμὲ κεῖνος ἕλῃ ταναήκεϊ χαλκῷ,
τεύχεα συλήσας φερέτω κοίλας ἐπὶ νῆας,
σῶμα δὲ οἴκαδ᾽ ἐμὸν δόμεναι πάλιν, ὄφρα πυρός με
Τρῶες καὶ Τρώων ἄλοχοι λελάχωσι θανόντα.
εἰ δέ κ᾽ ἐγὼ τὸν ἕλω, δώῃ δέ μοι εὖχος Ἀπόλλων,
τεύχεα συλήσας οἴσω προτὶ Ἴλιον ἱρήν,
καὶ κρεμόω προτὶ νηὸν Ἀπόλλωνος ἑκάτοιο,
τὸν δὲ νέκυν ἐπὶ νῆας ἐϋσσέλμους ἀποδώσω,
ὄφρα ἑ ταρχύσωσι κάρη κομόωντες Ἀχαιοί,
σῆμά τε οἱ χεύωσιν ἐπὶ πλατεῖ Ἑλλησπόντῳ.

Hector's "false oath" to Dolon (10.321–332).

"ἀλλ᾽ ἄγε μοι τὸ σκῆπτρον ἀνάσχεο, καί μοι ὄμοσσον
ἦ μὲν τοὺς ἵππους τε καὶ ἅρματα ποικίλα χαλκῷ
δωσέμεν, οἳ φορέουσιν ἀμύμονα Πηλεΐωνα,
σοὶ δ᾽ ἐγὼ οὐχ ἅλιος σκοπὸς ἔσσομαι οὐδ᾽ ἀπὸ δόξης·
τόφρα γὰρ ἐς στρατρὸν εἶμι διαμπερές, ὄφρ᾽ ἂν ἵκωμαι

νῆ᾽ Ἀγαμεμνονέην, ὅθι που μέλλουσιν ἄριστοι
Βουλὰς Βουλεύειν, ἢ φευγέμεν ἠὲ μάχεσθαι"
    "Ὣς φάθ᾽, ὁ δ᾽ ἐν χερσὶ σκῆπτρον λάβε καὶ οἱ ὅμοσσεν·
"ἴστω νῦν Ζεὺς αὐτός, ἐρίγδουπος πόσις Ἥρης,
μὴ μὲν τοῖς ἵπποισιν ἀνὴρ ἐποχήσεται ἄλλος
Τρώων, ἀλλά σέ φημι διαμπερὲς ἀγλαϊεῖσθαι."
    "Ὣς φάτο καί ῥ᾽ ἐπίορκον ἐτώμοσε, τὸν δ᾽ ὀρόθυνεν·

Hera swears that she will give to Hypnos a daughter of the Graces (14.270–276).

"Ὣς φάτο, χήρατο δ᾽" Ὕπνος, ἀμειβόμενος δὲ προσηύδα·
"ὄγρει νῦν μοι ὅμοσσον ἀάατον Στυγὸς ὕδωρ,
χειρὶ δὲ τῇ ἑτέρῃ μὲν ἕλε χθόνα πουλυβότειραν,
τῇ δ᾽ἑτέρῃ ἅλα μαρμαρέην, ἵνα νῶϊν ἅπαντες
μάτυροι ὦσ᾽ οἱ ἔνερθε θεοὶ Κρόνον ἀμφὶς ἐόντες,
ἦ μὲν ἐμοὶ δώσειν Χαρίτων μίαν ὁπλοτεράων,
Πασιθέην, ἧς τ᾽ αὐτὸς ἐέλδομαι ἤματα πάντα."

Hera swears not to have deceived Zeus (15.34–46)

"Ὣς φάτο, ῥίγησεν δὲ Βοῶις πότνια Ἥρη,
καί μιν φωνήσασ᾽ ἔπεα πτερόεντα προσηύδα·
"ἴστω νῦω τόδε Γαῖα καὶ Οὐρανὸς εὐρὺς ὕπερθε
καὶ τὸ κατειβόμενος Στυγὸς ὕδωρ, ὅς τε μέγιστος
ὅρκος δεινότατός τε πέλει μακάρεσσι θεοῖσι,
σή θ᾽ ἱερὴ κεφαλη καὶ νωΐτερον λέχος αὐτῶν
κουρίδιον, τὸ μὲν οὐκ ἂν ἐγώ ποτε μάψ ὀμόσαιμι·
μὴ δι᾽ ἐμὴν ἰότητα Ποσειδάων ἐνοσίχθων
πημαίνει Τρῶάς τε καὶ Ἕκτορα, τοῖσι δ᾽ ἀρήγει,
ἀλλά που αὐτὸν θυμὸς ἐποτρύνει καὶ ἀνώγει,
τειρομένους δ᾽ ἐπὶ νηυσὶν ἰδὼν ἐλέησεν Ἀχαιούς.
αὐτάρ τοι καὶ κείνῳ ἐγώ παραμυθησαίμην
τῇ ἴμεν καὶ ᾗ κεν δὴ σύ, κελαινεφές, ἡγεμονεύῃς."

Hera coaxes Zeus into making a great oath to allow dominion to a son born from his seed on this day, eventuating in the exile of *Atē* (Folly, Delusion) from heaven to earth (19.107–133).

τὸν δὲ δολοφρονέουσα προσηύδα πότνια Ἥρη·
'ψευστήσεις, οὐδ᾽ αὖτε τέλος μύθῳ ἐπιθήσεις.
εἰ δ᾽ ἄγε νῦν λμοι ὅμοσσον, Ὀλύμπιε, καρτερὸν ὅρκον,
ἦ μὲν τὸν πάντεσσι περικτιόνεσσιν ἀνάξειν,
ὅς κεν ἐπ᾽ ἤματι τῷδε πέσῃ μετὰ ποσσὶ γυναικὸς
τῶν ἀνδρῶν οἳ σῆς ἐξ αἵματός εἰσι γενέθλης.'

ὣς ἔφατο· Ζεὺς δ’ οὔ τι δολοφροσύνην ἐνόησεν,
ἀλλ’ ὄμοσεν μέγαν ὅρκον, ἔπειτα δὲ πολλὸν ἀάσθη.
Ἥρη δ’ ἀΐξασα λίπεν ῥίον Οὐλύμποιο,
καρπαλίμως δ’ ἵκετ’ Ἄργος Ἀχαιικόν, ἔνθ’ ἄρα ἤδη
ἰφθίμην ἄλοχον Σθενέλου Περσηϊάδαο.
ἡ δ’ ἐκύει φίλον υἱόν, ὁ δ’ ἕβδομος ἑστήκει μείς·
Ἀλκμήνης δ’ ἀπέπαυσε τόκον, σχέθε δ’ Εἰλειθυίας.
αὐτὴ δ’ ἀγγελέουσα Δία Κρονίωνα προσηύδα·
Ζεῦ πάτερ ἀργικέραυνε, ἔπος τί τοι ἐν φρεσὶ θήσω·
ἤδη ἀνὴρ γέγον’ ἐσθλός, ὃς Ἀργείοισιν ἀνάξει,
Εὐρυσθεύς, Σθενέλοιο πάϊς Περσηϊάδαο,
σὸν γένος· οὔ οἱ ἀεικὲς ἀνασσέμεν Ἀργείοισιν.’
ὣς φάτο, τὸν δ’ ἄχος ὀξὺ κατὰ φρένα τύψε βαθεῖαν·
αὐτίκα δ’ εἷλ’ Ἄτην κεφαλῆς λιπαροπλοκάμοιο
χωόμενος φρεσὶν ᾗσι, καὶ ὤμοσε καρτερὸν ὅρκον
μή ποτ’ ἐς Οὔλυμπόν τε καὶ οὐρανὸν ἀστερόεντα
αὖτις ἐλεύσεσθαι Ἄτην, ἣ πάντας ἀᾶται.
ὣς εἰπὼν ἔρριψεν ἀπ’ οὐρανοῦ ἀστερόεντος
χειρὶ περιστρέψας· τάχα δ’ ἵκετο ἔργ’ ἀνθρώπων.
τὴν αἰεὶ στενάχεσχ’, ὅθ’ ἑὸν φίλον υἱὸν ὁρῷτο
ἔργον ἀεικὲς ἔχοντα ὑπ’ Εὐρυσθῆος ἀέθων.

Odysseus encourages Agamemnon to swear an oath that he has not touched Briseis (19.171–183).

’αλλ’ ἄγε λαὸν μὲν σκέδασον καὶ δεῖπνον ἄνωχθι
ὅπλεσθαι· τὰ δὲ δῶρα ἄναξ ἀνδρῶν’ Ἀγαμέμνων
οἰσέτω ἐς μέσσην ἀγορήν, ἵνα πάντες Ἀχαιοὶ
ὀφθαλμοῖσιν ἴδωσι, σὺ δὲ φρεσὶ σῇσιν ἰανθῇς.
ὀμνυέτω δέ τοι ὅρκον ἐν Ἀργείοισιν ἀναστάς,
μή ποτε τῆς εὐνῆς ἐπιβήμεναι ἠδὲ μιγῆναι·
ἦ θέμις ἐστίν, ἄναξ, ἥ τ’ ἀνδρῶν ἤ τε γυναικῶν·
καὶ δὲ σοὶ αὐτῷ θυμὸς ἐνὶ φρεσὶν ἵλαος ἔστω.
αὐτὰρ ἔπειτά σε δαιτὶ ἐνὶ κλισίῃς ἀρεσάσθω
πιείρῃ, ἵνα μή τι δίκης ἐπιδευὲς ἐχῇσθα,
Ἀτρεΐδη, σὺ δ’ ἔπειτα δικαιότερος καὶ ἐπ’ ἄλλῳ
ἔσσεαι. οὐ μὲν γάρ τι νεμεσσητὸν βασιλῆα
ἄνδρ’ ἀπαρέσσασθαι, ὅτε τις πρότερος χαλεπήνῃ.”

Achilles is indignant that the Achaians think of eating before vengeance is paid, urges them to fast, and vows to fast until the fallen Achaians have been avenged (19.199–214).

“’Ἀτρεΐδη κύδιστε, ἄναξ ἀνδρῶν Ἀγάμεμνον,
ἄλλοτέ περ καὶ μᾶλλον ὀφέλλετε ταῦτα πένεσθαι,

ὁππότε τις μεταπαυσωλὴ πολέμοιο γένηται
καὶ μένος οὐ τόσον ἦσιν ἐνὶ στήθεσσιν ἐμοῖσι.
νῦν δ' οἱ μὲν κέαται δεδαϊγμένοι, οὓς ἐδάμασσεν
Ἕκτωρ Πριαμίδης, ὅτε οἱ Ζεὺς κῦδος ἔδωκεν,
ὑμεῖς δ' ἐς βρωτὺν ὀτρύνετον· ἦ τ' ἂν ἔγωγε
νῦν μὲν ἀνώγοιμι πτολεμίζειν υἷας Ἀχαιῶν
νήστιας ἀκμήνους, ἅμα δ' ἠελίῳ καταδύντι
τεύξεσθαι μέγα δόρπον, ἐπὴν τεισαίμεθα λώβην.
πρὶν δ' οὔ πως ἂν ἔμοιγε φίλον κατὰ λαιμὸν ἰείη
οὐ πόσις οὐδὲ βρῶσις, ἑταίρου τεθνηῶτος,
ὅς μοι ἐνὶ κλισίῃ δεδαϊγμένος ὀξέϊ χαλκῷ
κεῖται ἀνὰ πρόθυρον τετραμμένος, ἀμφὶ δ' ἑταῖροι
μύρονται· τό μοι οὔ τι μετὰ φρεσὶ ταῦτα μέμηλεν,
ἀλλὰ φόνος τε καὶ αἷμα καὶ ἀργαλέος στόνος ἀνδρῶν."

After bringing out the *apoina* for Achilles, Agamemnon makes an oath-sacrifice that he has not touched Briseis (19.250–268).

. . . Ταλθύβιος δὲ θεῷ ἐναλίγκιος αὐδὴν
κάπρον ἔχων ἐν χερσὶν παρίστατο ποιμένι λαῶν.
Ἀτρεΐδης δὲ ἐρυσσάμενος χείρεσσι μάχαιραν,
ἥ οἱ πὰρ ξίφεος μέγα κουλεὸν αἰὲν ἄωρτο,
κάπρον ἀπὸ τρίχας ἀρξάμενος, Διὶ χεῖρας ἀνασχών
εὔχετο· τοὶ δ' ἄρα πάντες ἐπ' αὐτόφιν ἧατο σιγῇ
Ἀργεῖοι κατὰ μοῖραν. ἀκούοντες Βασιλῆος.
εὐξάμενος δ' ἄρα εἶπεν ἰδὼν εἰς οὐρανὸν εὐρύν·
"ἴστω νῦν Ζεὺς πρῶτα, θεῶν ὕπατος καὶ ἄριστος,
Γῆ τε καὶ Ἠέλιός καὶ Ἐρινύες, αἵ θ' ὑπὸ γαῖαν
ἀνθρώπους τίνυνται, ὅτις κ' ἐπίορκον ὀμόσσῃ,
μὴ μὲν ἐγὼ κούρῃ Βρισηΐδι χεῖρ' ἐπένεικα,
οὔτ' εὐνῆς πρόφασιν κεχρημένος οὔτε τευ ἄλλου.
ἀλλ' ἔμεν' ἀπροτίμαστος ἐνὶ κλισίῃσιν ἐμῇσιν.
εἰ δέ τι τῶνδ' ἐπίορκον, ἐμοὶ θεοὶ ἄλγεα δοῖεν
πολλὰ μάλ', ὅσσα διδοῦσιν ὅτίς σφ' ἀλίτηται ὀμόσσας."
Ἦ, , καὶ ἀπὸ στομάχον κάπρου τάμε νηλέϊ χαλκῷ.
τὸν μὲν Ταλθύβιος πολιῆς ἁλὸς ἐς μέγα λαῖτμα
ρῖψ' ἐπιδινήσας, βόσιν ἰχθύσιν· . . .

Athene and Poseidon bind themselves to support Achilles, taking him by the hand (21.284–297).

Ὣς φάτο, τῷ δὲ μάλ' ὦκα Ποσειδάων καὶ Ἀθήνη
στήτην ἐγγὺς ἰόντε, δέμας δ' ἄνδρεσσιν ἐ ἴκτην,
χειρὶ δὲ χεῖρα λαβόντες ἐπιστώσαντ' ἐπέεσσι.
τοῖσι δὲ μύθων ἦρκε Ποσειδάων ἐνοσίχθων·

"Πηλεΐδη, μήτ' ἄρ τι λίην τρέε μήτε τι τάρβει·
τοίω γάρ τοι νῶϊ θεῶν ἐπιταρρόθω εἰμέν,
Ζηνὸς ἐπαινήσαντος, ἐγὼ καὶ Παλλὰς Ἀθήνη·
ὡς οὔ τοι ποταμῷ γε δαμήμεναι αἴσιμόν ἐστιν,
ἀλλ' ὅδε μὲν τάχα λωφήσει, σὺ δὲ εἴσεαι αὐτός·
αὐτάρ τοι πυκινῶς ὑποθησόμεθ', αἴ κε τίθηαι·
μὴ πρὶν παύειν χεῖρας ὁμοιίου πολέμοιο,
πρὶν κατὰ Ἰλιόφι κλυτὰ τείχεα λαὸν ἐέλσαι
Τρωϊκόν, ὅς κε φύγῃσι· σὺ δ' Ἕκτορι θυμὸν ἀπούρας
ἂψ ἐπὶ νῆας ἴμεν· δίδομεν δέ τοι εὖχος ἀρέσθαι."

River Xanthos is forced to swear an oath to Hera that he will not ward
off the day of ruin for the Trojans (21.372–376).

"ἀλλ' ἤτοι μὲν ἐγὼν ἀποπαύσομαι, εἰ σὺ κελεύεις,
παυέσθω δὲ καὶ οὗτος· ἐγὼ δ' ἐπὶ καὶ τόδ' ὀμοῦμαι,
μή ποτ' ἐπὶ Τρώεσσιν ἀλεξήσειν κακὸν ἦμαρ,
μήδ' ὁπότ' ἂν Τροίη μαλερῷ πυρὶ πᾶσα δάηται
καιομένη, καίωσι δ' ἀρήϊοι υἷες Ἀχαιῶν."

Hector contemplates an oath by senators to dissuade Achilles from killing
him (22.111–125).

εἰ δέ κεν ἀσπίδα μὲν καταθείομαι ὀμφαλόεσσαν
καὶ κόρυθα βριαρήν, δόρυ δὲ πρὸς τεῖχος ἐρείσας
αὐτὸς ἰὼν Ἀχιλῆος ἀμύμονος ἀντίος ἔλθω
καί οἱ ὑπόσχωμαι Ἑλένην καὶ κτήμαθ' ἅμ' αὐτῇ,
πάντα μάλ' ὅσσα τ' Ἀλέξανδρος κοίλης ἐνὶ νηυσὶν
ἠγάγετο Τροίηδ', ἥ τ' ἔπλετο νείκεος ἀρχή,
δωσέμεν Ἀτρεΐδῃσιν ἄγειν, ἅμα δ' ἀμφὶς Ἀχαιοῖς
ἀλλ' ἀποδάσσεσθαι, ὅσα τε πτόλις ἥδε κέκευθε·
Τρωσὶν δ' αὖ μετόπισθε γερούσιν ὅρκον ἕλωμαι
μή τι κατακρύψειν, ἀλλ' ἄνδιχα πάντα δάσασθαι
κτῆσιν ὅσην πτολίεθρον ἐπήρατον ἐντὸς ἐέργει·
ἀλλὰ τίη μοι ταῦτα φίλος διελέξατο θυμός;
μή μιν ἐγὼ μὲν ἵκωμαι ἰών, ὁ δέ μ' οὐκ ἐλεήσει
οὐδέ τί μ' αἰδέσεται, κτενέει δέ με γυμνὸν ἐόντα
αὔτως ὥς τε γυναῖκα, ἐπεί κ' ἀπὸ τεύχεα δύω.

Hector appeals to Achilles for an oath to respect each other's corpse
(22.252–259).

". . . νῦν αὖτέ με θυμὸς ἀνῆκε
στήμεναι ἀντία σεῖο· ἕλοιμί κεν, ἤ κεν ἁλοίην.
ἀλλ' ἄγε δεῦρο θεοὺς ἐπιδώμεθα· τοὶ γὰρ ἄριστοι

μάρτυροι ἔσσονται καὶ ἐπίσκοποι ἁρμονιάων·
οὐ γὰρ ἐγώ σ᾽ ἔκπαγλον ἀεικιῶ, αἴ κεν ἐμοὶ Ζεὺς
δώῃ καμμονίην, σὴν δὲ ψυχὴν ἀφέλωμαι·
ἀλλ᾽ ἐπεὶ ἄρ κέ σε συλήσω κλυτὰ τεύχε᾽, Ἀχιλλεῦ,
νεκρὸν Ἀχαιοῖσιν δώσω πάλιν· ὣς δὲ σὺ ῥέζειν."

Achilles rejects Hector's appeal for an oath (22.261–267).

"Ἕκτορ, μή μοι, ἄλαστε, συνημοσύνας ἀγόρευε·
ὡς οὐκ ἔστι λέουσι καὶ ἀνδράσιν ὅρκια πιστά,
οὐδὲ λύκοι τε καὶ ἄρνες ὁμόφρονα θυμὸν ἔχουσιν,
ἀλλὰ κακὰ φρονέουσι διαμπερὲς ἀλλήλουσιν,
ὣς οὐκ ἔστ᾽ ἐμὲ καὶ σὲ φιλήμεναι, οὐδέ τι νῶϊν
ὅρκια ἔσσονται, πρίν γ᾽ ἢ ἕτερόν γε πεσόντα
αἵματος ἆσαι Ἄρηα, ταλαύρινον πολεμιστήν."

Menelaos bids Antilochus to swear an oath that he did not cheat during
the chariot race at Patroklos's funeral games (23.582–585).

"Ἀντίλοχ᾽ εἰ δ᾽ ἄγε δεῦρο, διοτρεφές ἢ θέμις ἐστί,
στὰς ἵππων προπάροιθε καὶ ἄρματος, αὐτὰρ ἱμάσθλην
χερσὶν ἔχε ῥαδινήν, ᾗ περ τὸ πρόσθεν ἔλαυνες,
ἵππων ἁψάμενος γαιήοχον ἐννοσίγαιον
ὄμνυθι μὴ μὲν ἑκὼν τὸ ἐμὸν δόλῳ ἅρμα πεδῆσαι."

Achilles promises Priam to hold off the war until the Trojans can bury
Hector (23.668–672).

τὸν δ᾽ αὖτε προσέειπε ποδάρκης δῖος Ἀχιλλεύς·
"ἔσται τοι καὶ ταῦτα, γέρον Πρίαμ᾽, ὡς σὺ κελεύεις·
σχήσω γὰρ πόλεμον τόσσον χρόνον ὅσσον ἄνωγας."
Ὣς ἄρα φωνήσας ἐπὶ καρπῷ χεῖρα γέροντος
ἔλλαβε δεξιτερήν, μή πως δείσει᾽ ἐνὶ θυμῷ.

# BIBLIOGRAPHY

Alexiou, Margaret (1990) "Reappropriating Greek Sacrifice: *homo necans* or ἄνθρωπος θυσιάζων?" *Journal of Modern Greek Studies* 8: 97–123.

Alter, Robert (1996) *Genesis*. New York: W. W. Norton & Company.

Amodio, Mark C. (1998) "Contemporary Critical Approaches and Studies in Oral Tradition." In *Teaching Oral Traditions*. Ed. John Miles Foley. New York: The Modern Language Association. 95–105.

Andersen, O. (1976) "Some Thoughts on the Shield of Achilles." *Symbolae Osloenses* LI 5–18.

Archi, Alfonso (1973). "L'Organizzazione amministrative ittita e il regime delle offerte cultuali." *Or An* XII: 3 209–226.

Archi, Alfonso (2002) "Kizzuwatna Amid Anatolian and Syrian Cults." In *Anatolia Antica, Studi in memoria di Fiorella Imparati*, Vol. I. Ed. Stefano de Martino e Franca Pecchioli Daddi. Florence: Lo Gisma. 47–54

Archi, Alfonso (1975). "Il Culto Del Focolare presso gli Ittiti." *Studi micenei ed egeo-anatolici* XVI: 77–87.

Arend, Walter (1933) *Die Typischen Scenen bei Homer*. Problemata Forschungen zur Klassischen Philologie. Berlin: Weidmannsche Buchhandlung.

Austin, J. L. (1975) *How To Do Things with Words*. Cambridge: Harvard University Press (originally published 1962).

Bakker, Egbert and Florence Fabbricotti (1991) "Peripheral and Nuclear Semantics in Homeric Diction." *Mnemosyne* XLIV:1–2 63–84.

Bateson, Gregory (1972, 1985) *Steps to an Ecology of Mind*. New York: Ballantine Books (Random House).

Beckman, Gary (1983) *Hittite Birth Rituals*. Weisbaden: Otto Harrassowitz.

Beckman, Gary (1986) "Proverbs and Proverbial Allusions in Hittite." *Journal of Near Eastern Studies* 45 no. 1, 19–30.

Beckman, Gary (1996) *Hittite Diplomatic Texts*, Vol. I. Atlanta: Scholars Press.

Bell, Catherine (1992) *Ritual Theory, Ritual Practice*. New York: Oxford University Press.

Bickerman, E. J. (1976) "Couper une alliance," *Studies in Jewish and Christian History, Vol. I.* Leiden: E. J. Brill, 1–32.

Blickman, Daniel R. (1987) "Styx and the Justice of Zeus in Hesiod's Theogony." *Phoenix* 41 341–55.

Bloch, Maurice (1974) "Symbols, Song, Dance and Features of Articulation: Is Religion an Extreme Form of Traditional Authority?" *Archives Europeenes de Sociologie* 15, 55–81, cited by Catherine Bell (1992: 214–15).

Bloch, Maurice (1975) *Political Language and Oratory in Traditional Society.* London: Academy Press.

Bloch, Maurice (1992) *Prey into Hunter.* Cambridge: Cambridge University Press.

Bonnechere, Pierre (1999) "'La machaira etá' dissimulee dans le kanoun': quelques interrogations." *Revue des etudes anciennes* 101:1–2 21–35.

Bourdieu, Pierre (1991) *Language and Symbolic Power.* Trans. Gino Raymond and Matthew Adamson. Cambridge, MA: Harvard University Press.

Bowie, A. M. (1995) "Greek Sacrifice: Forms and Functions." In *The Greek World.* Ed. Anton Powell. London: Routledge. 463–82.

Bruitt Zaidman, Louise, and Schmitt Pantel, Pauline (1989, 1992, 1994) *Religion in the Ancient Greek City* (Cambridge: Cambridge University Press).

Burkert, Walter (1983) *Homo Necans.* Trans. Peter Bing. Berkeley: University of California Press.

Burkert, Walter (1985) *Greek Religion.* Cambridge, MA: Harvard University Press.

Burkert, Walter (1987) "Offerings in Perspective: Surrender, Distribution, Exchange." In *Gifts to the Gods: Proceedings of the Uppsala Symposium 1985.* Ed. J. Linders and G. Nordquist, Acta Universitatis Upsaliensis: Boreas 15 43–50.

Burkert, Walter (1992) *The Orientalizing Revolution.* Cambridge, MA: Harvard University Press.

Burkert, Walter (1996) *Creation of the Sacred.* Cambridge, MA: Harvard University Press.

Charpin, Dominique (1996) "Manger un serment." *Jurer et Maudire: practiques politiques et usages juridiques du serment dans le Proche-Orient ancient.* Paris: L'Harmattan. Mediterranees 10–11 85–96.

Chirassi-Colombo, Ileana (1975) "I doni di Demeter: mito e ideologia nella Grecia arcaica." In *Studi Triestine di Antichita' in Onore di Luigia Achillea Stella.* Trieste: Universitá' degli studi antichi di Trieste.

deHeusch, Luc (1985) *Sacrifice in Africa: A Structuralist Approach.* Bloomington: Indiana University Press.

Detienne, Marcel (1994) *The Gardens of Adonis: Spices in Greek Mythology.* Trans. Janet Lloyd. Princeton: Princeton University Press.

Detienne, Marcel (1989) "Culinary Practices and the Spirit of Sacrifice." In *The Cuisine of Sacrifice among the Greeks.* Ed. Marcel Detienne and Jean-Pierre Vernant. Chicago: University of Chicago Press. 1–20.

Duckworth, George (1933) *Foreshadowing and Suspense in the Epics of Homer, Apollonius, and Vergil.* Princeton: Princeton University Press.

Durkheim, Emile (1915) *The Elementary Forms of Religious Life.* Trans. Joseph Ward Swain. New York: The Free Press.

Edwards, Mark (1975) "Type-Scenes and Homeric Hospitality," *Transactions of the American Philological Association* 105: 51–72.

Edwards, Mark (1987) *Homer, Poet of the Iliad.* Baltimore: Johns Hopkins University Press.

Edwards, Mark (1991) *The Iliad: A Commentary. Vol. V.* Cambridge: Cambridge University Press.

Eilberg-Schwartz, Howard (1990) *The Savage in Judaism.* Bloomington: Indiana University Press.

Faraone, Christopher (1993) "Molten Wax, Spilt Wine and Mutilated Animals: Sympathetic Magic in Near Eastern and Early Greek Oath Ceremonies." *Journal of Hellenic Studies* cxiii 60–80.

Fenik, Bernard (1968) *Typical Battle Scenes in the Iliad.* Wiesbaden: Franz Sterlag.

Fernandez, James W. (1972) "Persuasions and Performances: Of the Beast in Every Body . . . and the Metaphors of Everyman." *Daedalus* 101:1. 39–59.

Fernandez, James W. (1977) "The Performance of Ritual Metaphors." In *The Social Use of Metaphor.* Ed. J. David Sapir and J. Christopher Crocker. Philadelphia: University of Pennsylvania Press. 100–31.

Finet, A. (1993) "Le sacrifice de l'ane en Mesopotamie." *Ritual and Sacrifice in the Ancient Near East.* Ed. J. Quaegebeur. Leuven: Orientalia Louvaniensia Analecta 55, Leuven: Uitgeverij Peeters en Departement Oriëntalistiek, 135–42.

Floyd, Erwin (1989) "Homer and the Life-Producing Earth." *Classical World* 2 1ff.

Foley, Helene (1994) *The Homeric Hymn to Demeter.* Princeton: Princeton University Press.

Foley, John Miles (1990) *Traditional Oral Epic.* Berkeley: University of California Press.

Foley, John Miles (1991) *Immanent Art, from Structure to Meaning in Traditional Oral Epic.* Bloomington: Indiana University Press.

Foley, John Miles (1997) "Oral Tradition and Its Implications." In *A New Companion to Homer.* Ed. Ian Morris & Barry Powell. Leiden: E. J. Brill. 146–73.

Freud, Sigmund (1946) "The Infantile Recurrence of Totemism." In *Totem and Taboo.* New York: Random House, Vintage Books. Originally published by E. J. Brill 1918.

Gadamer, Hans-Georg (1976) *Philosophical Hermeneutics.* Berkeley: University of California Press.

Geertz, Clifford (1972) "Deep Play: Notes on the Balinese Cockfight." *Daedalus* 101:1 1–71.

George, Andrew (1999) *The Epic of Gilgamesh, A New Translation.* Oxford: Oxford University Press.

George, Andrew (2003) *The Babylonian Gilgamesh Epic, Vols. I and II.* Oxford: Oxford University Press.

Giorgieri, Mauro (2001) "Aspetti magico-religiosi del giuramento presso gli ittiti e i Greci." In *La questione delle influenze vicino-orientali sulla religione greca.* Ed. Sergio Ribichini, Maria Rocchi, Paolo Xelle. Rome: Consiglio Naziowale delle Recerche. 421–40.

Giorgieri, Mauro (2002) "Birra, acqua ed olio: paralleli sirianni e neo-assiri ad un giuramento ittita." In *Anatolia Antica, Studi in memoria di Fiorella Imparati.* Vol. 1, Ed. Stefano de Martino e Franca Pecchioli Daddi. Florence: Lo Gisma. 299–320.

Girard, René (1977) *Violence and the Sacred.* Trans. Patrick Gregory. Baltimore: Johns Hopkins University Press.

Girard, Rene (2000, 1996) *The Girard Reader.* Ed. James G. Williams. New York: Crossroads.

Giudorizzi, Giulio (2002) "Uno scudo pieno di sangue." In *I Sette A Tebe. Dal mito alla letterature.* Bologna: Patrone Editore. 63–72.

Gottwald, Norman (forthcoming) "Proto-Globalization and Proto-Secularization in Ancient Israel," forthcoming in *Out of the Cloister a Festschrift in Honor of William G. Dever.* Ed. S. Gitin, J. E. Wright, and J. P. Dessel. Winona Lake, IN: Eisenbrauns, in press.

Gould, John (1973). "Hiketeia." *Journal of Hellenistic Studies* 93 74–103.

Gouldner, Alvin W. (1960) "The Norm of Reciprocity: A Preliminary Statement." *American Sociological Review* 25:161–78.

Graf, Fritz (1980) "Milch, Honig und Wein." In *Perennitas, Studi in Onore di Angelo Brelich.* Ed. G. Piccaluga. Rome: Edizione dell'Ateneo.

Graf, Fritz (1997) *Magic in the Ancient World.* Trans. Franklin Philip. Cambridge, MA: Harvard University Press.

Gray, John Glen (1970) *The Warriors, Reflections on Men in Battle.* New York: Harper & Row (First published 1959).

Griffin, Jasper (1980, 1990) *Homer on Life and Death.* Oxford: Clarendon Press.

Griffiths, Alan (1985) "A Ram Called Patroklos." *Bulletin of the Institute of Classical Studies* 32: 49–50 (plus plates).

Griffiths, Alan (1989) "Patroklos the Ram (Again)." *Bulletin of the Institute of Classical Studies* 36: 139 (plus plate).

Grottanelli, Cristiano (1988) "Uccidere, donare, mangiare. Problematiche attuali dei sacrificio antico." In *Sacrificio nel mondo antico.* Ed. C. Grottanelli and N. F. Parese. Roma–Bari: Laterza. 3–53.

Gunter, Ann C. (1990) "Models of the Orient in the Art History of the Orientalizing Period." In *Achaemenid History V: The Roots of the European Tradition.* Ed. S. Sancisi-Weerdenburg and J. W. Drijvers, Leiden: Nederlands Instrutuut Voor Het Nabije Oosten. 131–47.

Gurney, O. R. (1976) *Some Aspects of Hittite Religion*. Oxford: Oxford University Press.

Guthrie, W. K. C. (1955) *The Greeks and Their Gods*. Boston: Beacon Press.

Güterbock, Hans (1996) "Troy in Hittite Texts? Wilusa, Ahhiyawa and Hittite History." In *Troy and the Trojan War*. Ed. Machteld J. Mellink. Bryn Mawr, PA: Bryn Mawr College. 33–44.

Güterbock, Hans G. and Herry A. Hoffner, Eds. (1980) *The Hittite Dictionary*, Vol.3, Fascicle 1. Chicago: The Oriental Institute of the University of Chicago.

Hedges, Chris (2002) *War Is a Force that Gives Us Meaning*. New York: Random House Books.

Herman, Gabriel (1987) *Ritualized Friendship and the Greek City*. Cambridge: Cambridge University Press.

Heubeck, Alfred (1986) "Erinus in der archaischen Epik." *Glotta* 64. 145–65.

Higbie, Carolyn (1990) *Measure and Music: Enjambcment and Sentence Structure in the Iliad*. Oxford: Clarendon Press.

Hillers, Delbert (1964) *Treaty-Curses and the Old Testament Prophets*. Rome: Pontifical Biblical Institute.

Hiltebeitel, Alf (1990) *The Ritual of Battle*. New York: SUNY Press.

Hoffner, Jr., Harry A. (1973) "Incest, Sodomy and Bestiality in the Ancient Near East." *Alter Orient und Altest Testament* Vol. 22 81–90.

Hoffner, Jr., Harry A. (1990) *Hittite Myths*. Society of Biblical Literature Vol. 2. Atlanta: Scholars' Press.

Holloway, Steven W. (2002) *Assur Is King! Assur Is King! Religion in the Exercise of Power in the Neo-Assyrian Empire*. Leiden: E. J. Brill.

Hughes, Dennis (1991) *Human Sacrifice in Ancient Greece*. London: Routledge.

Huizinga, Johann (1950) *Homo Ludens, A Study of the Play-Element in Culture*. Boston: Beacon Press.

Jameson, Michael H. (1988) "Sacrifice and Ritual: Greece." In *Civilization of the Ancient Mediterranean*. Ed. Michael Grant and Rachel Kitzinger. Schribner. 959–79.

Janko, Richard (1992) *The Iliad: A Commentary, Vol. IV*. Cambridge: Cambridge University Press.

Jensen, Adolf E. (1951) *Myth and Cult among Primitive Peoples*. Trans. Marianna Tax Choldin and Wolfgang Weissleder. Reprinted 1963. Chicago: University of Chicago Press.

Johnson, Mark (1981) "Introduction: Metaphor in the Philosophical Tradition." In *Philosophical Perspectives on Metaphor*. Minneapolis: Universat of Minnesota Press, 3–47.

Juergensmeyer, Mark (2000) *Terror in the Mind of God*. Berkeley: University of California Press.

Karavites, Peter (1992) *Promise-Giving and Treaty-Making*. Leiden: E. J. Brill.

Kiparsky, Paul. (1976) "Oral Poetry: Some Linguistic and Typological Consider-ations." In *Oral Literature and the Formula.* Ed. Stoz and Shannon. Ann Arbor, MI: Center for the Coordination of Ancient ·and Modern Studies. 73–105.

Kirk, G. S. (1985) *The Iliad: A Commentary, Vol. I.* Cambridge: Cambridge University Press.

Kitts, Margo (1992) "The Sacrifice of Lykaon in Iliad 21:1–25" *Mētis* 7(1–2) 161–176.

Kitts, Margo (1994) "Two Expressions for Human Mortality in the Epics of Homer." *History of Religions* November: 132–51.

Kitts, Margo (1999) "Killing, Healing, and the Hidden Motif of Oath-Sacrifice in Iliad 21." *Journal of Ritual Studies* 13:2 42–57.

Kitts, Margo (2000) "The Wide Bosom of the Sea as a Place of Death: Maternal and Sacrificial Imagery in Iliad 21." *Literature and Theology* 14:2, 103–24.

Kitts, Margo (2002) "Sacrificial Violence in the Iliad." *Journal of Ritual Studies* 16:1 19–39.

Kitts, Margo (2003) "Not Barren Is the Blood of Lambs: Homeric Oath-Sacrifice as Metaphorical Transformation." *Kernos, Revue internationale et pluridisciplinaire de religion grecque ancienne,* 16: 17–34.

Lakoff, George, with Mark Johnson (1980) *Metaphors We Live By.* Chicago: University of Chicago.

Lakoff, George, with Mark Johnson (1981) "Conceptual Metaphor in Ever-day Language." In *Philosophical Perspectives on Metaphor.* Ed. Mark Johnson. Minneapolis: University of Minnesota Press. 286–328.

Langer, Susanne (1951) *Philosophy in a New Key.* New York: New American Library. Quoted in Tambiah (1979: 125).

Lateiner, Donald (1995) *Sardonic Smile, Nonverbal Behavior in Homeric Epic.* Ann Arbor: University of Michigan Press.

Launderville, Dale (2003) *Piety and Politics, The Dynamics of Royal Authority in Homeric Greece, Biblical Israel, and Old Babylonian Mesopotamia.* Grand Rapids, MI: Eerdmans.

Lebrun, Rene (1993) "Aspects particuliers du sacrifice dans le monde Hittite. In *Ritual and Sacrifice in the Ancient Near East.* Ed. J. Quaegebeur. Leuven: Uitgeverij Peeters en Departement Orientalistick 225–53.

Lévi-Strauss, Claude (1981) *The Naked Man.* Trans. John and Doreen Weight-man. New York: Harper & Row. French *L'Homme Nu* (Librarie Plon 1971).

Liddell & Scott (1968) *A Greek English Lexicon,* Oxford: Clarendon Press.

Lord, Albert (1960) *The Singer of Tales.* Cambridge, MA: Harvard University Press.

Lorenz, Konrad Z. (1952) *King Solomon's Ring.* Trans. Majorie Kerr Wilson. New York: Harper & Row.

Lowenstam, Steven (1981) *The Death of Patroklos, A Study in Typology.* Konigstein/Ts: Hain.

Luckenbill, Daniel David (1968) *Ancient Records of Assyria and Babylonia, Vol. I* (originally published 1926, University of Chicago); *Ancient Records of Assyria and Babylonia, Vol. II* (originally published 1927, University of Chicago). New York: Greenwood Press 1968.

Lynn-George, Michael (1993) "Aspects of the Epic Vocabulary of Vulnerability." *Colby Quarterly* XXIX:3 197–221.

Magdalene, F. Rachel (1995) "Ancient Near Eastern Treaty-Curses and the Ultimate Texts of Terror: A Study of the Language of Divine Sexual Abuse in the Prophetic Corpus." In *A Feminist Companion to the Latter Prophets*. Ed. Athalya Bremmer. Sheffield: Sheffield Academic Press. 326–52.

Malina, Bruce J. (1996) "Mediterranean Sacrifice: Dimensions of Domestic and Political Religion." *Biblical Theology Bulletin* 26:26–44.

Martin, Richard P. (1983) *Healing, Sacrifice, and Battle*. Innsbruck: Innsbrucker Beitrage zur Sprachwissenschaft #41.

Martin, Richard P. (1989) *The Language of Heroes*. Ithaca: Cornell University Press.

Martin, Richard P. (1993) "Telemachus and the Last Hero Song." *Colby Quarterly* XXIX:3 222–40.

Matthews, Victor (2000) *Old Testament Themes*. St. Louis: Chalice Press.

McCarthy, Dennis J. (1966) *Der Gottesbund im Alten Testament*. Stuttgart: Verlag Katholische Bibelwerk.

McTernan, Oliver (2003) *Violence in God's Name*. New York: Orbis Books.

Michel, Cecile (1996) "Hommes et femmes pretent serment a l'epoque paleo-assyrienne." In *Jurer et Maudire: practiques politiques et usages juridiques du serment dans le Proche-Orient ancient*. Paris: L'Harmattan. (Méditerranées 10/11) 109–18.

Mikalson, Jon D. (1991) *Honor Thy Gods*. Chapel Hill: University of North Carolina Press.

Milbank, John (1996) "Stories of Sacrifice." *Modern Theology* 12:1 27–56.

Mondi, Robert (1990) "Greek Mythic Thought in the Light of the Near East." In *Approaches to Greek Myth*. Ed. Lowell Edmunds. Baltimore: Johns Hopkins University Press. 142–98.

Morris, Sarah (1995) "The Sacrifice of Astyanax: Near Eastern Contributions to the Siege of Troy." In *The Ages of Homer: A Tribute to Emily Townsend Vermeule*. Ed. Jane B. Carter and Sarah P. Morris. Austin: University of Texas. 221–44.

Morris, Sarah (1997) "Homer and the Near East." In *A New Companion to Homer*. Ed. Ian Morris and Barry Powell. Leiden: E. J. Brill. 599–623.

Morrison, J. V. (1991) "The Function and Context of Homeric Prayers: A Narrative Perspective." *Hermes* 139 145–57.

Muellner, Leonard (1976) *The Meaning of Homeric [Euchomai] Through Its Formulas*. Innsbruck: Institut fur Sprachwissenschaft der Universitat Innsbruck.

Nagler, Michael (1974) *Spontaneity and Tradition*. Berkeley: University of California Press.

Nagy, Gregory (1979) *The Best of the Achaeans*. Baltimore: Johns Hopkins University Press.

Nagy, Gregory (1990) "Formula and Meter." In *Greek Mythology and Poetics*. Ithaca, NY: Cornell University Press.

Nagy, Gregory (1996) *Poetry as Performance*. Cambridge: Cambridge University Press. 107–52.

Niditch, Susan (1993) *War in the Hebrew Bible*. New York: Oxford University Press.

O'Brien. Tim (1990) "How To Tell a True War Story." *The Things They Carried*. Boston: Houghton Mifflin. 75–91.

Ong, Walter (1977) *Interfaces of the Word*. London: Cornell University Press.

Otten, Heinrich (1981) *Die Apologie Hattusilis III, Studien zu den Bogazkoy-Texten*, Heft 24. Wiesbaden: Otto Harrassowitz.

Otto, Rudolf (1958) *The Idea of the Holy: An Inquiry into the Non-Rational Factor in the Idea of the Divine and Its Relation to the Rational*. Trans. John W. Harvey. London: Oxford University Press.

Parpola, Simo, and Watanabe, Kazuko, Eds. (1988) *State Archives of Assyria, Vol. II, Neo-Assyrian Treaties and Loyalty Oaths*. Helsinki: The Neo-Assyrian Text Corpus Project and the Helsinki Press, 9.

Parry, Milman (1987a) "Enjambement in Homeric Verse." In *The Making of Homeric Verse*. Ed. Adam Parry. New York: Oxford University Press. 252–65.

Parry, Milman (1987b) *The Making of Homeric Verse, The Collected Papers of Milman Parry*. Ed. Adam Parry. New York: Oxford University Press.

Pecchioli-Daddi, Franca (1982) *Mestieri, professioni e dignita' nel'Anatolia ittita*. Roma: Edizioni dell'Ateneo.

Plescia, Joseph (1970) *The Oath and Perjury in Ancient Greece*. Tallahassee: Florida State University Press.

Ponchia, Simonetta (1987) "Analogie, Metafore, e Similitudini nelle iscrizioni reali assire: Semantica e Ideologia." *Oriens Antiquus* XXVI:3–4. 223–55.

Puhvel, Jaan (1991) *Homer and Hittite*. Innsbruck: Inst. f. Sprachwiss. d. Univ. 9–12.

Rappaport, Roy A. (1979) "The Obvious Aspects of Ritual." In *Ecology, Meaning and Religion*. Berkeley, CA: North Atlantic. 175–80. Reprinted in *Readings in Ritual Studies*, Ed. Ronald Grimes. Upper Saddle River, NJ: Prentice Hall 427–40.

Rappaport, Roy A. (1999) *Ritual and Religion in the Making of Humanity*. Cambridge: Cambridge University Press.

Reece, Steve (1993) *The Stranger's Welcome*. Ann Arbor: University of Michigan Press.

Ricoeur, Paul (1977) *The Rule of Metaphor*. Toronto: University of Toronto Press.

Ricoeur, Paul (1981a) "The Metaphorical Process as Cognition, Imagination, and Feeling." In *Philosophical Perspectives on Metaphor*. Ed. Mark Johnson.

Minneapolis: University of Minnesota Press, 228–47. Reprinted from *Critical Inquiry* 5:1 (1978) 143–59.

Ricoeur, Paul (1981b) *Hermeneutics and the Human Sciences: Essays on Language, Action and Interpretation.* Ed. & trans. John B. Thompson. Cambridge: Cambridge University Press.

Robertson-Smith, W. (1957) *The Religion of the Semites.* New York: Meridian Books.

Sabbatucci, Dario (1978) *It Mito, Il Rito e La Storia.* Rome: Bulzoni.

Seaford, Richard (1994) *Reciprocity and Ritual.* Oxford: Clarendon Press.

Searle, John R. (1974) *Speech Acts.* London: Cambridge University Press (originally published 1969).

Segal, Charles (1971) *The Theme of the Mutilation of the Corpse in the Iliad.* Mnemosyne, Biblioteca Classica Batava, Supp. 17. Leiden: E. J. Brill.

Sinos, Dale S. (1980) *Achilles, Patroklos and the Meaning of Philos.* Innsbruck: Innsburcker Beitrage zur Sprachwissenschaft.

Smith, Pierre (1979) "Aspects of the Organization of Rites." In *Between Belief and Transgression.* Trans. John Leavitt. Ed. M. Izard and P. Smith. Chicago: Chicago University Press. 103–28.

Sourvinou-Inwood, Christiane (1995) *Reading Greek Death.* Oxford: Clarendon Press.

Stefanini, Ruggero (2002) "Toward a Diachronic Reconstruction of the Linguistic Map of Ancient Anatolia." *Anatolia Antica 11: Studi in Memoria di Fiorella Imparati.* Florence: LoGisma. 783–806.

Stegemann, Wolfgang (2001) "Sacrifice as Metaphor." In *Social Scientific Models for Interpreting the Bible, Essays by the Context Group in Honor of Bruce J. Malina.* Ed. John J. Pilch. Leiden: E. J. Brill. 310–27.

Stengel, Paul (1920) *Die Griechischen Kultusaltertumer.* Munich: Oskar Beck, 136–38.

Stengel, Paul (1972) *Opferbrauch Der Griechen.* Darmstadt: Wissenschaftliche Buchgesellschaft. 78–85.

Stowers, Stanley K. (1995) "Greeks Who Sacrifice and Those Who Do Not: Toward an Anthropology of Greek Religion." *The Social World of the First Christians: Essays in Honor of Wayne A. Meeks.* Ed. L. Michael White and O. Larry Yarbrough. Minneapolis: Augsburg Fortress Press. 293–333.

Tambiah, Stanley J. (1968). "The Magic Power of Words." *Man* 3:2 175–208.

Tambiah, Stanley J. (1979) "A Performative Approach to Ritual." In *Proceedings of the British Academy*, Vol. 65. Oxford: Oxford University Press.

Taplin, Oliver (1980) "The Shield of Achilles within the Iliad." *Greece and Rome* 27 1–23. Rep. in *Homer, Critical Assessments*, Vol. III. Ed. I. M. F. de Jong. London: Routledge 1999. 179–200.

Taplin, Oliver (1992) *Homeric Soundings.* Oxford: Clarendon Press.

Thornton, Agathe (1984) *Homer's Iliad: Its Composition and the Motif of Supplication*. Gottingen: Vandenhoeck and Ruprecht, H.81.

Turner, Mark (1994) "Design for a Theory of Meaning." In *The Nature and Ontogenesis of Meaning*. Ed. W. Overton and D. Palermo. Mahwah, NJ: Lawrence Erlbaum Associates.

Turner, Victor (1974) *Dramas, Fields, and Metaphors: Symbolic Action in Human Society*. Ithaca, NY: Cornell University Press.

Turner, Victor (1977) "Sacrifice as Quintessential Process, Prophylaxis or Abandonment?" *History of Religions* 16:3 189–215.

Turner, Victor (1990) "Comparative Epic and Saga," p. 7 (unpublished essay). Quoted by Alf Hiltebeitel, *The Ritual of Battle* (New York: SUNY) 37.

Unal, Ahmet (1988a) "The Role of Magic in Ancient Anatolian Religion." In *Essays on Anatolian Studies in the Second Millennium BC, Vol. III*. Ed. HIH Prince Takahido Mikasa. Wiesbaden: Otto Harrassowitz. 52–85.

Unal, Ahmet (1988b) "Hittite Architect and a Rope-Climbing Ritual." *Turk Tarih Kurumu Belleten* LII:205. 1469–1503.

Valeri, Valerio (1985) *Kingship and Sacrifice*. Trans. Paula Wissing. Chicago: University of Chicago Press.

Van Brock, Nadia (1959) "Substitution Rituelle." *Revue Hittite et Asianique* 65 117–46.

van den Hout, Theo (2002) "Another View of Hittite Literature." *Anatolia Antica* 11: *Studi in Memoria di Fiorella Imparati*. Florence: LoGisma. 857–78.

Vernant, J-P. (1977, 1994 – English editions) "Introduction." In *The Gardens of Adonis*. By Marcel Detienne. Princeton: Princeton University Press. i–xl.

Vernant, J-P. (1983) *Myth and Thought Among the Greeks*. London: Routledge & Kegan Paul.

Vernant, J-P. (1989) "Culinary Practices and the Spirit of Sacrifice." In *The Cuisine of Sacrifice among the Greeks*. Ed. J-P. Vernant and M. Detienne. Chicago: University of Chicago Press 1989. 1–20.

Vidal-Naquet, Pierre (1986) *The Black Hunter; Forms of Thought and Forms of Society in the Greek World*. Trans. Andrew Szagedy-Mazak. Baltimore: Johns Hopkins University Press.

Visser, Edzard (1988) "Formulae or Single Words?" *Würzburger Jahrbücher fur die Altertumswissenschaft* 14 21–37.

von Rad, Gerhard (1958, 1991) *Holy War in Ancient Israel*. Trans. Marva J. Dawn. Grand Rapids, MI: Eerdmans.

Wallace, Anthony (1966) "Ritual as Revitalization." In *Religion, an Anthropological View*. New York: Random House.

Weinfeld, Moshe (1970) "The Covenant of Grant in the Old Testament and in the Ancient Near East," *Journal of the American Oriental Society* 90 184–203.

Weinfeld, Moshe (1973a) "'Rider of the Clouds' and 'Gatherer of the Clouds.'" *Journal of the Ancient Near Eastern Society* 5: 421–26.

Weinfeld, Moshe (1973b) "Covenant Terminology in the Ancient Near East and Its Influence on the West." *Journal of the American Oriental Society* 93.2: 190–99.

Weinfeld, Moshe (1990) "The Common Heritage of Covenantal Traditions in the Ancient World." In *I Trattai nel mondo antico, forma, ideologica, funzione.* Ed. Luciano Canfora, Mario Liverani, Carlo Zaccagnini. Rome: L'Erinna di Bretschneider. 175–91.

Weinfeld, Moshe (1993) "Covenant Making in Anatolia and Mesopotamia." *Journal of the Ancient Near Eastern Society* 22:135–39.

Weitenberg, Jos (1991) "The Meaning of the Expression 'To Become a Wolf' in Hittite." In *Perspectives on Indo-European Language, Culture and Religion, Studies in Honor of Edgar C. Polome'*, Vol. 1. Ed. Roger Pearson. Monograph Number Seven. *Journal of Indo-European Studies*, McLean, VA. 189–98.

Wilson, Donna F. (2002) *Ransom, Revenge, and Heroic Identity in the Iliad.* Cambridge: Cambridge University Press.

Zeitlin, Froma I. (1966) "The Motif of the Corrupted Sacrifice in Aeschylus' Oresteia." *Transactions of the American Philological Association* 96, 463–508.

Zimbalist Rosaldo, Michelle (1975) "It's All Uphill: The Creative Metaphors of Ilongot Magical Spells." In *Sociocultural Dimensions of Language Use.* Ed. Mary Sanches and B. G. Blount. New York: Academic Press. Quoted in Tambiah (1979) at 138.

# INDEX

Achilles, 2, 11, 14, 27, 29, 30, 31, 36, 55,
    68, 81, 94, 97, 102, 106, 126, 134,
    138, 145, 166, 176, 190, 191, 194,
    195, 201, 203, 204, 213, 217
    and Agamemnon, 31, 58, 62, 90, 91,
        94, 127, 149, 153
    and Kalchas, 93, 98, 102–103, 176
    and Patroklos, 58, 93, 106–111, 135,
        141–142, 158, 169–170, 183
    and Lykaon, 63–65, 91, 154, 155,
        162–168, 170
    and Hector, 36, 53, 58, 67, 84
Acchiyawa, 131
adoption motif, 88–90, 149
Agamemnon, 14, 15, 16, 27, 29, 30, 31,
    67, 76, 93, 95, 102, 112, 113, 119,
    120, 125, 126–127, 128, 133, 135,
    144–145, 147, 148, 149, 150, 157,
    161, 169, 172, 174, 185, 189, 205,
    206, 211, 213
    and Achilles. See Achilles
Alexiou, Magaret, 35, 42–43
Apollo, 4, 55, 87, 102, 134, 144–145, 166,
    188, 204
apodeirotomeō, 66, 69, 190
Ares, 4, 56, 69, 190, 204
Ashur, 4, 198, 204–205, 206, 208,
    214
Ashurbanipal, 55, 136, 159, 161, 192, 205,
    206, 207, 208
Assyrian, including Neo-Assyrian, 6, 7, 9,
    10, 12, 77, 111
Atē, 27, 76, 91, 101, 102, 126, 149

Athene, 4, 56, 58, 69, 75, 78, 80, 88,
    128–129, 135, 145, 188, 190, 191,
    194, 204
Austin, J. L., 28, 97

Bateson, Gregory, 72
Bell, Catherine, 30, 35, 36, 66, 172
Bible, passages from, 6, 7, 10, 54, 68,
    78–79, 81–82, 83, 88, 89, 94, 95,
    100, 111, 129, 137, 142, 160, 161,
    193, 196, 197, 207, 210, 211, 213
Bickerman, E. J., 3, 6, 132, 140, 143,
    149–151
Bloch, Maurice, 4, 5, 30, 32–33, 36, 63,
    122, 180
blood, 13
boar, sacrifice of, 15, 117, 118, 120, 127,
    128, 129, 140, 151, 155, 166, 168
Bourdieu, Pierre, 30, 34, 62
Briseis, 31
Burkert, Walter, 17, 18, 35, 36, 48, 128,
    140, 143, 165

calembour, 48
castration, 128
cholos, 69, 70, 158
commensal sacrifice, 1, 18, 36, 188
commissive statements, 28, 29, 81, 82
curses, 15, 54, 55, 58, 79–89, 94, 97,
    99–100, 102, 106, 111, 112–114, 118,
    119, 120, 133, 146, 148, 157, 161,
    165, 174, 175, 188, 199–200, 207,
    208–215, 217

David and Jonathan, 83, 86
deHeusch, Luc, 36
*deirotomeō*. See *apodeirotomeō* and *tamnō*
Demeter, 59, 97
  meal of, 56–58, 162, 163. *See also* hearth
Detienne, Marcel. *See* Vernant, J.-P.
Diomedes, 56, 81, 83, 87, 95, 109, 134, 135, 145, 190, 202
disarming before oath, 101–102, 124

earth, as oath-sanctioning element, 98
Enlil, 4
*epitinō*, 65
Erinyes, 15, 90–91, 117, 119, 126, 146, 147, 148, 169, 171
Esarhaddon, 54, 136, 160, 161, 167, 192, 199, 207, 208
*euchomai*. *See* prayer

Faraone, Christopher, 99
fasting for vengenace, 98
Fernandez, John, 10, 35, 36, 41–42, 71, 72, 115, 171, 172, 178, 187, 217
Foley, John Miles, 22
Freud, Sigmund, 35
friendship. *See philotēs*
funeral sacrifice, 3
Furies. *See* Erinyes

Gadamer, Hans-Georg, 4, 23, 24
Gaia, 93, 96, 119
gasping of victims, 12, 13, 102, 133, 156, 158, 176, 177, 180–182, 186
Geertz, Clifford, 34
Gilgamesh, 107
Girard, René, 17, 35, 36
Glaukos, 81, 83, 87
Gray, John Glen, 54
Graf, Fritz, 143–144
Griffiths, Alan, 109
guestfriendship, 57, 81, 83–85, 87, 88, 173. *See also philotēs*
Gunter, Ann, 7, 9

Hades, 58, 94, 170
hair, 119, 120, 123, 140–144, 174
hand, taking by the, 79–84, 97, 102
  ritual gesture with, 79, 83, 101, 116, 127, 133–134, 135, 144–145

Hattusilis, 78, 79, 89, 191
hearth, 57, 59–60, 61
Hector, 11, 12, 15, 52, 55, 56, 76, 81, 84, 87, 95, 101, 102, 109, 110, 114, 116, 124, 144, 172, 190, 199–200, 201, 203, 204, 215
  and Achilles, *see* Achilles
Helen, 50
Helios, 96, 97, 119, 128, 147, 174
Hera, 40, 51–52, 76, 93, 95, 96, 101, 102, 113
Heracles, 76
*herem*, 3, 213
*herkos*, 25
Herman, Gabriel, 81, 82, 83
hermeneutics, 23
Hesiod, 25, 44, 97, 99–100, 108
Heubeck, Alfred, 90, 91–96
*hikētēs*, 163, 168
Hippodamos, 177–178, 181, 182, 183
Hittites, 6, 7, 8, 9, 10, 51, 59, 77, 78–79, 82, 86, 87, 88, 89, 95, 96, 97, 100, 107, 111, 131–133, 137
*horkia*, 18, 36, 52, 73, 84, 87, 88, 113
  *horkia pista*, 85, 127, 147, 172
  *horkos*, 6, 25
  *horkos temnein*, 6
horses, 12, 91, 101, 183
Huizinga, Johan, 178
human sacrifice. See *tamnō* and *apodeirotomeō*
Hypnos, 95, 96, 101

illocution. *See* speech act
intertextuality, 4, 5, 19, 21, 151
Ishtar (various forms), 4, 56, 78, 79, 191–192, 205, 207, 208

Jakobson, Roman, 4, 21, 71, 167–168, 180
Jensen, Adolf, 35, 180, 185
Johnson, Lakoff, and Turner, 4, 24
Juergensmeyer, Mark, 2

Kalchas. *See* Achilles
Karavites, Peter, 2, 5, 6, 51, 52, 61, 84–88, 90
Kiparsky, Paul, 48

Lakoff, George. *See* Johnson
lambs, 118, 128, 135, 140, 151, 156–168, 174, 176, 180, 184, 186, 187
Lévi-Strauss, Claude, 35
libations, 16, 59, 101, 102, 116, 118, 120, 143, 145, 149, 157, 164. *See also* pouring oaths
liturgical order, 6, 39–40, 43–44, 46, 47, 48, 62, 74, 94, 121, 139–140, 145, 155, 187, 216
Lord, Albert, 37
Lowenstam, Steven, 79, 107–108
lying, 25
Lykaon, 11, 57, 58. *See* Achilles and Lykaon

*machaira*, 15, 117, 118–119, 120, 123
magic words, 26, 60, 72, 87, 99–100, 176
Marduk, 4, 55, 56, 63
Martin, Richard, 113, 138
Meleagros, 91, 94, 101
Menelaos, 78, 88, 96, 101, 113, 117, 128–129, 173, 174, 175, 183, 188, 215
*mēnis*, 29, 57, 66, 126, 189, 195
metaphorical transformation, 10, 18, 19, 156–168, 170, 171, 175, 179. *See also* Fernandez, James
Mondi, Robert, 49
Muellner, Leonard, 61, 120, 121, 147, 153, 164, 165, 166–167, 174
Mursilis, 209

Nagler, Michael, 45–46, 48, 121, 154, 166–167
Nagy, Gregory, 48, 107, 153
natural disaster, 54–56
*nelei chalkō*, 15, 118, 119, 120, 138, 151, 158, 176
Nergal, 4
Nestor, 29, 30, 56, 58, 61, 81, 88, 95, 102, 133, 135, 154

Odysseus, 2, 26, 29, 30, 98, 99, 102, 109, 125, 133, 134, 135, 140, 145, 154, 189, 202–203
Old Woman, as Hittite ritual persona, 79, 100
Ong, Walter, 48

oral traditional theory, 4, 19, 21, 22, 23, 120
Ouranos, 93, 96

Parry, Milman, 48, 113, 154
Patroklos, 11, 12, 69, 72, 81, 109, 134, 157, 183, 200. *See also* Achilles
Pausanias, 43
performative, 28
Persephone, 94
*philotēs*, 2, 52, 76, 84–88, 90, 91–96, 110, 124–125, 172–173
    *philotēta kai horkia pista*, 85–87
Phoinix, 68, 90, 94, 109
*phonē*, 1, 36
*pistoō*, 6
pitiless bronze. See *nelei chalkō*
*poinē*, 7, 18, 58, 65–71, 149, 157, 158–162, 167, 171, 217
Polydoros, 11
Poseidon, 30, 55, 80, 90, 93, 96, 98, 101, 127, 181, 188, 189, 201, 204–205
pouring oaths, 15
prayer, 15, 117, 119, 120, 123, 133, 144–145, 147, 153, 165, 168
Priam, 11, 12, 14, 81, 112, 125, 134, 135, 144, 176, 211, 213

Radcliffe-Brown, A. Reginald, 33
Rappaport, Roy A., 4, 5, 6, 7, 21, 24, 26, 27, 28, 30, 32, 35, 36, 38, 42, 44, 62, 63, 71, 74, 75, 82, 90, 92, 99, 101, 121, 122, 139, 145, 169, 172, 185, 187, 216
raw-flesh-eater, 54–56
Ricoeur, Paul, 4, 10, 22, 36, 46, 93, 115, 157, 176
ritual register, 32–34, 38, 49, 74, 122–123, 146, 148, 152–155, 166, 175, 180, 186, 216
ritual fiction, 93, 116, 176, 179, 185, 187
Ritual fixity. *See* liturgical orders
ritual gesture, 42–43
ritual leitmotif, 3, 10, 42, 65, 72, 159, 171, 173, 217
ritual patterns, 33–34, 36–37, 45, 119
River Scamander, 55, 201
River Styx, 93, 96, 97, 101

River Tartaressos, 97
Robertson Smith, W., 18

Sargon II, 55, 192, 197, 199–200, 202, 208, 212
Sarpedon, 11
scepter, 98, 101, 102–107, 110
semantic domains of ritual, 17, 19
Sennacharib, 159, 198, 199, 212, 214
sense of ritual, 40, 42
Shalmaneser III, 82
Shamash, 192, 202–203
Sinos, Dale, 107
Smith, Pierre, 178, 185
speech acts, 46, 62, 123, 146–151, 174, 180
*sphazdō*, 13
Stengel, Paul, 104, 128, 132, 140, 143
Styx. *See* River Styx
sun-goddess of Arinna, 4, 96, 191
sun-goddess of the earth, 79, 100
Suppiliuluma, 51, 78–82, 89

Tambiah, 4, 5, 26, 27, 33, 34, 35, 36, 45, 74, 98, 100, 121, 143, 147, 148–149, 172, 180, 186, 187
*tamnō*, 15, 119, 140, 157–158
terrorism, 2
*therapon*, 83–85, 106–111, 141–142
Thetis, 65, 68, 97, 109
*thumos*, 15, 119, 120, 155, 156, 158, 176, 177, 180
*thusia. See* commensal sacrifice

*timē*, 66
truce, 31
Tudhaliya IV, 82, 85–86, 89, 209
Turner, Victor, 11, 35, 37
typical scene, 45–48, 75, 115, 120, 216

Valeri, Valerio, 4, 5, 20, 21, 71, 167, 172, 180, 187
van Brock, Nadia, 107
vengeance, 10, 12, 58, 111, 168, 170, 175. *See* also *poinē*
Vernant Jean-Pierre, 17, 18, 35
Visser, Edzard, 48

Weinfeld, Moshe, 1, 2, 6, 49, 77, 82, 85, 88, 89, 90, 102, 132
Wilson, Donna, 66
Wilusa, 90, 91–96
womb-bond. *See* Eryines

*xeinia. See* guestfriendship

Yahweh, 4, 56–63, 95
yawning earth. *See* earth

Zeus Katachthonios, 94
Zeus, 15, 16, 25, 27, 40, 52, 55, 57, 68, 70, 75, 76, 81, 83, 88, 90, 93–94, 96, 97, 101, 102, 105, 110, 112, 113, 117, 119, 125, 126, 127, 128, 129, 134, 135, 144–145, 146, 147, 149, 154, 161, 169, 170, 173, 174, 175, 185, 188, 189, 190, 194, 195, 203, 204, 205